Cognition and
Psychotherapy

Cognition and Psychotherapy

Edited by

MICHAEL J. MAHONEY

University of California
Santa Barbara, California

and

ARTHUR FREEMAN

Center for Cognitive Therapy
University of Pennsylvania
Philadelphia, Pennsylvania

Plenum Press • New York and London

Library of Congress Cataloging in Publication Data

Main entry under title:

Cognition and psychotherapy.

Includes bibliographies and index.
1. Cognitive therapy. I. Mahoney, Michael J. II. Freeman, Arthur M. [DNLM: 1. Cognition. 2. Psychotherapy. WM 420 C6755]
RC489.C63C6   1985   616.89′14   85-3370
ISBN 0-306-41858-4

To Aaron T. Beck
valued friend, colleague, and pioneer
in the cognitive clinical sciences

Contributors

SILVANO ARIETI, Late of New York Medical College and William Alanson White Institute of Psychiatry, Psychoanalysis, and Psychology, New York, New York.

ALBERT BANDURA, Stanford University, Building 420, Jordan Hall, Stanford, California

AARON T. BECK, Department of Psychiatry, University of Pennsylvania, 133 South 36th Street, Room 602, Philadelphia, Pennsylvania

JOHN BOWLBY, Tavistock Institute, 120 Belsize Lane, London, England

RALPH M. CROWLEY, Late of William Alanson White Institute of Psychiatry, Psychoanalysis, and Psychology, New York, New York

ALBERT ELLIS, Institute for Rational Emotive Therapy, 45 East 65th Street, New York, New York

JEROME D. FRANK, Department of Psychiatry, The Johns Hopkins University Medical School, Baltimore, Maryland

VIKTOR E. FRANKL, University of Vienna Medical School, 1 Mariannengasse, Vienna, Austria

ARTHUR FREEMAN, Department of Psychiatry, University of Pennsylvania, 133 South 36th Street, Room 602, Philadelphia, Pennsylvania

VITTORIO F. GUIDANO, Center for Cognitive Psychotherapy, Via degli Scipioni 245, Rome, Italy

LUIS JOYCE-MONIZ, Faculty of Psychology, University of Lisbon, Rua Pinheiro Chagas 17, Lisbon, Portugal

GIANNI LIOTTI, Center for Cognitive Psychotherapy, Via degli Scipioni 245, Rome, Italy

MICHAEL J. MAHONEY, Counseling Psychology, University of California, Santa Barbara, California

VICTOR E. RAIMY, Clinical Psychologist in private practice, 6770 Hawaii Kai Dr., Honolulu, Hawaii

MARIO RENDON, Montefiore Hospital and Medical Center, 3412 Bainbridge Avenue, Bronx, New York

BERNARD SHULMAN, Stone Medical Center, 2800 North Sheridan Road, Chicago, Illinois

Preface

For almost three millennia, philosophy and its more pragmatic offspring, psychology and the cognitive sciences, have struggled to understand the complex principles reflected in the patterned operations of the human mind. What is knowledge? How does it relate to what we feel and do? What are the fundamental processes underlying attention, perception, intention, learning, memory, and consciousness? How are thought, feeling, and action related, and what are the practical implications of our current knowledge for the everyday priorities of parenting, education, and counseling? Such meaningful and fascinating questions lie at the heart of contemporary attempts to build a stronger working alliance among the fields of epistemology (theories of knowledge), the cognitive sciences, and psychotherapy.

The proliferation and pervasiveness of what some have called "cognitivism" throughout all quarters of modern psychology represent a phenomenon of paradigmatic proportions. The (re-)emergence of cognitive concepts and perspectives—whether portrayed as revolutionary (reactive) or evolutionary (developmental) in nature—marks what may well be the single most formative theme in late twentieth-century psychology. Skeptics of the cognitive movement, if it may be so called, can readily note the necessary limits and liabilities of naive forms of metaphysics and mentalism. The history of human ideas is writ large in the polarities of "in here" and "out there"—from Plato, Pythagoras, and Kant to Locke, Bacon, and Watson. What appears to be different among modern cognitive proponents, however, is a willingness to transcend the polarity levels of analysis in favor of more comprehensive and complex models of human adaptation and development. Mind and body, not to mention self and environment, are no longer viewed as reciprocals in the symbolic functions describing human experience. We are clearly both the subject and object of inquiry, the changer and the changed, and the only thinking, feeling, acting organism known to be capable of self-consciousness.

There are, to be sure, a wide range of theories and models that attempt to order the scientific and clinical literatures bearing on the nature of the cognitive processes that lie at the heart of human neuro-functions. There is some convergence worthy of attention, and there are nontrivial differences that also warrant consideration. In this volume we have asked recognized specialists from the major ideological schools to address the role and conceptualization of cognitive processes in psychotherapy. The opening chapter by Mahoney offers a metatheoretical survey of convergent themes—approximations toward principles—noted across approaches to psychotherapy.

The quest for basic principles and effective ingredients in psychotherapy is pursued even further by Jerome D. Frank in Chapter 2. The roles of relationship, rationale, and ritual in effective counseling are emphasized by Frank, as is the elusive dimension of hope and morale. This interest in the person's confidence and perceived capacities is then more thoroughly analyzed in Albert Bandura's influential theory of self-efficacy (Chapter 3). His theory links the sense of self-efficacy with the performance, persistence, and resilience of coping behaviors. Bandura endorses a social learning theory interpretation of the sources of information about personal efficacy, namely, self-observation, vicarious learning, persuasion, and physiological cues.

Chapters 4 and 5 are by Luis Joyce-Moniz of Portugal and Vittorio F. Guidano and Gianni Liotti of Rome, respectively. All three represent *structuralist* and *constructivist* cognitive theorists. Joyce-Moniz calls for more attention to the unique personal epistemology of each client and the need for an integrative model of cognitive structures and processes that transcend techniques. Guidano and Liotti share some fascinating conjectures and demonstrations of a constructivist, process-oriented model of personal realities and their formation. Chapter 5 offers an overview of their approach, which combines evolutionary epistemology with attachment theory in tracing personal trajectories of affective development, disorder, and treatment.

This theme is itself expanded in Chapter 6 by John Bowlby, the author of attachment theory. There is growing evidence that certain patterns of early problems in attachment appear to leave an enduring vulnerability to emotional distress and dysfunction. As Bowlby aptly notes, however, we have been relatively neglectful of research on developmental psychopathology. Such research could refine our understanding of the developmental origins and psychological functions of a syndrome and thereby enhance our capacity not only to understand better our clients, but also to guide them through developmental struggles.

In Chapter 7 Victor Raimy offers a valuable contribution on the role of misconceptions or misunderstandings in the generation and maintenance of personal problems. Dr. Raimy calls for a cognitive-behavioral eclecticism, noting that "finding and changing faulty beliefs that interfere with adjustment is a highly specific and concrete therapeutic activity, even though it may be accomplished in many different ways." Cognition is seen in a somewhat different light by the late Silvano Arieti in his discussion of "Cognition in Psychoanalysis" (Chapter 8). While offering his own valuable conjectures on cognitive organization, Arieti laments the fact that "cognition is or has been, up to now, the Cinderella of psychoanalysis in psychiatry. No other field of the psyche has been so consistently neglected by clinicians and theoreticians alike." In Chapter 9 Bernard Shulman aptly notes that Alfred Adler's theory of individual psychology represented one of the earliest statements of a cognitive constructivist view. The development of a life-style or *schema* through formative social interactions remains a core assumption of several modern cognitive perspectives.

Viktor Frankl, the founder of logotherapy, is the author of Chapter 10, which traces his early theoretical development and interactions with Freud and Adler. Frankl offers a stimulating distinction between *paradoxical intention* and *symptom prescription* and concludes with some provocative thoughts on the roles of *detachment* and *self-transcendance* in psychological development. Somewhat parallel themes are addressed in Chapter 11 by Mario Rendon. Rendon discusses Karen Horney's role in the early appreciation and analysis of self-relationships that are, of course, developed, maintained, and modified in the context of human relationships. Horney and Frankl both emphasize self-realization as a motivational component in the struggle to be freed of neurotic preoccupations.

The last three chapters were reserved for three of the most influential pioneering figures in the cognitive clinical sciences—Harry Stack Sullivan, Albert Ellis, and Aaron T. Beck. The late Ralph Crowley documents the cognitive emphases of Sullivan's interpersonal theory and credits Sullivan with recognizing the inseparability of the cognitive, conative, and affective elements of experience. These elements are more explicitly addressed by Dr. Ellis in his expansion of a foundational aspect of rational-emotive therapy, namely, relationships among the "ABCs" of experience—(A) activating events, (B) beliefs, and (C) consequences. Ellis joins other contemporary experts who view these elements as complexly interactive.

In the final chapter, Beck, to whom this volume is affectionately dedicated, offers a survey of integrative convergences among proponents of cognitive therapy, behavior therapy, psychoanalysis, and pharmacotherapy. Noting that the phenomenon of depression can be viewed from each of these perspectives, Dr. Beck notes:

> The various perspectives have varying degrees of explanatory power. By relating them to each other, we can attempt to construct an integrated model that will have greater explanatory power than the individual perspectives.

We hope that this volume will contribute to such ongoing exchange among cognitive clinical scientists and practitioners.

Grateful acknowledgments are due many people who helped make this volume possible. First and foremost, we wish to thank our contributors for helping to breathe life into this project. Their ideas, framed so well in their contributions, will be a source of interest, discussion, and debate for years to come. Eliot Werner, our editor at Plenum, offered ideas and encouragement through the initiation and development phases of this project. Likewise, without the hard work and perseverance of Tina Inforzato and Sandy Ranio, this volume would not exist. Their abilities to turn the written or spoken word into typescript and to bear with our multiple revisions have been greatly appreciated.

An undertaking of this sort almost by definition means that time, energy, and attention must be shifted from other activities, interactions, and relationships. Karen M. Simon has offered not only her support and encouragement, but has also served as a sounding board for the ideas that I have developed (AF). Sean Mahoney and Teresa Nezworski also offered welcome support (MJM).

The editors were saddened by the recent death of Ralph M. Crowley. Psychiatry has lost an important contributor to the literature, a highly respected teacher, and a skilled clinician.

Our final acknowledgments go to our clients and our students, from whom we gratefully continue to learn. May we all find inspiration in the everyday struggles to change, to live more fully, and to help as best we can.

MICHAEL J. MAHONEY
ARTHUR FREEMAN

Contents

PART I

CHAPTER 1

Psychotherapy and Human Change Processes

MICHAEL J. MAHONEY

The patterns and parameters of human change processes remain one of the oldest and most intriguing themes of thoughtful inquiry. Our libraries are filled with an inseparable mixture of fictional and non-fictional expressions and analyses of change and stability in human lives. And throughout these writings are pervasive assumptions about human nature, epistemology, and certain tacit universals of experience and existence (Durant & Durant, 1970; Foucault, 1970; Friedman, 1967, 1974; Polanyi, 1966; Russell, 1945). The persistence of our quest for knowledge—and especially knowledge about ourselves—is probably a reflection of formidable inclinations toward both meaning and power. Francis Bacon observed that "knowledge is power." The nature of that power was stated more explicitly in the ancient Chinese volume, the *I Ching* or *Book of Changes* (Wilhelm & Baynes, 1950, p. 243):

> If we know the laws of change, we can precalculate in regard to it, and freedom of action thereupon becomes possible.

Our philosophic, scientific, and artistic literatures offer an expansive array of proposed laws or patterns of change, each with its prescriptions and proscriptions for living.

Only in the last century, however, have we come to appreciate more fully that the laws of change are interdependently reflected in the laws describing microscopic and macroscopic processes. The increasing recognition of this participatory system can be witnessed in

---

MICHAEL J. MAHONEY • Counseling Psychology, University of California, Santa Barbara, California 93106.

areas as disparate as self-efficacy theory (Bandura, 1977), politics and economics (Hayek, 1967, 1978), biosocial evolution (Campbell, 1979; Wilson, 1975, 1978), and even the ordering processes of history and science themselves (Foucault, 1970; Weimer, 1979). It is therefore not surprising that many advocates of human potential and world peace are now turning their attention to the pivotal significance of personal change in cultural transformation (Ferguson, 1980; Land, 1973; Leonard, 1972).

But the average consumer of psychotherapy does not seek our services in altruistic hopes of facilitating cultural transformation. Although its meanings and measures seem to be shifting away from earlier connotations of pathology and personal inadequacy, psychotherapy continues to draw much of its energy from the covalent resources of human pain and human hope. Our socially sanctioned role as therapists is that of a guide and assistant—each of us using our individualized and ever-changing theoretical sextants to gauge movement and direction. And, from our privileged role as helpers, we must often witness the breadth and depth of human suffering, the awesome tenacity of human courage, and the humbling limitations of our own understanding. After sixteen years of studying, teaching, and practicing psychotherapy, I am increasingly impressed with both the capacity and the constrictiveness of human change processes.

PREFATORY REMARKS

This is perhaps a good point at which to insert some structural intentions for the observations that follow. To begin with, I am not writing as a representative of any particular school of thought, conventional or emergent. It has become increasingly clear in recent commentaries on eclecticism and convergence that the theoretical substrate of psychotherapy is undergoing widespread reappraisal (Garfield & Kurtz, 1976, 1977; Goldfried, 1980). Although I feel a deep sense of respect for the dialectics that are already underway between various schools of thought, I cannot honestly claim a comfortable niche in their contact. The point here is that I do not mean to present my remarks as emanating from an established theoretical corner. They are my impressions as a student and practitioner of psychotherapy.

A second prefatory remark has to do with the divergence between my present reflections on human change processes and what has been traditionally considered the literature and domain of psychotherapy process. Many models and instruments have been proposed as viable analyses and measures of therapeutic change (Burton, 1976; Howard & Orlinsky, 1972; Kiesler, 1973; Mahoney, 1980a; Orlinsky & Howard, 1978). I believe that these contributions have been most valuable in highlighting their individual limitations. Molecular analyses of communication patterns within sessions have yielded results that have been heuristically unsatisfying. Whether the reasons be instrument error, unwieldy magnification, or something else, the complexities of human change have not been adequately captured or conveyed by precise dissections of therapeutic transcripts. At the other extreme, the holistic complexity of personal development has been beautifully rendered by numerous "big picture" artists, but many of these megamodels seem to sacrifice disorderly particulars in the service of universal generalizations. I am not sure where to place my own contribution to all this—except perhaps by negation. I will not offer encyclopedic reviews of the molecular process research, nor will I pretend to offer a new megamodel of change. Instead, my remarks will be directed at five related themes that, in my opinion, are relevant to human change processes. Since I believe that psychotherapy process is an arbitrary subset of more fundamental processes of personal development and change, I will use the broader category as the admittedly spacious arena for my observations.

Finally, the comments that follow are an intentional hybrid of theoretical conjectures and clinical impressions. I have tried to communicate some of the assumptions and emerging hypotheses that guide my behavior as a therapist and stimulate my inquiries as a researcher. I have assumed that those who might find my work useful would be interested in both its practical and its theoretical dimensions. I have therefore attempted to illustrate some of my conjectures with clinical material. I am indebted to my clients not only for allowing me to share these experiences with you but also for helping me refine my theoretical impressions in the challenging reality of our exchanges. Although the library and laboratory have been valuable instructors in my life, the limitations of their lessons have been most clearly revealed to me in the context of my attempts to facilitate change in myself and others. Like many of my colleagues, I often despair at the size of the gap between our theoretical maps and the experiential territory they are supposed to represent. As I shall reiterate, there are strong arguments from the fields of epistemology and cognitive psychology to the effect that our ability to create adequate models of human experience may ultimately result in a deeper appreciation of how limited our models must be and how instrumental our maps are in defining, distorting, and directing our endless explorations. All of this notwithstanding, I have become increasingly engaged by the challenge and responsiblity of studying our patterns of stability and change. Although my clients have often disabused me of some treasured and entrenched illusions about process, the sting of their lessons has been amply compensated for by their intimate gifts of honesty, complexity, and courage.

Since I will be weaving through some wide-ranging areas of relevance, let me offer a crude sketch of the directions I will be taking. My remarks have been organized with the aid of five themes. I will begin by arguing that a fundamental challenge in our efforts to understand and direct our lives is the *problem of meaning*. Within that context I will discuss the significance of viewing the central nervous system as an organ of order and the implications of conceptualizing therapeutic change in terms of changes in personal meaning. My second focus will take us into the centuries-old debate about mechanistic determinism and personal causation. Under the rubric of *constructive ontology* I will share my impressions of this feud in an analysis of "the new look" in cognitive psychology and epistemology. The main assertion there will deal with our active role in cocreating the personal realities to which we react. To understand more adequately the nature of our contribution to individual meaning structures, I will then have to examine the processes of ordering and knowing. This realm is modestly understood, and my remarks there will be brief. In studying the evolution of complex phenomena and the organization of our nervous systems, I shall endorse the concept of *heterarchical structuralism*—the functional stratification of our experiential processes. I will briefly touch upon the convergent implications of several themes in neurobiology, psychoanalysis, cognitive psychology, and social evolution.

Up to this point the thrust of my remarks will have been (1) that personal experience is extensively embedded in an individual context of meaning, (2) that we are active participants in the creation and change of our meaningful contexts, and (3) that an adequate appreciation of this perspective requires an analysis of stratified ordering processes in the nervous system. Many of the themes developed in these first three areas will be reintegrated in the fourth and fifth. Under *oscillative processes in development* I will present some conjectures on the dynamics of change and on the essential tensions which define our experience of stability and mutation. Our myriad strategies for dealing with disequilibrium in ourselves and in our clients will afford me the opportunity to comment on such topics as the role of attention in change, the importance of resistance processes, and the tyranny of techniques in our attempts to help people change. I will conclude the main part of my paper with a section on *participatory vitalism* and the role of self-empowering hope in adaptation and change. My final remarks will translate all of this discussion into some questions and impressions about the practice of psychotherapy and the investigation of human change processes.

PHENOMENOLOGY AND THE PRIMACY OF MEANING

The first theme I shall emphasize is deceptive in its simplicity. It is the fundamental proposition that human experience is imbued with the pursuit, construction, and alteration of meaning. Bartlett (1932) proposed a similar notion in his documentation of the extent to which humans display an "effort after meaning." That we seek and create meaning, however, need not imply that our lives reflect a tropism toward some transcendant plane of ultimate ideals. By its very nature, meaning is a highly personal and idiosyncratic phenomenon. Except where our research instruments have sacrificed individual differences as trivial or troublesome, we seldom report identical perceptions of ostensibly identical events. This phenomenological variance may itself be a reflection of an embedded evolutionary wisdom at both the individual and collective levels.

At an individual level, the primacy of meaning does not necessarily lead to a retrenchment in phenomenalism or existential solipsism. Although we may each inhabit a private universe of personal meanings, we also share an extensive part of our world with other people. Indeed, much of our social intercourse is directed at defining discrepancies among received views of reality and dealing with them. Reality and meaningfulness have long been companion concepts, and their closeness is hardly coincidental. Threats to a meaning structure are often experienced as threats to reality by its adherents (Berger & Luckman, 1967). The primacy of meaning and this protection against its change are as much a reflection on our nervous systems as on the social systems in which they have developed.

ORDER AND CONTRAST

Most contemporary observers of human behavior seem to concur in the notion that the brain and nervous system facilitate adaptation and growth through mechanisms that entail classification, contrast, and meaning. Studies into the paleoneurology of our intelligence suggest that we bear the burden and blessing of a long and challenging biosocial evolution (Campbell, 1975; Jerison, 1973, 1976). Similarly, the literature of cognitive psychology and psychobiology seem to be converging toward some intriguing implications that have relevance for our understanding and practice of psychotherapy (cf. Davidson & Davidson, 1980; Schwartz, 1978; Shaw & Bransford, 1977; Weimer & Palermo, 1974, 1981). The evolution of the nervous system was apparently influenced by its adaptive ability to order, organize, and "translate" experience into pragmatic action. The extant data on human perception and thought also suggest that much of our consciousness is dependent upon some form of contrast. As Foucault (1970) and others have noted, order may be constructed from a variety of patterns which share the critical feature of classificatory contrast. The content of knowing, if not its process, is tethered by such focalizing contrasts as agent and action, figure and ground, known and unknown. This dependency on contrast could be illustrated at many levels of information processing. For example, we could look at the meaning of the term *change* and discover that its definition is tied up with notions of stability, and vice versa. This type of definition is an illustration of conceptual contrast. A more primitive example might take the form of perceptual contrast patterns. Most of us look for a pattern in all visual arrays, only dimly aware that we actively evaluate a variety of potential tacit meanings. Our active role in perception will be a topic in the next section. For the moment, we need only note the search for order, the inclination to classify and assign meaning. This process is facilitated, of course, when different patterns of contrast are explored.

Contrast may also be illustrated in the less sensate realm of logic. The laws of identity and the excluded middle form the cornerstone of Aristotelian logic. The law of identity ($a = a$, $a \neq not-a$) is an arbitrary vote for symbolic permanence. It protects the stability of a meaning within the boundaries of a given proposition. The law of the excluded middle states that a proposition must be either true or false; it cannot be both. It can, of course, be neither; but this conclusion usually renders the proposition literally meaning-less. Much of our moment-to-moment experience is imbued with this contrast-laden quest for meaning.[1] One irony here is that we seek order through

---

[1]There is at least one sense in which Eastern philosophies seem to invoke a more subtle form of contrast in their logic. Where Western notions of truth require the absence of self-contradictory assertions, some Eastern perspectives define *truth* as the harmonic assimilation of opposites. In these systems, the contrast between truth and untruth is more frequently expressed as a contrast between whole and part rather than consistency and contradiction.

contrast and, although we seem to gravitate toward consistency and invariance, we also learn most from the limits and contrasts of our experiential categories (Foucalt, 1970; Hayek, 1952a, 1952b, 1978). In at least one sense, we represent open ordering systems which are "naturally" inclined to seek certain kinds of closure. Consistency and contrast seem to be our fundamental domains of exchange with the world.

CONTEXTUAL THEORIES OF MEANING

Translating this concept into the more familiar realm of our everyday contact with psychotherapy clients, we must first reiterate the importance of gauging the assumptive worlds which give meaning and significance to personal experience (Beck, 1976; Frank, 1973; Guidano & Liotti, 1983; Raimy, 1975). Unless we appreciate the patterns by which individuals order their realities, we are unlikely to understand fully their requests for help. According to contextual theories of meaning (cf. Bransford & McCarrell, 1974; Jenkins, 1974; MacNamara, 1981; Pepper, 1942), the meaning of any given particular depends upon the context from which it is viewed. A vertical line may be read as a *one* or an *el* depending on whether it is surrounded by letters or digits. Similarly, an experience may be granted different meanings from the vantage point of different contexts.

The everyday significance of this point was brought home to me several years ago in a family-style program for predelinquent children. I was working with a six-year-old black boy who was bright, sensitive, and abandoned. Over a period of years, he had come to reject his racial heritage and to torture himself with his blackness. A devout racist, he insisted that white people were inherently better than blacks. I was a live-in teaching parent and wanted to help this boy, Taylor, not only to accept but also to take pride in his ancestry. I had been encouraging him to acknowledge and express some of the resentment he felt for other blacks, but progress had been painfully slow. Finally, after a flash of inspiration, I invited two personable and affectionate friends to join us for dinner—a black businessman and his white wife. Taylor was politely distant throughout dinner and refused to talk to our guests. I was puzzled. That night when I went in to kiss him good-night, I found myself confronting two tear-filled eyes. It took me several minutes to recognize the naiveté of my plan. While I had been orchestrating an *in vivo* illustration of racial equality and raceless affection, Taylor had been watching a very different spectacle. Where I had seen two adults impervious to the hues of their skin, my six-year-old friend had seen a successful black man who had rejected his own race in favor of a white wife. Our contexts were different, and with them the derivative meanings. That night I also learned that hugs can communicate some things much better than words.

The contexts by which an individual orders experience may well be one of the most challenging and promising targets of effective psychotherapy. It is apparent that we are capable of shifting some of our frames of reference (Goffman, 1974) and that we are actively involved in the choice of some contexts. Thus, as Proffitt (1976) has illustrated, we seem to contract or "buy into" a particular framework from which to order experience. We purchase consistency and order by inventing or borrowing a context that captures and organizes our current experience patterns (Proffitt & Halwes, 1981). In this sense, meaning is accompanied by closure and by limiting reference points. In cases of chronic dysphoria these frameworks, I believe, are imbued with painful assumptions and self-fulfilling prophecies (Jones, 1977). Although there are wide individual variations, we should not overlook the possibililty of common meaning structures within similar displays of self-preoccupation. For example, we should not be surprised to find that persons who seek therapy report danger and disappointment in their lives. Although I am skeptical of attempts to map universal schemata corresponding to discrete nosological categories, my skepticism rests with our diagnostic categories as much as with our individual differences. The invariance within the variance is often fascinating, however, and it deserves our attention as researchers.

The practical relevance of the primacy of meaning has only recently begun to receive recognition in our experimental endeavors. While many workers have shifted their attention from the ostensive stimulus to the "stimulus as perceived" (Mahoney, 1974), the significance of that shift for our understanding of human change processes is still being evaluated. The data suggest that the significance may be quite impressive. In her review of the role of perceived control in subjective distress, for example, Thompson (1981) concludes that "reactions to potentially stressful events depend on their meaning for the individual" (p. 89). She goes on to note that our various strategies of cognitive and behavioral control may derive their power by changing the meaning of an event and its corresponding emotional and behavioral concomitants. Thompson's (1981) recommendations for future research are noteworthy:

> The challenge now is to discover the types of meanings that can be used
> and to explore how to help individuals develop the ability to assign meanings that will be the most beneficial to them. (p. 99)

The point is that most forms of personal distress and its treatment rely on the primacy of meaning and the centrality of meaning change in personal change. The implication for research into the contexts and contracts by which we assign and alter meaning need only be noted.

I like to remind myself and my clients that our personal frameworks for meaning did not evolve in a function-free vacuum. No matter how painful and limiting our personal realities, they are the legacy of valuable developmental choices. We have adapted to idiosyncratic patterns of genetic potential, affectional bonds, and environmental possibilites. It is, of course, distressing to witness the widespread display of unnecessary suffering and avoidable constraints on personal freedom. But I believe we must also learn to respect our old and fallible constructions of self and reality as having been functional allies in our earlier attempts to cope with the vicissitudes of life. I shall return to this point in a later section when we take up the concept of healthy resistance.

CONSTRUCTIVE ONTOLOGY

Thus far I have argued that the problem of meaning is fundamental to our understanding of human experience. I have not, however, offered a reference point from which to study the meaning of meaning. Cogent analyses of this concept have already been offered by a number of capable philosophers and scientists (Bransford & McCarrell, 1974; Frankl, 1978; Jenkins, 1974; Klemke, 1981; Pepper, 1942; Proffitt, 1976). There is one sense in which meaning—as the fiber of ordered value—can never be understood. Until we develop less dependency on contrast in our knowing processes, we are unlikely to appreciate the pervasiveness of meaning in our adaptation. We can, of course, divide experiences along categories of relative quantity of meaning—from most to least meaningful—but the dimension itself will still lack a figure–ground contrast.

The definitional difficulty is common to all branches of science and philosophy. One valuable lesson from our centuries of studying epistemology, cosmology, and the nature of explanation has been the ultimate retreat of our analyses into some form of commitment—an arational leap of faith or trust in the wisdom, stability, or pragmatics of one's basic assumptions. This was the theme in Bartley's (1962) revolutionary volume on the nature of rationality and knowing processes. Our philosophical quests for uncaused causes, unexplained explainers, and undefined definers may well remind us of a saying sometimes attributed to Schopenhauer, that "philosophy is the systematic misuse of a set of symbols specifically designed for that purpose." They have led us repeatedly back to ourselves, confronting our quest for the mysteries of human stabilization and change—or, perhaps preferably, the maintenance of integrity and the dynamics of lifelong human development. I therefore find the meaning of meaning much less engaging than the processes operative in its development and change. A discussion of these processes brings us to yet another arena of interdisciplinary convergence.

LEARNING AND MEMORY

As central as they are to the enterprise we call psychology, the concepts of learning and memory remain two of the most elusive fundamentals in our knowledge. We have made undeniable progress in these areas, but I do not know too many psychologists who feel comfortable with the adequacy of our understanding. Only in the last decade have we begun to move away from obtuse laboratory analogues and restrictive instruments of analysis. In my opinion, that move is long overdue. Clearly, the old experimental chambers of animal learning research and the early emphasis on associative learning in our memory laboratories have left us with a stockpile of potentially valuable details on micro-processes. But they have also diverted us from some very compelling and challenging questions about dynamic patterns of stability and change in a complex and open system.

It seems increasingly obvious that we are active participants in our environmental exchanges. Examples of this "reciprocal determinism" are abundant (Bandura, 1978; Jones, 1977; Mahoney, 1974; in press; Reda & Mahoney, 1984). These complex patterns of attention, action, and reaction illustrate our participation in the ongoing exchange between person and environment. In my present argument for constructive ontology I am concurring with some recent insights into our participation in the development and maintenance of functional ordering schemes—or schemata—that place limitations on the realm of assimilable experience.

If humans are, indeed, active participants in the reality constructions that shape their lives, we are well advised to study the processes involved in that participatory construction. Behavioristic and cybernetic models generally fall short in their analyses because of their metatheories of classical or strict determinism and, in the case of radical behaviorism, their anachronistic notions about the nature of scientific inquiry (Mahoney, 1984).[2] Whatever else it may require, an adequate analysis of human learning and memory processes must consider the complexities of an open system that acts upon the information encountered and alters it. And this statement brings us to the new look in human knowing processes.

COGNITIVE PSYCHOLOGY

There have been many debates about what constitutes a bonafide revolution in science (Kuhn, 1962, 1970a, 1970b; Lakatos & Musgrave, 1970, Weimer, 1979). Without pursuing that tangent, let me suggest that we are witnesses of and participants in an exciting generation of change and development in our theories of human experience. This change is most apparent in the renewal of interest in cognition and in the role of psychological processes in our scientific constructions of reality. Since I have addressed the new look in epistemology in other works (Mahoney, 1976, 1979, 1981), I shall confine my present remarks to cognitive psychology and the recent expansion of cognitivism in clinical psychology. Cognitive theories and therapies are increasingly in vogue and are being looked to for novel suggestions on stubborn issues in psychotherapy. Until quite recently, the bulk of these cognitive approaches have placed rationality and self-encouragement/instruction at the core of their theories and therapies. The positive, self-affirming theme is more salient in some than in others, but it renders many of these therapies reminiscent of the "mind-cure movement" which William James noted with both alarm and fascination at the turn of the century (James, 1901/1958). Writers such as Dubois (1906, 1908, 1911), Janet (1898) and Vaihinger (1911) were laying foundations for what would later become today's rational and cognitive therapies. Their basic features, according to James, were that they were "deliberately optimistic" and "largely suggestive," often conveying "an intuitive belief in the all-saving power of healthy-minded attitudes" (p. 88).

Much of my own writing and research has been in rational and cognitive therapies, and it is therefore not surprising that I would call attention to their promise. But much of what is being popularized

---

[2]The difference between *determinate* and *deterministic* metatheories has been addressed by such writers as Hayek (1967, 1978) and Weimer (1981a, 1981b). Briefly, a determinate perspective recognizes the operation of rules and ordered relationships, but it does not claim the ability to forecast particular outcomes. Deterministic perspectives, however, often presume a linear sequence of discrete particulars (hence the label of "billiard ball determinism").

in today's wave of cognitivism seems superficially mediational and unnecessarily restrictive in its notions of contemporary cognitive psychology. I do not believe that the simple cueing, recitation, or reinforcement of "positive self-statements" or the rationalistic "reconstruction" of explicit beliefs are optimal or sufficient approaches for facilitating significant and enduring personal development (Mahoney, 1974, 1980b). These interventions on explicit surface structures are, I believe, a welcome movement toward the refinement of our understanding, but I think we should be careful not to over rationalize a developing system (the person) that contains powerful and primitive prerational modes of knowing and adapting to its world (Mahoney, in press). Cognitive and cognitive-behavioral therapies are, in my opinion, fertile and progressive movements within the profession, but some of the limitations of their first assumptions are already apparent.

The "cognitive revolution" (Dember, 1974) has not been confined to expansions of cognitive notions in our various specializations. While the rest of psychology has been becoming energetically more cognitive, cognitive psychology has taken a dramatic step toward becoming more *motoric*. The step has hardly been unanimous, but those who have suggested it are beginning to offer some fascinating reappraisals of our notions of attention, perception, memory, and action.

Conventional models of cognition have portrayed the human brain as an active but subservient witness to experience—a logical collector of pieces to a large puzzle. This model is reflected in an emphasis on sensory input and associationism and preoccupation with stimulus–response analyses. In commenting on these sensory metatheories of cognition, Weimer (1977) wrote the following:

> Common to these positions is an implicit notion that cognition is to be understood "from the outside inward," that it is a matter of the structuring of sensory information by intrinsically sensory systems, and that the products of cognition must somehow subsequently be married (in a peculiar sort of shotgun wedding) to action. (p. 270)

It is this leap from input to output that has stymied associationism ever since its inception. How does the human brain manage to "translate" sensation to perception, let alone action? This puzzle was posed by Hoffding in his critique of associationism in 1891 and is thus called the Hoffding step. How does sensory input become meaningful? And what are the transformational processes that turn the lead of perception into the gold of behavioral adaptation?

Sensory metatheories of cognition would have us follow the stimulus from sensory receptors through perceptual filters, iconic stores, the crowded streets of short- and long-term memory, and finally into some cybernetic mechanism or executive routine that decides upon and intitates a reaction. The problem of a central controlling mechanism—in other words, the ageless problem of the homunculus—is alive and well in these earlier information-processing models.

The newer models of human cognition are called motor theories because they emphasize the active and instrumental role of the person in all cognitive processes. Where sensory theories emphasize the role of *feedback* in learning, motor theories combine feedback mechanisms with *feedforward mechanisms*. The latter might be likened to variably flexible intentions for experience which serve to protect and expand its current structure. Feedforward mechanisms are actually preontological in the sense that they place limits on the nature and range of assimilable experience. Their hypothesized operation is consistent with a sizable literature in cognitive psychology as well as with some recent neurological findings that the cortex transmits information "downstream to subcortical structures for preprocessing" (Weimer, 1977, p. 275). Contemporary representatives of these motor theories include Guidane (this volume), Hayek (1952b), Shaw and Bransford (1977), Turvey (1974), and Weimer (1977). Although they could be illustrated in a number of ways, feedforward mechanisms are most familiar to the clinician when they are compared with projection processes. When one examines Figure 1, for example, one is tempted to view it as yet another rendition of Rorschach. One of the more enjoyable interpretations of this figure suggested that it depicts Popeye kissing Olive Oyl. An experienced psychometrician may be in-

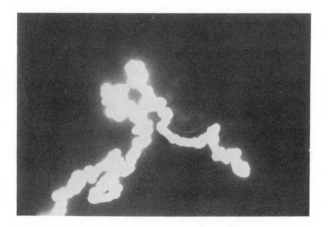

FIGURE 1. An illustration of feedforward mechanisms.

clined to edit and censor meanings fed forward, especially if projection is viewed as an externalization of rejected parts of the personality. The stimuli used for conventional projective testing have no real (i.e., absolute) meaning—indeed, it is their ambiguity that is presumed to warrant the responsibility for meaning assignment to the respondent. In the present illustration, however, my ambiguous stimulus does have some real-world contact in that I know how it was created. Where other persons may construct various perceptions of the figure, I am at least partially tethered by memories of a full moon over Nantucket and this crude first attempt at a hand-held time exposure photograph.

MECHANISM, MYSTICISM, AND MOTOR THEORIES

The significance of motor theories and feedforward mechanisms goes far beyond that conjectured by Kant and Freud in their respective writings on synthetic *a priori* knowledge and the projection of personal realities onto external configurations. We coauthor the scripts of our lives, so to speak, within the confines of our senses and our idiosyncratic ordering processes. When we confront the extent of our participation in the meaning of our experience patterns, the relevance of constructive ontology for adjustment becomes more obvious. Do we sometimes do to ourselves what we fear our environment may do? Do we self-spectate, self-judge, and self-doubt *because* we fear public inspection, social evaluation, and mistrust? I doubt that the cause-and-effect process is that simple, yet there are clear implications for constraints and freedoms within the dynamic cocreation of our personal fates and our reactions to their vicissitudes.

Epictetus may have been wise in invoking us to examine our attitudes toward an experience more closely than the experience itself. That invitation—made some 20 centuries ago—was a startling call to process as contrasted to content. *Content* and *process* are terms that serve here to illustrate what I believe could be one of the most progresssive paradigm shifts in contemporary psychology—namely, the transcendence of a lively theoretical dialectic between the mechanists and the mystics.

The mechanists are typified by behaviorists, cyberneticians, and other specialists in closed systems. Their studies of the molecular determinants of predictable behavior are a potentially valuable asset in our self-understanding. Their focus, however, is on the role of the person as a transducer of energy. Their flow diagrams are essentially linear, associative, and anchored at both ends in the public domain of observable stimuli and observable responses.

The mystics, on the other hand, are illustrated in their extremes by cosmogenic theories in which the person is a channel and/or a generator of energy. Some of these models reframe personal responsiblity as a karmic assignment, and many grant the individual generous capacities for intelligence and well-being. Reality as seen by the conscious "outer mind" is often portrayed by these writers as a patently crude and confining illustration that recedes only for those who seek and attain enlightenment. In some forms, mystical ontology asserts that we are active agents in the material existence of objects.[3]

The essence of the contrast here may ultimately rest on tacit assumptions of an epistemological sort. The mechanists seem to view reality as a matrix of discrete causal events, while the mystics seem to like fluid, probabilistic, and holistic metaphors. One group likes to view the world from without, the other from within. I do not pretend to have an unequivocal resolution to this debate, but I do have some opinions on the warrant for their assumptions and claims. Without belaboring the specific contentions of the mechanists, mystics, and motor theorists, I would argue that, at the present time, the motor theorists appear to offer a "progressive problem shift" (Lakatos, 1970) without violating too much of the embedded wisdom of the two extremes. It might be more accurate to bring motor theories into this dialogue not as a contender so much as a commentator on the contrast. We are indeed the sculptors of our experience, but we must work within tangible boundaries of our individual scaffoldings and limited powers. There is a noteworthy consistency between motor theories of cognition and some of the more modest renditions of transpersonal psychology (cf. Walsh & Vaughan, 1980). In one sense, they are strange companions, but their paths of inquiry seem to have brought them along parallel directions. Personally, I find the extreme mechanistic approaches the least credible, followed at variable distances by the mystics. Conceptually, I sleep with the motor theories, but I keep an eye open.

The point of the foregoing discussion is that constructive ontology—the phenomen of active participation in our reality constructions—appears to be a viable and working hypothesis. As Cris Wil-

---

[3]There is some irony in the fact that John Wheeler, the astrophysicist who coined the term "black hole," has given unintentional ammunition to proponents of holographic and mystical models of the universe (Brush, 1980). Wheeler's interpretation of recent developments in quantum mechanics suggests that "our consciousness affects that which we are conscious of" (Brush, p. 432)—a statement that understandably invites the interest of parapsychologists. According to Wheeler, we are contributors to a "participatory universe." For a discussion of some of the confusions and complexities in this argument, see Weimer (1981a).

liamson notes in one of her songs, we are both "the changer and the changed." How often have we observed or suspected that our clients are unwitting culprits in their own life crises? How often do we witness repetitive patterns of dysfunction and distress that are fueled and directed by idiosyncratic patterns of contracted meaning?

In this sense, one of our major tasks as therapists and theorists lies in the realm of identifying the structures and processes through which our clients construct and construe their everyday existence. Motor theories do not provide a miraculous solution to the problem of translating awareness into action. They do, however, highlight the extent to which our experience is tacitly prepared for us by our central nervous system, and they manage to escape the aforementioned problem of a homunculus by challenging the differentiation of input from output and decentralizing control processes within the individual. Motor theories also suggest that a promising direction for research on intervention strategies may involve a shift away from what the therapist does *to* the client and toward what the client is actively involved in *doing* to and with himself or herself.

HETERARCHICAL STRUCTURALISM

My third major theme deals with the nature and form of relationships within and among our central nervous system (CNS) ordering processes. This theme is one which bears important implications for our models of relatively stable patterns of individuality and unconscious processes and for the omnipresent issues of motivation and resistance in psychotherapy.

The nervous system can be viewed as a survival-enhancing structure the primary functions of which include the maintenance of basic life-support systems. The senses—enteroceptive and exteroceptive—provide the brain with much of is information about internal and external realities, but we must appreciate the variable influence of feedforward mechanisms in constructing, focusing, and assimilating that information. As Hayek (1952b) and others have noted, we seem to be neurologically "wired" to classify our experiences and to transform the "buzzing booming confusion" of sensation into some codified and dynamic *representation* of the world. Research on memory and forgetting is basically directed at investigating our intriguing abilities to transcend spatiotemporal boundaries by means of these hypothesized internal representations. Not surprisingly, we find that our learning and memory abilities are themselves related to certain skills of categorization and condensation. Performances with meaningful material are almost always superior to those obtained when the test materials cannot be assimilated by prior ordering systems.

The point I am moving toward here might be paraphrased by saying that our CNS ordering processes are themselves ordered. They are not only organized and holistically integrated, but they also appear to be functionally stratified. Of course, this stratification is one of the central features of the myriad perspectives subsumed under the rubric of structuralism. For present purposes, I am using the term *hierarchial structuralism* to refer to the contention that our knowing processes are functionally stratified. Put another way, there appear to be patterns of nonreciprocal interaction within the holistic interdependence of the human nervous system. Our theories of language, of personality, and even of the physical universe are imbued with reflections of presumed stratification. We talk about cardinal and surface traits, primary and secondary reinforcement, primary and secondary thinking processes, and deep and surface structures. Here the validity of our models may be less relevant than the frequency with which our brains seem to impose stratification and structure on experience. It should be noted that our conceptions of hierarchy, structure, and stratification are often imbued with the excess connotations of linearity, unidirectional (slave–master) influence, and discrete presumably central regulatory processes. These are *not* intended here, and I shall therefore opt to use the less familiar but more accurate term of *heterarchy* to refer to the decentralized distribution of knowledge and the emergence of what we shall call control from an endless internal coalition and competition among interdependent systems of systems (Hayek, 1967, 1978; Jantsch, 1980; Pattee, 1973, Weimer, 1981a, b).

STRUCTURALISM AND COGNITIVISM

The theme of structuralism is one that invites both contention and confusion in that it often invokes mixed metaphors and semantic ambiguities. Since many of us rely on our visual system to instantiate the concept of structure, we may find ourselves limited and misled by some of the nuances of that system. Some of these problems seem to be receding, however, in recent analyses of the development and dynamics of complex systems. The growing acknowledgment of an interdependence between structure and function is evident in literatures that span several disciplines. Most pertinent here are the structural analyses that have become increasingly popular in personal and

socialized belief systems and in the analyses of hierarchial and heterarchical structure in biological evolution (e.g., Ayala & Dobzhansky, 1974; Campbell, 1974, 1975; Goldstein & Blackman, 1978; Kuhn,
1970a; Lakatos, 1970; Pattee, 1973; Zeleny, 1980). For the sake of
brevity, let me move past the interdisciplinary convergences here and
focus on the potential significance of this notion for our work as
therapists.

To begin with, the idea of ordinations within CNS ordering processes suggests that some of these processes may be more fundamental than others. This notion is hardly new or alien to theorists who
are comfortable with stratified or layered models of human consciousness (Valle & von Eckartsberg, 1981). It is more likely to present
problems for those writers who question the value of inferred mediational processes in our analyses of behavior. For them, stratified
mediational processes are simply a deeper and more costly excursion
into an infinite abyss. Thus, in *About Behaviorism* Skinner (1974)
argues:

> A small part of [one's] inner world can be felt or introspectively observed,
> but it is not an essential part, . . . and the role assigned to it has been
> vastly overrated. . . . It is impossible to estimate the havoc [that theories
> about internal states and processes] have wreaked . . . [upon] effort(s) to
> describe or explain human behavior. (pp. xii–xiii)

The increasing skirmishes between behaviorists and cognitivists are
a reflection of issues that run much deeper than the epistemological
wisdom of operationism, the logical warrant for parsimony, and the
essence of scientific method. Beneath the surface arguments are recurrent hints of tacit assumptions about determinism, personal causation, teleonomy, and the complexity of CNS processes that comprise
and potentiate human experience (Mahoney, 1984).

I digress on this point partly to separate structuralism from cognitivism and partly to preview a forthcoming assertion. In 1974, I
attempted a comparison of nondmediational and mediational models
of human behavior (Mahoney, 1974). My conclusion at that time was
a cautiously optimistic endorsement of the value of cognitive psychology for clinical work. As previously noted, we have recently witnessed a remarkable growth of interest in clinically relevant cognitive
processes and cognitive-behavioral therapies. Several aspects of this
cognitive revolution have concerned me (Mahoney, 1980b), but my
fascination with CNS ordering processes remains undaunted. Far from
being "vastly overrated" (Skinner, 1974), the "inner world" is probably the least understood and potentially most revealing frontier in
contemporary science. Although I sometimes worry that the extreme

cognitivists may try to seal themselves within the organism in an inverted reflection of their behavioral colleagues, I generally trust that we are moving toward a less dichotomous set of vantage points from which to examine ourselves.

Although the cognitive-behavioral therapies have gone in the direction of integrating intrapersonal and external influence processes, I believe that our models still have a long way to go. Private speech, self-statements, and communicable fantasies are apparently important elements in personal adaptation and growth (Beck, 1976; Mahoney, 1974; Mahoney & Arnkoff, 1978; Meichenbaum, 1977; Pope & Singer, 1978; Singer, 1974; Singer & Pope, 1978). As noted earlier, however, our analyses of CNS ordering processes cannot hope to be adequate so long as we treat the most easily measured surface structures as if they were the whole of human consciousness. Words and other public expressions of inner experience are generally crude and distorting representations of our phenomenology. In a quest for public consensus, such as that of science, we are fortunate to have these expressions, however, crude they may be. But we are committing a costly error of translation if we equate what our clients say with what they think and how they feel. Similarly, our preoccupations with cognitive contents may be diverting attention from the critical patterns in cognitive processes. The valuable data base of surface structures—or observable particulars—need not be abandoned in order to expand our analyses into the more elusive and yet more basic structures and dynamics of human experience.

Unconscious Processes

With this assertion we have entered the territories of depth psychology, linguistics, transformational theories, and unconscious processes—a tropical jungle the diversity and fertility of which offer ample opportunities for entanglement, confusion, and obfuscation. I have argued elsewhere that unconscious processes—or, more accurately, tacit ordering processes in the CNS—seem to be increasingly difficult to ignore given the extant arguments and data (e.g., Bowlby, 1979b (this volume); Hayek, 1952b, 1978; Mahoney, 1980a, 1980b; Nisbett & Wilson, 1977; Polanyi, 1966; Shaw & Bransford, 1977; Shevrin & Dickman, 1980; Weimer, 1977). In his stimulating analysis of the structure and functions of the nervous system, Hayek (1952b, 1978) leaves little doubt as to the centrality of unconscious processes in everyday experience. For example, in his discussion of "the primacy of the abstract" (1978), his propositions are spelled out quite clearly:

> The contention which I want to expound and defend here is that . . . all
> the conscious experience that we regard as relatively concrete and pri-
> mary, in particular all sensations, perceptions and images, are the product
> of a super-imposition of many "classifications" of the events perceived. . . .
> What I contend, in short, is that the mind must be capable of performing
> abstract operations in order to be able to perceive particulars, and that
> this capacity appears long before we can speak of a conscious awareness
> of particulars. . . . When we want to explain what makes us tick, we must
> start with the abstract relations governing the order which, as a whole,
> gives particulars their distinct place. (pp. 36–37)

The most obvious implication of this kind of analysis is one that has
been defended and attacked since the turn of the century—namely,
that the scope of our inquiry must be broad enough to accomodate
experiences that are not consciously experienced.

On a more personal and pragmatic level, there is also the invitation to reappraise our assumptions and proscriptions in this domain. Elsewhere I have outlined in more detail my own earlier resistance to the notion of unconscious processes (Mahoney, 1980b). It
took several years for me to recognize these prejudices and achieve
some measure of emancipation from them, and I suspect that there
are still others that will present themselves from time to time. Many
social scientists are understandably reluctant to shift their focus from
public observables to the seemingly less secure realm of private processes. There are arguments for parsimony, arguments against explanatory fictions, and threatening implications that these cognitivist
excursions into mentation are a dangerous step away from science.

I believe that these arguments are well intentioned and that one
can, indeed, point to historical instances wherein the invocation of
tacit mediational processes has apparently encouraged more obfuscation than progress. At the same time, I think we would be naive
and reckless in our theory construction either to deny their potential
significance or to allow our theories to be confined by Freud's (or
anyone else's) notions of unconscious processes. Although there may
not be an adequate contemporary theory of deep structures or processes, I believe that there is some valuable wisdom in the extant
speculations on such foundational systems and processes in experience (Ellenberger, 1970).

I shall illustrate—though hardly justify—my own increased respect for unconscious processes by sharing some clinical experiences.
Several years ago, when I began to explore more open-ended assessment techniques with my clients, I was impressed with the richness
of their self-reports. They offered some hints of ordering patterns that
had not been apparent in their earlier records of private speech pat-

terns. Until then, my clients' self-monitoring assignments had been structured in accordance with my own theoretical assumptions about their belief systems. The emphasis in my clinical assessment had been clearly rationalistic, and much of my attention in therapy was directed at the identification and change of maladaptive beliefs. The novelty and the potential relevance of their responses to my newer techniques were sufficient, however, to pique my clincial and scientific interests, and I was soon encouraging clients to share segments of their "stream of consciousness" during our sessions. The essence of my technique was not unlike that of free association except that I used a gentle induction of trusting relaxation and would occasionally interrupt a client's report to illustrate and/or encourage significant themes.[4] Because of the utility of this procedure in offering *in vivo* instantiations of tacit world views, I now explore the benefits of "streaming" with many of my clients. An extensive literature on some dimensions of this process already exists (Klinger, 1971; Pope & Singer, 1978; Singer & Pope, 1978). In an effort to increase the clinical utility of these streams, several colleagues and I have been working toward developing a system of classifying their contents and patterns.

Another contribution to my increased respect for unconscious processes has come from explorations of my own feedforward mechanisms. I do not claim to be intimately familiar with and accepting of those processes, but I have become increasingly respectful of their influence in my personal and professional life. Over the years, I have tried to expose myself to a wide range of theoretical models. My research on psychological processes in science reflects this interest in personal and social processes in knowing. I have tried to remain open to the value of heterogeneity and tacit features of invariance. Besides having some genuine personal motives, I have been interested in gleaning the embedded bits of wisdom in our attempts to help each other. My experiences in psychotherapy workshops, retreats, and individual therapies have deepened my appreciation for my own tacit scaffoldings. A hopeful skeptic, I have had the privilege of exploring both the experiential and the theoretical dimensions of these different approaches. In the process of learning about them, of course, I have also learned a lot about myself. For example, I came to recognize a tacit resistance to "non-talking cures"—the evocative therapies and other interventions that deviated from my comfortable role as a spectating therapist. I also became aware of my continual testing of a

---

[4]This technique may be similar to some of the experimental procedures used by Kulpe and Buhler in their early investigations of imageless thought. It is described in more detail elsewhere (Mahoney, 1983, in press).

therapy in ways that subtly reduced its chances of infiltrating my core assumptions about change. And I came to appreciate the persistence, pervasiveness, and self-protectiveness of some chronic patterns of self-world interactions.

These are hardly earthshaking insights, and they may not have the rhetorical force of a few dramatized case histories. My remarks serve only to expand a point that has already fueled our dialectics for quite some time—namely, that our "normal waking consciousness" may, in the words of William James (1901/1958) be "but one special type of consciousness" (p. 298). The nature, functions, and patterns of other types of experience present a formidable problem for depth psychologies. Heterarchical structuralism suggests that our understanding of human experience might be enriched by a more balanced appreciation of fundamental ordering processes and their associated expressions. Needless to say, the challenge is a formidable one, and it is all the more complicated by its immersion in paradign politics and by the myopia that always makes difficult the forecasting of a progressive problem shift (Lakatos, 1970).

The declining popularity of orthodox psychoanalysis (Garfield & Kurtz, 1976) could reflect a rejection of unconscious determinants in our causal analyses. Such a rejection might be both premature and excessive if we place any stock whatsoever in the cutting edge of contemporary psychobiology, epistemology, and cognitive psychology. And the most central question, in my opinion, is not one of salvage: that is, what should we retain of Freud's hypotheses? In some ways, the new look offered by today's structuralists may require some sweeping shifts in old notions of determinism and causation. As a brief illustration, one of Hayek's (1978) passing comments on the "sub-conscious" will suffice:

> It is generally taken for granted that in some sense conscious experience constitutes the highest level in the hierarchy of mental events, and that what is not conscious has remained sub-conscious because it has not yet risen to that level. . . . If my conception is correct . . . [we are not aware of much that happens in our mind] not because it proceeds at too low a level but because it proceeds at too high a level. It would seem more appropriate to call such processes not sub-conscious but super-conscious, because they govern the conscious processes without appearing in them. (p. 45)

This perspective challenges the idea that adaptation and growth entail the moving of unconscious material "upward" into awareness. Indeed, it highlights the naiveté of two-dimensional structuralism as well as some of our tacit arrogance about the role of awareness in experience. A message that seems to be frequently repeated by modern structuralists has already been noted here in reference to meaning change and psychotherapy—namely, that an adequate analysis must address process as well as content.

Related to the theme of hierarchical structuralism is the emergent hypothesis that there may be a correlation between stratification and mutability. The essential schemata for experience—those that bear on such issues as the trustworthiness of sense data, identity, causation, values, and self-world relationships—this core of schemata is probably more difficult to change than more peripheral or specialized ordering processes (Mahoney, 1980b). This greater resistance to change may derive from their chronological primacy in the developing organism. Experiences that occur early in the lifespan—especially if they are autonomically intense and repeated—seem to leave a noticeable mark on the developing person (Ainsworth, 1979; Bowlby, 1973, 1979a; Sroufe, 1979). Such experiences need not be critical or insurmountable to constitute formative influences in the development of personal meaning structures. (For the vying opinions on this issue, see Kagan, 1976; Kagan, Kearsley, & Zelazo, 1978; Lipsitt, 1979; and Rutter, 1972.) That such early experiences are formative is all too apparent in psychotherapy clients.

It is also apparent that change, when it is effected, seems to consolidate rather than eliminate prior patterns of adaptation. As reflected in our literatures on extinction, relapse, and recidivism, earlier patterns of thought, feeling, and action are seldom eradicated. Instead, they appear to be competing candidates for experience, and they often seem to win the competition during stressful or novel episodes in a client's struggle toward personal change. In a manner that may reflect the wisdom of individuality within evolution, new scaffoldings for experience may offer an option to override previous schematic patterns. When the override is experienced as a failure, the organism wisely falls back on old and familar schemata for its directives.

OSCILLATIVE PROCESSES IN CHANGE

Retracing my remarks thus far, I have talked about the primacy of meaning, personal responsiblity in the construction of meaning, and the stratification of our CNS ordering processes. In this section, I shall try to pull these themes together. Our earlier discussion of meaning noted that human consciousness appears to be permeated with contrasts and polarities. The main conjecture in this section is that these contrasts may be related to the experience of disequilibrium and the energization of human change processes. Although binary cybernetic metaphors seem less than adequate in describing our internal processes, in another sense the concept of contrast may offer some helpful directions for our theorizing.

Let us return for a moment to the assertion that the nervous system is an organ of classification and order. This assertion presumes an ability to differentiate and relate—to identify perceptual invariants (Gibson, 1966) and to create functional, pragmatic, or meaningful webs of relationship among our representations of reality. Polanyi (1966), Hayek (1952b, 1978), and others have cogently argued that our awareness of the tacit or abstract rules employed by the nervous system may be inherently limited by our abilities to classify, correlate, and—in a sense—perceive our own ordering patterns. Also, our most respected models of our universe invoke sharp contrasts between such categories as matter and energy, part and whole, good and evil, reality and unreality. This is not to say that there are no gray areas between a set of polarities, but only to note the frequency with which we rely on contrasting reference points to stabilize and define a dimension.

This same reliance on certain kinds of contrast may well be operative in our personal constructions of reality and in our capacities for change. Just as Kuhn (1977) has come to defend the role of an "essential tension" in the dynamic progression of scientific thought, we may find ourselves confronting a similar concept in the realm of personal thought. If so, this concept could have implications for the processes of change in and outside psychotherapy. If meaning change lies at the heart of personal change—and if meaning is itself a fedforward relationship between our CNS scaffolding and the furniture of experience—then personal change may involve some tacit and explicit restructurings of our assimilating processes. In ways reminiscent of Herbert's and Piaget's concepts of assimilation and accommodation, our exchanges with the world around us may involve dynamic expansions of our conceptual scaffoldings.

EQUILIBRIUM AND EMOTIONAL PROCESSES

The concepts of equilibrium and disequilibrium permeate our psychological theories and our therapeutic interventions. We acknowledge that the human nervous system appears to have incorporated a "negative feedback logic" in its structure and functions.

The lower-brain and midbrain structures seem to be wired to protect homeostasis. When we are within the limits of acceptable deviation from our "set points," we are more likely to be experiencing the equanimity of equilibrium. When we violate the boundaries of that contrast, however, we enter the domain of disequilibrium and usually initiate actions to restore balance to our *milieu intérieur* (Bernard, 1865/1957). This same metaphor permeates our theories of personality and psychotherapy in that our clients' most common request— and a therapist's most comfortable goal—is usually equilibration. In psychotherapy, the elusive balance that is sought is most often located in the domain of emotive processes. I shall therefore comment briefly on some of the ramifications of that emphasis.

To begin with, I share the concern expressed by several existential and humanistic therapists about the extent to which contemporary psychotherapies have assented to a static equilibration model of personal well-being (e.g., Bugental, 1965, 1978; Maslow, 1971). When clients request our assistance in reducing and controlling the pain and debilitation of their personal struggles, I believe our most humane intentions lie in the direction of that assistance. What seems less certain is whether our attention should remain unilaterally focused at the level of emotional control. Virtually all of our intervention attempts stem from a metatheory that uses harmony, balance, or equanimity as its tacit direction. I have recently begun to wonder whether that direction—as precious as I believe it may be to our well-being—fully captures the dynamics of our human predicament. In our attempts rapidly to reduce emotional turbulence, I sometimes wonder if we are not rushing to quiet the messenger long before we have comprehended the message. The bulk of our specifiable techniques for helping seems to be aimed at achieving emotional satisfaction, directly or indirectly, without our more fully examining the role of contrasts and feelings in our personal experience.

Few psychologists would question the importance of studying the nature and functions of emotionality in human development (cf. Lewis & Rosenbaum, 1978; Plutchik & Kellerman, 1980; Yarrow, 1979; Zajonc, 1980). It seems clear that emotional changes are bound up with significant personal changes. It is also clear that we manifest a long-standing tradition of conceptualizing emotions as both expressions and driving forces in those changes. What I find most intriguing at the moment are the hypothesized oscillative processes that superordinate the emotive ones. By "oscillative" I do not necessarily mean temporal shifts in valence or configuration, although oscillative patterns are readily apparent in our adaptation (Aschoff, 1981; Ferguson,

1980; Land, 1973). In its present use *oscillative* refers to the dynamic tension between contrasts in our ordering processes. Parallel notions can be found in Kuhn's (1977) concept of essential tension, meta-theories of dialectics, opponent-process theories of motivation (e.g., Solomon, 1980), two-factor learning theory (Mowrer, 1960a), axiology (theories of value), and a wide range of metatheories that echo the yin and yang of a holistic approach.

The extant strategies for dealing with emotional contrasts appear to fall into one or more of the following categories:

1. *Discharge*, which is evidenced in evocative and cathartic therapies (Nichols & Zax, 1977)
2. *Control*, which is really a superordinate concept for those therapies that pit the person against his or her emotive processes
3. *Denial*, which is usually accomplished by a diversion of the experienced energy
4. *Confrontation*, which overlaps with the first two in its acknowledgment and engagement with emotive processes (cf. Rachman, 1980)
5. *Reframing*, which attempts to redefine the contrast
6. *Transcendance*, in which the contrast is not only redefined, but also used to move the system forward

My remarks here are not intended to endorse a particular strategy so much as to reflect upon all of them. I do, however, want to comment on what appear to be converging paths in our secular wanderings. For example, consider the following commentary on the processes of change:

> General kinds of "cognitive pendulums" or systematic shifts with development apply.... Among these are: (1) shifts from rapid acquisition of new skills and rules to limited growth while old skills and rules are repeatedly applied, and (2) shifts from one quality to its opposite, as from broad to narrow, from stable to unstable, and from loosely-related components to a highly integrated and complex level.

Out of context, these could be the words of a cognitive theorist or a transcendentalist. In reality, they are a rendition of pendulum theory in developmental linguistics (Nelson & Nelson, 1978, p. 226).

Another gem of apparent convergence comes from the worlds of physics and chemistry. For his revolutionary theory of dissipative structures Ilya Prigogine (1980) was recently awarded a Nobel prize. Aside from challenging the second law of thermodynamics and our revered concept of entropy, Prigogine's theory comments on the role of oscillative contrasts in the development of any open system. His theory and data suggest that disequilibrium—when it reaches a crit-

ical criterion—helps to drive an open system in the direction of restructuring its ordering processes. The initial structures for assimilating and balancing energy contrasts must transform in order to
accommodate the disequilibrium. The principle underlying dissipative self-organizaton, called "order through fluctuations," has already
stimulated some intriguing hypotheses about personal and social development (cf. Ferguson, 1980; Jantsch, 1980; Zeleny, 1980). The process of dissipative self-organization is one that clearly reflects the
spontaneous development of progressively higher levels of order within
the system.

When I first learned of Prigogine's work, I was struck by its parallels in psychotherapy. I was particularly interested in the processes
of transformation, hoping that the fields of chemistry and physics
might offer some useful metaphors for my work in helping clients to
restructure—or, perhaps more accurately, develop—their tacit constructions of self (identity), world (reality), and their interrelationships. Of particular heuristic and practical interest was the idea that
episodes of psychological disequilibrium may reflect and/or stimulate
fundamental restructuring processes in the central nervous system.
If this is the case, our analyses must withdraw to a molar vantage
point, and our efforts to achieve rapid emotional equilibration must
be reappraised. This line of thinking is buttressed by a growing number of oscillative theories in personal and systems development (cf.
Ayala & Dobzhansky, 1974; Campbell, 1975; Capra, 1975; Davidson
& Davidson, 1980; Ferguson, 1980; Ford, Note 2; Hayek, 1952b, 1978;
Kuhn, 1977; Lakatos & Musgrave, 1970; Land, 1973; Leonard, 1972;
Mahoney, 1981; Pribram, 1980; Progoff, 1975; Russell, 1945; Weimer,
1977, 1979, 1984; Zukav, 1979). Therapists who have focused on transformational processes in change have suggested that our therapeutic
interventions may be more helpful when they direct the energy of
crisis toward basic reconstructions of personal meaning. Joy (1978),
for example, comments as follow:

> Realizing that the specific problem of the client is only the shadow of a
> much deeper pattern dynamic, the Transformational therapist does not
> start at the problem level, the level at which the client perceives the
> difficulty. Instead, the Transformational therapist tries to comprehend
> the pattern level of consciousness, which is manifesting the "problem,"
> and to focus the transmutational energy there. Nothing of much value . . .
> will happen if the client's awareness is allowed to remain in the per-
> spective of the problem. (p. 216)

Joy describes the three major paths to problem resolution outlined
by the Tibetan Buddhist approach: (1) *transmutation*, which is roughly
equivalent to a restructuring of cognitive-experiential processes through

the development of higher-order scaffolding; (2) *ennoblement*, which consists in reframing the problem as an important life task; and (3) *distanced manifestation*, which entails a joint effort to allow the problem to manifest itself fully while one simultaneously disidentifies from it. A fourth strategy, evidently not endorsed by the Tibetan Buddhists, is simply to wear the problem out. As Joy (1978) aptly notes, this strategy seems to be the unfortunate predicament of all too many psychotherapy clients.

An intriguing question for researchers interested in oscillative processes and personal change has to do with the parameters and patterns involved in the transformation of meaning. Emotional arousal has long been recognized as a facilitator of belief change (Frank, 1973; Nichols & Zax, 1977; Sargant, 1957). The necessity and functions of affective disequilibrium remain only modestly understood, however. Should the psychotherapy client be encouraged to develop skills for coping with such dysphoria or for controlling it? Should the disequilibrium be "ennobled" and the problem reframed? What are the effects of symptom prescription on the meaning assigned to personal distress?[5] The developing literatures on autopoiesis and dissipative structures suggest that spontaneously ordering open systems may become locked into unprogressive and even regressive cycles of instability or stagnation when their self-organizing processes are thwarted (cf. Jantsch, 1980; Prigogine, 1980; Zeleny, 1980). Is there warrant to draw a parallel here to the client who is stuck in a chronic pattern of self-defeating efforts which seem to transform the solution into a problem? These are issues that warrant our thoughtful attention.

ATTENTION AND EFFORT

To illustrate further the potential relevance of oscillative processes for our theoretical investments, I shall conclude this section with some emergent hunches about the interrelationships among our arbitrary dimensions of contrast, value, meaning, and emotionality. First, it would not be surprising to find that attentional processes lie at the heart of therapeutic change. With their apparent connection to our concepts of vilgilance, meaning, and the direction of experi-

---

[5]One must be careful to distinguish between the therapeutic strategies of *symptom prescription* (Watzlawick, 1978) and *paradoxical intention* (Frankl, 1978 and this volume). As I understand them, the latter places more emphasis on the functional *intent* of problematic patterns rather than the nature of enactment of the specific "symptoms" *per se*.

ence, these processes appear to premonitor and construct the focal areas of our moment-to-moment engagements in life.

Despite the probable role of attentional processes in meaning change, however, I doubt whether significant personal change can be effected by means of superficial strategies of stimulus control and focalized meditation. Since attentional processes are likely to be a reflection of fundamental ordering processes, there may be more practical yield in those approaches that attempt to sketch the metastructures to which attention is subservient. The literatures of paradoxical intention, symptom prescription, and psychological reversals, for example, point to the limited mutability of both the contents and processes of attention (Apter, 1982; Bandler & Grinder, 1975, 1979; Frankl, 1978 and this volume; Haley, 1973; Raskin & Klein, 1976; Sveback and Stoyva, 1980; Watzlawick, 1978). My hunch is that therapies that look above and beneath attentional processes may yield more promise than those that restrict their focus to that dimension. This is not, however, an invitation to narcissistic depth. I agree with Kopp (1978) that although the unexamined life may not be worth living, "the unlived life is not worth examining" (p. 72). A balanced appreciation of the dynamic interplay between feedforward and feedback mechanisms may be our most reasonable hope at this time.

A second theme that is placed in focus by oscillative processes is the role of effort and surrender in personal well-being. Contemporary Western ideologies continue to reflect an impatient preoccupation with increasing the boundaries of personal causation (Fogle, 1978). We long to control our feelings, our actions, and our lives (cf. Perlmuter & Monty, 1979), and our attempts to do so often involve attentive effort (cf. Pribram & McGuinness, 1975). Embedded in our desperate quest for control is a metatheory of personal and public freedom. And much of that freedom is libertarian in flavor: it seeks freedom from its contexts rather than freedom within them (Hayek, 1978; Weimer, 1984). The net message to our cultural participants is to try harder. Little wonder, then, that we appear to lead the world in dysphoria and stress-related diseases. The Eastern alternative to effort is surrender, a relatively passive intentionality that attempts to integrate and utilize the contrasting powers of internal and external influence. By many Western readers, *surrender* is read as *defeat* and equated with a submissive deference to fatalistic processes. The accuracy of this translation is questionable, however, inasmuch as the meaning of trans-paradigmatic concepts can never be accurately grasped from the context of a foreign perspective (cf. Radnitzky, 1981; Walsh, 1980).

The practical implications of the effort–surrender issue merit our close attention. To me, the relevance of this issue is most apparent in disorders that involve sympathetic-parasympathetic conflicts—anxiety, insomnia, and several sexual dysfunctions. Here there are clearly times when effort seems to get in the way of progress, and I am comfortable encouraging patience, gentleness, and some kind of self-trust. But does this pattern extend beyond the above-mentioned instances of autonomic coordination? At this point, I must say I don't know. In all honesty, however, I would add that I have been actively exploring this possibility in my work as a therapist and that I have been encouraged by the results to date (Mahoney, in press). My most credible successes have thus far come in areas wherein a client has been struggling with apparent resistance processes. I shall therefore close this section with a few comments on the significance of these processes for meaningful change.

RESISTANCE

Let us begin by respectfully separating this concept from its Freudian legacy. Although there are clear parallels, my use of the term *resistance* derives more from cognitive psychology, psychobiology, and clinical practice than from classical psychoanalytic theory. The reality of resistance also appears to be less controversial than its meaning. Our vast literatures on stress reduction, lifestyle change, and psychotherapy appear to converge on the difficulty of and resistance to personal change. Relatively little clinical experience is needed to confront the ambivalence behind many therapeutic undertakings. This conflict about change can be experienced and expressed in many different ways. Resistance processes are often most apparent when significant meaning structures are being challenged. This resistance may occur early in therapy, but it is more common when disequilibrium is intense and demanding. The parallel to dissipative structures and to critical instability thresholds is a tempting one to draw in that resistance to change seems to intensify with the demands for that change. My first point here is to comment on the wisdom of such resistance in a heterarchically structured complex system. There is a sensed survival value in protecting and perpetuating old reality constructions, especially those which have been central to our experience. These constructions may well feedforward an active reluctance to be examined or changed.

In his insightful analysis of what a scientist may experience during the revolution and evolution of paradigms, Lakatos (1970) offered an intriguing interdisciplinary comment on intrapersonal resistance processes. He argues that the hard core of a belief system is functionally surrounded by a protective belt the function of which is to divert reality tests away from the hard core. This diversion is accomplished by two opponent subprocesses of the protective belt—a "negative heuristic" that directs one away from certain paths of engagement and a "positive heuristic" that encourages patterns that do not threaten the hard core of a paradigm. How many of us have seen comparable processes in ourselves and our clients? How often do we foreclose on credibility before experiencing the returns of an excursion beyond familiar ordering patterns? And how often are our clients locked into so-called neurotic patterns of insecurity by rejecting old scaffoldings almost as vigorously as they avoid alternative ones?[6]

Freud is said to have abandoned hypnosis because it sidestepped the processes of resistance. My own experiences as a therapist have led me to agree cautiously that a vast amount of personal energy seems to be channeled into the avoidance of certain changes. For example, several of my clients seemed to have identified with their problems to the point that symptomatic improvements were frightening assaults on identity. When I asked one chronically depressed man what he thought it would take for him to change, he answered, "I guess I would have to be someone else." After several months of therapy, another woman reported experiencing unprecedented periods of well-being but lamented that they could not be authentic if *she* were experiencing them.[7] The same woman offered a vivid illustration of the protective role of resistance to the examination or change of core ordering processes. When we first began to work intensively

---

[6]It is interesting to speculate that the "protective belt" postulated by Lakatos may involve many of the ego functions hypothesized by personality theorists. Western metatheories encourage a strengthening of the ego, while many Eastern ideologies contend that the ego must be weakened and stripped away in healthy development. A structuralist compromise might take the form of redirecting the protective focus of such processes so that a higher order structure can emerge.

[7]In cases wherein symptomatology has merged with personal identity, techniques of distancing or disidentification may be valuable. These techniques, which are espoused by a wide range of therapies, encourage the individual to develop a boundary between identity—the dynamic integrity of the whole system—and the momentary particulars of experience. They may also aid in extricating a person from a meaning structure to the point that the structure can be recognized as a formerly tacit operational scheme. The problem with distancing techniques may be akin to that noted in our discussion of effort and surrender, however—viz., their appropriateness may vary with time, the nature of the problem, and personality components. They may also accentuate and amplify issues of identity and control.

on the process as well as on the content of her depression, I used
stream of consciousness as both an assessment and reactive examination of her attentional patterns. During her second experience with
streaming, she experienced intense terror and bolted upright from
the exercise. My inquiries revealed that she was experiencing what
she called "tunnels." She described these tunnels as follows:

> They come in when I'm in trouble. They keep me away from things and
> they won't let anything in . . . just enough to function.

When I asked her if she could draw one, she said that they were not
really visual. Part of the time she felt the presence of a tunnel, but
only occasionally did she "see" something resembling one. As depicted by her drawing in Figure 2, it was—in her own words—more
like seeing *through* them." Our later work in therapy led both of us
to conclude that the experience of her tunnels varied with her examination of some of her most basic assumptions. In later months,
she experienced the tunnel phenomenon many times as she moved
through our therapy sessions and her own change processes. These
experiences became less frequent as our work progressed, but their
intensity and patterns seem to reflect the protection given to our
fundamental ordering processes.

FIGURE 2. A client's rendition of perceptual defense "tunnels."

My strategy for dealing with cognitive entrenchment processes is not unlike that espoused by others who have voiced a respect for the role of resistance in therapy (e.g., Bugenthal, 1978; Haley, 1973). I try to deal with it in a manner that reduces the need for entrenchment, that recognizes developmental patterns or styles of coping (Bowlby, 1979a), and that channels that same protective energy in the service of a progressive shift in personal paradigms (Mahoney, in press). Several years ago I believed that these shifts might be accomplished by means of precipitous "cognitive clicks" similar to those experienced in such figure–ground transformations as the Necker cube (see Figure 3; Mahoney, 1974). More recently I have come to appreciate that those clicks are seldom developmentally climactic. They seem to be important reflections of shifts in personal meaning, but they are not tantamount to an enduring and sufficient transformation of the overall system. More often than not, they are experienced as startling perceptual/phenomenological shifts that reflect increasing flexibility and ambiguity in the individual's reality constructions.

This is not to deny, of course, that such experiences may occasionally suggest a transformation of formidable personal significance. This finding was illustrated for me in the case of a woman who had been severely incapacitated by agoraphobia for almost six years. Two years of psychoanalysis had apparently exacerbated the problem. Although she had reached terminal behavior on a cognitive-behav-

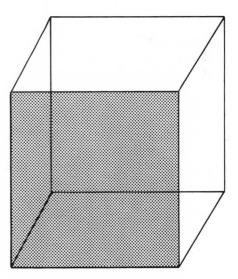

FIGURE 3. The Necker cube.

ioral program of therapy, her subjective distress and incapacitation remained extreme. During almost two years of work with me, she reported intense "waves" of autonomic arousal and cognitive disequilibrium. These culminated in a brief period of diffuse affect and courageous personal struggle, after which the agoraphobia suddenly dissipated. When I asked her to describe her experience, I was struck by the magnitude of the shift:

> You know, [parts of my past] seem like a dream . . . in the sense of its being hard to remember *that* life as anything but so far away in both time and mind—it's hard even to feel it anymore—I *remember*, but it's like . . . the whole thing . . . was just this 5- or 6-year interruption in my life.

Precipitous shifts like this one are relatively rare both in and outside psychotherapy, perhaps because of the self-protective aspects of core CNS ordering processes. From my own limited experience with significant personal transformations, such shifts appear to be correlated with long and intense engagement with formerly tacit features of one's hard core (cf. Bugental, 1978; Guidano & Liotti, 1983).

If we hope to expand our understanding of human change processes, we must respect the inherent self-protective mechanisms within complex open systems. With that understanding, we may learn better to recognize our clients' multifaceted "escapes from freedom" (Fromm, 1941) and to facilitate their attempts to overcome the limitations of prior meaning structures.

PARTICIPATORY VITALISM

The fifth and final theme for my remarks has to do with the concept of hope and its role in personal change and well-being. Although its absence is often acknowledged as a factor in affective disorders, hope remains one of those ethereal topics that has escaped serious scientific attention.[8] In recent years it has begun to make so ubiquitous an appearance in our theories that one wonders how long we can continue to overlook it. In Burton's (1976) collection of contemporary theories of psychotherapy process, for example, we find the theme of hope permeating the thinking of some of our most respected authorities. Marmor speaks of the role of "faith, hope, and expectancy" in a client, and Salzman titles his contribution "The Will to Change." Bandura's (1976) comments reflect his growing re-

[8]It is noteworthy that Mowrer's (1960a, 1960b) two-factor learning theory incorporated hope and fear as central and related elements in motivation and learning.

spect for "self-efficacy" and the parameters determing self-percep-
tions of adequacy. Frank (1976) offers the thesis that "a major function
of all schools of psychotherapy is to restore morale" (p. 73). Viewing
demoralization as a frequent characteristic of persons who seek therapy, he argues that a successful therapy must be able to combat
"feelings of helplessness, hopelessness, impotence, and isolation" (1976,
p. 79; see also Frank, this volume). A parallel endorsement of autonomy, self-direction, and personal adequacy is offered by Strupp and
by theorists representing a number of other approaches.

The apparent consensus on the role of hope in psychotherapy
may not be surprising given the frequency with which we encounter
this concept in philosophy, religion, biography, and fiction (Barrett,
1967; Durant & Durant, 1970; Friedman, 1967, 1974; Hendin, 1978;
Russell, 1945). Whatever it is, hope appears to be a perennial theme
in our analyses of the human condition. I bring it into the present
discussion because I believe that its importance merits reiteration. I
would also like to believe that contemporary psychology can make a
valuable contribution to our understanding of its role in personal
well-being.

Let me begin by offering a tentative definition of hope as an
expectation of or trust in the satisfactory value of future experience.
Rather than dwell on the semantics of the concept, I shall plunge
more directly toward some pragmatics. My main contention here can
be outlined as follows: *Since we appear to be active participants in
constructing and influencing the realities which, in turn, shape us, we
bear some responsiblity for the nature of our exchanges with the world.*
Our control is, of course, often limited, so that the boundaries of
causal responsiblilty—as contrasted with physical and social accountability—may fluctuate dynamically across exchanges. Hope appears to be an influential factor in our multifaceted involvements
with life processes at individual and social levels. To the extent that
we value such involvements, we are well advised to respect the power
of hope and our own role in its generative processes.

TELEONOMY AND GROWTH

The concept of hope cannot be adequately addressed without
touching upon its connections with such themes as love, faith, humanism, and vitalism. As Friedman (1967, 1974) has so aptly noted
in his analyses of the "hidden human image," our everyday exchanges
with each other, ourselves, and the world around us are richly imbued
with a web of assumptions about human nature, cosmology, deter-

minism, existential absurdities, pragmatics, and so forth. One of the themes that seems to recur quite frequently in our widely varying ideologies is that of *vitalism* or, in the language of evolutionary biologists, *teleonomy* (Ayala & Dobzhansky, 1974). At the risk of over-simplification, teleonomy refers to the inherent ordering processes which serve to direct the maintenance and growth of open systems. Whereas teleology implies a tacit or explicit destination, teleonomy connotes more of a flexible direction. I say "flexible" because inherent ordering processes must always contend with unpredictable constraints in their expression. Thus, in his attempt to integrate the wisdom of biological reductionism and evolutionary vitalism, Campbell (1974) notes that our development—as persons and systems—is influenced by our encounters with selective "natural laws" which often stimulate and preserve novel patterns of adaptation.

Notions of growth, negentropy, and dynamic processes in development have, of course, been recorded for centuries. Henri Bergson developed the first clear philosophy of vitalism when he linked reality, life and values to an *élan vital*, or vital force, which might be described in the lyric words of Kahlil Gibran (1923) as "life longing after itself." Although vitalism was soon overshadowed by the movements toward existentialism, positivism, and pragmatism, its continued presence is not difficult to discern in our poetry, fiction, and reflections on human directions (e.g. Barrett, 1967; Ferguson, 1980; Hendin, 1978). As Friedman (1967) and others have noted, Bergson's idealistic rendition of vitalism committed "the fatal error of assuming that any movement onward is also upward" (p. 72). Although we may be wise to respect and value the teleonomic dimensions in our lives, we must also contend with the existential responsibilities inherent in the processes of living. Hence, the heading of "participatory vitalism." We are participants in the dynamic exchange that constitutes a human life. We are simultaneously cause and effect, choice and chance, figure and ground. Our understanding is incomplete, our power often limited, and yet the demands of life remain frequently unsympathetic.

This is where hope may be recognized as an elusive ether that permeates all perseverance. Our studies into human suffering leave little doubt about the preciousness of hope, while our records of war and destruction tell us that misguided hope can also be directed in the service of inhumane goals. Out of all the life forms on our planet, we appear to be most capable of transcending time and space. We remember, consciously and otherwise, the constructed lessons of past experience, and we lean toward our future with a preparatory mixture of hope and fear. I concur with Frank (1974, 1976, this volume) that the people who most often seek our assistance in psychotherapy suffer from an imbalance in these inclinations. That imbalance is often understandable in light of their life history and personal sensitivities. I also believe that their dysphoria is often a valuable element in energizing and directing their lives. But without hope there is little engagement in either life or change, and without engagement there is little left that we recognize as human.

RESPONSIBLE HOPE

Significant personal change is seldom achieved without sacrifice, suffering, and a kind of loneliness that eludes description. In reflecting on his own energetic life as a philosopher, humanitarian, and human being, Russell (1967) noted the preciousness of human love in relieving "that terrible loneliness in which one shivering consciousness looks over the rim of the world into the cold unfathomable lifeless abyss." The loneliness and suffering experienced by psychotherapy clients often seems to emanate from a kindred dimension. It is during these periods of core vulnerability and need that we may recognize both the value and the importance of our role as therapists.

The processes of psychotherapy are indistinguishable from more generic processes of change, and they are therefore operative before and after our privileged exchanges with a client. In this sense, it is difficult to imagine those processes being completed or finished within any given period of personal development. Within the time-limited relationship that constitutes intensive psychotherapy, however, there is often a need to deal with attributions of power and the wellsprings of hope. As tempting as it may seem to be placed on a pedestal by a client, client attributions that excessively credit the therapist's person, theory, or techniques may jeopardize a client's appreciations of his or her own role in both the development and transformation of a change crisis. This is not to diminish the value of professional assistance nor to overrate the boundaries of clients' personal causation. There is, indeed, an important role for balanced reciprocity of respect. My point here is that the "retreat to authorities" (Bartley, 1962) must eventually find itself in the personal arena of commitment and trust. A client who trusts in my competency as a therapist, for example, must first trust in his or her skill in the selection of a trustee. The analysis, when pursued far enough, always returns us to "home"— to personal meaning structures and their pragmatic obligations. Psychotherapy, when pursued toward its optimal yield, usually finds the client acknowledging his or her readiness to move forward in life without regular professional assistance and with a deeper appreciation of personal resources.

REFLECTIONS AND CONCLUDING REMARKS

I have reflected along five interrelated themes—the primacy of meaning, the role of feedforward mechanisms in our constructions of meaning, the stratification of our ordering systems, oscillative processes in stability and change, and the value of responsible hope. Although my remarks have sometimes approached the arrogance of a formal hypothesis, they have usually remained tentative and discursive. Those familiar with my work will not be surprised by that tentativeness. I am a cautious optimist, and my remarks probably emanate from some tacit structures well removed from my awareness. I do have the opportunity to edit my remarks, of course, so I accept responsiblity for what I have said in this attempted account of my present thoughts and intuitions about therapy.

One of the primary goals of this paper has been to raise questions about the fundamental processes of human change. Progressive inquiry always leads to more questions than answers, more opening than closure. Rather than summarize or review my remarks, let me therefore conclude with a few emergent questions and a brief commentary on the conduct of psychotherapy. My questions begin with some fundamentals and move toward particulars:

1. How might we improve our understanding of change processes? Is our current scientific knowledge being avoidably constrained by theoretical filters, inappropriate assessments, and technical tyranny?

2. To what extent are we aware of tacit feedforward processes in our conceptions and enactments of therapy? How would the quality of our therapy be influenced by our becoming more or less parochial in our ideological boundaries?

3. To what extent do our graduate training programs offer students the most meaningful and relevant experiences for their careers as helping professionals?

4. What would be the effects of widening our conceptions of science to accommodate qualitative as well as quantitative research?

5. What would be the effects of moving away from molecular techniques and toward the study of therapy in its broader context as a personal and cultural exchange?

6. What are the most important questions for directing our research programs?

Questions like these may prove helpful in refining our understanding of human change processes. My own responses to them would necessarily reflect a deepening appreciation of the complexity and potential of human growth processes. In my privileged role as a socially sanctioned professional life counselor, I have sensed the formidable depth and breadth of a person's capacities for adaptation and development. I have tried, sometimes unsuccessfully, to help people free themselves from stubborn patterns of suffering and self-limitation. But I have also had the honor of witnessing moderate and occasionally dramatic changes in my clients—changes in self-concept, reality constructions, and the fluctuating interface of these crude constructs. I have never "cured" a client of a mental disease; I do not know what that would be like. But I have seen people transcend and transform painful constraints on their personal freedom, and the experience has been both humbling and inspiring.

The fact that clients' progress has seldom been painless or rapid makes me worry about the implications of the recent trend toward prescriptive brevity in psychotherapy. With the growing emphasis on accountability by government and health care agencies, there comes a temptation to dilute our therapies and to define success in terms of what we can achieve in less than 20 sessions. Occasionally, that is plenty of time; sometimes it is just what the client needed. But what do we do about persons who are struggling with "tenured" core schemata that constrict or complicate their lives? What do we do about the clients who need more time? I believe we are in trouble when the length of therapy is equated with its quality. Some clients, and admittedly some of us therapists, need more time than others. That is reality. We are naive if we believe we can force human change processes into certain statutes of limitation.

I believe that psychotherapy can offer helpful assistance in human adaptation and development; that it can be a catalyst for the kinds of transformations, sharp and subtle, that nurture a life toward a fuller expression of its identity in the dynamic contexts of an open system. The kind of psychotherapy I am talking about remains an elusive ideal for today's practitioners. It has not been captured by any of the competing ideologies. Nor does it lie hidden behind our annual progression of new techniques. Techniques are valuable but crude expressions; they are ritualized communications about *our* constructions of reality and *our* intentions for our clients (Mahoney, in press). It is *beneath* our techniques—in the murky realm of those constructions and intentions— that we may sense our grasp of human change processes. And it is beneath the familiarity of our role as therapists that we may come to sense and appreciate our privileged role as guides, counselors, and observers of the human pilgrimage.

I shall therefore close with an acknowledgment of the unity of our intent, if not of our methods. In the next few decades, psychotherapy may well face one of its most formative challenges. In my opinion, that challenge is not in the demand for demonstrated impact. Instead, it is in our reaction to those demands. Unless we are prepared to meet those demands with a courage born of conviction, we may risk compromising our humanitarian foundations. Relevance, effectiveness, and cost-efficiency are legitimate requests, but let us not lose sight of the fundamental issues of value on which they are based. However it may be conceptualized or enacted, psychotherapy reflects both an intention and a commitment to helping people. Let us not overlook either of these in the debates on our status as a science, art, or service. I believe that we already have much to *offer* and that the responsiblities of having a "window on the human soul" (Bugental, 1978) have never been so apparent. Let us therefore agree to share our experiences in ways that respect and foster the life processes to which our profession is committed. We will best serve our profession and our clients when we act with integrity on our best intentions.

ACKNOWLEDGMENTS

I am grateful to my clients, colleagues, and students for their valuable contributions.

REFERENCES

Ainsworth, M. D. S. Infant—mother attachment. *American Psychologist*, 1979, *34*, 932–937.

Apter, M. J. *The experience of motivation: A theory of psychological reversals*. New York: Academic Press, 1982.

Aschoff, J. (Ed.). *Handbook of behavioral neurobiology. Vol. 4. Biological rhythms*. New York: Plenum Press, 1981.

Ayala, F. J., & Dobzhansky, T. (Eds.). *Studies in the philosophy of biology: Reduction and related problems*. Berkeley: University of California Press, 1974.

Bandler, R., & Grinder, J. *The structure of magic: A book about language and therapy* (2 vols.). Palo Alto, CA: Science and Behavior Books, 1975.

Bandler, R., & Grinder, J. *Frogs into princes: Neurolinguistic programming*. Moab, VT: Real People Press, 1979.

Bandura, A. Social learning perspective on behavior change. In A. Burton (Ed.), *What makes behavior change possible?* New York: Brunner/Mazel, 1976.

Bandura, A. Self-efficacy: Toward a unifying theory of behavioral change. *Psychological Review*, 1977, *84*, 191–215.

Bandura, A. The self system in reciprocal determinism. *American Psychologist*, 1978, *33*, 344–358

Barrett, W. *The illusion of technique*. New York: Doubleday, 1967.

Bartlett, F. C. *Remembering*. Cambridge: Cambridge University Press, 1932.

Bartley, W. W., *The retreat to commitment*. New York: Knopf, 1962.

Beck, A. T. *Cognitive therapy and the emotional disorders*. New York: International Universities Press, 1976.

Berger, P. L., & Luckman, T. *The social construction of reality: A treatise in the sociology of knowledge*. Garden City, NY: Anchor, 1967.

Bernard, C. *An introduction to the study of experimental medicine*. New York: Dover, 1957. (Originally published, 1865).

Bowlby, J. *Separation: Anxiety and anger*. New York: Basic Books, 1973.

Bowlby, J. *The making and breaking of affectional bonds*. London: Tavistock, 1979. (a)

Bowlby, J. Knowing what you are not supposed to know and feeling what you are not supposed to feel. *Canadian Journal of Psychiatry*, 1979, *24*, 403–408. (b) (Reprinted in this volume.)

Bransford, J. D. & McCarrell, N. S. A sketch of a cognitive approach to comprehension: Some thoughts about understanding what it means to comprehend. In W. B. Weimer & D. S. Palermo (Eds.), *Cognition and the symbolic processes* (Vol. 1). Hillsdale, NJ: Erlbaum, 1974.

Brush, S. G. The chimerical cat: Philosophy of quantum mechanics in historical perspective. *Social Studies of Science*, 1980, *10*, 393–447.

Bugental, J. F. T. *The search for authenticity: An existential-analytic approach to psychotherapy*. New York: Holt, Rinehart, & Winston, 1965.

Bugental, J. F. T. *Psychotherapy and process: The fundamentals of an existential-humanistic approach*. Reading, MA: Addison-Wesley, 1978.

Burton, A. (Ed.). *What makes behavior change possible?* New York: Brunner/Mazel, 1976.

Campbell, D. T. Evolutionary epistemology. In P. A. Schilpp (Ed.), *The philosophy of Karl Popper* (Vol. 14, Books I and II). *The Library of living philosophers*. LaSalle, IL: Open Court Publishing, 1974.

Campbell, D. T. On the conflicts between biological and social evolution and between psychology and moral tradition. *American Psychologist*, 1975, *30*, 1103–1126.

Capra, F. *The tao of physics*. New York: Bantam, 1975.

Davidson, J. M., & Davidson, R. J. (Eds.). *The psychobiology of consciousness*. New York: Plenum Press, 1980.

Dember, W. N. Motivation and the cognitive revolution. *American Psychologist*, 1974, *29*, 161–168.

Dubois, P. *The influence of the mind on the body*. New York: Funk & Wagnalls, 1906.

Dubois, P. *The psychic treatment of nervous disorders*. New York: Funk & Wagnalls, 1908.

Dubois, P. *The education of self*. New York: Funk & Wagnalls, 1911.

Durant, W., & Durant, A. *Interpretations of life: A survey of contemporary literature*. New York: Simon & Schuster, 1970.

Ellenberger, H. F. *The discovery of the unconscious*. New York: Basic Books, 1970.

Ferguson, M. *The Aquarian conspiracy: Personal and social transformation in the 1980s*. Los Angeles: J. P. Tarcher, 1980.

Fogle, D. O. Learned helplessness and learned restlessness. *Psychotherapy: Theory, Research and Practice*, 1978, *15*, 39–47.

44 MICHAEL J. MAHONEY

Ford, D. H. *The organization and development of human behavior: A living systems perspective*. 1984. Manuscript in preparation.

Foucault, M. *The order of things: An archeology of the human sciences*. New York: Random House, 1970.

Frank, J. D. *Persuasion and healing* (2nd ed.). Baltimore, MD: Johns Hopkins University Press, 1973.

Frank, J. D. Psychotherapy: The restoration of morale. *American Journal of Psychiatry*, 1974, *131*, 271–274.

Frank, J. D. Restoration of morale and behavior change. In A. Burton (Ed.), *What makes behavior change possibe?* New York: Brunner/Mazel, 1976.

Frankl, V. E. *The unheard cry for meaning; Psychotherapy and humanism*. New York: Simon & Schuster, 1978.

Friedman, M. *To deny our nothingness: Contemporary images of man*. Chicago: University of Chicago Press, 1967.

Friedman, M. *The hidden human image*. New York: Dell, 1974.

Fromm, E. *Escape from freedom*, New York: Holt, Rinehart, & Winston, 1941.

Garfield, S. L., & Kurtz, R. Clinical psychologists in the 1970s. *American Psychologist*, 1976, *31*, 1–9.

Garfield, S. L., & Kurtz, R. A study of eclectic views. *Journal of Consulting and Clinical Psychology*, 1977, *45*, 78–83.

Gibran, K. *The prophet*. New York: Knopf, 1923.

Gibson, J. J. *The senses considered as perceptual systems*. Boston: Houghton Mifflin, 1966.

Goffman, E. *Frame analysis: An essay on the organization of experience*. New York: Harper, 1974.

Goldfried, M. R. Toward the delineation of therapeutic change principles. *American Psychologist*, 1980, *35*, 991–999.

Goldstein, K. M., & Blackman, S. *Cognitive style: Five approaches and relevant research*. New York: Wiley, 1978.

Guidano, V. F., & Liotti, G. *Cognitive processes and emotional disorders: A structural approach to psychotherapy*. New York: Guilford, 1983.

Haley, J. *Uncommon therapy*. New York: Norton, 1973.

Hayek, F. A. *The counter-revolution of science: Studies on the abuse of reason*. New York: Free Press, 1952. (a)

Hayek, F. A. *The sensory order*. Chicago: University of Chicago Press, 1952 (b)

Hayek, F. A. *Studies in philosophy, politics, economics*. Chicago: University of Chicago Press, 1967.

Hayek, F. A. *New studies in philosophy, politics, economics, and the history of ideas*. Chicago: University of Chicago Press, 1978.

Hendin, J. *Vulnerable people: A view of American fiction since 1945*. Oxford: Oxford University Press, 1978.

Howard, K. L., & Orlinsky, D. E. Psychotherapeutic process. *Annual Review of Psychology*, 1972, *23*, 615–668.

James, W. *The varieties of religious experience*. New York: New American Library, 1958. (Originally published, 1901.)

Janet, P. *Neurosis and fixed ideas*. Paris: Alcan, 1898.

Jantsch, E. The unifying paradigm behind autopoiesis, dissipative structures, hyper- and ultracycles. In M. Zeleny (Ed.), *Autopoiesis, dissipative structures, and spontaneous social orders*. Washington, DC: American Association for the Advancement of Science, 1980.

Jenkins, J. J. Remember that old theory of memory? Well, forget it! *American Psychologist*, 1974, *29*, 785–795.

Jerison, H. J. *Evolution of the brain and intelligence*. New York: Wiley, 1973.

Jerison, H. J. Paleoneurology and the evolution of mind. *Scientific American*, 1976, *234*, 90–101

Jones, R. A. *Self-fulfilling prophecies: Social, psychological, and physiological effects of expectancies*. Hillsdale, NJ: Erlbaum, 1977.

Joy, W. B. *Joy's way: A map for the transformational journey*. Los Angeles: J. P. Tarcher, 1978.

Kagan, J. Resiliency and continuity in psychological development. In A. M. Clarke and A. D. B. Clarke (Eds.), *Early experience: Myth and evidence*. New York: Free Press, 1976.

Kagan, J., Kearsley, R. B., & Zelazo, P. R. *Infancy: Its place in human development*. Cambridge, MA: Harvard University Press, 1978.

Kiesler, D. J. *The process of psychotherapy: Empirical foundations and systems of analysis*. Chicago: Aldine, 1973.

Klemke, E. D. (Ed.). *The meaning of life*. Oxford: Oxford University Press, 1981.

Klinger, E. *Structure and functions of fantasy*. New York: Wiley, 1971

Kopp, S. *An end to innocence: Facing life without illusions*. New York: Bantam, 1978.

Kuhn, T. S. *The structure of scientific revolutions*. Chicago: University of Chicago Press, 1962.

Kuhn, T. S. Logic of discovery or psychology of research? In I. Lakatos and A. Musgrave (Eds.), *Criticism and the growth of knowledge*. Cambridge: Cambridge University Press, 1970. (a)

Kuhn, T. S. Reflections on my critics. In I. Lakatos and A. Musgrave (Eds.), *Criticism and the growth of knowledge*. Cambridge: Cambridge University Press, 1970. (b)

Kuhn, T. S. *The essential tension*. Chicago: University of Chicago Press, 1977.

Lakatos I. Falsification and the methodology of scientific research programmes. In I. Lakatos & A. Musgrave (Eds.), *Criticism and the growth of knowledge*. Cambridge: Cambridge University Press, 1970.

Lakatos, I., & Musgrave, A. (Eds.). *Criticism and the growth of knowledge*. Cambridge: Cambridge University Press, 1970.

Land, G. T. L. *Grow or die: The unifying principle of transformation*. New York: Dell, 1973.

Leonard, G. B., *The transformation: A guide to the inevitable changes in humankind*. Los Angeles: J. P. Tarcher, 1972.

Lewis, M., & Rosenbaum, L. A. (Eds.). *The development of affect*. New York: Plenum Press, 1978.

Lipsitt, L. P. Critical conditions in infancy: A psychological perspective. *American Psychologist*, 1979, *34*, 973–980.

MacNamara, J. Meaning. In W. B. Weimer and D. S. Palermo (Eds.), *Cognition and the symbolic processes* (Vol. 2). Hillsdale, NJ: Erlbaum, 1981.

Mahoney, M. J. *Cognition and behavior modification*. Cambridge, MA: Ballinger, 1974.

Mahoney, M. J. *Scientist as subject: The psychological imperative*. Cambridge, MA: Ballinger, 1976.

Mahoney, M. J. Psychology of the scientist: An evaluative review. *Social Studies of Science*, 1979, *9*, 349–375.

Mahoney, M. J. (Ed.). *Psychotherapy process: Current issues and future directions*. New York: Plenum Press, 1980. (a)

Mahoney, M. J. Psychotherapy and the structure of personal revolutions. In M. J.

Mahoney (Ed.), *Psychotherapy process: Current issues and future directions.* New York: Plenum Press, 1980. (b)

Mahoney, M. J. Clinical psychology and scientific inquiry. *International Journal of Psychology*, 1981, *16*, 157–274.

Mahoney, M. J. *Stream of consciousness: A therapeutic application.* (videotape) Bellefonte, PA: Personal Empowerment Programs, 1983.

Mahoney, M. J. Behaviorism, cognitivism, and human change processes. In M. A. Reda & M. J. Mahoney (Eds.), *Cognitive psychotherapies: Recent developments in theory, research, and practice.* Cambridge, MA: Ballinger, 1984, pp. 3–30.

Mahoney, M. J. *Personal change processes: Notes on the facilitation of human development.* New York: Basic Books, in press.

Mahoney, M. J., & Arnkoff, D. B. Cognitive and self-control therapies. In S. L. Garfield and A. E. Bergin (Eds.), *Handbook of psychotherapy and behavior change* (2nd ed.). New York: Wiley, 1978.

Marmor, J. Common operational factors in diverse approaches to behavior change. In A. Burton (Ed.), *What makes behavior change possible?* New York: Brunner/Mazel, 1976.

Maslow, A. H. *The farther reaches of human nature.* New York: Viking, 1971.

Meichenbaum, D. *Cognitive behavior modification.* New York: Plenum Press, 1977.

Mowrer, O. H. *Learning theory and behavior.* New York: Wiley, 1960. (a)

Mowrer, O. H. *Learning theory and the symbolic processes.* New York: Wiley, 1960. (b)

Nelson, K. E., & Nelson, K. Cognitive pendulums and their linguistic realization. In K. E. Nelson (Ed.), *Children's language* (Vol. 1).New York: Gardner Press, 1978.

Nichols, M. P., & Zax, M. *Catharsis in psychotherapy.* New York: Gardner Press, 1977.

Nisbett, R. E., & Wilson, T. D. Telling more than we can know: Verbal reports on mental processes. *Psychological Review*, 1977, *84*, 231–259.

Orlinsky, D. E., & Howard, K. I. The relationship of process to outcome in psychotherapy. In S. L. Garfield & A. E. Bergin (Eds.), *Handbook of psychotherapy and behavior change* (2nd ed.). New York: Wiley, 1978.

Pattee, H. H. (Ed.). *Hierarchy theory: The challenge of complex systems.* New York: George Braziller, 1973.

Pepper, S. C. *World hypotheses: A study in evidence.* Berkeley, CA: University of California Press, 1942.

Perlmuter, L. C., & Monty, R. A. (Eds.). *Choice and perceived control.* Hillsdale, NJ: Erlbaum, 1979.

Plutchik, R., & Kellerman, H. *Emotion: Theory, research, and experience* (vol. 1). New York: Academic Press, 1980.

Polanyi, M. *The tacit dimension.* New York: Doubleday, 1966.

Pope, K. S., & Singer, J. L. *The stream of consciousness: Scientific investigations into the flow of human experience.* New York: Plenum, Press, 1978.

Pribram, K. H., Mind, brain, and consciousness: The organization of competence and conduct. In J. S. Davidson & R. J. Davidson (Eds.), *The psychobiology of consciousness.* New York: Plenum Press, 1980.

Pribram, K. H., & McGuinness, D. Arousal, activation and effort in the control of attention. *Psychological Review*, 1975, *82*, 116–149.

Prigogine, I. *From being to becoming: Time and complexity in the physical sciences.* San Francisco: Freeman, 1980.

Proffitt, D. R. *Demonstrations to investigate the meaning of everyday experience.* Unpublished doctoral dissertation. The Pennsylvania State University, 1976.

Proffitt, D. R., & Halwes, T. Categorical perception: A contractual approach. In W. B.

Weimer and D. S. Palermo (Eds.), *Cognition and the symbolic processes* (Vol. 2). Hillsdale, NJ: Erlbaum, 1981.

Progoff, I. *At a journal workshop.* New York: Dialogue House Library, 1975.

Rachman, S. Emotional processing. *Behaviour Research and Therapy*, 1980, *18*, 51–60

Radnitzky, G. The complementarity of western and oriental philosophy. *Social Science*, 1981, *56*, 82–87.

Raimy, V. *Misunderstandings of the self.* San Francisco: Jossey-Bass, 1975.

Raskin, D. E., & Klein, Z. E. Losing a symptom through keeping it: A review of paradoxical treatment techniques and rationale. *Archives of General Psychiatry*, 1976, *33*, 548–555.

Reda, M. A., & Mahoney, M. J. (Eds.). *Cognitive psychotherapies: Recent developments in theory, research, and practice.* Cambridge, MA: Ballinger, 1984.

Russell, B. *A history of western philosophy.* New York: Simon & Schuster, 1945.

Russell, B. *The autobiography of Bertrand Russell.* London: George Allen and Unwin, 1967.

Rutter, M. *Maternal deprivation reassessed.* Baltimore: Penguin, 1972.

Salzman, L. The will to change. In A. Burton (Ed.), *What makes behavior change possible?* New York: Brunner/Mazel, 1976.

Sargant, W. *Battle for the mind*, New York: Harper & Row, 1957.

Schwartz, G. E. Psychobiological foundations of psychotherapy and behavior change. In S. L. Garfield & A. E. Bergin (Eds.), *Handbook of psychotherapy and behavior change* (2nd ed.). New York: Wiley, 1978.

Shaw, R., & Bransford, J. (Eds.). *Perceiving, acting, and knowing: Toward an ecological psychology.* Hillsdale, NJ: Erlbaum, 1977.

Shevrin, H., & Dickman, S. The psychological unconscious: A necessary assumption for all psychological theory? *American Psychologist*, 1980, *35*, 421–434.

Singer, J. L. *Imagery and daydream techniques in psychotherapy and behavior modification.* New York: Academic Press, 1974.

Singer, J. L., & Pope, K. S. (Eds.). *The power of human imagination: New methods in psychotherapy.* New York: Plenum Press, 1978.

Skinner, B. F. *About behaviorism.* New York: Knopf, 1974.

Solomon, R. L. The opponent-process theory of acquired motivation: The costs of pleasure and the benefits of pain. *American Psychologist*, 1980, *35*, 691–712.

Sroufe, L. A. The coherence of individual development: Early care, attachment, and subsequent developmental issues. *American Psychologist*, 1979, *34*, 834–841.

Strupp, H. H. The nature of the therapeutic influence and its basic ingredients. In A. Burton (Ed.), *What makes behavior change possible?* New York: Brunner/Mazel, 1976.

Svebak, S., & Stoyva, H. High arousal can be pleasant and exciting: The theory of psychological reversals. *Biofeedback and Self-Regulation*, 1980, *5*, 439–444.

Thompson, S. C. Will it hurt less if I can control it? A complex answer to a simple question. *Psychological Bulletin*, 1981, *90*, 89–101.

Turvey, M. T. Constructive theory, perceptual systems, and tacit knowledge. In W. B. Weimer and D. S. Palermo (Eds.), *Cognition and the symbolic processes* (Vol. 1). Hillsdale, NJ: Erlbaum, 1974.

Vaihinger, H. *The philosophy of as if.* Berlin: Reuther & Reichard, 1911.

Valle, R. S., & von Eckartsberg, R. (Eds.). *The metaphors of consciousness.* New York: Plenum Press, 1981.

Walsh, R. M. The consciousness disciplines and the behavioral sciences: Questions of comparison and assessment. *American Journal of Psychiatry*, 1980, *137*, 663–673.

Walsh, R. N., & Vaughan, F. (Eds.). *Beyond ego: Transpersonal dimensions in psychology.* Los Angeles: J. P. Tarcher, 1980.

Watzlawick, P. *Change: The language of therapeutic communication.* New York: Basic Books, 1978.

Weimer, W. B. A conceptual framework for cognitive psychology: Motor theories of the mind. In R. Shaw & J. Bransford (Eds.), *Perceiving, acting, and knowing.* Hillsdale, NJ: Erlbaum, 1977.

Weimer, W. B. *Notes on the methodology of scientific research.* Hillsdale, NJ: Erlbaum, 1979.

Weimer, W. B. Ambiguity and the future of psychology: *Meditations Leibniziennes.* In W. B. Weimer and D. S. Palermo (Eds.), *Cognition and the symbolic processes* (Vol. 2). Hillsdale, NJ: Erlbaum, 1981. (a)

Weimer, W. B. Hayek's approach to the problems of complex phenomena: An introduction to the theoretical psychology of *The Sensory Order.* In W. B. Weimer and D. S. Palermo (Eds.), *Cognition and the symbolic processes* (vol. 2). Hillsdale, NJ: Erlbaum, 1981. (b)

Weimer, W. B. *Rationalist constructivism, scientism, and the study of man and society,* 1984. Manuscript in preparation.

Weimer, W. B. & Palermo, D. S. (Eds.), *Cognition and the symbolic processes* (Vol. 1). Hillsdale, NJ: Erlbaum, 1974.

Weimer, W. B. & Palermo, D. S. (Eds.), *Cognition and the symbolic processes* (Vol. 2.). Hillsdale, NJ: Erlbaum, 1981.

Wilhelm, R. & Baynes C. F. (trans.). *The I Ching or book of changes.* Princeton: Princeton University Press, 1950.

Wilson, E. O. *Sociobiology: the new synthesis.* Cambridge, MA: Harvard University Press, 1975.

Wilson, E. O. *On human nature.* New York: Bantam, 1978.

Yarrow, L. J. Emotional development. *American Psychologist,* 1979, *34,* 973–980.

Zajonc, R. B. Feeling and thinking: Preferences need no inferences. *American Psychologist,* 1980, *35,* 151–175.

Zeleny, M. (Ed.), *Autopoiesis, dissipative structures, and spontaneous social orders.* Washington, DC: American Association for the Advancement of Science, 1980.

Zukav, G. *The dancing Wu Li masters: An overview of the new physics.* New York: William Morrow, 1979.

CHAPTER 2

Therapeutic Components Shared by All Psychotherapies

JEROME D. FRANK

The field of psychotherapy in the United States has presented a be-
wildering array of theories and techniques accompanied by a deaf-
ening cacophony of rival claims. A recent comprehensive review of
the field requires over 250 pages simply to describe extant approaches
(Wolberg, 1977). Now, however, observers are beginning to detect
increasing signs that representatives of different schools are willing
to acknowledge the potential value of a range of techniques and to
show increasing flexibility in applying them (Goldfried & Padawer,
1983).

These stirrings of rapprochement reflect a growing recognition
that all psychotherapeutic procedures share certain healing components which account for a considerable proportion of their effectiveness, so that practitioners of different schools may usefully learn
from each other. In order to contribute to this welcome development, in this paper I shall consider healing components mobilized
by all forms of psychotherapy and the ways these components may
work.

All psychotherapeutic methods are elaborations and variations

This is a revised version of an invited address to the American Psychological Association
and is reprinted with kind permission. The original version appeared in J. H. Harvey
and M. M. Parks (Eds.), *The Master Lecture Series. Vol. 1: Psychotherapy Research and
Behavior Change.* Washington, D.C.: American Psychological Association, 1982; pp.
73–122. Copyright 1982 by the American Psychological Association. Reprinted by permission of the publisher and author.

JEROME D. FRANK • Department of Psychiatry, The Johns Hopkins University Medical
School, Baltimore, Maryland 21205.

of age-old procedures of psychological healing. These include confession, atonement and absolution, encouragement, positive and negative reinforcements, modeling, and promulgation of a particular set of values. These methods become embedded in theories as to the causes and cures of various conditions which often become highly elaborated.

In view of their use of time-tested healing procedures, it is not surprising that all psychotherapies have many features in common. Those features which distinguish them from each other, however, receive special emphasis in the pluralistic, competitive American society. Since the prestige and the financial security of psychotherapists depend to a considerable extent on their being able to show that their particular theory and method are more successful than those of their rivals, they inevitably emphasize their differences; and each therapist attributes his or her successes to those conceptual and procedural features that distinguish that theory and method from its competitors rather than to the features that all share.

Let me now offer a definition of psychotherapy that is sufficiently broad to include everything that goes by that term but excludes informal help from relatives, friends, and bartenders. Psychotherapy is a planned, emotionally charged, confiding interaction between a trained, socially sanctioned healer and a sufferer. During this interaction the healer seeks to relieve the sufferer's distress and disability through symbolic communications, primarily words but also sometimes bodily activities. The healer may or may not involve the patient's relatives and others in the healing rituals. Psychotherapy also often includes helping the patient to accept and endure suffering as an inevitable aspect of life that can be used as an opportunity for personal growth.

DISTINGUISHING FEATURES OF PSYCHOTHERAPY

Before proceeding further, let us pause briefly to consider the features that distinguish psychotherapy thus defined from other forms of giving and receiving help. The psychotherapist has credentials as a healer. These are provided by society at large in the form of licensure or other official recognition. The therapist has earned this recognition by having undergone special training, usually prolonged, which entitles him or her to the status symbol of an academic degree. Therapists lacking such generally recognized credentials are sanctioned by the particular sect or cult they represent. Persons who go to them thereby imply that they accept the validity of these sanctions.

It is assumed that, whatever his or her credentials, the therapist is not attempting to gratify any personal needs or make any personal emotional demands on the patient. Nor need the patient guard his own responses for fear of hurting the therapist. In these respects the therapist differs fundamentally from family members or friends. Finally, psychotherapeutic procedures, in contrast to informal help, are guided by conceptual schemes which prescribe specific rituals.

In different societies, psychotherapy reflects not only a society's conceptualizations of illness and health but also its values. In American psychotherapy, for example, patient and therapist are generally required to work at some form of mutual activity to justify their spending time together, and increased autonomy is regarded as an important feature of mental health. Hindus find these attitudes astonishing. For them, simply being together is a worthwhile end in itself, and dependency on others is a valued feature of life (Neki, 1973; Pande, 1968).

An aspect of the American world view shared by most psychotherapists is the high prestige accorded to science. As a result, psychotherapists of most schools, from psychoanalysis to behavior modification, claim that their procedures are grounded on scientific evidence. The extent to which psychotherapists view themselves as applied scientists, or at least wish to be seen as such, was brought home to me many years ago at a conference attended by leading exponents of different psychotherapeutic schools. Each speaker introduced his or her presentation by a genuflection toward science. One showed kymographic tracings, another referred to work on rats, and a third displayed anatomical charts—all of which had only tenuous relevance to the therapies they were presenting.

The scientific world view assumes that man is part of the animal kingdom which, like all of nature, is ruled by natural laws. Human behavior, thinking, and feeling are determined and constrained by genetic endowment, biologically based needs, and the effects of beneficial and harmful environmental influences. Therapy consists of the application of special techniques to combat maladaptive patterns and encourage more appropriate ones.

The American psychotherapeutic scene also includes a minority but influential viewpoint, termed humanist or existential, that rejects the scientific view of man. According to this view, the essence of being human is the right and the capacity for self-determination, guided by purposes, values, and options. Out of our free will we can give our lives meaning even in the face of inevitable death. The essence of therapy is a particular kind of relationship, the "encounter," which cannot be objectively described. Existential-humanist therapists describe what they do in such terms as "relating to the patient as one existence communicating with another," or "entering the world of the patient with reverent love," or "merging with the patient." Through this total acceptance, the patient comes to value his or her own uniqueness, becomes free to exert choice, to make commitments, and to find a meaning in life (Seguin, 1965).

A basic assumption of all psychotherapies is that humans react to their interpretation of events, which may not correspond to events as they are in reality. All psychotherapies, therefore, try to alter favorably patients' views of themselves, their relations with others, and their system of values. To this extent psychotherapies resemble both religion (Szasz, 1978) and rhetoric. To enhance their credibility, psychotherapists try to project the same personal qualities as rhetoricians, such as perceived expertness, trustworthiness, and attractiveness; and they use many of the same rhetorical devices, such as metaphors and sensory images, to focus the patients' attention "on ideas central to the therapeutic message and . . . [make them] appear more . . . believable" (Glaser, 1980, p. 331; see also Frank, 1980).

Psychotherapy also has analogies to other arts, music, for example. Like the practitioner of any art, the psychotherapist must master a certain amount of scientific and technical information, but this mastery takes one only so far. For example, a composer or performer must know something of the rules of harmony and of the physical principles of pitch and volume, but the application of scientific method will never be able to explain a Mozart or to determine whether the music of Cole Porter is better than that of Richard Rodgers. To be sure, one can analyze their songs in terms of patterns of harmony, pitch, and volume and administer any number of rating scales to cohorts of listeners; but this information casts little, if any, light on the nature of their aesthetic impact. To the extent that the analogy is valid, determining scientifically whether, let us say, Gestalt therapy is preferable to Transactional Analysis should prove equally futile.

LIMITATIONS OF RESEARCH

A brief consideration of the limitations of research in psychotherapy may not be inappropriate here. An authority on research in psychology has recently concluded that "psychology is . . . a collectivity of studies of various casts, some few of which may qualify as science, while most do not. . . . Extensive and important sectors of psychological study require modes of inquiry rather more like those of the humanities than the sciences" (Koch, 1981, pp. 268–269).

One of these important sectors is psychotherapy, which presents special difficulties to the researcher. These difficulties permit only modest hopes as to the extent to which application of the scientific method will lead to insights that will improve psychotherapies.

A general problem which plagues all psychological experiments is that humans respond to their interpretations of situations and the subject's interpretation of the experimental situation may differ strikingly from the one that the experimenter thinks has been created (Orne, 1969). Thus the experimental findings may reflect the subject's efforts to comply with what he or she thinks the experimenter wants rather than reflecting a response to the experimental conditions. In psychotherapy this problem is aggravated because the patient typically experiences strong "evaluation apprehension," which has been shown to increase a psychological subject's susceptibility to influence by the experimenter's unspoken expectations (Rosenberg, 1969). In psychotherapy, the patient depends on the therapist for relief, which would be expected to enhance this susceptibility. Therefore, it is particularly difficult to disentangle how much of a patient's apparent response to psychotherapy is an effort to meet the therapist's expectations.

Psychotherapy is just one more influence operating briefly and intermittently on the patient in the context of his ongoing life experiences. At best psychotherapeutic interviews represent only infrequent, intermittent, brief personal contacts wedged in among innumerable others. What goes on between sessions may be more important in determining outcome than what occurs during sessions. Also psychotherapy and ongoing life experiences may interact in complex ways because a change in the patient's outlook or behavior brought about by psychotherapy inevitably affects the attitudes of others toward him and these attitudes may reinforce or counteract the changes induced by therapy. Mere acceptance of the patient for psychiatric treatment, for example, may lead family members to change their view of the individual from a person who is lazy or bad to one who is sick, with corresponding favorable changes in their attitudes toward the patient. Conversely, if the patient's symptoms or deviant behaviors contribute to the equilibrium of the family, losing these symptoms or behaviors might lead other family members to sabotage treatment. Thus it may be difficult to assess the relative extent to which patients' changes during psychotherapy are attributable to the treatment itself, to factors outside it, and to the interaction between treatment and outside factors.

At a more fundamental level, some important experiences in psychotherapy may in principle be unamenable to scientific study because they occur in altered states of consciousness, in ways not accessible to the senses, and in levels of reality differing from the everyday one (LeShan, 1974; Smith, 1977).

When we return from this uncomfortable line of thought to more familiar ground, we find that psychotherapy research bristles with practical difficulties such as the dearth of suitable patients and experienced therapists, inadequate ways of classifying patients and describing therapies, and problems of measuring outcome. These difficulties create an often irresistible temptation to choose research problems on the basis on methodological simplicity rather than on intrinsic interest.

Finally, motivational problems, especially in therapists, create difficulties. Not only are therapists' personal and financial security and status wrapped up in the success of their methods, but much of their success may depend on personal qualities. So therapists are understandably reluctant to submit themselves to investigations which could reveal that they have attributes which militate against therapeutic success. Such a finding could be devastating not only to their pocketbooks but also to their self-esteem.

All in all, it is no wonder that, despite the outstanding ability of many researchers in psychotherapy, findings by and large have been tentative and disappointing. Reviews of psychotherapy research studies characteristically bemoan their lack of impact on practice and conclude with comments on their inadequacies and the need for further research.

Actually, my impression is that most innovative psychotherapeutic procedures are really derived from clinical experience and the discoverer then seeks to support them by laboratory analogies. The great nineteenth century German psychiatrist, Emil Kraepelin, for example, described his treatment for "dread neurosis"—what we would call "generalized anxiety disorder"—in terms that could easily be translated into a combination of reciprocal inhibition and operant conditioning (Diefendorf, 1915, p. 400).

Perhaps the greatest contribution of the scientific method is that it requires the experimenter to take negative findings seriously. As a result, the scientific study of psychotherapy has performed a useful function by rescuing common sense from the clutches of dogmatic theories. A good example of such a rescue has been the overemphasis on unconscious processes by certain schools and the insistence by others that subjective symbolic processes are irrelevant, both of which have had to yield to scientific evidence that conscious cognitive processes are important features of human functioning—a blatant truism, one might say, but one that certain people have been reluctant to accept.

The preceding discussion is by way of justifying that in this presentation, although I shall cite research findings as far as possible, I shamelessly admit that my conclusions are based at least as much on reflection about my own and others' clinical experience as they are on experiments. Research findings are offered as illustrations of points rather than as proofs of their validity.

GENERALIZATIONS ABOUT OUTCOMES OF PSYCHOTHERAPIES

To open the discussion of therapeutic features common to all types of psychotherapy, let me briefly state four generalizations that are relatively firmly established. The first is that patients who receive any form of psychotherapy do somewhat better than controls observed over the same period of time who have received no formal psychotherapy, which does not, of course, exclude their having benefited from informal helping contacts with others (Sloane, Staples, Cristol, Yorkston, & Whipple, 1975; Smith, Glass, & Miller, 1980). Second, follow-up studies appear to show consistently that, whatever the form of therapy, most patients who show initial improvement maintain it (Liberman, 1978b). Moreover, when two therapies yield differences in outcome at the close of treatment, with rare exceptions these differences disappear over time, and the closing of the gap seems to depend more on patients who receive the less successful therapy catching up than on both groups regressing equally toward the mean (Gelder, Marks, & Wolff, 1967; Liberman, 1978b). This result suggests that the main beneficial effect of psychotherapy with many patients may be to accelerate improvement that would have occurred eventually in any case. Third, more of the determinants of therapeutic success lie in the personal qualities of and the interaction between patient and therapist than in the particular therapeutic method used. Finally, there are a few conditions in which the therapeutic method does make a significant difference in outcome. Behavior therapies seem to be somewhat more effective for phobias, compulsions, and obesity and sexual problems than are less focused therapies.

Of particular interest from the standpoint of the hypothesis to be offered presently is that cognitive therapy, which seeks to combat negative cognitions about oneself, the future, and one's relationships with other people, seems particularly effective with depressed patients (Rush, Beck, Kovacs, & Hollon, 1977). The efficacy of all procedures, however, depends on the establishment of a good therapeutic relationship between the patient and the therapist. No method works in the absence of this relationship.

With increasing refinement of categorization of patients and their symptom pictures, more precise delineation of therapies, and more clearly differentiated measures of outcome, further advantages of specific therapies for specific conditions may yet be found. It does seem safe to conclude, however, that features shared by all therapies account for an appreciable amount of the improvement observed in most psychiatric patients who respond at all (Frank, 1973).

DEMORALIZATION HYPOTHESIS

If the preceding conclusion is so, patients, whatever their symptoms, must share a type of distress that responds to the components common to all schools of psychotherapy. A plausible hypothesis is that patients seek psychotherapy not for symptoms alone but for symptoms coupled with demoralization, a state of mind characterized by one or more of the following: subjective incompetence, loss of self-esteem, alienation, hopelessness (feeling that no one can help), or helplessness (feeling that other people could help but will not). These states of mind are often aggravated by cognitive unclarity as to the meaning and seriousness of the symptoms, not uncommonly accompanied by a sense of loss of control, leading to a fear of going crazy.

Demoralization occurs when, because of lack of certain skills or confusion of goals, an individual becomes persistently unable to master situations which both the individual and others expect him or her to handle or when the individual experiences continued distress which he or she cannot adequately explain or alleviate. Demoralization may be summed up as a feeling of subjective incompetence, coupled with distress (deFigueiredo & Frank, 1982; Frank, 1974).

One must add that not all demoralized people get into treatment and not all patients in psychotherapy are demoralized. Sometimes patients are brought to treatment not because they are demoralized, but because people around them are: for example, the parents of sociopaths or the spouses of alcoholics. This mention of alcoholics is a reminder that some people, such as skid row alcoholics, are too demoralized even to seek help. Finally, of course, a small proportion of patients seek treatment for specific symptoms without otherwise being demoralized because they have heard that behavior therapy will cure their phobia of heights.

The most common symptoms of demoralization presented by patients in psychotherapy are subjective or behavioral manifestations such as, on the one hand, anxiety, depression, and loneliness or, on the other, conflict with significant persons such as spouse, boss, or children. Anxiety and depression or loss of self-esteem are the symptoms most common among psychiatric outpatients and most responsive to treatment (Smith *et al.*, 1980).

Whatever their source or nature, all symptoms interact with demoralization in various ways. They reduce a person's coping capacity, predisposing the individual to demoralizing failures. Whether the symptom be schizophrenic thought disorder, reactive depression, or obsessional ritual, it may cause the patient to be defeated by problems of living that asymptomatic persons handle with ease. Furthermore, to the extent that the patient believes them to be unique, psychiatric symptoms contribute to demoralization by heightening feelings of alienation. Finally, symptoms wax and wane with the degree of demoralization; thus schizophrenics' thinking becomes more disorganized when they are anxious, and obsessions and compulsions become worse when the patients are depressed.

Most patients present themselves with specific symptoms, and both they and their therapists assume that psychotherapy is aimed primarily at relieving these symptoms. Such patients do indeed exist, but for the great bulk, I suggest, much of the improvement resulting from any form of psychotherapy lies in its ability to restore the patient's morale, with the resulting diminution or disappearance of symptoms. One must add, of course, that alleviation of the patient's symptoms may be the best way to restore morale.

Indirect evidence for the demoralization hypothesis comes from several sources. One source consists of studies comparing cohorts of persons who seek or have sought psychotherapy with those who have not. Studies of college students (Galassi & Galassi, 1973), alumni out of college for 25 years (Vaillant, 1972), and ordinary citizens in England and America (Kellner & Sheffield, 1973) showed that the treated had a higher incidence or greater severity of social isolation, helplessness, or sense of failure or unworthiness—all symptoms of demoralization—than the untreated.

The strongest empirical support has been supplied by the surveys of Bruce and Barbara Dohrenwend, who have devised a set of scales to determine the extent of psychiatric symptoms and clinical impairment in the general population (Dohrenwend, Shrout, Egri, & Mendlsohn, 1980). To their surprise, they found that eight of their scales correlated as highly with each other as their internal reliabilities would permit; that is, they all appeared to measure a single dimension. These scales included features of demoralization such as anxiety, sadness, hopelessness, and low self-esteem (Dohrenwend, Oksenberg, Shrout, Dohrenwend, & Cook, 1979). About one fourth of the persons in the population they surveyed were estimated to be demoralized according to this criterion. Of these about one half were also clinically impaired (Link & Dohrenwend, 1980). The finding most supportive of the hypothesis was that about four-fifths of clinically impaired outpatients scored above the cut-off point on a scale that later was found to correlate about .90 with the demoralization scales (Dohrenwend & Crandall, 1970).

Surveys of reported emotional distress and presence or absence of supportive social networks provide further indirect evidence for the demoralization hypothesis. A general population survey found that persons who possess such a network are much less likely to be distressed by severe environmental stresses than those who are not so supported (Henderson, Byrne, & Duncan-Jones, 1981). In response to a similar survey, members who had joined a religious cult reported a sharp decline in anxiety, depression, and general emotional problems and attributed this decline primarily to emotional support from all the group members (Galanter, 1978). Apparently emotional support from others protects individuals from demoralization.

Quite different indirect support for the demoralization hypothesis is that many patients come to psychotherapy only after other forms of relief have failed. At least these inference seems justified by the finding in one setting that patients did not appear until six months to two years after their symptoms first appeared (T. B. Karasu, personal communication, July 24, 1981). A study of college students' use of a university's psychological services similarly found out "the decision to actually use psychotherapy was likely to come only after ineffective attempts to cope with the problem one's self or with the help of a close friend or relative" (Farber & Geller, 1977, p. 306).

That demoralization may account for the emergence of specific symptoms in the course of psychoanalysis is suggested by a detailed content analysis of psychoanalytic sessions which showed that complaints of migraine headaches were reported in a context of lack of self-control, hopelessness, and helplessness, and stomach pains in a context of helplessness and anxiety (Luborsky & Auerbach, 1969).

Further indirect support for the demoralization hypothesis is that many patients improve very quickly in therapy, suggesting that their favorable response is to the reassuring aspects of the therapeutic situation itself rather than to the particular procedure. In clinic settings the mean number of therapeutic interviews is between five and six (Garfield, 1978, pp. 195–197). This finding is usually interpreted to mean that many patients who are in need of psychotherapy reject it. Undoubtedly this interpretation is true of some. Others, however, probably stop because they have obtained sufficient symptom relief and no longer feel the need to continue. Unfortunately, patients who drop out of therapy early are not usually called back for reassessment. In one study which did call them back, the average symptomatic relief was found to be just as great in those who dropped out before their fourth session as in those who had received 6 months of therapy (Frank, Gliedman, Imber, Stone, & Nash, 1959).

A finding with the same implications is that about three-fourths of psychiatric outpatients on a waiting list for four months were rated as improved. During this period, their only contact was an occasional telephone call from a research associate to ensure that they would wait for the assigned treatment (Sloane et al., 1975). Apparently some patients gain relief from any contact in a therapeutic setting, probably because they perceive the contact as therapy.

SHARED THERAPEUTIC COMPONENTS

Turning at last to the shared therapeutic components of all forms of psychotherapy, we find that most forms can be viewed as means of directly or indirectly combating demoralization. The list which follows, with minor variations, is similar to those components propounded by many therapists (Goldfried & Padawer, 1983; Marmor, 1976; Rosenzweig, 1936).

1. *An emotionally charged, confiding relationship with a helping person*, often with the participation of a group. With some possible minor exceptions, the relationship with the therapist is a necessary, and perhaps often a sufficient, condition for improvement in any kind

of psychotherapy (Rogers, 1957). As Sloane *et al.* (1975, p. 225) found, "Successful patients rated the personal interaction with the therapist as the single most important part of their treatment."

Especially thought provoking in this connection is the finding that male college students in time-limited psychotherapy experienced as much improvement, on the average, when treated by college professors chosen for their ability to form understanding relationships as when treated by highly experienced psychotherapists (Strupp & Hadley, 1979).

Patients let themselves become dependent on the therapist for help because of their confidence in the therapist's competence and good will. This dependence is reinforced by the patient's knowledge of the therapist's training, by the setting of treatment, and by the congruence of the therapist's approach with the patient's expectations. While the therapist's status or reputation in the patient's eyes may initially determine the therapist's ascendency, success of therapy depends on the therapist's ability to convey to the patient that the therapist cares about the patient, is competent to help, and has no ulterior motives (Gurman, 1977)—an attitude summed up by one eminent psychotherapist by the term "therapeutic Eros" (Seguin, 1965).

2. *A healing setting*, which has at least two therapeutic functions in itself. First, it heightens the therapist's prestige and strengthens the patient's expectation of help by symbolizing the therapist's role as a healer, whether the setting is a clinic in a prestigious hospital or a private office complete with bookshelves, impressive desk, couch, and easy chair. Often the setting also contains evidence of the therapist's training such as diplomas and pictures of his or her teachers. Second, the setting provides safety. Surrounded by its walls, patients know they can let themselves go within wide limits, dare to reveal aspects of themselves that they have concealed from others, and discuss various alternatives for future behavior without commitment and without any consequences outside the office.

3. *Rationale, conceptual scheme, or myth* that provides a plausible explanation for the patient's symptoms and prescribes a ritual or procedure for resolving them.

4. *A ritual* that requires active participation of both patient and therapist and that is believed by both to be the means of restoring the patient's health.

The words *myth* and *ritual* are used advisedly to emphasize that, although typically expressed in scientific terms, therapeutic rationales and procedures cannot be disproved. Successes are taken as proof of their validity, often erroneously, whereas failures are explained away. "No form of therapy has even been initiated without a claim that it had unique therapeutic advantages. And no form of therapy has ever been abandoned because of its failure to live up to these claims" (M. B. Parloff quoted in Hilts, 1980). To my knowledge, no therapeutic school has ever disbanded because it concluded that another's doctrine and method was superior.

An often overlooked function of therapeutic rituals is to provide a face-saving excuse for the patient to abandon a symptom or complaint when ready to do so. To relinquish a symptom without an adequate external reason would carry the implication that it was trivial or that the patient had produced it for some ulterior motive. The more spectacular the ritual, the greater its usefulness from the individual's standpoint. This circumstance necessitates caution in attributing remission of a symptom to a particular maneuver. The patient might have been ready to relinquish the symptom for other reasons, and the role of the procedure may simply have been to serve as the occasion for doing so.

FUNCTIONS OF MYTH AND RITUAL

All therapeutic myths and rituals, irrespective of differences in specific content, have in common functions that combat demoralization by strengthening the therapeutic relationship, inspiring expectations of help, providing new learning experiences, arousing the patient emotionally, enhancing the sense of mastery or self-efficacy, and affording opportunities for rehearsal and practice. Let us consider each of these briefly in turn.

1. *Strengthening the therapeutic relationship, thereby combating the patient's sense of alienation.* A shared belief system is essential to the formation and maintenance of groups, so the adherence of therapist and patient to the same therapeutic myth creates a powerful bond between them. Within this context, the therapist's continued acceptance of the patient after the patient has "confessed" combats the latter's demoralizing feelings of alienation, especially if, as is usually the case, the therapist represents a group. The ritual serves to maintain the patient–therapist bond, especially over stretches when nothing much seems to be happening. By giving patient and therapist something to do together, the ritual sustains mutual interest. The

chief problem of Strupp's kindly college professors (Strupp & Hadley, 1979), was that they sometimes ran out of things to talk about, a predicament never reported by the experienced therapists.

2. *Inspiring and maintaining the patient's expectation of help.* By inspiring expectations of help, myths and rituals not only keep the patient coming to treatment but also may be powerful morale builders and symptom relievers in themselves (Friedman, 1963; Jacobson, 1968; Uhlenhuth & Duncan, 1968). The arousal of hope may also account for the findings in several studies that "the best predictor of later benefits is ... expectations of early benefits expressed in the early sessions" (Luborsky, 1976, p. 107).

Several colleagues and I were put on the track of the importance of positive expectations in the relief of symptoms by the results of our first study of psychotherapy. In this study we compared the effects on symptoms and social behavior of six months of one of three forms of psychotherapy: group therapy, individual therapy once a week, or minimal contact treatment not more than one-half hour every two weeks. We found that patients in all three therapies showed equal symptom reduction on the average, but so did those who had dropped out of treatment within the first four interviews (Frank *et al.*, 1959). Symptom reduction, therefore, seemed in large part a response to the hope of relief engendered by being offered treatment. We decided to explore this theory by studying the effects of placebos on psychiatric symptoms, since this effect must depend solely on arousing the patient's positive expectations through administering an inert medication which symbolizes the physician's role (Frank, Nash, Stone, & Imber, 1963).

The experiment called for research personnel to administer a discomfort scale, followed by a half-hour series of tests aimed at discovering personality attributes related to placebo responsiveness. Then the discomfort scale was readministered, and it was followed by an administration of the placebo. After another half hour, during which the placebo was given time to "work" and the patient received additional tests, the discomfort scale was again administered. The patients were kept on the placebo for two weeks, the discomfort scale being administered at the end of each week, and then the placebo was discontinued. Figure 1 illustrates the findings. We can see that the biggest drop in discomfort occurred before the administration of the placebo, that the reduction in discomfort was largely maintained at one and two weeks and, for those patients whom we were able to recall after three years, the average discomfort was still lower than it was at the time of admission to treatment.

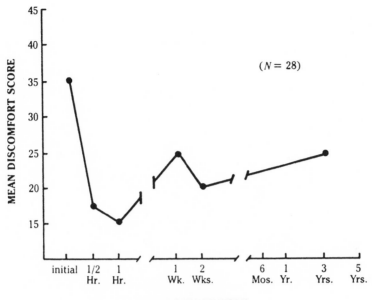

FIGURE 1. Changes in mean discomfort over time following administration of placebo. Placebo administered at the half hour. From *Effective Ingredients of Successful Psychotherapy* by J. D. Frank, R. Hoehn-Saric, S. D. Imber, B. L. Liberman, and A. R. Stone. Copyright 1978 by Brunner/Mazel. Reprinted by permission.

A comparison of symptom reduction by psychotherapy and by placebo is illustrated in Figure 2, which portrays the findings from two groups of patients, one of which had initially received a placebo and the other six months of psychotherapy, who were recalled after three years because of some recurrence of symptoms. At this point, both groups received a placebo and their discomfort level was checked one or two weeks later. You will note that the initial average drop in discomfort was virtually identical after six months of psychotherapy and after the administration of a placebo for a week. On being give a placebo three years later, both groups showed the same average drop, which was the same as the initial drop in discomfort with six months of psychotherapy.

An important point is that, although the mean drop in discomfort was the same after three years as it was initially, the responses of individual patients on the two occasions were widely different. Some responded the first time and not the second, and vice versa. This finding is evidence that responsiveness to placebos depends not so

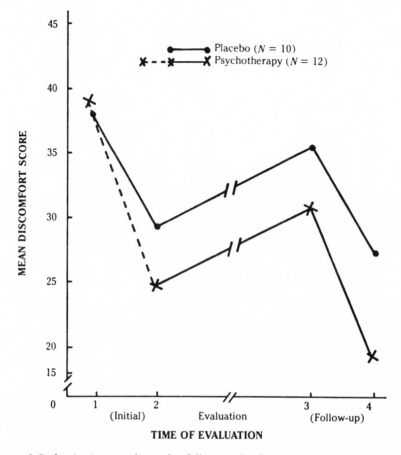

FIGURE 2. Reduction in mean discomfort following placebo and psychotherapy. Interval between 1 and 2 is one week in the placebo study, 6 months in the psychotherapy study. Interval between 2 and 3 is 3 years in both studies. Interval between 3 and 4 is one week in the placebo study, 2 weeks in the psychotherapy study. From *Effective Ingredients of Successful Psychotherapy* by J. D. Frank, R. Hoehn-Saric, S. D. Imber, B. L. Liberman, and A. R. Stone. Copyright 1978 by Brunner/Mazel. Reprinted by permission.

much on a personal trait as on the interaction of the immediate state of the patient with factors in the environment, an observation that has been confirmed by other studies (Liberman, 1964).

The response after three years also rules out a possible interpretation of the very rapid relief of discomfort with the initial placebo group, namely, that their initial mean discomfort score was artificially heightened by their apprehension as to what was to transpire. Although this apprehension may have had some effect, it could not explain all of the drop, since it would not operate with patients who three years previously had received, and therefore were familiar with, psychotherapy.

To be therapeutically effective, hope for improvement must be linked in the patient's mind to specific processes of therapy as well as outcome (Imber, Pande, Frank, Hoehn-Saric, Stone, & Wargo, 1970; Wilkins, 1979). This link could be taken for granted by purveyors of traditional therapies like psychoanalysis because most patients came to them already familiar with their procedures (Kadushin, 1969). Introducers of new or unfamiliar therapies regularly spend considerable time and effort at the start teaching the patient their particular therapeutic game and shaping the patient's expectations accordingly.

These considerations led me and several colleagues to devise a controlled experiment comparing the results of four months of therapy between patients who first received a preliminary "role induction interview" designed to coordinate their expectations with what they would receive and patients who were treated identically but did not have the preparatory interview (Hoehn-Saric, Frank, Imber, Nash, & Battle, 1964; Nash, Hoehn-Saric, Battle, Stone, Imber, & Frank, 1965).

The purposes of the role-induction interview were (1) to clarify the processes of treatment; (2) to assure the patient that treatment would be helpful; (3) to dispel unrealistic hopes (thereby guarding against disillusionment); and (4) to help the patient behave in a way that accorded with the therapist's image of a good patient, thereby indirectly heightening the latter's interest and optimism.

As a group, patients receiving the role-induction interview showed more appropriate behavior in therapy and had a better outcome than the controls. This finding has been replicated in another setting (Sloane, Cristol, Pepernick, & Staples, 1970). It should be emphasized that by leading the patients to behave better in therapy, the role-induction interview made them more attractive to the therapists, thereby improving the patient–therapist relationship.

3. *Providing new learning experiences.* These new learning experiences can enhance morale by enabling patients to discover potentially helpful alternate ways of looking at themselves and their problems and to develop alternate values. In this connection, improvement in therapy seems to go along with movement of the patient's values toward those of the therapist (Pande & Gart, 1968; Parloff, Goldstein, & Iflund, 1960; Rosenthal, 1955).

Learning may occur in several ways, including instruction,

modeling (Bandura, 1969), operant conditioning (in which the therapist's responses serve as positive or negative reinforcers), and exposure to new emotionally charged experiences, including transference reactions and emotional arousal by attempts to change contingencies governing behavior.

The more numerous and more intense the experiential, as opposed to the purely cognitive, components of learning, the more likely they are to be followed by changes in the patient's attitudes or behavior. It is a truism that intellectual insight alone is essentially powerless to effect change. This brings us to the fourth therapeutic ingredient common to all therapeutic conceptualizatons and rituals, emotional arousal.

4. *Arousing emotions.* Such arousal is essential to therapeutic change in at least three ways. It supplies the motive power to undertake the effort and to undergo the suffering usually involved in attempts to change one's attitudes and behavior, facilitates attitude change, and enhances sensitivity to environmental influences. If the emotional arousal is unpleasant, it leads the patient to search actively for relief. When this occurs in therapy, the patient naturally turns to the therapist. Arousal intense enough to be disorganizing further increases this dependence and in addition may facilitate the achievement of a better personality integration by breaking up old patterns.

Eliciting intense emotions characterizes almost all healing rituals in nonindustrialized societies. In the West, the popularity of such approaches waxes and wanes. In the recent past these approaches emerged in Mesmerism and Freudian abreaction, and currently they are flourishing under various labels such as implosive therapy (Stampfl, 1976), primal therapy (Janov, 1970), reevaluation counseling (Jackins, 1965), bioenergetics (Lowen, 1975), and many, many more.

Influenced by the *Zeitgeist,* my colleagues and I conducted a series of experiments on emotional arousal and susceptibility to attitude change (Hoehn-Saric, 1978). To produce arousal we first used small doses of ether given by drip inhalation, because of the preanesthesia excitatory stage it produces in most persons. The semantic differential (Osgood, Suci, & Tannenbaum, 1957), which permits the ratings of meanings of a given concept on a set of bipolar scales, was used as the measure of attitude change. In consultation with their therapists during interview therapy, patients selected a "focal" concept that the therapist would try to shift and others that the therapist would not try to change (the patients were not told which concepts the therapist would try to shift). Examples of focal concepts were "my mother's influence on me" and "my tolerance of imperfections in persons close to me." In a preliminary uncontrolled experiment, patients received three interviews under a slow-drip administration of ether a week and a half apart, and the therapist tried to shift only the focal concept during or immediately after the excitatory phase. The focal concept shifted cumulatively in the predicted direction, and the shift achieved statistical significance after the third interview, as compared to the shift in the initial session without ether. The other concepts remained unchanged throughout.

We next devised a controlled experiment in which the purpose and those patients who received ether were unknown to the therapists. The experimental room smelled of ether for all patients. The results, although less striking than in the preliminary study, confirmed our premise.

Since ether produces confusion, which might account for the patients' increased susceptibility to influence, we repeated the experiment using inhalation of vapor containing adrenalin (which stimulates the sympathetic nervous system without clouding consciousness), with essentially the same result.

In all these studies the effects on patients' attitudes were transitory; that is, the concepts soon reverted to their original positions. Perhaps this reversion is related to the repeated decline of interest in abreactive techniques after a wave of popularity. Although emotional arousal may facilitate attitude change, something else seems to be needed to maintain the change. If one may generalize from this observation, which is consistent with others, it may be important to distinguish factors that produce therapeutic change from those that sustain it (Liberman, 1978a).

From the perspective of the demoralization hypothesis, the therapeutic effect of intense emotional arousal may be in its demonstration to patients that they can stand, at high intensity, emotions which they feared and which therefore caused them to avoid or escape from situations that threatened to arouse them. Surviving such an experience would strengthen self-confidence directly and also encourage a patient to enter and cope successfully with these feared situations, thereby indirectly further bolstering morale.

Thus the maintenance of improvement following emotional flooding may depend on the ability of this procedure to enhance the patient's sense of mastery (Liberman, 1978a) or self-efficacy (Bandura, 1977), to which I now turn.

5. *Enhancing the patient's sense of mastery or self-efficacy.* Self-esteem and personal security depend to a considerable degree on a sense of being able to exert some control over the reactions of others

toward oneself as well as over one's own inner states. Inability to control feelings, thoughts, and impulses not only is demoralizing in itself but also impedes one's ability to control others by preempting too much attention and distorting one's perceptions and behavior. The feeling of loss of control gives rise to emotions such as anxiety which aggravate and are aggravated by the specific symptoms or problems for which the person ostensibly seeks psychotherapy. All schools of psychotherapy seek to bolster the patient's sense of mastery in at least two ways: (1) by providing the patient with a conceptual scheme that labels and explains symptoms and supplies the rationale for the treatment program and (2) by giving the individual experiences of success.

Since the verbal apparatus is a human being's chief tool for analyzing and organizing experience, the conceptual scheme increases the patient's sense of control by making sense out of experineces that had seemed haphazard, confusing, or inexplicable and giving names to them. This effect has been termed the principle of Rumpelstiltskin (Torrey, 1972) after the fairy tale in which the queen broke the wicked dwarf's power over her by guessing his name.

To have this effect, interpretations, which are the primary means of transmitting the conceptual framework, need not necessarily be correct but may merely be plausible. One therapist demonstrated this concept by offering six "all-purpose" interpretations to four patients in intensive psychotherapy. An example of such an interpretation is "You seem to live your life as though you were apologizing all the time." The same series of interpretations, spaced about a month apart, was given to all four patients. In 20 of these 24 instances, the patients responded with a drop in anxiety level. All patients experienced this move from the "preinterpreted" to the "postinterpreted" state at least once (Mendel, 1964).

Experiences of success, a major source of enhanced self-efficacy, are implicit in all psychotherapeutic procedures. Verbally adept patients get them from achieving new insights, behaviorally oriented patients from carrying out increasingly anxiety-laden behaviors. As we have already mentioned, by demonstrating to the patient that he or she can withstand at their maximal intensity the emotions he or she fears, emotional flooding techniques yield powerful experiences of success.

Furthermore, performances which the patient regards as due to his or her own efforts would be expected to reflect more strongly on an individual's self-esteem than those which the patient attributes to factors beyond his or her control, such as a medication or the help of someone else. In recognition of this expectation, psychotherapists of all persuasions convey to the patient the progress is the result of the individual's own efforts. Nondirective therapists disclaim any credit for the patient's acquiring new insights, and directive ones stress that the patient's gains depends on his or her ability to carry out the prescribed procedures.

6. *Providing opportunities for practice.* A final morale-enhancing feature of all psychotherapies is that they provide opportunities and incentives for internalizing and reinforcing therapeutic gains through repeated testing both within and outside the therapeutic session.

For completeness, it should be mentioned that group therapies involve the same morale-building principles as individual ones, often to a greater degree. The presence of other patients and the emergence of processes specific to groups introduce additional ways of combating the alienation that accompanies demoralization and provide different opportunities for cognitive and experiential learning and for practicing what has been learned. They also provide more occasions for emotional arousal and more opportunities to achieve a sense of mastery through weathering the stresses of group interactions. Finally, as social microcosms more closely resembling real life than individual interview situations, groups facilitate transfer of what has been learned to daily living.

DETERMINANTS OF THERAPEUTIC SUCCESS

The most powerful determinants of the success of any therapeutic encounter probably lie in properties of the patient, the therapist and the particular patient–therapist pair rather than in the therapeutic procedure. Despite its importance, this area presents particular problems for research, as already indicated, so research findings are scanty and, for the most part, simply confirm clinical impressions. This situation enables me to be mercifully brief.

There is general agreement that the good patient is characterized by sufficient distress to be motivated for treatment and by the capacity to profit from a helping relationship. Strupp (1976) suggests that to be able to so profit, the patient must have had sufficiently rewarding experiences with his or her own parents so that the patient has developed "the capacity to profit from and change as a result of the forces operating in a 'good' human relationship" (p. 99).

Patients with a good prognosis are characterized, in addition, by such terms as good ego strength, coping capacity, or personality assets. An illuminating approach to therapeutically favorable personal qualities is provided by Harrower (1965). On the basis of a follow-up study of 622 patients in psychoanalysis or analytically oriented therapy, she was able to devise an index of mental-health potential based on score patterns on projective tests that correlated highly with improvement as judged retrospectively by the patients' therapists. Mental-health potential included capacity for emotional warmth and friendliness, adequate intellectual control combined with freedom and spontaneity, inner resources, and intuitive empathy for others. In short, the psychologically healthier the patient is at the start, the better the prognosis for response to treatment.

One would like to know much more about factors determining ability to profit from specific therapeutic procedures. For example, Malan (1976) presents evidence that "motivation for insight" may be important for the success of brief psychoanalytically oriented psychotherapy. A promising lead is classification of patients in terms of locus of control—that is, whether the person sees control of his or her life as lying primarily within or outside of self (Rotter, 1966; Seeman & Evans, 1962). In one study, my colleagues and I stumbled on an interesting interaction between locus of control, therapeutic improvement, and the source to which patients were led to attribute their improved performance in therapy-linked tasks (that is, whether their improvement in therapy was attributed to their own efforts or to the effect of taking a placebo pill). The internally controlled patients did significantly better than the externally controlled in the first condition, but the results were reversed in the second (Liberman, 1978a; see Figure 3). Studies of the relation between locus of control and responses to a variety of therapies are accumulating (Friedman & Dies, 1975; Ollendick & Murphy, 1977).

In examining the therapeutic qualities of therapists, we find that the success rate of therapists varies widely, even within the same therapeutic school. For example, in a study of encounter groups that used at least two therapists from each of several therapeutic schools, Lieberman, Yalom, and Miles (1973) found that the best and the worst outcomes were in groups conducted by therapists belonging to the same school. Participants in encounter groups are sufficiently similar to those in therapy groups to justify applying this finding to them. In a retrospective analysis of 150 women treated by 16 male and 10 female therapists, Orlinsky and Howard (1980) found that two-thirds of the patients of the most successful therapists were much improved and none were worse, whereas for the least successful only one-third were much improved and one-third were worse. As to what qualities

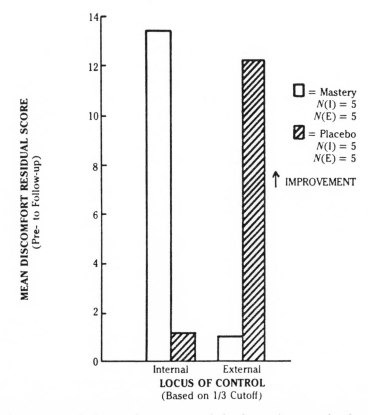

FIGURE 3. HSCL residual scores for mastery and placebo conditions with reference to initial mastery orientation (high residual scores reflect greater maintenance of improvement). From *Effective Ingredients of Successful Psychotherapy* by J. D. Frank, R. Hoehn-Saric, S. D. Imber, B. L. Liberman, and A. R. Stone. Copyright 1978 by Brunner/Mazel. Reprinted by permission.

of therapists account for differences in therapeutic success, however, our understanding has not progressed beyond the empathy, warmth, and genuineness found by Rogers and his school (1957) to be helpful with neurotics and the active personal participation perhaps related to success with schizophrenics (Dent, 1978; Whitehorn & Betz, 1975); and the ability to generalize about these findings remains questionable (Parloff, Waskow, & Wolfe, 1978).

To return to our analogy of psychotherapy with music, we find that psychotherapists, like muscial performers, seem to vary in innate talent, which in most can be enhanced by training. Almost anyone can learn to play the piano; but no amount of training can produce a Horowitz or a Rubinstein, nor can it turn someone who is tone-deaf into a violinist. Analogously, some therapists seem to obtain extraordinary results while the patients of a few do no better, or even fare worse, than if they had received no treatment at all. It would be highly desirable to weed out these "tone-deaf" therapists early in training, thereby preventing harm to patients and sparing the therapists from misery; but, unfortunately, adequate screening methods for this purpose do not yet exist.

My own hunch, which I mention with some trepidation, is that the most gifted therapists may have telepathic, clairvoyant, or other parapsychological abilities (Ehrenwald, 1966, 1978; Freud, 1964; Jung, 1963). They may, in addition, possess something that is similar to the ability to speed plant growth (Grad, 1967) or to produce spectacular auras on Kirlian photographs (Krippner & Rubin, 1973) and that can only be termed "healing power." Any researcher who attempts to study such phenomena risks his reputation as a reliable scientist, so their pursuit can be recommended only to the most intrepid. The rewards, however, might be great.

Descending to more solid ground, we see that the therapeutic relationship is, of course, a two-way street; therefore efforts to determine aspects of patients and therapists which make good or poor therapeutic matches should be promising. Again, information about this is very scanty, but thought-provoking. For example, it appears that with hospitalized chronic schizophrenics, composed therapists work best with anxious patients, therapists comfortable with aggression work well with hostile patients, grandparental therapists do well with seductive patients, and therapists comfortable with depression do well with depressed schizophrenics (Gunderson, 1978). Hardly a world-shaking finding, you will say, but it is a beginning.

The study of women in therapy mentioned earlier (Orlinksy & Howard, 1980) unearthed some interesting leads. The differential success rate of therapists appeared to be due primarily to interaction of patient–therapist pairs rather than to properties of the therapist alone, except that experience appeared to operate across the board. Therapists with less than six years' experience, compared with those with more, had twice as many patients who were unchanged or worse and only half as many who were considerably improved. The role of experience in therapeutic success, however, remains moot (Parloff *et al.*, 1978). Of more interest is the fact that although the sex of the therapist made no difference overall, young single women benefited more from women therapists, suggesting that men may have been somewhat threatening to them. Conversely, the only female patients who did better with the men were parents without partners. Could it be that the therapists represented to them a potential new partner?

Finally, the level of conceptualization may prove highly relevant to the matching of patients with therapists (Carr, 1970). Although no conclusive findings have emerged, it seems probable that persons who conceptualize at relatively concrete levels respond best with structured therapies in a structured environment. Furthermore, studies of smokers (Best, 1975), psychiatric outpatients treated by medical students, alcoholics, college students, and delinquents all found that patients whose conceptual level was similar to that of their therapist did better than those for whom there was a mismatch (Posthuma & Carr, 1975).

CONCLUSION

In concluding, let me attempt to correct a common misunderstanding of the demoralization hypothesis, namely that, since features shared by all therapies that combat demoralization account for much of their effectiveness, training is unnecessary. The point I have sought to make is that healing factors mobilized by all techniques contribute significantly to the outcome of any specific one.

Through personal characteristics and past experiences, however, some patients may be more attuned to behavioral, cognitive, abreactive, hypnotic, or other procedures. Thus it remains probable that certain specific techniques are more effective for some patients, or even for some symptoms, than others.

But even in the unlikely eventuality that all therapeutic techniques prove to be fully interchangeable, this substitutability would not mean that mastery of one or more is unnecessary. Such an unwarranted conclusion confuses the content of therapeutic conceptualizations and procedures with their function. Some therapeutically gifted persons, to be sure, can be effective with very little formal training, but most of us need to master at least one therapeutic rationale and ritual. Because the techniques are irrefutable and are supported by a like-minded group to which the therapist belongs (Festinger, 1957), they maintain the therapist's sense of competence, especially in the face of inevitable therapeutic failures. As one young adherent of a psychotherapeutic school remarked, "Even if the patient doesn't get better, you know you are doing the right thing." This attitude indirectly strengthens the patient's confidence in the therapist as a person who knows what he or she is doing.

If any moral can be drawn from this presentation, it is that the choice of procedures should be guided by the therapist's personal predilections. Some therapists are effective hypnotists; others are not. Some welcome emotional displays; others shy away from them. Some work best with groups, others in the privacy of the dyad. Some enjoy exploring psyches; others prefer to try to change behavior. Ideally, from this standpoint, training programs should expose trainees to a range of rationales and procedures and encourage them to select those which are most congenial to their own personalities. The greater the number of approaches that the therapist can handle, the wider the range of patients he or she will be able to help.

SUMMARY

Whatever their specific symptoms, patients coming to psychotherapy are also demoralized; and much of patients' disability and distress is caused by this demoralization. The sources of demoralization, whether a general response or a response to specific stress situations, insofar as it is amenable to psychotherapy, spring from warping experiences in the patients' past histories. These experiences result in three interacting, mutually reinforcing components: intrapsychic conflicts coupled with low self-esteem, distorted perception of others, and deficient coping skills. In conjunction, these components engender failure experiences or other distressing emotions that further undermine morale.

All psychotherapies aim to break the resulting vicious circle and to restore morale by providing experiences with a helping person that offer general encouragement and support, in addition to sometimes combating specific perceptual distortions and maladaptive behaviors.

The effectiveness of any psychotherapy with a specific patient depends on the morale-building features it shares with all other psychotherapies as well as its specific rationale and procedures. The relative contribution of these depends on the role of demoralization in the production or exacerbation of the patient's symptoms. Selection of technique is usually best guided less by the symptoms than by the personal characteristics and predilections of therapist and patient. The more closely these accord with each other and with the type of therapy, the better the prospects for a successful outcome.

REFERENCES

Bandura, A. *Principles of behavior modification.* New York: Holt, Rinehart & Winston, 1969.

Bandura, A. Self-efficacy: Toward a unifying theory of behavioral change. *Psychological Review*, 1977, *84*, 191–215.

Best, J. A. Tailoring smoking withdrawal procedures to personality and motivational differences. *Journal of Consulting and Clinical Psychology*, 1975, *43*, 1–8.

Carr, J. E. Differentiation similarity of patient and therapist and the outcome of psychotherapy. *Journal of Abnormal Psychology*, 1970, *76*, 361–369.

deFigueiredo, J., & Frank, J. D. Subjective incompetence, the clinical hallmark of demoralization. Unpublished manuscript, 1981.

Dent, J. K. *Exploring the psychological therapies through the personalities of effective therapists.* Publication No. ADM 77-527. Washington, DC: U.S. Government Printing Office, 1978.

Diefendorf, A. R. *Clinical psychiatry: A textbook for students and physicians abstracted and adapted from the 7th German edition of Kraepelin's "Lehrbuch der Psychiatrie."* New York: Macmillan, 1915.

Dohrenwend, B. P., & Crandall, D. L. Psychiatric symptoms in community, clinic and mental hospital groups. *American Journal of Psychiatry*, 1970, *126*, 1611–1621.

Dohrenwend, B. P., Oksenberg, L., Shrout, P. E., Dohrenwend, B. S., & Cook, D. What brief psychiatric screening scales measure. In S. Sudman (Ed.), *Proceedings of the 3rd biennial conference on health survey research methods, May, 1979.* Washington, DC: U.S. Department of Health & Human Services DHHS Publication No. (PHS) 81-3268, 1979, pp. 188–198.

Dohrenwend, B. P., Shrout, P. E., Egri, G., & Mendlsohn, F. S. Nonspecific psychological distress and other dimensions of psychopathology: Measures for use in the general population. *Archives of General Psychiatry*, 1980, *37*, 1229–1236.

Ehrenwald, J. *Psychotherapy: Myth and method.* New York: Grune & Stratton, 1966.

Ehrenwald, J. *The ESP experience: A psychiatric validation.* New York: Basic Books, 1978.

Farber, B. A., & Geller, J. D. Student attitudes toward psychotherapy. *Journal of the American College Health Association*, 1977, *25*, 301–307.

Festinger, L. *A theory of cognitive dissonance.* Evanston, IL: Row, Peterson, 1957.

Frank, J. D. *Persuasion and healing* (2nd ed.). Baltimore: John Hopkins University Press, 1973.

Frank, J. D. Psychotherapy: The restoration of morale. *American Journal of Psychiatry*, 1974, *131*, 271–274.

Frank, J. D. Aristotle as psychotherapist. In M. J. Mahoney (Ed.), *Psychotherapy process: Current issues and future directions.* New York: Plenum Press, 1980.

Frank, J. D., Gliedman, L. H., Imber, S. D., Stone, A. R., & Nash, E. H. Patients' expectancies and relearning as factors determining improvement in psychotherapy. *American Journal of Psychiatry*, 1959, *115*, 961–968.

Frank, J. D., Nash, E. H., Stone, A. R., & Imber, S. D. Immediate and long-term symptomatic course of psychiatric outpatients. *American Journal of Psychiatry*, 1963, *120*, 429–439.

Frank, J. D., Hoehn-Saric, R., Imber, S. D., Liberman, B. L., and Stone, A. R. *Effective Ingredients of Successful Psychotherapy.* New York: Brunner/Mazel, 1978.

Freud, S. Dreams and occultism. In J. Strachey (Ed.), *The complete psychological works of Sigmund Freud.* London: Hogarth, 1964.

Friedman, H. J. Patient expectancy and symptom reduction. *Archives of General Psychiatry*, 1963, *8*, 61–67.

Friedman, M. L., & Dies, R. R. Reactions of internal and external test-anxious students to counseling and behavior therapies. *Journal of Consulting and Clinical Psychology*, 1975, *42*, 921.

Galanter, M. The "relief effect": A sociobiological model for neurotic distress and large-group therapy. *American Journal of Psychiatry*, 1978, *135*, 588–591.

Galassi, J. P., & Galassi, M. D. Alienation in college students: A comparison of counseling seekers and nonseekers. *Journal of Counseling Psychology*, 1973, *20*, 44–49.

Garfield, S. L. Research on client variables in psychotherapy. In S. L. Garfield & A. E. Bergin (Eds.), *Handbook of psychotherapy and behavior change: An empirical analysis* (2nd ed.). New York: Wiley, 1978.

Gelder, M. G., Marks, I. M., & Wolff, H. H. Desensitization and psychotherapy in phobic states: A controlled inquiry. *British Journal of Psychiatry*, 1967, *113*, 53–73.

Glaser, S. R. Rhetoric and psychotherapy. In M. J. Mahoney (Ed.), *Psychotherapy process: Current issues and future directions*. New York: Plenum Press, 1980.

Goldfried, M. R., & Padawer, W. Current status and future directions in psychotherapy. In M. R. Goldfried (Ed.), *Converging themes in the practice of psychotherapy*. New York: Springer, 1983.

Grad, B. The "laying on of hands": Implications for psychotherapy, gentling, and the placebo effect. *Journal of the American Society for Psychical Research*, 1967, *61*, 286–305.

Gunderson, J. C. Patient–therapist matching: A research evaluation. *American Journal of Psychiatry*, 1978, *135*, 1193–1197.

Gurman, A. S. The patient's perception of the therapeutic relationship. In A. S. Gurman & A. M. Razin (Eds.), *Effective psychotherapy: A handbook of research*. New York: Pergamon, 1977.

Harrower, M. *Psychodiagnostic testing: An empirical approach*. Springfield, IL: Thomas, 1965.

Henderson, S., Byrne, D. G., & Duncan-Jones, P. *Neurosis and the social environment*. New York: Academic Press, 1981.

Hilts, P. J. Psychotherapy put on couch by government. *Washington Post*, September 14, 1980, Section A, pp. 1, 12.

Hoehn-Saric, R. Emotional arousal, attitude change, and psychotherapy. In J. D. Frank, R. Hoehn-Saric, S. D. Imber, & A. R. Stone, *Effective ingredients of successful psychotherapy*. New York: Brunner/Mazel, 1978.

Hoehn-Saric, R., Frank, J. D., Imber, S. D., Nash, E. H., & Battle, C. C. Systematic preparation of patients for psychotherapy. I. Effects on therapy behavior and outcome. *Journal of Psychiatry Research*, 1964, *2*, 267–281.

Imber, S. D., Pande, S. K., Frank, J. D., Hoehn-Saric, R., Stone, A. R., & Wargo, D. G. Time-focused role induction: Report of an instructive failure. *Journal of Nervous and Mental Disease*, 1970, *150*, 27–30.

Jackins, H. *The human side of human beings*. Seattle: Rational Island Publishers, 1965.

Jacobson, G. The briefest psychiatric encounter. *Archives of General Psychiatry*, 1968, *18*, 718–724.

Janov, A. *The primal scream: Primal therapy, the cure for neurosis*. New York: Putnam, 1970.

Jung, C. G. *Memories, dreams and reflections*. New York: Vintage, 1963.

Kadushin, K. *Why people go to psychiatrists*. New York: Atherton, 1969.

Kellner, R., & Sheffield, B. F. The one-week prevalence of symptoms in neurotic patients and normals. *American Journal of Psychiatry*, 1973, *130*, 102–105.

Koch, S. The nature and limits of psychological knowledge: Lessons of a century *qua* "science." *American Psychologist*, 1981, *36*, 257–269.

Krippner, S., & Rubin, D. (Eds.). *Galaxies of life: The human aura in acupuncture and Kirlian photography.* New York: Gordon & Breach, 1973.

LeShan, L. *The medium, the mystic, and the physicist: Toward a general theory of the paranormal.* New York: Viking, 1974.

Liberman, B. L. The role of mastery in psychotherapy: Maintenance of improvement and prescriptive change. In J. D. Frank, R. Hoehn-Saric, S. D. Imber, B. L. Liberman, & A. R. Stone, *Effective ingredients of successful psychotherapy.* New York: Brunner/Mazel, 1978. (a)

Liberman, B. L. The maintenance and persistence of change: Long-term follow-up investigations of psychotherapy. In J. D. Frank, R. Hoehn-Saric, S. D. Imber, B. L. Liberman, & A. R. Stone, *Effective ingredients of successful psychotherapy.* New York: Brunner/Mazel, 1978. (b)

Liberman, R. An experimental study of the placebo response under three different situations of pain. *Journal of Psychiatric Research*, 1964, *2*, 233–246.

Lieberman, M. A., Yalom, I. D., & Miles, M. D. *Encounter groups: First facts.* New York: Basic Books, 1973.

Link, B., & Dohrenwend, B. P. Formulation of hypotheses about the true prevalence of demoralization in the United States. In B. P. Dohrenwend, B. S. Dohrenwend, M. S. Gould, B. Link, R. Neugebauer, & R. Wunsch-Hitzig (Eds.), *Mental illness in the United States: Epidemiological estimates.* New York: Praeger, 1980.

Lowen, A. *Bioenergetics.* New York: Doward, McCann, & Geoghegan, 1975.

Luborsky, L. Helping alliances in psychotherapy. In J. L. Claghorn (Ed.), *Successful psychotherapy.* New York: Brunner/Mazel, 1976.

Luborsky, L., & Auerbach, A. H. The symptom-context method: Quantitative studies of symptom formation in psychotherapy. *Journal of the American Psychoanalytical Association*, 1969, *17*, 68–99.

Malan, D. H. *Toward the validation of dynamic psychotherapy: A replication.* New York: Plenum Press, 1976.

Marmor, J. Common operational factors in diverse approaches to behavior change. In A. Burton (Eds.), *What makes behavior change possible?* New York: Brunner/Mazel, 1976.

Mendel, W. M. The phenomenon of interpretation. *American Journal of Psychoanalysis*, 1964, *24*, 184–189.

Nash, E. H., Hoehn-Saric, R., Battle, C. C., Stone, A. R., Imber, S. D., & Frank, J. D. Systematic preparation of patients for short-term psychotherapy. II. Relation to characteristics of patient, therapist and the psychotherapeutic process. *Journal of Nervous and Mental Disease*, 1965, *140*, 374–383.

Neki, J. S. Guru–chela relationship: The possibility of a therapeutic paradigm. *American Journal of Orthopsychiatry*, 1973, *32*, 755–766.

Ollendick, T. H., & Murphy, M. J. Differential effectiveness of muscular and cognitive relaxation as a function of locus of control. *Journal of Behavioral Therapy and Experimental Psychiatry*, 1977, *8*, 223–228.

Orlinsky, D. E., & Howard, K. I. Gender and psychotherapeutic outcome. In A. Brodsky & R. T. Har-Mustin (Eds.), *Women and psychotherapy.* New York: Guilford Press, 1980.

Orne, M. T. Demand characteristics and the concept of quasi-controls. In R. Rosenthan & R. L. Rosnow (Eds.), *Artifact in behavioral research*. New York: Academic Press, 1969.

Osgood, C. E., Suci, G. J., & Tannenbaum, P. H. *The measurement of meaning*. Urbana: University of Illinois Press, 1957.

Pande, S. K. The mystique of "Western" psychotherapy: An Eastern view. *Journal of Nervous and Mental Disease*, 1968, *146*, 425–432.

Pande, S. K., & Gart, J. J. A method to quantify reciprocal influence between therapist and patient in psychotherapy. In J. Shlien, H. F. Hunt, J. D. Matarazzo, & C. Savage (Eds.), *Research in psychotherapy*. Washington, DC: American Psychological Association, 1968.

Parloff, M. B., Waskow, I. E., & Wolfe, B. E. Research on therapist variables in relation to process and outcome. In S. L. Garfield & A. E. Bergin (Eds.), *Handbook of psychotherapy and behavior change*. New York: Wiley, 1978.

Parloff, M. B., Goldstein, N., & Iflund, B. Communication of values and therapeutic change. *Archives of General Psychiatry*, 1960, *2*, 300–304.

Posthuma, A. B., & Carr, J. E. Differentiation matching in psychotherapy. *Canadian Psychological Review*, 1975, *16*, 35–43.

Rogers, C. R. The necessary and sufficient conditions of therapeutic personality change. *Journal of Consulting Psychology*, 1957, *21*, 95–103.

Rosenberg, M. J. The conditions and consequences of evaluation apprehension. In R. Rosenthal & R. L. Rosnow (Eds.), *Artifact in behavioral research*. New York: Academic Press, 1969.

Rosenthal, D. Changes in some moral values following psychotherapy *Journal of Consulting Psychology*, 1955, *19*, 431–436.

Rosenzweig, S. Some implicit common factors in diverse methods of psychotherapy. *American Journal of Orthopsychiatry*, 1936, *6*, 412–415.

Rotter, J. B. Generalized expectancies for internal vs. external control of reinforcement. *Psychological Monographs*, 1966, *80*, (1, Whole No. 609).

Rush, A. J., Beck, A. T., Kovacs, M., & Hollon, S. Comparative effects of cognitive therapy and pharmacotherapy in the treatment of depressed outpatients. *Cognitive Therapy and Research*, 1977, *1*, 17–37.

Seeman, M., & Evans, J. W. Alienation and learning in a hospital setting. *American Sociological Review*, 1962, *27*, 772–782.

Seguin, C. A. *Love and psychotherapy*. New York: Libra Publishers, 1965.

Sloane, R. B., Cristol, A. H., Pepernick, M. C., & Staples, F. R. Role preparation and expectation of improvement in psychotherapy. *Journal of Nervous and Mental Disease*, 1970, *150*, 18–26.

Sloane, R. B., Staples, F. R., Cristol, A. H., Yorkston, N. J., & Whipple, K. *Psychotherapy versus behavior therapy*. Cambridge, MA: Harvard University Press, 1975.

Smith, H. *Forgotten truth: The primordial tradition*. New York: Harper Colophon, 1977.

Smith, N. L., Glass, G. V., & Miller, T. I. *Benefits of psychotherapy*. Baltimore: Johns Hopkins University Press, 1980.

Stampfl, T. G. Implosive therapy. In P. Olsen (Ed.), *Emotional flooding*. New York: Human Sciences Press, 1976.

Strupp, H. H. The nature of the therapeutic influence and its basic ingredients. In A. Burton (Ed.), *What makes behavior change possible?* New York: Brunner/Mazel, 1976.

Strupp, H. H., & Hadley, S. W. Specific vs. nonspecific factors in psychotherapy: A controlled study of outcome. *Archives of General Psychiatry*, 1979, *36*, 1125–1136.

Szasz, T. S. *The myth of psychotherapy: Mental healing as religion, rhetoric, and repression.* New York: Anchor, 1978.

Torrey, E. F. *The mind game.* New York: Emerson Hall, 1972.

Uhlenhuth, E. H., & Duncan, D. B. Subjective change with medical student therapists: II. Some determinants of change in psychoneurotic outpatients. *Archives of General Psychiatry,* 1968, *18,* 186–198.

Vaillant, G. E. Why men seek psychotherapy, I: Results of a survey of college students. *American Journal of Psychiatry,* 1972, *129,* 645–651.

Whitehorn, J. C., & Betz, B. *Effective psychotherapy with the schizophrenic patient.* New York: Jason Aronson, 1975.

Wilkins, W. Expectancies in therapy research: Discriminating among heterogeneous non-specifics. *Journal of Consulting and Clinical Psychology,* 1979, *47,* 837–845.

Wolberg, L. R. *The technique of psychotherapy* (3rd ed.). New York: Grune & Stratton, 1977.

CHAPTER 3

Model of Causality in Social Learning Theory

ALBERT BANDURA

Many theories have been proposed over the years to explain human behavior. The basic conceptions of human nature they adopt and the causal processes they postulate require careful examination for several reasons. What theorists believe people to be determines which aspects of human functioning they explore most thoroughly and which they leave unexamined. Conceptions of human nature thus focus inquiry on selected processes and are in turn strengthened by findings of paradigms embodying the particular view. For example, theorists who exclude the capacity for self-direction from their view of human potentialities confine their research to external sources of influence and indeed find that behavior is often influenced by extrinsic outcomes. Theorists who view humans as possessing self-directing capabilities employ paradigms that shed light on how people make causal contribution to their own motivation and action through the exercise of self-influence.

The view of human nature embodied in psychological theories is more than a philosophical issue. As psychological knowledge gained through study is put into practice, the conceptions on which social technologies rest have even vaster implications. They can affect which human potentialities will be cultivated and which will be underdeveloped. In this way, conceptions of human nature can influence what

ALBERT BANDURA • Stanford University, Building 420, Jordan Hall, Stanford, California 94305.

people become. This article is devoted mainly to the model of human nature and causality embodied in social learning theory.

TRIADIC RECIPROCAL DETERMINISM

ONE-SIDED DETERMINATION

Human behavior has often been explained in terms of a one-sided determinism in which either environmental forces or internal dispositions are depicted as acting unidirectionally to produce behavior. As empirical evidence accumulated on the bidirectionality of influence, theorists increasingly subscribed to some form of interactional model of causality. Behavior is now commonly viewed as a product of personal and situational influences (Bandura, 1978; Bowers, 1973, Cairns, 1979; Endler & Magnusson, 1976). It is no longer interactionism, but the type of interaction advocated, that is the central issue in dispute. Interactive processes have been conceptualized in at least three different ways, as summarized in Figure 1. Two of these formulations subscribe to a one-sided interactionism with respect to behavior.

ONE-SIDED INTERACTIONISM

In the unidirectional view of interaction, persons and situations are treated as independent entities that somehow combine to produce

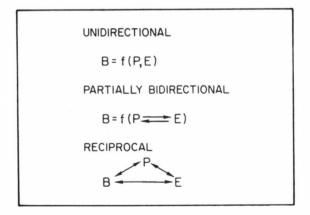

FIGURE 1. Schematic representation of three alternative conceptions of interaction. *B* signifies behavior, *P* the cognitive and other internal events that can affect perceptions and actions, and *E* the external environment.

behavior. This model of causality does not adequately represent interactive processes because personal and environmental factors do not function as independent determinants; rather, they determine each other.

The partially bidirectional conception of interaction acknowledges that persons and situations affect each other. But it treats influences relating to behavior as flowing in only one direction—the person–situation interchange unidirectionally produces the behavior, but behavior itself contributes nothing to the ongoing transaction. A major deficiency of this type of view is that behavior is not produced by the union of a behaviorless person and a situation. It is mainly through their actions that people influence situations which, in turn, affect their thoughts, emotional reactions, and behavior. Behavior is an interacting determinant, not a detached by-product that plays no role in transactions between persons and situations.

Triadic Reciprocality

Social learning theory favors a conception of interaction based on triadic reciprocality (Bandura, 1977a, 1982b). In this model of reciprocal determinism, behavior, cognitive and other personal factors, and environmental influences all operate as interlocking determinants that affect each other bidirectionally. Reciprocality does not mean that the two sides of the influence are of equal strength. Nor is the patterning and strength of mutual influences fixed in reciprocal causation. The relative influence exerted by the three sources of interlocking determinants will vary for different activities, different individuals, and different circumstances.

It would be exceedingly difficult to study all aspects of triadic reciprocality simultaneously. Hence, different branches of psychology study different segments of it. Clarifying the interactional links between the various subsystems advances understanding of how the superordinate system operates. Cognitive psychologists, who explore the interaction between thought and action, examine how conceptions, beliefs, self-percepts, and intentions give shape and direction to behavior. What people think, believe, and feel affects how they behave. The natural and extrinsic effects of their actions, in turn, partly determine their thought patterns and affective reactions (Bandura, 1982; Bower, 1975; Neisser, 1976).

Social psychologists center much of their attention on the segment of reciprocality between the person and the environment in the triadic system. They explore how thoughts, feelings, and behavioral competencies are modified through modeling, tuition, or social persuasion (Bandura, 1977a; Rosenthal & Zimmerman, 1978; Zimbardo, Ebbesen, & Maslach, 1977). People also evoke different reactions from their social environment by their physical characteristics and their social roles and statuses. The processes by which people's perceptions of each other influence the course of their interactions has been a subject of major concern to researchers working within the field of person perception (Schneider, Hastorf, & Ellsworth, 1979; Snyder, 1981).

Of all the various segments in the triadic interlocking system, the reciprocal relationship between behavior and environmental events has received the greatest attention. Indeed, some theories focus exclusively on this portion of reciprocity in the explanation of behavior (Skinner, 1974). In the transactions of everyday life, behavior alters environmental conditions and is, in turn, altered by the very conditions it creates (Cairns, 1979; Patterson, 1976; Thomas & Malone, 1979). To understand fully the interactive relation between behavior and environment the analysis must include cognitive determinants that also operate bidirectionally in the triadic interlocking system. This requires tapping what people are thinking as they perform responses and experience their effects.

DETERMINISM AND FORTUITOUS DETERMINANTS OF LIFE PATHS

Analysis of determinism in terms of triadic reciprocality of influence sheds light on how people are influenced by, and influencers of, the events with which they happen to have contact. But there is a fortuitous element in the events they are likely to encounter in their daily lives. People are often brought together through a fortuitous constellation of events, when their paths would otherwise never have crossed. In a chance encounter the separate paths in which people are moving have their own chain of causal determinants, but their intersection occurs fortuitously rather than through deliberate plan. The profusion of separate chains of events provides innumerable opportunities for fortuitous intersections. It is such chance encounters that often play a prominent role in shaping the course of career pursuits, marital partnerships, and other important aspects of human lives (Bandura, 1982c).

Some chance encounters touch people only lightly, others leave more lasting effects, and still others thrust people into new trajectories of life. Psychology cannot foretell the occurrence of fortuitous encounters, however sophisticated its knowledge of human behavior.

The unforeseeability and branching power of fortuitous influences make the specific course of lives neither easily predictable nor easily socially engineerable. Fortuity of influence does not mean that behavior is undetermined. Fortuitous influences may be unforeseeable, but having occurred they enter as evident factors in causal chains in the same way as prearranged ones do.

A science of psychology does not have much to say about the occurrence of fortuitous intersections, except that personal dispositions and social structures and affiliations make some types of encounters more probable than others. However, psychology can provide the basis for predicting the nature, scope, and strength of the impact they will have on human lives. The way in which personal attributes and environmental properties act reciprocally to determine the branching power of chance encounters has been extensively analyzed elsewhere (Bandura, 1982c) and will not be reviewed here.

FREEDOM AND DETERMINISM

In philosophical discourses, freedom is often considered antithetical to determinism. When viewed from a social learning perspective, there is no incompatibility between freedom and determinism. Freedom is not conceived negatively as the absence of influences or simply the lack of external constraints. Rather, it is defined positively in terms of the exercise of self-influence. This is achieved through thought, the skills at one's command, and other tools of self-influence which choice of action requires. Self-generated influences operate deterministically on behavior as do external sources of influence. Given the same environmental conditions, persons who have the capabilities for exercising many options and are adept at regulating their own behavior will experience greater freedom than will those whose means of personal agency are limited. It is because self-influence operates deterministically on action that some measure of freedom is possible.

Nor is determinism incompatible with personal responsibility. Behavior always involves choices from among the various options one can pursue in a particular situation. In the face of situational inducements to behave in a particular way, persons can, and do, choose to behave otherwise by exerting self-influence. Obviously they are not the sole source of determinants but they do contribute causality to their own actions which shape the nature of their situations. Because persons can exercise some degree of control over how circumstances will influence their actions, they cannot be entirely ab-

solved of the responsibility of their behavior. Partial personal causality of action involves at least partial responsibility for it.

DISTINCTIVE HUMAN CAPABILITIES

In the social learning view people are neither driven by inner
forces nor automatically shaped and controlled by external stimuli.
As we have already seen, they function as a reciprocally contributing
influence to their own motivation and behavior within a system of
interacting influences. Persons are characterized within this perspective in terms of a number of basic capabilities, to which we turn
next.

SYMBOLIZING CAPABILITY

The remarkable capacity to use symbols provides humans with
a powerful means of creating and regulating environmental events
that touch virtually every aspect of their lives. It is through symbols
that people process and transform transient experiences into internal
models that serve as guides for future action. Through symbols they
similarly give meaning, form, and continuance to the experiences
they have lived through.

By drawing on their knowledge and thinking skills people can
generate innovative courses of action. Rather than solve problems
solely by performing options and suffering the costs of missteps, people usually test possible solutions symbolically and discard or retain
them on the basis of calculated consequences before plunging into
action. An advanced cognitive capability coupled with the remarkable
flexibility of symbolization enables people to create ideas that transcend their sensory experiences. Through the medium of symbols they
can communicate with others at any distance in time and space. Other
distinctive human characteristics to be discussed shortly are similarly founded on symbolic capability.

To say that people base many of their actions on thought does
not necessarily mean they are always objectively rational. Rationality
depends on reasoning skills which are not always well developed or
used effectively. Even if people know how to reason logically they
make faulty judgments when they base their inferences on inadequate
information or fail to consider the full consequences of different choices.
Moreover, they often misread events in ways that give rise to faulty
conceptions about themselves and the world around them. When they
act on their misconceptions, which appear subjectively rational given
their errant basis, such persons are viewed by others as behaving in

an unreasoning, if not downright foolish, manner. Thought can thus be a source of human failing and distress as well as human accomplishment.

Analysis of how thought enters into the determination of behavior touches on fundamental issues concerning the mind–body relationship. In social learning theory, thoughts are construed as higher neural processes that activate visceral, motoric, and other physical processes which can in turn affect thought processes. Ideational and neural terms are different ways of representing the same brain processes, as identity theorists have argued for years. Thoughts are causative but not immaterial. Bunge (1980) presents a detailed analysis of cognitive processes as a set of brain activities in plastic neural sytems of the cerebral cortex and interprets psychophysical relations as involving reciprocal actions between specialized subsystems of the organism.

The view that cognitive events are neural occurrences does not mean that psychological laws regarding cognitive functioning must be reduced to neurophysiological ones. Quite the contrary. It is important to distinguish between cortical systems and the personal and social means by which they can be orchestrated for diverse purposes. Knowing how cortical neurons function in learning does not tell one much about how best to present and organize instructional contents, how to code them for memory representation, and how to motivate learners to attend to, process, and rehearse what they are learning. Nor does understanding of how the brain works furnish rules on how to construct learning conditions best suited to cultivate skills needed to become a successful parent, teacher, or politician.

The events needed to produce the neural occurrences underlying complex human behavior are either external to the organism or are cognitively generated. The laws of psychology therefore concern the environmental structuring and cognitive generation of influences for given purposes. Although psychological laws cannot violate what is known about the physiological system that subserves them, they need to be pursued in their own right. Were one to embark on the road to reductionism, the journey would successively traverse biology and chemistry and would eventually end in particles of atomic nuclei with neither the intermediate locales nor the final stop supplying the psychological laws of human behavior.

FORETHOUGHT CAPABILITY

People are not simply reactors to their immediate environment or steered by remnants of their past. Most of their behavior, being purposive, is under forethought control. They anticipate likely consequences of prospective actions, set goals for themselves, and otherwise plan courses of action that lead to valued futures. Through such exercise of forethought, people motivate themselves and guide their actions anticipatorily. By reducing the impact of immediate influences, forethought can support foresightful behavior even when present conditions are not especially conducive to it.

The capability for intentional and purposive action is rooted in symbolic activity. Future events cannot serve as determinants of behavior but their cognitive representation can have strong causal impact on present actions. Thus, for example, images of desirable futures foster the type of behavior likely to bring about their realization. By representing foreseeable outcomes symbolically, future consequences can be converted into current motivators and regulators of foresightful behavior. In social learning analyses of telic or purposive mechanisms through goals and outcomes projected forward in time, the future gains causal influence by being represented cognitively in the present.

Because outcomes affect behavior largely through the mediation of thought, consequences alone often produce little change in behavior until people become aware of what actions are being rewarded or punished (Bandura, 1969; Brewer, 1974). The way in which behavior is influenced by its effects also depends on the judgments people form about the rules governing outcomes, the meaning they attribute to the outcomes, and beliefs about how their actions are likely to change future outcomes over the course of time (Bandura, 1977a; Baron, Kaufman, & Stauber, 1969; Dulany, 1968).

When belief differs from actuality, which is not uncommon, behavior is weakly controlled by its consequences until repeated experience instills realistic expectations. But it is not always one's beliefs that change in the direction of social reality. Acting on erroneous expectations can alter how others behave, thus shaping the social reality in the direction of the beliefs (Snyder, 1981).

VICARIOUS CAPABILITY

Psychological theories have traditionally assumed that learning can occur only by performing responses and experiencing their effects. Learning through action was thus given major, if not exclusive, priority. In actuality, virtually all learning phenomena resulting from direct experience occur on a vicarious basis by observing other people's behavior and its consequences for them (Bandura, 1977a; Rosenthal, 1984; Rosenthal & Zimmerman, 1978; Sukemune, Haruki,

& Kashiwagi, 1977). The capacity to learn by observation enables people to acquire rules and integrated patterns of behavior without having to form them gradually by tedious trial and error. The constraints of time, resources, and mobility impose severe limits on the types of situations and activities that can be explored directly. Through social modeling people can draw on vast sources of information, exhibited and authored by others, for expanding their knowledge and skills.

Abbreviating the acquisition process through observational learning is vital for both development and survival. Because mistakes can produce costly or even fatal consequences, the prospects for survival would be slim indeed if one could learn only from the consequences of trial and error. For this reason, one does not teach children to swim, adolescents to drive automobiles, and novice medical students to perform surgery by having them discover the appropriate behavior through the consequences of their hit-and-miss efforts. The more costly and hazardous the possible errors, the heavier is the dependence on observational learning in the functional organization of behavior.

Humans come with few inborn patterns. This remarkable plasticity places heavy demands on learning functions. People must develop their basic capabilities over an extended period, and they must continue to master new competencies to fulfill changing demands throughout their lifespan. It therefore comes as no surprise that humans evolved an advanced vicarious capability. Apart from the question of survival, it is difficult to imagine a social transmission process in which the language, life-styles, and institutional practices of a culture are taught to each new member by selective reinforcement of whatever behaviors happen to occur, without the benefit of models who exemplify the cultural patterns.

Most psychological theories were formulated long before the advent of enormous advances in the technology of communication. As a result, they give insufficient attention to the increasingly powerful role the symbolic environment plays in present-day human lives. Indeed, in many aspects of living, televised vicarious influence has supplanted the primacy of direct experience. Whether it be thought patterns, values, attitudes, or styles of behavior, life increasingly models the media.

The video system feeding off telecommunications satellites has become the dominant vehicle for disseminating symbolic environments. Further developments in cable systems that permit two-way communication, laser transmission with its enormous information-

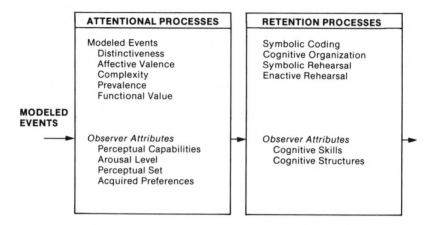

FIGURE 2. Subprocesses governing observational learning.

carrying capacity, and computer delivery systems with vast stored choices will provide households with diverse symbolic environments to serve almost any purpose. These extraordinary changes in communication technologies are restructuring how we live our lives. Diversity and ready choice of symbolic environments allow greater leeway for self-directedness to affect the course of personal development.

In the social learning view, observational learning is governed by four component processes which are depicted in Figure 2. *Attentional processes* determine what is selectively observed in the profusion of modeling influences and what information is extracted from ongoing modeled events. The process of attention is not simply a matter of absorbing sensory information that happens to impinge upon the organism. Rather, it involves self-directed exploration of the environment and construction of meaningful perceptions from ongoing modeled events. Perceptions are guided by preconceptions. Observers' cognitive competencies and perceptual sets dispose them to look for some things over others. Their expectations not only channel what they look for but partly affect what features they extract from observations and how they interpret what they see and hear.

People cannot be much influenced by observation of modeled activities if they do not remember them. A second major subfunction governing observational learning concerns *retention processes*. Retention involves an active process of transforming and restructuring information about events. Observational learning relies mainly upon two representational systems—imaginal and verbal. After modeled

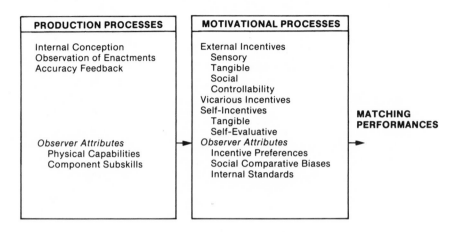

activities have been coded into images and readily utilizable verbal symbols, these conceptions function as guides for subsequent action. Cognitive rehearsal also serves as an important memory aid. If symbolic conceptions of modeled events are not rehearsed when first observed, they are vulnerable to loss from memory (Bandura & Jeffery, 1973).

In the third subfunction in modeling—the *behavioral production process*—symbolic conceptions are translated into appropriate actions. Behavioral production primarily involves a conception matching process in which feedback from action is compared against the conceptual model. The behavior is then modified on the basis of the comparative information to achieve close correspondence between conception and action. Feedback is not of much aid if it occurs before an adequate conceptual representation is formed (Carroll & Bandura, 1982). Lack of an internal conception to serve as a comparative standard limits the extent to which performance feedback can be used correctively.

The fourth subfunction in modeling concerns *motivational processes.* Social learning theory distinguishes between acquisition and performance. This distinction is emphasized because people do not perform everything they learn. Performance of observationally learned behavior is influenced by three major types of incentives—direct, vicarious, and self-produced. People are more likely to exhibit modeled behavior if it results in valued outcomes than if it has unrewarding or punishing effects. Observed consequences influence the perform-

ance of modeled behavior in much the same way as do directly experienced consequences (Bandura, 1977a; Thelen & Rennie, 1972).
Seeing modeled behavior succeed for others increases the tendency
to behave in similar ways, whereas seeing modeled behavior punished
decreases like tendencies. The impact of observed consequences depends on observers' inferences that they would experience similar or
unlike outcomes for engaging in the modeled activities. The self-evaluative reactions people generate toward their own actions also regulate which observationally learned activities will be performed (Hicks,
1971). They express what they find self-satisfying and exclude what
they personally disapprove.

SELF-REGULATORY CAPABILITY

Another distinctive feature of social learning theory is the central
role it assigns to self-regulatory functions. People do not behave just
to suit the preferences of others. Much of their behavior is motivated
and regulated through internal standards and self-evaluative reactions to their own actions. An act therefore includes among its determinants self-produced influences.

Figure 3 depicts the three main subfunctions in the self-regulation

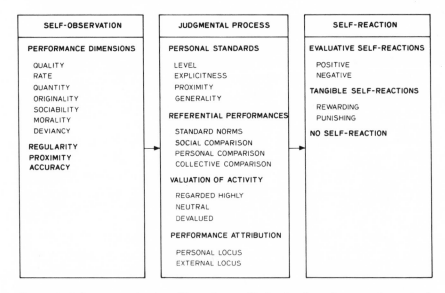

FIGURE 3. Subprocesses in the self-regulaton of behavior through internal standards
and self-incentives.

of behavior through internal standards and self-incentives. The first subfunction concerns the selective observation of one's own behavior on dimensions that are relevant in particular situations. Behavior produces self-reactions through a judgmental function relying on several subsidiary processes which include comparisons of perceived conduct to internal standards and the performances of others, valuation of the activities in which one is engaged, and cognitive appraisals of the personal and situational factors affecting one's performance. Performance appraisals set the occasion for self-produced consequences. Favorable judgments give rise to positive self-reactions, whereas unfavorable appraisals activate negative self-reactions.

Self-evaluative incentives operate as motivational devices rather than as automatic strengtheners of behavior (Bandura, 1977a; Locke, Shaw, Saari, & Latham, 1981). When people commit themselves to explicit standards or goals, perceived negative discrepancies between what they do and what they seek to achieve create self-dissatisfactions that serve as motivational inducements for change. Both the anticipated self-satisfactions for matching accomplishments and self-dissatisfactions with insufficient ones provide incentives for action.

Activation of self-evaluative processes through internal comparison requires both personal standards and knowledge of the level of one's performance. Neither knowledge of performance without standards nor standards without performance knowledge provides a basis for self-evaluative reactions and thus has little motivational effect (Bandura & Cervone, 1983). Whether negative discrepancies are motivating or discouraging is partly determined by people's perceptions of their efficacy to attain the standards they set for themselves. Those who have a low sense of efficacy are easily discouraged by failure, whereas those who are assured of their capabilities intensify their efforts when their performances fall short and persist until they succeed. Research examining these cognitive processes reveals that effects of goal systems on motivation are indeed mediated through self-evaluative and self-efficacy mechanisms (Bandura & Cervone, 1983). Personal goals are most highly motivating when persons are self-dissatisfied with substandard performances but are highly self-assured in their efficacy to achieve their self-prescribed goals.

Social learning theory distinguishes between distal goals and proximal subgoals. End goals influence the activity paths that are chosen, but they are too far removed in time to function as effective incentives and guides for present action. Focus on the distant future makes it easy to temporize and to slacken efforts in the present. It is proximal subgoals that effectively mobilize effort and direct what one does in the here and now. Attainable subgoals leading toward aspiring ultimate goals thus create the most favorable conditions for continuing self-motivation. Such proximal self-motivators cultivate competence, expand self-percepts of efficacy, and foster intrinsic interest in activities (Bandura & Schunk, 1981).

After social and moral standards of conduct are adopted, anticipatory self-condemning reactions for violating personal standards ordinarily serve as self-deterrents against reprehensible acts. But development of self-regulatory capabilities does not create an invariant control mechanism within a person. Self-evaluative regulators do not operate unless activated, and many factors affect the selective activation and disengagement of internal control. There are various means by which self-evaluative reactions can be dissociated from censurable behavior or even enlisted in its service. Figure 4 shows the several points in the process at which the disengagement can occur.

One set of disengagement practices operates at the level of the behavior. What is culpable can be made honorable by moral justification that portrays the conduct as serving moral ends, by euphemistic language that confers a respectable status on reprehensible activities, and by advantageous comparison with more deplorable behavior. Another set of dissociative practices operates by obscuring, through displacement or diffusion of responsibility, the relationship

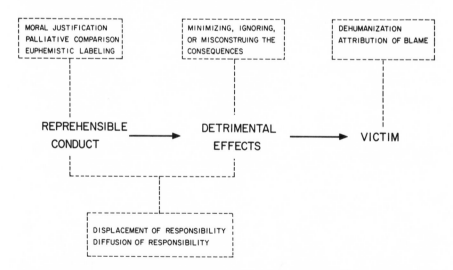

FIGURE 4. Mechanisms through which behavior is disengaged from self-evaluative consequences at different points in the process.

between actions and the effects they cause. Self-prohibiting reactions are weak when personal agency can be easily disowned. Additional ways of weakening self-deterring reactions operate through disregard or misrepresentation of consequences of actions. The final set of dissociative practices serve self-exonerative purposes by dehumanizing and attributing blame to those who are maltreated. Because self-regulatory functions can be selectively activated and disengaged, internal standards do not always safeguard against harmful conduct.

SELF-REFLECTIVE CAPABILITY

If there is any characteristic that is distinctively human, it is the capability for reflective self-consciousness. This enables people to analyze their experiences and to think about their own thought processes. By reflecting on their varied experiences and on what they know, they can derive generic knowledge about themselves and the world around them. People not only gain understanding through reflection, they evaluate and alter their own thinking. In verifying thought through self-reflective means, they monitor their ideas, act on them or predict occurrences from them, judge from the results the adequacy of their thoughts, and change them accordingly. While such metacognitive activities usually foster veridical thought (Flavell, 1978), they can produce faulty thought patterns as well through reciprocal causation. Forceful actions arising from erroneous beliefs often create social effects that confirm the misbeliefs (Snyder, 1980).

Among the types of thoughts that affect action, none is more central or pervasive than people's judgments of their capabilities to deal effectively with different realities. The self-efficacy mechanism plays a central role in human agency (Bandura, 1977b, 1982a). Self-judgments of operative capabilities function as one set of proximal determinants of how people behave, their thought patterns, and the emotional reactions they experience in taxing situations. In their daily lives people continuously have to make decisions about what courses of action to pursue and how long to continue those they have undertaken. Because acting on misjudgments of personal efficacy can produce adverse consequences, accurate appraisal of one's own capabilities has considerable functional value.

It is partly on the basis of self-percepts of efficacy that people choose what to do, how much effort to invest in activities, and how long to persevere in the face of disappointing results. People's judgments of their capabilities additionally influence their thought patterns and emotional reactions during anticipatory and actual transactions with the environment. Those who judge themselves inefficacious in coping with environmental demands dwell upon their personal deficiencies and imagine potential difficulties as more formidable than they really are (Beck, 1976; Lazarus & Launier, 1978; Meichenbaum, 1977; Sarason, 1975). Such self-doubts create stress and impair performance by diverting attention from how best to proceed with undertakings to concerns over failings and mishaps. In contrast, persons who have a strong sense of efficacy deploy their attention and effort to the demands of the situation and are spurred by obstacles to greater effort.

Judgments of self-efficacy, whether accurate or faulty, are based on four principal sources of information. These include performance attainments; vicarious experiences of observing the performances of others; verbal persuasion and allied types of social influences that one possesses certain capabilities; and physiological states from which people partly judge their capableness, strength, and vulnerability. In the self-appraisal of efficacy these different sources of efficacy information must be processed and weighed through self-referent thought. Acting on one's self-percepts of efficacy brings successes or missteps requiring further self-reappraisals of operative competencies. The self-knowledge which underlies the exercise of many facets of personal agency is largely the product of such reflective self-appraisal.

Self-reflectivity entails shifting the perspective of the same agent rather than reifying different internal agents or selves regulating each other. Thus, in their daily transactions people act on their thoughts and later analyze how well their thoughts have served them in managing events. But it is the one and the same person who is doing the thinking and later evaluating the adequacy of one's knowledge, thinking skills, and action strategies. The shift in perspective does not transform one from an agent to an object. One is just as much an agent reflecting on one's experiences as in executing the original courses of action.

THE NATURE OF HUMAN NATURE

Seen from the social learning perspective, human nature is characterized by a vast potentiality that can be fashioned by direct and observational experience into a variety of forms within biological limits. To say that a major distinguishing mark of humans is their endowed plasticity is not to say that they have no nature or that they come structureless (Midgley, 1978). The plasticity which is intrinsic to the nature of humans depends upon neurophysiological mechanisms and structures that have evolved over time. These advanced neural systems for processing, retaining, and using coded information provide the capacity for those very characteristics that are distinctly human—generative symbolization, forethought, evaluative self-regulation, reflective self-consciousness, and symbolic communication.

Nor does plasticity mean that behavior is entirely the product of current experience. Some innately organized patterns of behavior are present at birth, others appear after a period of maturation. One does not teach crying and sucking to infants and walking to toddlers. Nor does one have to teach somatic motivators arising from tissue deficits and aversive events or have to create somatic rewards. Infants come equipped with some attentional selectivities as well (von Cranach, Foppa, LePenies, & Ploog, 1979). These neural programs for basic physiological functions are the product of accumulated ancestral experiences that are stored in genetic codes.

Most patterns of human behavior are organized by individual experience rather than provided ready-made by inborn programming. Although human thought and conduct may be fashioned largely through experience, innately determined factors enter to some degree into every form of behavior. Genetic factors affect behavioral potentialities. Both experiential and physiological factors interact, often in intricate ways, in determining behavior. The level of psychological and physiological development, of course, limits what can be acquired at any given time. But it is because of their considerable plasticity and cognizing powers that humans have an unparalled capability to become many things.

REFERENCES

Bandura, A. *Principles of behavior modification.* New York: Holt, Rinehart & Winston, 1969.

Bandura, A. *Social learning theory.* Englewood Cliffs, N.J.: Prentice-Hall, 1977. (a)

Bandura, A. Self-efficacy: Toward a unifying theory of behavioral change. *Psychological Review,* 1977, *84,* 191–215. (b)

Bandura, A. The self system in reciprocal determinism. *American Psychologist,* 1978, *33,* 344–358.

Bandura, A. Self-efficacy mechanism in human agency. *American Psychologist,* 1982, *37,* 122–147. (a)

Bandura, A. The self and mechanisms of agency. In J. Suls (Ed.), *Psychological perspectives on the self* (Vol. 1). Hillsdale, N.J.: Erlbaum, 1982. (b)

Bandura, A. The psychology of chance encounters and life paths. *American Psychologist,* 1982, *37,* 747–755. (c)

Bandura, A., & Cervone, D. Self-evaluative and self-efficacy mechanisms in the motivational effects of goal systems. *Journal of Personality and Social Psychology*, 1983, *45*, 1017–1028.

Bandura, A., & Jeffery, R. W. role of symbolic coding and rehearsal processes in observational learning. *Journal of Personality and Social Psychology*, 1973, *26*, 122–130.

Bandura, A., & Schunk, D. H. Cultivating competence, self-efficacy, and intrinsic interest through proximal self-motivation. *Journal of Personality and Social Psychology*, 1981, *41*, 586–598.

Baron, A., Kaufman, A., & Stauber, K. A. Effects of instructions and reinforcement-feedback on human operant behavior maintained by fixed-interval reinforcement. *Journal of the Experimental Analysis of Behavior*, 1969, *12*, 701–712.

Beck, A. T. *Cognitive therapy and the emotional disorders.* New York: International Universities Press, 1976.

Bower, G. H. Cognitive psychology: An introduction. In W. K. Estes (Ed.)., *Handbook of learning and cognition.* Hillsdale, N.J.: Erlbaum, 1975.

Bowers, K. S. Situationism in psychology: An analysis and a critique. *Psychological Review*, 1973, *80*, 307–336.

Brewer, W. F. There is no convincing evidence for operant or classical conditioning in adult humans. In W. B. Weimer & D. S. Palermo (Eds.), *Cognition and the symbolic processes.* Hillsdale, N.J.: Erlbaum, 1974.

Bunge, M. *The mind–body problem: A psychobiological approach.* Oxford: Pergamon Press, 1980.

Cairns, R. B. (Ed.). *The analysis of social interactions: Methods, issues, and illustrations.* Hillsdale, N.J.: Erlbaum, 1979.

Carroll, W. R., & Bandura, A. The role of visual monitoring in observational learning of action patterns: Making the unobservable observable. *Journal of Motor Behavior*, 1982, *14*, 153–167.

Dulany, D. E. Awareness, rules, and propositional control: A confrontation with S–R behavior theory. In T. R. Dixon & D. L. Horton (Eds.), *Verbal behavior and general behavior theory.* Englewood Cliffs, N.J.: Prentice-Hall, 1968.

Endler, N. S., & Magnusson, D. (Eds.). *Interactional psychology and personality.* Washington, D.C.: Hemisphere, 1976.

Flavell, J. H. Metacognitive development. In J. M. Scandura & C. J. Brainerd (Eds.), *Structural/process theories of complex human behavior.* Alphen a. d. Rijn, The Netherlands: Sijthoff and Nordhoff, 1978.

Hicks, D. J. Girls' attitudes toward modeled behaviors and the content of imitative private play. *Child Development*, 1971, *42*, 139–147.

Lazarus, R. S., & Launier, R. Stress-related transactions between person and environment. In L. A. Pervin & M. Lewis (Eds.), *Perspectives in interactional psychology.* New York: Plenum Press, 1978.

Locke, E. A., Shaw, K. N., Saari, L. M., & Latham, G. P. Goal setting and task performance: 1969–1980. *Psychological Bulletin*, 1981, *90*, 125–152.

Meichenbaum, D. H. *Cognitive-behavior modification: An integrative approach.* New York: Plenum Press, 1977.

Midgely, M. *Beast and man: The roots of human nature.* Ithaca, N.Y.: Cornell University Press, 1978.

Neisser, U. *Cognition and reality: Principles and implications of cognitive psychology.* San Francisco: Freeman, 1976.

Patterson, G. R. The aggressive child: Victim and architect of a coercive system. In E. J. Mash, L. A. Hamerlynck, & L. C. Handy (Eds.), *Behavior modification and families.* New York: Brunner/Mazel, 1976.

Rosenthal, T. L. Cognitive social learning theory. In N. S. Endler & J. McVicker Hunt (Eds.), *Personality and the behavior disorders* (rev. ed.). New York: Wiley, 1984.

Rosenthal, T. L., & Zimmerman, B. J. *Social learning and cognition*. New York: Academic Press, 1978.

Sarason, I. G. Anxiety and self-preoccupation. In I. G. Sarason & C. D. Spielberger (Eds.), *Stress and anxiety* (Vol. 2). Washington, D.C.: Hemisphere, 1975.

Schneider, D. J., Hastorf, A. H., & Ellsworth, P. C. *Person perception* (2nd ed.). Reading, Mass.: Addison-Wesley, 1979.

Skinner, B. F. *About behaviorism*. New York: Knopf, 1974.

Snyder, M. Seek, and ye shall find: Testing hypotheses about other people. In E. T. Higgins, C. P. Herman, & M. P. Zanna (Eds.), *Social cognition: The Ontario symposium on personality and social psychology* (Vol. 1). Hillsdale, N.J.: Erlbaum, 1980.

Snyder, M. On the self-perpetuating nature of social stereotypes. In D. L. Hamilton (Ed.), *Cognitive processes in stereotyping and intergroup behavior*. Hillsdale, N.J.: Erlbaum, 1981.

Sukemune, S., Haruki, Y., & Kashiwagi, K. Studies on social learning in Japan. *American Psychologist*, 1977, *32*, 924–933.

Thelen, M. H., & Rennie, D. L. The effect of vicarious reinforcement on imitation: A review of the literature. In B. H. Maher (Ed.), *Progress in experimental personality research* (Vol. 6). New York: Academic Press, 1972.

Thomas, E. A. C., & Malone, T. W. On the dynamics of two-person interactions. *Psychological Review*, 1979, *86*, 331–360.

von Cranach, M., Foppa, K., Lepenies, W., & Ploog, D. (Eds.). *Human ethology: Claims and limits of a new discipline*. Cambridge, England: Cambridge University Press, 1979.

Zimbardo, P. G., Ebbesen, E. B., & Maslach, C. *Influencing attitudes and changing behavior*. Reading, Mass.: Addison-Wesley, 1977.

CHAPTER 4

A Constructivistic Foundation for Cognitive Therapy

VITTORIO F. GUIDANO and GIANNI LIOTTI

Psychotherapy as a cultural achievement emerging in the last century lacks a coherent, unitary, epistemological program; this lack of a program explains the steady proliferation of competing approaches. The cognitive approach has represented, for many students, the promise of a new integrating paradigm. However, the proliferation of a number of cognitive therapies, along with the present inability of clinicians engaged in this kind of therapy to define a theoretical framework capable of including the basic contributions of developmental, experimental, and clinical psychology, seems to indicate that the cognitive approach, too, could fall into epistemological confusion. The theoretical framework delineated in the first section of our chapter is not only relevant to everyday clinical practice but also leads to a model of cognitive organization that can be used as a guideline for clinical research and psychotherapeutic work. Our second section deals with a clinical study of agoraphobia and suggests connections between the theoretical model and clinical practice.

THEORETICAL OVERVIEW

A CONSTRUCTIVISTIC FRAMEWORK

Preliminary Epistemological Remarks

The elaboration of a constructivistic framework stems from a set of basic assumptions resting on a background of evolutionary epis-

---

VITTORIO F. GUIDANO and GIANNI LIOTTI • Center for Cognitive Psychotherapy, Via degli Scipioni 245, Rome, Italy 00192.

temology (cf. Campbell, 1974; Lorenz, 1973; Popper, 1972; Popper & Eccles, 1977) and are briefly outlined.

Knowledge as an Evolutionary Result. A biological conception of the origin of knowledge allows one to define it as a specific field of natural science (i.e., it permits us to draw a definite separation from the fields of philosophy or metaphysics, which have thus far frequently been employed in studying human knowledge processes); consequently, it becomes possible to study and plan research about knowledge using the same procedure applied to modern scientific methodology: an experimentally falsifiable approach testing the hypotheses arising from the interaction of available, tenable theories and emerging observational data.

Moreover, the concept that knowledge structures are evolutionary patterns of information gathering and processing, progressively shaped in response to challenging environmental pressures, implies that the organisms' activity is the key feature of their interaction with the world (cf. Popper, 1975). Hence, knowledge evolution appears to be an ongoing process, unfolding in its progressive elaboration of environment-modeled templates, able to order and decode incoming experience, since ordering and decoding are the essential devices for effective survival. In short, organisms are theories of their environment, as Weimer (1975) cogently put it.

Knowledge as an Interactive Process. If knowledge processes are emergent, interactive products of the ongoing match between the knowing subject and reality, then knowledge itself appears to be very far from a mere sensorial copy of reality (empiricism), as well as far from a mere unfolding of schemata already preformed in the individual (innatism). On the contrary, knowledge appears to be a progressive, hierarchic construction of models of reality where, step by step, the furniture of experience is moulded inside knowledge structures by the ordering activity carried out by the knowing subject. On this premise, speculative problems such as "How true may our knowledge be?" or "How real is reality?" seem inconsequential. Indeed, the structured models of reality determine the patterns with which the individual can see and conceive the world, thus substantially contributing to defining the very form reality assumes in each experience.

If we consider knowledge as an interactive construction of reality, the truth appears as the limit—as it were—toward which we tend, without ever reaching it.

Knowledge Development as Biased by Self-organizing Abilities of Human Mental Processing. Far from being an impersonal construction, human knowledge is imbued with and biased by all the invariant aspects (evolutionary and cultural constraints) that define human nature and consequently determine the human way of knowing reality.

Thus, the development of a full sense of self-identity—and the inherent feeling of uniqueness and historical continuity—seems to be a hallmark of human knowing systems and, from its beginning, is intertwined with a parallel development of more abstract and integrating levels of knowledge processes. Given the present state of scientific knowledge, it seems logical to look at the evolutionary emergence of the principle of biologic individuation (considered as a selective device increasing survival possibilities) as fundamental for the subsequent evolution of selfhood (Popper & Eccles, 1977). In other words, the emergence of self-identity coincides with the acquisition of cognitive skills in order to shift from a biological to a psychological individuation, following the parallel emergence of higher cortical processes. An evolutionary perspective allows us to look at the progressive construction of the selfhood structures[1] along with levels of knowledge that are increasingly more complex and integrated, as the human way of developing the functional continuity carried out by self-organizing abilities common to living systems (cf. Ferracin *et al.*, 1978).

Toward a Constructive Sketch of Knowledge Processes

Motor Theories of Mind. The basic feature of human interaction with the world is the construction of models of reality which are able to arrange and regulate reality itself. From this perspective, the mind appears to be an active, constructive system, capable of producing not only its output but also, to a large extent, the input it receives, including the basic sensations underlying the construction of itself. That is why, in recent years, there has been a gradually felt need to shift the conceptualization of the mind toward the so-called motor theories (Weimer, 1977) and drop conventional empiricist sensory theories that depict the mind as a mere collector of sensations, which implies the simplistic assumption that the order with which we are

[1]From a constructivistic perspective the approach to the self is very different from proposed self-concept theories in that it attempts to enlarge the empiricistic paradigm by admitting the presence of centralized cognitive mediators of behavior (cf. Broughton & Riegel, 1977). The basic difference consists in regarding the self not as a *self-concept*—i.e., like an entity connecting experience and behavior—but as a *concept of selfhood* (cf. Broughton, 1981) continuously remodeling and restructuring itself—that is, *as a process* accounting for the basic feature of human knowledge: its reflexive nature.

acquainted actually belong to reality (cf. Hayek, 1952, 1978; Piaget, 1970; Popper, 1972). Therefore, if mind is to be considered as a system of abstraction rules bringing about a relational order of events, in order to produce experience and behavior (cf. Weimer, 1981, p. 265), two essential aspects should be taken into account in an attempt to outline a model of knowledge processes: (a) Centrality of unconscious processes in the arrangement of our everyday experience (cf. Franks, 1974; Polanyi, 1966; Reber & Lewis, 1977; Turvey, 1974; Weimer, 1973). Deep, tacit processes of mental activity abstract the key features of the ongoing interaction with reality while simultaneously elaborating an apprehensional frame capable of processing the incoming input and to construct experience accordingly. (b) Deep-surface distinction. Although the apprehensional frame is essential for the production of experience, it never occurs within experience. Consequently, it is obvious that there is another basic level in knowledge processes in which ordering rules, provided by the tacit frame, are converted and manipulated into explicit knowledge (e.g., expectations, thought procedures, etc.).

A Two-Level Model of Knowledge Processes. Increasing convergent evidence (Airenti, Bara, & Colombetti, 1980, 1982; Tulving, 1972; Weimer, 1975) shows that deep-surface aspects of mental processing are the expression of a structural differentiation between two closely interconnected levels of knowledge processes. These knowledge processes give stability and consistency to both understanding processes carried out in everyday experience, and to organizational processes structuring knowledge during its temporal evolution.[2]

According to this model (see Figure 1), cognition is the emergent result of the ongoing match between incoming information and contextual schemata resulting from the first- and second-level interaction (tacit-explicit knowledge relationship).

Tacit-explicit knowledge is, in its structure, a feedforward rela-

---

[2]Actually, data emerging from experimental psychology in the last decades have suggested the existence of preconscious, anticipatory cognitive structures: general concepts like Bartlett's *schemata* (1932) or the *mental sets* so widely used by cybernetic approaches in neurophysiology and neuropsychology (cf. Miller, Galanter, Pribram, 1960; Pribram, 1971), to mention only some examples. However, only in recent years, with the availability of a pardigm of human mind as an information-processing system (cf. Haugeland, 1981; Newell & Simon, 1972) and of epistemological approaches reproposing the problem of knowing as recognizing (cf. Kuhn, 1962; Lakatos, 1974; Polanyi, 1966; Weimer, 1973), have we been allowed to collect within a unitary framework data and hypotheses concerning the existence of a precognitive level while at the same time abstracting precognition from the fields of metaphysics and parapsychology to which it had almost exclusively belonged up to that time.

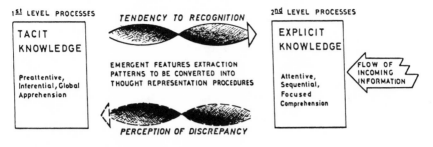

FIGURE 1

tionship—aimed at the recognition of incoming information by means of contextual schemata selected for it—and endowed with feedback systems of control capable of keeping the level of discrepancies emerging during the procedure below a critical point. Beyond this point the elaboration of revised contextual schemata able to carry out new recognition trials begins.

The forward motion in time of the tacit-explicit relationship is characterized by the elaboration of even more complex and integrated systems of explicit knowledge out of the incoming modulation of contextual frames, provided by tacit ordering processes, and paralleling the variability of the ongoing interaction with the world.

Tacit-Explicit Knowledge Relationship

The procedure by which tacit knowledge is converted into explicit knowledge is a constructive, generative process rather than a simple one-to-one mapping (Reber & Lewis, 1977): tacit abstract relations are mapped out through analogical-analytical thought procedures bringing about the structuring of a set of explicit relations (e.g., beliefs, problem-solving procedures, and so on) through which experience can be organized in specific understanding patterns. The basic features of this generative process are summarized.

Search for Consistency Appears to Be the Main Regulator of the Whole Process. That is, the matching procedure is biased by a tendency first to recognize and then to shape incoming information into available, preexisting knowledge structures, while the possibility of modifying the available decoding structures is mainly elicited by the perception of discrepancies arising from the disproving of recognition trials. The search for consistency seems to be specific to the epistemic subject, whereas the development of disproving capabilities—and the parallel development of linguistic capacities—is an emergent feature of higher cortical levels recently attained in the evolutionary process. Therefore, the essential characteristic of human knowledge is to pursue order through contrast, thus reaching progressively more fully integrated and comprehensive recognition patterns by learning to select and assimilate new incoming data—i.e., by continuously remodeling the ability to perceive the range of discrepancies so as to further elaborate preexisting knowledge structures. Thus, if constructive abilities are the hallmark that characterizes the interaction of an active mind with reality, consistency (i.e., the tendency toward recognition) and discrepancy are the domains of exchange in which that interaction takes place (cf. Mahoney, 1982).

Synchronous Aspects of Tacit-Explicit Relationship. Cognition can be regarded as an ongoing, emergent result of the fedforward tacit-explicit knowledge relationship, controlled by the dynamic consistency-discrepancy balance, where the tendency toward recognition is the basic procedure for assimilating new details and enlarging knowledge (understanding processes), and perception of discrepancy is the main regulator allowing the restructuring of preexisting schemata, with the production of more fully integrated ones (discovery processes). Discovery processes, although discontinuous in their structuring, are essential for the production of new aspects of conceptual, explicit knowledge, in that they bring about a further elaboration of consistency-discrepancy domains along with which understanding processes can further proceed.

The Temporal Becoming of the Tacit-Explicit Relationship. The structure and level of selfhood conceptions reached during the temporal evolution of knowledge can be regarded as emergent results of the fedforward relationship between tacit self-knowledge and its representational models in the ongoing match with incoming experimental data (see the section below on knowledge organization).

In its temporal becoming as well, the tacit-explicit knowledge relationship is controlled throughout its development by the dynamic consistency-discrepancy balance. The search for consistency (maintenance processes) is the basic procedure for structuring and stabilizing available levels of self-identity and self-awareness, and emotional perturbations aroused by the perception of discrepancies are the main regulators eliciting a restructuring of more fully integrated levels of self-identity and self-awareness (change processes).

THE ORGANIZATION OF DEVELOPMENTAL PROCESSES

The self-organizing abilities of human knowledge processes represent the principal continuous thread around which knowledge structures assume, over time, an overall, coherent functional organization. In other words, the structure of self-knowledge, progressively emerging during development, must be considered as the integrating element of the whole process. Through the gradual structuring of self-knowledge, organismic processes inherent in development (cognitive growth and emotional differentiation) and environmental conditions (patterns of family interaction and characteristics of social network) that shape and regulate individual learning assume idiosyncratic forms and definite relationships, thus allowing the developing child to undergo changes without losing functional continuity. Hence a satisfying description of development should be unitary, because, as Sroufe (1979) cogently argues, the whole coherence of a developing child can be captured only by looking at his total functioning.

Learning to Be a Self

Although human beings are born with a complex repertoire predisposing them to arrange incoming information in a selfhood fashion, a child at this stage is not yet a "self." The attainment of self-knowledge is in itself an active learning process stemming from a specific set of evolutionary constraints. Thus, "learning to be a self" (Popper & Eccles, 1977) represents the basic process through which a human organism learns to recognize itself, progressively unifies knowledge about itself into a definite self-identity, and eventually puts its self-identity at the center of reality, that is, at the center of all its knowledge.

The essential features regulating the "learning to be a self-process," and accounting for its unique emergent properties, can be outlined as follows:

Reflective Nature of Self-knowledge. The well-known theory that human beings acquire self-knowledge through interaction with other people (e.g., Cooley, 1902; Mead, 1934) is at present supported by increasing evidence coming mainly from research on primates (cf. Hayes & Nissen, 1971; Hill, Bundy, Gallup, & McClure, 1970; Linden, 1974) and from studies on inborn human errors (Curtiss et al., 1974; von Senden, 1960). An infant learns to know by exploring and actively interacting with his or her own environment, and people are undoubtedly the most important objects in this environment (cf. Brazelton, 1974; Lewis & Lee-Painter, 1974). Mainly from the qualitative aspects of ongoing interactions with people in his or her development environment does the child become progressively able to recognize invariant aspects by which he or she can define and evaluate himself as a person. Popper gives the following definition of this phenomenon,

known as the "looking-glass" effect:[3] "Just as we learn to see ourselves in a mirror, so the child becomes conscious of himself by seeing
his reflection in the mirror of other people's consciousness of himself"
(Popper & Eccles, 1977, p. 110).

Indeed, the reflective feature of human knowledge seems to rely
directly on the evolutionary emergence of bidirectional properties of
human consciousness (Gallup, 1977), according to which all information is simultaneously processed along two different levels: awareness (having an experience) and reflexive awareness (being aware of
having an experience). In other words, the emergence of new properties of consciousness imposes a peculiar constraint on human
knowledge: the presence of a reflective-interactive mechanism as a
basic process in knowledge development and organization (Bickhard,
1980).

*The Structuring of Knowledge of Self and the World as a Unitary
Process.* From what we have described above, it should be clear that
every human being from the very beginning actively processes two
flows of stimuli that, though belonging to different levels, are always
simultaneous: perception of the world and self-perception. Thus, any
information about the outside world always and inevitably corresponds to information about self. In this way the elaboration of knowledge appears to be a unitary process that occurs through a dynamic
interplay of two polarities, the self and the world, which can be met-
aphorically equated to the two sides of a coin: a subject's self-knowledge always involves his or her conception of reality, and conversely,
every conception of reality is directly connected to the subject's view
of self.

Attachment Theory as an Integrative Paradigm of Human Development

As a logical consequence of the assumption that human knowledge is imbued with interactive-reflective properties, a crucial role

---

[3]Although we consider the looking-glass effect absolutely fundamental for the acquisition of self-knowledge, we do not agree with the environmentalist formulation that
the construction of self is essentially a social acquisition (cf. Gergen, 1977). According
to this viewpoint, self-knowledge is the outcome of social roles and of the knowledge
of ourselves that the social environment imposes upon us; in other words, we are
what society makes us believe we are. As Hamlyn (1977) has appropriately argued,
in this formulation the *content* of knowledge is confused with the *conditions* necessary
for its development; indeed, if interaction with others is an indispensable condition
for the acquisition of self-knowledge, the subject's own activity in selecting and shaping the content of this knowledge cannot be overlooked.

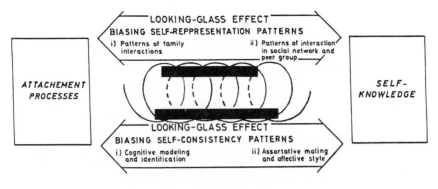

FIGURE 2

is attributed to interpersonal and relational domains in the development of self-knowledge. We therefore agree with Ainsworth *et al.* (1978) in considering attachment theory (cf. Bowlby, 1969, 1973, 1980) as a sort of explanatory theory supplying a structured framework for understanding and organizing observational and experimental data already available, that is, a new integrating paradigm of human development that gives us an inclusive and organized vision of all factors that contribute to the structuring of self-knowlege.

Attachment Styles and Developing Self-knowledge. The qualitative aspects of attachment patterns between the child and his or her caregivers will reflect themselves in different structural aspects of the child's developing self-knowledge, the looking-glass effect being the main mechanism of this process. In other words, if the parents, as a mirror, supply the child with an image of himself, it does not remain a mere sensorial datum, but rather directs and coordinates self-recognition patterns until the child is able to perceive himself consistently with that image. As Lewis and Brooks-Gunn (1979, p. 230) put it, "Any knowledge gained about the other also must be gained about the self." Self-recognition patterns, so established, work as a set of basic rules enabling the child to elaborate the invariant aspects upon which the perception of self and others relies. Moreover, from the beginning the gradual structuring of self-knowledge is constantly biasing—within the possibilities of a slow cognitive growth—the child's ongoing perception of incoming information through the selection of specific domains of exchange in his interaction with experience. Therefore, the quality of early attachment is obviously fundamental for healthy development (Sroufe, 1979; cf. Bowlby, 1977; Guidano & Liotti, 1982, chap. 5, for clinical applications). However, it may be useful to recall that the role of attachment in the development of self-knowledge is by no means limited to the early period. Indeed, attachment and parental proximity have distinctive features for human beings unprecedented in the rest of the zoological world. On the one hand, the process goes on for years, usually long after adolescence. On the other hand, the quality of attachment itself becomes even more complex and articulated in the course of development: From mere physical attachment in early infancy it evolves toward a structured relationship, intensely charged with emotions, that becomes one of the essential media for the shaping of self-conceptions, following the gradual emergence of cognitive abilities (e.g., modeling and identification processes; cf. Guidano & Liotti, 1982). Hence, attachment becomes, in the course of development, a highly structured vehicle through which increasingly complex and unlimited information about oneself and the surrounding reality becomes available. Put succinctly, attachment should be regarded as an organizing construct, the value of which lies in its integrative power (Sroufe & Waters, 1977).

Therefore, each person will spend a long period of his life in close contact with his family environment.[4] Needless to say, the conceptions of interpersonal relationships which guided parental attachment behavior are not likely to have changed significantly in the meanwhile. Thus, self-conceptions constructed since early infancy will in all probability develop through constant confirmations since the individual continues to experience the same relations that first allowed the definition of those conceptions.

Cognitive Growth. Cognitive growth essentially consists of ascending to higher structural levels of knowing, through the invariant sequence of Piaget's developmental stages (cf. Bickhard, 1980; Flavell, 1963; Piaget, 1970). Paralleling the stage-like attainment of higher semantic levels of information processing, the reflective dimension of consciousness is organized in progressively more complex levels, with the formation of increasingly more comprehensive and inte-

---

[4]The mother's role in children's development was probably overemphasized because of the influence of early psychodynamic models and based on the obvious observation that mothers usually spend more time with infants than fathers do. This idea has been reconsidered in recent years. Schaffer and Emerson (1964), in introducing their "intense attachment" concept, stressed the fact that an attentive, stimulating father could be first in the hierarchy of attachment figures in spite of the mother's greater availability. Futhermore, studies of the father's role have demonstrated the importance of this figure for a developing child, from infancy to adolescence (cf. Lamb, 1976; Lynn, 1974). This is further documented by the effects that his absence may have on cognitive and emotional development (cf. Biller, 1974).

grated selfhood structures, in approaching adolescence and youth (Montemayor & Eisen, 1977). The progressive disengagement of the person's thought from the situational "here and now," as well as from the immediacy of his experiences of self, is perhaps the most outstanding feature of the slowly unfolding cognitive abilities. As a result of this metacognitive development (cf. Flavell, 1978, 1979), a distancing and decentering occurs in the relationship between the developing subject and the world, allowing a gradual shift from an immediate and absolute conception of reality to an inferred, relativistic representation of the world.

Structured self-knowledge is the principal integrative element of the whole of cognitive growth, providing the discontinuous, progressive emergence of cognitive abilities with functional continuity. This functional continuity is carried out simultaneously at two different levels: (a) specific domains of exchange are selected in the ongoing interaction with experience, depending on the nature and quality of self-knowledge structured so far, and (b) inside the selected specific experience domains, structured self-knowledge keeps biasing invariant aspects of meaning which characterize the first overall apprehension phase of knowledge processes, and coordinates both the modality of recognition patterns (understanding processes) and the corresponding range of discrepancy perceptions (discovering processes), thus regulating the structure and content that knowledge will progressively assume.

Emotional Differentiation. It is most likely that, since earlier phases of development, the child is equipped with both the primary qualitiy of feelings and the ability to express them through expressive motor mechanisms (Brazelton *et al.*, 1974; Eibl-Eibesfeldt, 1972, 1979). Starting from these intense, undifferentiated, and rather uncontrollable basic feelings, emotions undergo a constant blending, becoming more subtle and articulated, abounding in specific meanings, and progressively more subject to cognitive control. As a result of such a differentiation during the course of development, the range of emotional experiences is greatly increased, allowing every individual to react to different, multiform environmental situations with a variety of emotional tones which provide an ongoing modulation of information about his internal style.

At present, increasing evidence suggests that emotions be regarded as an organized and complex experience the dynamic unity of which can be captured only by shifting to a more fully integrated level of observation (cf. Yarrow, 1979).

From this perspective, the concept of emotional schemata proposed by Leventhal (1979) can be considered as a tentative, integrative model which is able to account for the correlations between the many components of emotional experience (perception, imagery, memory, etc.). The essential feature of the emotional schemata model is the relevance given to an emotional memory mechanism active during emotional processing. It is a relatively concrete memory of an analogical nature,[5] principally composed of images that include key perceptual features of emotion-eliciting situations, representations of expressive patterns, and the motor and visceral reactions that accompany these situations. Such an integrative model offers some promising perspectives for understanding emotional development: (a) It could represent an effective device for explaining the progressive integration, occurring in the course of development, between inborn patterns of emotional reactions and acquired emotional differentiation. (b) It permits us to look at emotional differentiation as an ongoing matching process between preformed emotional schemata and incoming feelings. The search for congruity (recognition patterns) would act as the main regulator, giving functional continuity to the temporal progression of the whole process, while the perception of discrepancy acts as the main elicitor for differentiating new emotional domains. Again, the structuring of self-knowledge represents the integrating element of the whole process, in that it determines the qualitative aspects of recognition–discrepancy patterns involved in emotional differentiation; that is, it selects the type of emotional schemata that will act as "criterion images" in building more fully integrated patterns for the differentiation and recognition of one's own emotional states and of feelings expressed by others.

Intercorrelation between Cognition and Emotion. The functional parallelism between cognition and emotion is based on a complex, bidirectional, interactive process (Yarrow,1979) of which we wish to point out only the following aspects: (a) The content and structure of the cognitive level reached influence, to a large extent, the quality of the decodable emotional range and consequently the capacity for labeling and decoding one's own and others' feelings. (b) Feelings greatly influence the global apprehension phase of knowledge processes at the first level (biasing perception, attention, and so on) and, in a more indirect way, the subsequent explicit second-level processes by influencing modalities of thought representation and direction

---

[5]Leventhal's (1979) emotional memory mechanism closely parallels the concept of episodic memory introduced by Tulving (1972) in his differentiation between semantic and episodic storage. This division of memory into two different logical levels may have significant implications for psychopathology, as Bowlby (1980, p. 61–64) incisively points out.

problem-solving procedures. Finally, since emotions are activated in similar ways by intense or incongruous stimuli, emotional experiences can be seen as a preferential detector of discrepancies in the whole development and organization of knowledge.

Development as a Series of Progressive Steps in Self-knowledge Reorganization

Developmental stages can be considered as a progressive series of qualitative transformations beginning with the structuring of elementary patterns of self-recognition and ending with the emergence of a structured self-identity. In this step-like procedure, each emerging conception of self depends in its structuring on the level previously reached and in turn determines the possible direction in which the next can develop. Thus, each emerging self-conception is new in form (i.e., structure), not just in content (cf. Broughton, 1981), and is the expression of the whole structural reorganization involving the reflective dimension of consciousness, paralleling the ascension to higher structural levels of knowing.

The main stages in the development of self-knowledge can be sketched out as follows (for a more detailed exposition cf. Guidano & Liotti, 1982):

Infancy and Preschool Years (from about 2½ to 5 Years of Age). The level of cognitive growth available at this stage allows for the elaboration of a primordial nucleus of self-knowledge, that is, the structuring of a basic set of deep structural relations providing the invariant patterns of self-world recognition and biasing further self-knowledge development by selecting a specific set of meaning domains.

Childhood (Roughly Corresponding to the Primary School Age). The available level of cognitive growth (Piagetian concrete operations) permits the development of an increasing representational ordering of incoming experience, characterized by its "immediate" concrete quality. In short, this stage is marked by a "realistic" understanding of reality, in which the emergence of self-conceptions essentially results in the discovery of the self as "an object" (Dickstein, 1977).

Adolescence and Youth (from about 12 to 18 Years of Age). The available level of cognitive growth (Piagetian formal operations) allows us to consider the self on the one hand as an already existing agency and on the other hand as something to be discovered through a process of self-reflection. In other words, adulthood starts as epistemological understanding of reality (Chandler, 1975) in which the self emerges as "a knower" (Dickstein, 1977) endowed with a full sense of personal identity and actively structuring its life planning.

KNOWLEDGE ORGANIZATION: A DESCRIPTIVE MODEL

Introductory Remarks

The essential problem in the elaboration of a model of knowledge organization concerns the definition of a structural relationship in which both knowledge distinction (i.e., deep and surface aspects) and knowledge content (i.e., deep tacit rules, beliefs, problem-solving procedures, etc.) assume an overall, fedforward, organizational pattern equipped with feedback systems of control able to undergo reorganizational changes in its temporal becoming without losing its functional continuity. On this subject, the structural analysis proposed by Lakatos (1974), which considers the knowledge stored in a scientific theory to be organized as a research program, may prove to be a useful conceptual device, when formal analogies, recognizable at the epistemological level, are completely retranslated at the individual, self-organizing level of human knowledge processes (cf. Guidano & Liotti, 1982). A model of knowledge organization derived from such a perspective can be described as follows:

1. A human cognitive system is assumed to be analogous to a theory of the world considered as an open structure capable of supplying a heuristic representation of self and reality and consequently a "research program" to be followed (i.e., a fedforward relationship with incoming experience which affords the structuring of a life program during its temporal becoming).

2. The partitioning of knowledge into tacit and explicit aspects, which has emerged in recent years as a central theme both for cognitive science (Airenti *et al.*, 1980; Tulving, 1972) and cognitive therapy (Arnkoff, 1980; Mahoney, 1980, 1981), is also a distinctive feature of Lakatos's conceptions of the structure of scientific knowledge. Therefore, assuming that knowledge is organized along two different structural levels, we shall speak of a *metaphysical hard-core* (tacit deep structures) and of representational models of self and reality (surface structures) deriving from it.

3. In a model thus conceived, the emphasis on rationality is relatively reduced and metaphysical or dogmatic aspects (i.e., tacit ordering processes) are stressed, pointing out the tendency to seek confirmations as the basic procedure for further knowledge acquisitions.

Structural and Functional Aspects of Knowledge Organization

Metaphysical Hard Core. This is the first, tacit level of knowledge elaboration of a human cognitive system. The tacit knowledge con-

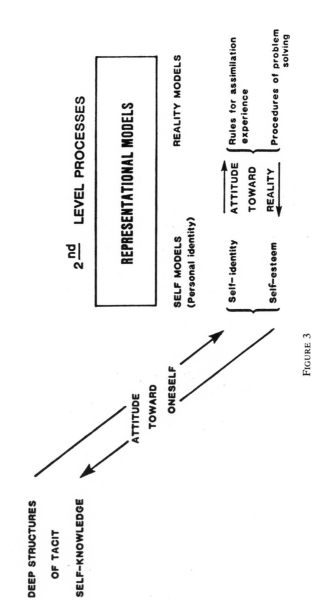

FIGURE 3

tained at this level can basically be regarded as hierarchically arranged sets of schemata representing the structural frames of reference which organize the flow of incoming information. In other words, they work as sets of deep rules through which a person is tacitly and directly provided with frames of reference. On these frames rest the invariant patterns of oneness structuring self-perception and the invariant patterns of feature extraction used to detect regularities by which the world is perceived in the same consistent way. Briefly, the functional aspects of the tacit level of knowledge organization can be outlined as follows (cf. Airenti *et al.*, 1980, 1982; Guidano & Liotti, 1982):

1. The metaphysical hard core's most striking feature is perhaps its ability progressively to elaborate new frames of reference (i.e., more and more abstract tacit rules) for the subsequent insertion and manipulation of representational models of reality. The insertion of a set of deep rules in representational models is always a constructive process in which analytical and analogical thought procedures, fedforward by the tacit level, provide scaffolding for the furniture of experience in emergent representational models of self and reality. Thus, the heuristic possibilities of a specific metaphysical hard core depend on its structural aspects and determine the set of worlds that are possible for that particular individual.

2. Deep structures of self-knowledge, through feeling tones and feeling memories (emotional schemata) processed during the course of development, direct and coordinate most of the individual's emotional and imaginative life. Particularly, fedforward mechanisms which regulate the progressive structuring of specific patterns used for decoding one's feelings limit the nature and range of assimilable experiences and so define for the individual the range of all possible subjective experiences. We agree with Hamlyn (1977) in believing that a complete theory of self-knowledge (which we are far from having achieved at present) should include a conceptual model of the "regulators" that preside over the development and organization of emotional experiences.

Representational Models

These are a set of explicit models of self and reality stemming from the core schemata and produced by imaginal (cf. Kieras, 1978; Pylyshyn, 1973) and verbal (cf. Meichenbaum, 1977; Wason & Johnson-Laird, 1972) thought procedures based upon incoming experience. Compared to the more abstract tacit level of knowledge organization, representational models give a more incomplete and limited image of self and the world. In other words, *not all* the knowledge contained in the metaphysical hard core is used in building explicit models, nor is the knowledge content pertaining to ongoing models of self and reality represented in the stream of consciousness with all its details and at every moment. Though represented each time in an episodic way—depending on individual needs and on the events that the individual is in fact experiencing—explicit knowledge generally fits the tacit knowledge level on which it depends, with minimal incongruities.

Personal identity. This cognitive structure is to be regarded as the emergent conceptualized polarity of the ongoing relationship between the individual level of explicit self-awareness and the tacit metaphysical hard core (see below). Essentially, it consists of a whole arrangement of beliefs, memories, and thought processes about self, producing a coherent self-image and a sense of personal unity and continuity in time. Although personal identity is fundamentally an inferred theory of oneself, biased by one's own tacit self-knowledge, it represents the basic frame of reference which every subject becomes able to monitor constantly as he evaluates himself in relation to incoming experience. A structured self-identity, in particular, provides a set of basic expectations, directing the individual's patterns of self-perception and self-evaluation, consistent with the selected self-image. The degree of congruence existing between beliefs about one's own value on the one hand and estimates of one's own behavior and emotions on the other corresponds to the degree of self-acceptability and self-esteem. Therefore, self-esteem implies the theory of emotions to which one adheres in the relationship one establishes with oneself. This theory defines the range of emotions that one can recognize as one's own, the way one labels and controls them, and the circumstances and ways in which one can express them. Consequently, only feelings belonging to the selected emotional range will be properly labeled and experienced as emotions, while unrecognizable feelings are likely to be experienced as externally caused, "strange" phenomena (e.g., somatic complaints, modifications of normal levels of awareness). Theoretical and clinical speculations implied in these remarks are left to the reader.

Models of Reality. Substantially, these cognitive structures actually form representational models of the outside world. It is important to keep in mind that models of reality are the individual's *only* possibility of establishing a relationship with the outside world. In other terms, the human knowing system cannot discriminate between external events and their internal representation (cf. Airenti *et al.*, 1982). The epistemological consequences implied in taking this perspective are likely to provide fruitful implications for both cognitive psychology (cf. Liotti & Reda, 1981; Shaw & Bransford, 1977; Weimer & Palermo, 1974, 1981) and for cognitive therapy (cf. Beck, 1976; Guidano & Liotti, 1982; Mahoney, 1981). It is important to notice that models of reality represent not only the perceived world but also any possible imagined world, since any imaginative procedure works on data which are consistent with deep structures.

The construction of reality-models, though biased by tacit self-knowledge, is constantly regulated by personal identity structures so as to build representational aspects of the outside world consistent with interactional attitudes toward reality defined by the self-image. This regulating activity is carried out mainly by controlling the executive procedures of the basic set of rules upon which rests the coherence and stability of reality models: (a) Rules that coordinate the assimilation of experience: these determine which domains of experience are to be held as significant, and the patterns of integration of these experiences within preformed knowledge structures. (b) Rules that coordinate problem-solving procedures: different types of logical problem-solving procedures (cf. Bara, 1980) are employed in defining both the nature of significant problems and the strategy for dealing with them.

Functional Aspects of Knowledge Organization

The essential feature of the model we have described so far consists of considering the different structural levels of knowledge as organized in an overall fedforward relationship and having feedback systems of control. While tacit self-knowledge constantly biases the temporal progression of knowledge processes, structured personal identity appears to be the main regulator of the whole process. Indeed, as shown in Figure 3, any new set of deep relations can be inserted and manipulated in reality models and therefore becomes an effective way of interacting with the world—only *through* personal identity structures. Thus the level of self-awareness reached is an essential variable that regulates the possibilities of representing more abstract, challenging deep structures and influences to a large extent the quality of knowledge levels set forth by forward oscillative processes. It should be noted (see Figure 3) that the controlling function exercised by personal identity is carried out through two basic structural relationships:

Attitude toward Oneself. This defines the ongoing relationship between the explicit self-image and the tacit self-knowledge. Although deep structures correspond to the subject's essential, unavoidable way of being "all that he is made of" he formalizes his existence in a definite way through the structuring of a specific personal identity— "all that he makes of himself". This formalization takes place through a dynamic relationship between the elements of the deep structures (e.g., invariant tacit rules, emotional schemata) and the emergent cognitive abilities (e.g., concept formation, decentering, and distancing). This relationship, through which each one of us makes himself out of what he is, unfolds by a continuous process of inner reconstructions. Personal identity structuring, being the emergent conceptualized polarity of this relationship, is regulated to a large extent by the features of self-awareness as they are expressed by structured patterns of the attitude toward oneself.[6] In other words, thought processes concerned with self-image principally indicate selective ways of processing internal information rather than the tacit self-knowledge that directly affects us. As a consequence, we cannot expect introspection to provide an open window on deep-structure processes, but rather on a biased model of them.

Attitude toward Reality. This defines the ongoing structural relationship by which personal identity carries out its regulatory function in the interaction with incoming experience, making the subject's plans and behaviors consistent with the quality of the attitude toward oneself that he was able to structure. The structuring of an attitude toward reality, therefore, is hierarchically dependent on the structure reached by the attitude toward oneself; that is, our way of seeing reality—and ourselves inside reality—essentially depends upon how we see and conceive of ourselves.

---

[6]In our opinion, future research on individual patterns of the attitude toward oneself could supply an altogether new perspective on the relationship between tacit self-knowledge and its representative models, including the problem of self-awareness. At present, although systematic investigations on this topic are not available, several lines of research can be identified: (a) Interesting data can be obtained chiefly from attempts to delineate descriptive models of attitude toward oneself, such as "blindness to oneself" characterized by a refusal to structure an integrated attitude toward oneself—leading to superficial levels of self-awareness—through an overriding attention to the actual environment, and a "standing back from oneself," a sort of self-evaluating attitude by which the individual seems to be always "a step behind himself," constantly watching and judging his own emotions and performances. (b) A developmental line of research is aimed at the definition of a comprehensive model of cognitive processes involved in the coherent development of specific patterns of self-awareness. The information-processing approach to defense recently proposed by Bowlby (1980, chapter 4) can be regarded as one of the most brilliant contributions to this research perspective.

KNOWLEDGE ORGANIZATION: MAINTENANCE AND CHANGE PROCESSES

The dynamic equilibrium that characterizes the temporal evolution of knowledge unfolds through fedforward oscillative[7] processes involving a discontinuous emergence of progressively more fully integrated models of self and reality. This oscillative procedure rests on the basic mechanism underlying the unfolding of knowledge processes: a discontinuous structuring of more integrated sets of invariant rules, as the emergent result of the ongoing ordering of incoming experience. Subsequent attempts to convert emergent core schemata into beliefs and thought procedures—change processes—are regulated and modeled, step by step, by maintenance processes aimed at preserving the functional continuity and the sense of oneness belonging to selfhood structures. In order to allow any consistent degree of modification in the concepts of self and reality, the individual must gradually elaborate an alternative self-image without experiencing interruptions in his structured sense of subjective continuity. Any interruption would represent a loss of one's very sense of reality. Thus, maintenance and change processes, rather than opposite polarities, are to be considered as interplaying and overlapping processes that, though simultaneous, show different modalities during the temporal becoming of knowledge: While maintenance processes are continuous, change processes are continuous only as challenges or possibilities and are discontinuous in their occurrence.

Maintenance Processes

Maintenance processes are expressions of the regulatory function controlled by personal identity. Though extremely variable in their procedures, they are all founded on a basic underlying feature: They

---

[7] It should be kept quite clear that the temporal evolution of knowledge is not a smooth, continuous process but rather a discontinuous, step-like one. The passage from one step to the next is in turn a relatively unpredictable process, both in the ways and the time of its occurring. The term *oscillative* therefore is meant to indicate this uncertainty pattern that characterizes the procedure of humam change processes (cf. Mahoney, 1981, for similar uses of this term). As a matter of fact, convergent evidence that oscillative patterns take place in the emergence of organizational changes during the temporal evolution of any open system is currently supplied by several disciplines; for example, epistemology, in articulating a scientific paradigm (cf. Kuhn, 1962; Lakatos, 1974); chemistry and physics, in describing the development of dissipative, self-organized structures (cf. Nicolis & Prigogine, 1977; Prigogine, 1978), and systems issuing from the neodarwinistic paradigm, that are increasingly indicating the creative and constructive role of genetic recombination processes (cf. Jacob, 1977; Waddington, 1975).

bias the recognition–discrepancy balance, which regulates the on-going matching between the subject's preexisting knowledge and in-coming experience, by preforming recognition trials. In other words, these processes are essentially devoted to producing confirming evidence about the reliability of self and reality models employed in dealing with the world.

The attitudes toward oneself and reality, at different hierarchical levels, represent the structured relationships that supply a whole range of confirmations for personal identity structures.

Attitude toward Oneself. This represents the higher hierarchical level of confirmations that contribute to the maintenance of personal identity. In the ongoing match between tacit self-knowledge and perceived personal identity, each subject has virtually unlimited access to past or currently available information about himself that he intends to look for, and the subject himself sets the limits (cf. Bower & Gilligan, 1979; Markus, 1977; Mischel, Ebbesen, & Zeiss, 1976; Rogers, Kuiper, & Kirker, 1977; Rogers, Rogers, & Kuiper, 1979). Thus the attitude toward oneself increasingly takes on the features of a patterned relationship, capable of providing the subject with a stable and structured self-image, which in turn allows a continuous and coherent self-perception and self-evaluation during temporal becoming.

Attitude toward Reality. Confirmations of a lower level are used mainly to provide stability and coherence in the face of a changing reality to models of the world consistent with the subject's adopted self-image. The tendency to maintain one's own conceptions of the world is expressed not only by the wide use of confirmatory-biasing procedures in reasoning and problem solving (Mahoney & De-Monbreun, 1977; Wason, 1977): Idiosyncratic problem-solving strategies also permit the individual actively to manipulate environmental situations so as to produce events that are in keeping with the structured self-image. Swann and Read (1981, p. 371), in concluding the discussion of their experimental data, cogently remark: "Through such processes, people may create—both in their own minds and in the actual social environment—a social reality that verifies, validates, and sustains the very conceptions that initiate and guide these processes."

Change Processes

These are expressions of the fedforward mechanisms that characterize the directionality of knowledge processes. The basic feature underlying and unifying the variety of change patterns consists in the restructuring of models of self and reality by explicating available emerging deeper rules. Essential conditions that trigger and influence the whole process can be outlined as follows:

1. Since any tacit assumption must pass through personal identity to be inserted into representational models (see Figure 3), awareness is a necessary condition for converting tacit knowledge into beliefs and thought procedures (cf. Airenti *et al.*, 1981). Thus, the quality of self-awareness—expressed by the corresponding patterns of attitude toward oneself—largely influences the oscillative procedure and the final result of a change process.

2. The tendency to obtain confirmations has to be disproved by the perception of a discrepancy that thus becomes capable of eliciting a further degree of distancing and decentering from actual representational models and thus allows one to restructure them. The attitudes toward oneself and reality are, again, dynamic relationships through which a whole range of discrepancies becomes available: (a) Discrepancies arising from the attitude toward reality tend mainly to elicit oscillative procedures for surface change processes, that is, when a local change occurs in reality models without any appreciable restructuring in the personal identity. However, since change processes are unitary in their differentiation, a deep change may be elicited by what, at least apparently, was only a limited change of one's concepts of the world. (b) Discrepancies arising from the attitude toward oneself essentially tend to elicit oscillative procedures for deep change processes, that is, they do so when a local change occurs in personal identity with a consequent restructuring of reality models.

Deep Change

From this perspective, deep change processes—ranging from a limited restructuring of personal identity to true personal revolutions (Mahoney, 1980)—correspond to changes in patterns of attitudes toward oneself, as a result of the reconstruction of sets of deeper rules emerging from tacit self-knowledge. The changed attitude toward oneself will consequently produce a modification of personal identity; this in turn will produce a restructuring of the attitude toward reality through which the world can be seen and dealt with in a different manner. The essential mechanism underlying a deep change, therefore, is the switching to a metalevel of knowledge representation elicited and regulated by the interaction of both environmental and deep pressures. A deep oscillative process, always charged with intense emotions, may have different effects on the temporal evolution of knowledge organization, depending on whether it has a progressive or a regressive nature.

Progressive Shift. The switching to a metalevel of knowledge representation is achieved when processing possibilities, determined by self-awareness patterns, somehow fit with incoming deep challenges. The emergence of a more fully integrated personal identity gives the possibility of: (a) labeling and decoding the arousal of emotions connected to the deep oscillative process, with a corresponding shift in self-awareness; (b) manipulating even more sophisticated reality models with also a corresponding progressive shift in experience assimilation.

Regressive Shift. The switching to a metalevel of knowledge representation is thwarted by a pattern of self-awareness that does not consent to the conversion of challenging core schemata into beliefs and thought procedures. The failure to reach a more integrated personal identity bears relevant consequences especially with regard to possible clinical applications: (a) Attempts to label and control the arousal of emotions related to the deep oscillative process by means of a proliferation of external *ad hoc* theories aimed at explaining overemotionality without altering one's own self-image. This obviously involves a regressive shift in self-awareness. (b) Consequently, in spite of unsuccessful predictions and outcomes, reality models become linked even more closely to stereotyped and repetitious imaginal representations and problem-solving procedures, with a corresonding regressive shift in experience assimilation.

Concluding Remarks

To conclude this theoretical outline we shall mention only some of the controversial points pertaining to the temporal evolution of knowledge organization.

1. One well-known problem concerns the correlation between abnormal early experiences and adult psychopathology, supported by many clinical and some statistical observations (cf. for example, Rutter, 1972, 1979). However, both the psychodynamic and the behavioral approach shared a mechanistic attitude toward the solution of this problem, though adopting different explanatory models (e.g., libidinal fixations versus conditioned learning schedules). From a constructivistic outlook, it becomes possible to consider the problem from an alternative perspective. Abnormal early experiences influ-

ence the structuring of tacit self-knowledge marked by a significantly high potential for a range of incongruities. Tacit incongruities may be revealed *only by the construction* of corresponding models that make them evident (Airenti *et al.*, 1982). In other words, the influence of early experiences on knowledge development and organization can be conceptualized as an active, constructive process the constructive capabilities of which unfold progressively in a stage-like procedure— requiring a rather long span of time—because of the gradual ascension to higher structural levels of knowing.

2. Another problem stems from the common observation that the control function carried out by personal identity tends to increase progressively with the passing of time: during juvenile and intermediate phases of life, a consistent restructuring of one's own identity is possible, whereas in late adulthood the possibilities of a significant identity change generally decrease. As Luckmann (1979) pointed out, personal identity tends to become a historical form of life. Indeed, various authors have used such terms as "plan of life" (Popper & Eccles, 1977) or "life theme" (Csikszentmihalyi & Beattie, 1979) to indicate the progressive unification that a human being's knowledge and actions assume in the course of his life. In fact, observing biographies, we usually get the impression that the individual, almost without realizing it, followed a sort of guiding track or, to use theatre terminology, a script.

It should be quite evident that in a constructivistic perspective the life theme is something progressively and dynamically constructed day by day, and year by year, on the basis of events that have characterized an individual's existence, of how he has interpreted and dealt with them, and of the consequences that derived from this process. The consequences of choices and actions, in turn, become further events that, unified in individual memory, allow the individual to build an even more uniform and comprehensive image of self and of life.

A CLINICAL STUDY IN THE CONSTRUCTIVISTIC PERSPECTIVE: AGORAPHOBIA

The theoretical principles and model of knowledge organization described so far are closely connected with our clinical activity. This study of agoraphobia is one instance of such connections. The choice of the agoraphobic syndrome as an example arises from our being especially familiar with it.[8]

THE AGORAPHOBIC SYNDROME: NOSOGRAPHICAL PROBLEMS

Any person who asks for therapeutic help to recover from a fear of leaving home or any other safe place *alone* is likely to receive a diagnosis of agoraphobia. Clinical experience shows that more accurate investigations of patients who suffer from this problem generally reveal many other disturbances. Table 1 gives a list of possible disturbances which in various combinations form the "agoraphobic syndrome" (Marks, 1969). Such a wide and diversified pool of disturbances poses the problem of describing the agoraphobic syndrome as distinguished from, or similar to, anxiety hysteria (cf. e.g., Fenichel, 1945, Chapter XI, 3), phobic-anxiety-depersonalization syndrome (Roth, 1959), "multiple phobias" and anxiety neurosis (cf. Beck, 1976, p. 179 for a brief discussion of problems presented by the latter differential diagnosis). As in other fields of psychiatric nosography, the question of diagnosing agoraphobia has two main aspects. On the one hand, descriptions of single clinical cases appear to be greatly uniform and internally consistent, and consequently it seems justified to ascribe them to a unitary condition, that is, to a pattern of behavior, feelings, attitudes, and thoughts obeying some set of rules (whether etiological, causal, social, or structural) capable of explaining origin and maintenance. On the other hand, it is not easy to specify this pattern and differentiate it from others more or less similar. Moreover, the set of lawful propositions that should strengthen and clarify the impression of invariance of the pattern itself across individual differences of single case studies from which that impression emerged remains elusive. To use medical terminology as a metaphor, the reliability of the diagnosis is uncertain until the disease's etiology and pathogenesis are known.

The great number of theories concerning the etiology and path-

---

[8]Observations of the characteristics of agoraphobia in this study are taken from a sample of 115 agoraphobic patients that we have treated with a group of collaborators over a ten-year period. The sample's composition and a more orderly account of the clinical observations collected during individual cognitive behavioral treatment of these patients can be found in Guidano & Liotti, 1982, which also contains clinical studies on other important neurotic syndromes (depression, eating disorders, obsessive-compulsive patterns) from the same constructivistic perspective.

TABLE 1. Agoraphobic Symptoms

1. Avoidance behavior	Leaving home, particularly alone Being alone in the house Crowded public places (movie houses, theaters, department stores, etc.) Public transportation (buses, subway, etc.) Traffic jams Long trips, air travels Sittings in barber's or beautician's chair Elevators, cablecars, and other closed-in, narrow places
2. Anxiety attacks	Subjective state of acute fear or panic Rapid heart, palpitation, precordial discomfort Nausea, vomiting, abdominal cramps, diarrhea, desire to urinate Dyspnea, feeling of choking or suffocation, hyperventilation Restlessness, tremulousness, muscule tension, weakness of limbs Parhestesia, numbness, dizziness, feelings of extreme weakness or fainting Perspiration, cold hands
3. Thought contents	Fantasies (particularly when the patient is forced into the avoided situations) of: • falling • losing consciousness • being unable to move, paralyzed • losing orientation in space • giving a pitiful display of himself or herself to bystanders • criticism, scorn, or indifference from onlookers toward the patient's suffering • going insane • dying Seeking of physical explanations for the distressing mental state Dependency problems Pessimistic views
4. Other possible disturbances	Difficulty in falling asleep Orgasmic dysfunction Theatrical or hysterical attitudes Depersonalization

ogenesis of agoraphobia shows how far we still are from having found a satisfactory solution to this diagnostic problem.[9]

In our opinion, a cognitivistic and constructivistic method of inquiry based on the theoretical outline contained in Part I on the one hand sanctions the statement that there is a unitary neurotic condition called agoraphobia and on the other hand allows us to integrate within a single model most observations and lines of reasoning expressed in the existing etiological theories of agoraphobia

[9]The following is a list of the most important causal theories of agoraphobia proposed up to the present day: (a) *Psychoanalytic theories*, based on the hypothesis of a displaced unconscious sexual temptation (cf. e.g, Fenichel, 1945; Katan, 1951), or of conflicts related to repressed hostile impulses towards the mother (Deutsch, 1929), or on the concept of a regression to developmental stages where strong unsolved needs of dependency existed (Weiss, 1964). (b) *Psychosomatic theories.* Roth (1959) postulates a specific cerebral mechanism, concerned with the regulation of awareness that chronically malfunctions in agoraphobia and explains depersonalization and panic attacks. Klein (1964) considers agoraphobia a masked endogenous depression caused by alterations of the biochemical regulation of moods. (c) *Attachment theory.* According to Bowlby (1973, chapter 19) "anxious attachment" is the cornerstone of the whole agoraphobic construction. The pattern of attachment of children having great difficulties in accepting short separations from their parents—caused by specific family interactions—persists in adulthood and can be aroused again by precipitating events often found at the onset of agoraphobia: expected separations from important attachment figures, losses, marital crises, etc. (d) *Interpersonal theories.* These maintain that there is a correlation between matrimonial interaction and the onset or persistence of agoraphobic disturbances. We know that spouses of neurotic patients tend to suffer from disturbed personalities more than the case could justify (Kreitman, 1962, 1964). This can be explained by the principle of pathogenic interaction or of assortative mating. Several surveys published suggest some of the ways in which general principles of pathogenic interaction between partners, or of assortative mating, can explain the origin and/or persistence of agoraphobic disturbances: c.f., for example, Fry, 1962; Hafner, 1977, 1979; Liotti & Guidano, 1976. (e) *Behavioristic theories.* According to these theories, early panic attacks (whose origin cannot be defined in terms of learning theory: see Marks, 1969, p. 93) may act as superreinforcers that facilitate phobic conditioning. A generalization of the stimulus and avoidance behavior, creating an obstacle to extinction processes, later contribute in shaping the agoraphobic behavior and maintaining it in time. (f) *Cognitive theories.* Beck and Rush (1975) and Beck (1976) suggested that the thought of losing control in front of strangers who are apt to judge negatively rather than to protect and the belief of constantly needing medical care because of one's supposedly unsound health are the main cognitive antecedents of agoraphobia behavior.

Ellis' opinion (1979) is that agoraphobes have a series of irrational beliefs concerning the need for being constantly approved by others, their own incapacity for tolerating painful emotions, and the idea that not readily obtaining what one wants is a terrible and insufferable thing. The interaction between these beliefs and resulting behaviors and emotions creates a cognitive trap capable of explaining the origin and persistence of agoraphobia.

(excluding perhaps psychosomatic and some psychoanalytic theories, which, however, do not seem to be necessarily incompatible with the outlook we are about to introduce). To support this statement, we will demonstrate that it is possible to give a *description* of agoraphobia satisfying the following conditions:

1. The great number of abnormal behavior patterns recognizable in the various cases can be connected to a limited number of definite *rules*.

2. Both tacit and explicit rules govern agoraphobic behavior. Mistakes in translating tacit knowledge into explicit knowledge are responsible for the difficulty encountered by patients in recognizing and eliminating the contradictions between different tacit rules, as these are revealed by particular life situations. This difficulty creates the tendency toward the self-maintenance of the syndrome.

3. Agoraphobic patients' developmental history can be reconstructed in order to define how the rules of their abnormal behavior were acquired and how particular classes of precipitating events and experiences may have revealed the internal incongruities of these rules, thereupon leading to overt symptoms.

RULES OF AGORAPHOBIC BEHAVIOR

If we read the first block of Table 1, we shall see at once that situations avoided by agoraphobics can be subsumed under two categories:

1. *Loneliness*, marked by the absence of a trustworthy companion in the immediate environment (e.g., being alone in the house, leaving home without an escort, being alone in a public place, and so on).

2. *Constriction*, that is, situations felt as limiting one's freedom of movement (e.g., traffic jams, elevators, crowded places, barber's chairs, public transportation vehicles when one cannot get off at one's will, etc.).[10]

[10]The dichotomous categorization of *loneliness stimuli* and *constriction stimuli* seemed to us the best way of summarizing the various phobic stimuli that we were able to detect in our 115 patients suffering from agoraphobia. Although we were not able to find in the psychiatric literature a dichotomous categorization similar to ours, an accurate reading of published clinical cases and of existing statistical studies revealed no data that were conflicting or incompatible with it. For example, Snaith (1968) published the scores obtained by 27 agoraphobic patients on items contained in a fear survey schedule. His results show that patients whose primary fear is of being out of the house also have a "most marked increase" (over 200%) of fear of traffic, crowds, and narrow streets, and an at least moderate increase (between 40% and 200%) of fear of being closed in.

The typical phobic avoidance behavior, therefore, can be described as obeying two rules, the first prescribing the avoidance of loneliness, the second to avoid constriction. Agoraphobic patients differ individually in their ability to describe these rules. However, even those who are unable spontaneously to express them in early therapy sessions will soon succeed in doing so if helped by the therapist (e.g., by means of a functional behavioral analysis). Consequently, these rules belong to the patient's explicit self-knowledge or, at least, they easily become a part of it.

Let us now consider causal theories held by patients about their avoidance behavior, and especially about their early panic attacks (or other kinds of unpleasant experiences), which first generated the avoidance behavior. The central, invariant aspect of such causal theories consists of the idea of a disease.

Some ascribe their phobic behavior to a somatic ailment, for instance, a possible weakness of the heart that may make them vulnerable to sudden "heart attacks," which they prove by citing frequent tachycardiac experiences. They insist that they must avoid being alone or being in places from which they cannot easily get away because they are afraid of not being helped by strangers or not being able to reach a hospital in case they are stricken by the feared "attack."

Others declare they feel threatened by a mental disease (often perceived as impending "madness") and that they feel the need for having trustworthy and familiar persons nearby to protect them in case the feeling of impending madness turns to a violent emotional crisis; these patients tend to justify their avoidance of public places especially when crowded, affirming that crowds give them a very alarming sense of confusion, or that they fear the judgment or actions of unknown bystanders after their fancied crisis of "madness."

Other agoraphobic patients, though admitting the emotional nature of disturbances associated with their avoidance behavior, express their fear that these emotions may cause sudden "madness crises" or may become too strong to be physically tolerated and will produce fainting, heart attack, and so on.

A close analysis of the imaginative contents and of the reasoning characterizing this disease theory shows another invariant aspect of agoraphobic cognition: the dreaded idea of *losing control*. (The reader will find a summary of the mentioned fantasies and reasonings in block 3 of Table 1).

Obviously, agoraphobics' causal theories about the nature of their disturbances are easily undermined by careful diagnostic and therapeutic investigations. Usually no medical confirmation is given to their fears of being ill, and their beliefs and explanations about their own behavior generally contain many logical inconsistencies. For a full understanding of the rules dominating agoraphobic behavior, we must therefore try to find out what tacit rules are behind these wrong causal attributions.[11]

AN INQUIRY INTO AGORAPHOBIC TACIT RULES

In the course of a cognitively oriented psychotherapy, we can follow three main paths for the identification of the tacit rules underlying agoraphobic behavior: define the interpersonal context in which early symptoms emerged; seek invariant aspects—among problem-solving procedures, rules for assimilating experience, and beliefs about personal identity—compatible with the idea of disease and the fear of losing control; analyze cognitive "resistances" to attempts at modifying, through behavior therapy and cognitive therapy techniques, the agoraphobic behavior and its explicit rules.

The Interpersonal Context of Agoraphobia

A wide range of clinical observations collected by researchers and therapists from varied orientations indicate that the onset of agoraphobia is connected with interpersonal contexts marked by modifications in the balance of the patient's affectional bonds. Roberts (1964, p. 194) reports the case of a housewife who became housebound after discovering that her husband was unfaithful and whose symptoms ceased when the man broke off his relationship with the other woman; she relapsed into agoraphobia five years later when her husband was again involved in an extramarital affair.

Wolpe (1976, p. 161) states that in his clinical experience one of the most common ways of developing fear reactions to physical loneliness stemmed from the presence of recurring fantasies of liberation from an unsatisfactory marriage, unfulfilled because of the great fear they evoke.

---

[11]Nisbett and Wilson (1977) collected significant evidence proving that people are often unable to formulate adequate causal theories about their ongoing cognitive processes. Agoraphobic patients are another example of "telling more than one can know," when they attribute to a disease the value of a causal explanation for their painful experiences.

Hafner (1979) reports on seven agoraphobic women married to abnormally jealous men. Milton and Hafner (1979) were also able to demonstrate a clear connection between growing dissatisfaction in marriage (as assessed by a marital questionnaire given to both patients and spouses) and worsening of the phobic disturbances.

Weiss (1964) has observed that agoraphobic symptoms are likely to emerge, in predisposed personalities, especially during phases of life when a person must make a move toward independence.

Bowlby (1973, Chapter 19) offered a theoretical basis for these and other observations (cf. Guidano & Liotti, 1982, Chapter 10, for a more exhaustive exposition of interpersonal problems connected with the origin and maintenance of agoraphobia) through the concept of "anxious attachment" and the description of family interaction patterns that seem to recur in the childhood of individuals subject to school phobia and agoraphobia.[12]

From the point of view of our inquiry about tacit rules dominating the agoraphobic behavior, these clinical observations can be usefully compared to disease-type causal theories with which patients explain their emotional suffering to themselves and others. On the one hand, there are indications (sometimes totally evident, as in the case of Roberts' patient) that early panic attacks coincided in time with an alteration in the balance of an affectional bond; on the other hand, the agoraphobic person will describe his or her disturbances as the symptoms of a disease rather than as an emotional reaction to this alteration. Agoraphobics, therefore, seem to have serious difficulties in using appropriate verbal labels for the emotional states they experience in the course of certain modifications in the balance of their affectional bonds. In other words, corresponding autonomic activation tends to be recognized as being due to morbid causes, external to personal identity. Since cognitive structures of personal identity represent the main regulator of individal knowledge growth processes, information potentially contained in these patterns of emotional arousal are largely unavailable to the patient. In terms suggested by Lakatos (1974, p. 28) in his research program metaphor, in

---

[12]The transition in a number of clinical cases from school phobia to agoraphobia was shown by Berg, Butler, and Hall (1976), among others. In our clinical sample this passage was evident in almost all cases wherein a significant alteration in the balance of affectional bonds could not be detected as the context of the agoraphobic onset. Unlike other authors, we consider growing dissatisfied toward a martial relationship an example of such alteration.

these circumstances we can expect the patient's entire cognitive organization to undergo a regressive shift.

The Agoraphobic Attitude toward Oneself and toward Reality

As we have seen, agoraphobes seem to be "blind" to certain personal emotional experiences somehow connected to the idea of loneliness and constriction, induced by alterations in the balance of affectional bonds.[13] Facing these experiences, they seem to take on an overcontrolling attitude. Most of their efforts are aimed at keeping control over their experiences, by avoiding environmental situations apt to evoke them and by interpreting feelings of autonomic arousal as the symptoms of a disease to be prevented and cured, rather than personal emotions to be causally explained. The fear of losing control—emerging from many fantasies and fragments of internal dialogue associated with phobic avoidance behaviors (fear of going mad, of fainting, of becoming incapable of controlling one's legs, and so on; see block 3, Table 1—is another sign of the overcontrolling attitude. Other disturbances frequently found in agoraphobics (orgasmic dysfunction, depersonalization: see block 4, Table 1) seem compatible with this attitude. Some female agoraphobics that we have treated explicitly expressed the idea that having an orgasm meant "losing control" and "being at the other's mercy." During the cognitive-behavioral analysis and treatment of some of our agoraphobic patients it was possible to identify a paradox (a sort of cognitive trap), apparently coresponsible, once the patient falls in it, for some depersonalization experiences. The paradox consists in self-describing emotional arousal as something external to the self, while at the same time striving to attain immediate control over that emotional arousal (see Guidano & Liotti, 1982, Chapter 10, note 15).

The tendency to overcontrol the expression of one's emotions and the course of interpersonal relationships also emerges in life situations not directly related to agoraphobic disturbances. These patients are prone to observe very carefully the contextual, nonverbal cues of interpersonal relationship and to use them to manipulate the relationship according to their need for company, protection, and control. Agoraphobic patients often tell the therapist that other people seldom

---

[13]Such attitudes toward oneself as self-deception and "blindness toward oneself" were described by Gur and Sackeim (1979) and by Hamlyn (1977). In a similar vein, but in a different language, a lack of self-nonself differentiation has been noticed in agoraphobics by "ego psychologists" such as Frances and Dunn (1975) and Rock and Goldberger (1978).

realize how strong their inner fear is; this is because their nonverbal expressiveness remains relatively unchanged even in the presence of an intense emotional arousal, or of ongoing cognitions focused on fear-inducing images and thoughts. Rules for everyday problem solving also largely depend on this basic controlling attitude. If we consider solutions generally adopted by agoraphobics for their everyday problems, we find they can be broadly classified into three groups: fight (a figure regarded as hostile); flight (from coercion, routines, etc.) or master (almost any other possible problematic situation). The solution will not likely consist of a more or less detached analysis of the problem's aspects, or in accepting the difficulty.

Finally, the overcontrolling attitude is easily observed in the course of attempts directly to modify the agoraphobic behavior with the use of behavior therapy techniques. Interested readers will find an accurate analysis of the types of behavioral or cognitive resistances of agoraphobic patients during cognitive-behavioral therapy in Chapter 10 of Guidano and Liotti, 1982. We shall use a clinical vignette from this book to illustrate this aspect of agoraphobic cognitive organization:

> Jimmy, after six months of treatment, managed to go skiing with his girlfriend, and even took the cablecar, which he had been unable to do for the past seven years. The cablecar stopped half-way. He panicked, but was soon able to "cope." He said to himself, "This is only my fear, not an impending tragedy," and "I can manage it." Fear almost disappeared. He was calmer than other people around him. Jimmy experienced a moment of triumph, but soon another thought came to mind, "I was able to control this phobic attack; shall I be able to control a bigger one?" In a few minutes, the thought, "This is only *my* fear," that had substantially decreased the unpleasant emotional arousal, was again changed so that the experience was attributed, as usual, to external causes: a "phobic attack" (note the idea of "disease" contained in the definition) that the self has the task of controlling.

On the basis of concepts delineated so far, we can postulate the existence of a set of deep rules generating the overcontrolling attitude and somehow related to alterations in the balance of affectional bonds. These deep rules are certainly tacit, since agoraphobics seem unable to establish a causal connection between the altered balance of their affectional bonds and the onset of their disturbances, although the two are temporarily and/or contextually correlated. Deep tacit rules are converted into surface rules: avoid loneliness and avoid constriction, through the mediation of improper causal theories concerning an imaginary impending illness. On the one hand, these improper causal theories soon assume characteristics compatible with the overcontrolling attitude toward oneself that seems typical of agoraphobics (i.e., representations, in the verbal and/or imaginative mode of thought, concerning the fear of losing control). On the other hand, they make it even more difficult to recognize and correct contradictions and paradoxes contained in the set of deep rules that generated both an overcontrolling attitude toward self and a personal identity unable to assimilate, as its own emotions, experiences connected to a specific alteration of the balance of affectional bonds coinciding with the syndromes' first appearance. To make use again of Lakatos's metaphor, we may say that the agoraphobic's causal theories are *ad hoc* theories, representing on the one hand a substantiation of the self-image selected (personal identity acquires the idea "I am ill") and resulting on the other hand in a regressive shift in experience assimilation (agoraphobics' possibilities of enriching their self-knowledge as subjects able to feel particular emotions in particular situations of interpersonal relationships and of freely exploring the surrounding environment are obviously more and more restricted). The metaphysical hard core (tacit knowledge structures) thus protected (that is, made hard to translate into explicit self-knowledge and therefore to correct or criticize) should plausibly concern alterations in the balance of affectional bonds not incompatible with loneliness and constriction avoidance rules that allow one to recognize the whole "research program."

Development of the Agoraphobic Knowledge Organization

Once we have acquired such an outline of the agoraphobic cognitive organization, the best way to rebuild, in detail, the set of deep tacit rules forming the foundation of the entire organization, is probably to retrace patients' developmental histories, focusing on domains of experience identified as nodal points of the whole structure: alterations in the balance of affectional bonds, loneliness, constriction, inclination to control (rather than understand) certain experiences, both personal and interpersonal, emerging in the interaction with other human beings.

We have already mentioned (see note 9) that Bowlby (1973, Chapter 19), through clinical evidence and theoretical speculations, was able tentatively to identify four patterns of pathogenic family interaction that may be etiologically related to the emergence of agoraphobic symptoms in the adult life of children who happened to grow up in such families. Statements made by 115 agoraphobic patients from our clinical sample in the course of reconstructing their developmental history strongly confirm the etiological value of family interaction patterns described by Bowlby. Recurring elements of these patterns were: *a serious limitation of the autonomous exploration of the extrafamiliar environment* imposed by the future agoraphobic's parents on the child and *a series of direct or indirect threats of desertion* received by the child (either for disciplinary purposes, or emerging from parents' quarrels, or in times of emotional crises of hypochondriac, anxious, depressed or seriously ill parents). As a general rule, the child's autonomous exploration is restricted, according to our patients' recollections, by means of a representation of the extrafamiliar environment (induced by parents' words) as a dangerous place, and/or the child's personal identity as being affected by specific shortcomings or feebleness.

Inquiries about this kind of interaction with the parents from childhood to adolescence, according to agoraphobic patients' memories, give the impression that patients were confronted with serious limitations of their spontaneous tendency to explore autonomously the extrafamiliar environment, while at the same time they had to define these limitations as a protection from imaginary dangers, resulting either from the interplay of ideas about the environment's hazards and ideas about their own weakness or inadequacy or from the representation of their condition as helpless, desperate children facing the threat of loneliness (cf. Guidano & Liotti, 1982).

If we consider the tendency toward autonomous environment exploration as an innate behavioral program (in the sense in which this term is used by ethologists), we may easily imagine the potential for intense emotional arousal deriving from its inhibition. But if the person experiencing the arousal must perceive it not as the consequence of coercion but rather as a part of a complex situation involving representations of loneliness, danger, and protection, emotional schemata for which the arousal itself becomes a part will inevitably contain *potential* conflicting and contradictory information. In the emotional schemata both loneliness and constriction are potentially represented, in a way, with opposite emotional markers. Loneliness is positive because it ensures the possibility of freedom and autonomous exploration and negative because it signals the lack of protection in the face of a dangerous new environment and of alleged personal weakness and inadequacy. Constriction from the activity of caregivers who hamper an autonomous exploration is obviously negative but it also has a positive connotation insofar as it implies protection in the face of imagined dangers and personal weaknesses.

Let us now suppose that instead of being able to express these conflicting logical implications of his experiences, the future agoraphobic tries to find a direct solution to his problems by developing more and more sophisticated controlling skills over his "weaknesses," over caregivers' behavior, and over possible dangers contained in novel extrafamiliar contingencies. The overcontrolling attitude toward oneself and toward reality thus formed will keep tacit the contradictory rules potentially present in developed emotional schemata and at the same time will allow a relative adjustment, as long as interpersonal relationships are kept relatively unchanged. But as soon as a critical alteration in the balance of affectional bonds occurs (see Bowlby, 1973, p. 309; Guidano & Liotti, 1982, Chapter 10, for a list of changes in family circumstances described so far in the literature as precipitating factors of acute agoraphobic symptoms), the partial adjustment is likely to be lost. The patient will then feel compelled to avoid both loneliness and constriction, but he will have to describe the danger he feels when not avoiding these situations as a consequence of the possibility of losing control rather than a part of his personal identity. The explicit knowledge of his personal identity was structured by the patient on the basis of a control over contradictory experiences connected to loneliness and constriction, rather than on an explicit knowledge of their origin.

Concluding Remarks

In our opinion, this model allows for a *description* of behavior, cognition, and developmental history typical of agoraphobia, compatible with most clinical observations published on the subject until this day, regardless of the observer's theoretical orientation. In addition, such description also undoubtedly contains *explanatory* elements, principally concerning:

1. The possibility of recognizing in some specific patterns of family interaction several etiological factors that concur in the development of a cognitive organization predisposed to agoraphobic disturbances.
2. The possibility of establishing a causal connection between precipitating events, acute symptoms of agoraphobia, and elements of cognitive organization (that now appear to oppose the old psychiatric concept of premorbid personality).
3. Consequently, the possibility of acknowledging the agoraphobic syndrome's quality as a distinct nosological entity (al-

though we are fully aware that the medical model is here used in a purely metaphorical sense).

4. The possibility of planning treatment and anticipating the effectiveness and proper timing of several therapeutic techniques proposed for agoraphobia.

Regarding this point, for example, our model of agoraphobia allows us to anticipate the failure of any therapeutic treatment if, at least in the early stages, the patients' overcontrolling attitude is not respected. Interventions requesting the agoraphobe to relax in the presence of other people (i.e., the therapist: systematic desensitization) are therefore likely to fail. But if the patient is allowed to control relaxation procedures (e.g., with the use of a biofeedback control system, see Chiari & Mosticoni, 1979) positive results become possible. We can also foresee that agoraphobic patients will duly assimilate any procedure for mastery over anxiety, for the good reason that this technique respects their tendency to solve every problem in terms of control, provided that such procedures do not threaten the protection–constriction balance established, because of the symptoms, in the relationship with an affectional partner (see Milton & Hafner, 1979).

Finally, a high rate of relapse can be expected in agoraphobic patients treated, with initial success, using cognitive behavior modification techniques, unless (a) they find a satisfactory protection-constriction balance in their affectional relationships and (b) they recognize and overcome, by undergoing a personal revolution during therapy (Mahoney, 1980), the restrictions forced on their personal identity by the overcontrolling attitude toward themselves.

We feel we can extend the conclusions of our clinical study of agoraphobia in a constructivistic perspective to other neurotic syndromes (see Guidano & Liotti, 1982). However, an even more important consideration should be noted. A constructivistic, structural model seems necessary, at this stage of our clinical knowledge, to collect into a single theoretical framework a series of observations on human behavior, cognition, and development which would otherwise remain fragmentary and offer clinicians little possibility for use in their everyday therapeutic activity. Obviously, this model makes no pretense of being true; it is merely intended to supply a means of inquiry comparable, as to the level of integration and logical complexity, to psychoanalytical theory; and at the same time it represents an effort to overcome ambiguities of concept and terminology and the separation between basic psychological and epistemological research which are the main shortcomings of the psychoanalytic procedure.

REFERENCES

Ainsworth, M. D. S., Blehar, M. C., Waters, E., & Wall, S. *Patterns of attachment.* Hillsdale, NJ: Erlbaum, 1978.

Airenti, G., Bara, B., & Colombetti, M. Semantic network representation of conceptual and episodic knowledge. In R. Trappl (Ed.), *Advances in cybernetics and system research (Vo. 2).* Washington, DC: Hemisphere Publications, 1980.

Airenti, G., Bara, B., & Colombetti, M. A two-level model of knowledge and belief. In R. Trappl (Ed.), *Proceedings of the Sixth E.M.C.S.R.* Amsterdam, North Holland, 1982.

Arnkoff, D. B. Psychotherapy from the perspective of cognitive theory. In M. J. Mahoney (Ed.), *Psychotherapy process.* New York: Plenum Press, 1980.

Bara, B. G. Changing connections between knowledge representation and problem solving. In M. Borillo (Ed.). *Représentation des connaissance et raisonnement dans les sciences de l'homme et de la société.* Le Chesnay: Éditions INRI-CRNS, 1980.

Bartlett, F. C. *Remembering.* Cambridge: Cambridge University Press, 1932.

Beck, A. T. *Cognitive therapy and the emotional disorders.* New York: International Universities Press, 1976.

Beck, A. T., & Rush, A. T. A cognitive model of anxiety formation and anxiety resolution. In I. D. Sarason & C. D. Spielberger (Eds.), *Stress and anxiety.* Washington, DC: Hemisphere Publications, 1975.

Berg, I., Butler, A., & Hall, G. The outcome of adolescent school phobia. *British Journal of Psychiatry*, 1976, *128*, 80–85.

Bickhard, M. H. A model of developmental and psychological processes. *Genetic Psychology Monographs*, 1940, *102*, 61–116.

Biller, H. B. *Paternal deprivation.* Lexington, MA: Lexington Books, D.C. Heath, 1974.

Bower, G. H., & Gilligan, S. G. Remembering information related to one's self. *Journal of Research in Personality*, 1979, *13*, 420–432.

Bowlby, J. *Attachment and loss* 2 vols. New York: Basic Books, 1973.

Bowlby, J. The making and breaking of affectional bonds: Etiology and psychopathology in the light of attachment theory. *British Journal of Psychiatry*, 1977, *130*, 201–210.

Bowlby, J. *Loss, sadness and depression.* London: Hogarth Press, 1980.

Brazelton, T. Berry. *Toddlers and parents.* New York: Delacorte Press, 1974.

Brazelton, T. Berry, Koslowski, B., & Main, M. The origins of reciprocity: The early mother-infant interaction. In M. Lewis & L. A. Rosenblum (Eds.), *The effect of the infant on its caregivers.* New York: Wiley, 1974.

Broughton, J. M. The divided self in adolescence. *Human Development*, 1981, *24*, 13–32.

Broughton, J. M., & Riegel, K. F. Developmental psychology and the self. *Annals of the New York Academy of Sciences*, 1977, *291*, 149–167.

Campbell, D. T. Evolutionary expistemology. In P. A. Schilpp (Ed.), *The philosophy of Karl Popper.* LaSalle, IL: The Library of Living Philosophers, 1974.

Chandler, M. J. Relativism and the problem of epistemological loneliness. *Human Development*, 1975, *18*, 171–180.

Chiari, G., & Mosticoni, R. The treatment of agoraphobia with biofeedback and systematic desensitization. *Journal of Behavior Therapy and Experimental Psychiatry*, 1979, *10*, 109–113.

Cooley, C. H. *Human nature and the social order*. New York: Scribner, 1902.

Csikszentmihalyi, M., & Beattie, O. V. Life themes: A theoretical and empirical exploration of their origins and effects. *Journal of Human Psychology*, 1979, *19*, 45–63.

Curtiss, S., Fromkin, V., Krshen, S., Rigler, D., & Rigler, M. The linguistic development of Genie. *Language*, 1974, *50*, 528–555.

Deutsch, H. The genesis of agoraphobia. *International Journal of Psychoanalysis*, 1929, *10*, 51–69.

Dickstein, E. Self and self-esteem: Theoretical foundations and their implications for research. *Human Development*, 1977, *20*, 129–140.

Eibl-Eibesfeldt, I. *Love and hate. The natural history of behavior patterns*. New York: Holt, Rinehart & Winston, 1972.

Eibl-Eibesfeldt, I. Ritual and ritualization from a biological perspective. In M. von Cranach, K. Foppa, W. Lepenies, & D. Ploog (Eds.), *Human ethology*. Cambridge: Cambridge University Press.

Ellis, A. A note on the treatment of agoraphobics with cognitive modification versus prolonged exposure in vivo. *Behavior Research and Therapy*, 1979, *17*, 162–164.

Fenichel, O. *The psychoanalytic theory of the neuroses*. New York: Norton, 1945.

Ferracin, A., Panichelli, E., Benassi, M., DiNallo, A., & Steindler, C. Self-organizing ability and living systems. *BioSystems*, 1978, *10*, 307–317.

Flavell, J. H. *The developmental psychology of Jean Piaget*. Princeton, NJ: Van Nostrand, 1963.

Flavell, J. H. Metacognitive development. In J. M. Scandura & C. J. Brainerd (Eds.), *Structural/process models of complex human behavior*. Amsterdam: Sijthoff & Noordhoff, 1978.

Flavell, J. H. Metacognition and cognitive monitoring. *American Psychologist*, 1979, *34*, 906–911.

Frances, A., & Dunn, P. The attachment-autonomy conflict in agoraphobia. *International Journal of Psychoanalysis*, 1975, *56*, 435–439.

Franks, J. J. Toward understanding understanding. In W. B. Weimer & D. S. Palermo (Eds.), *Cognition and the symbolic processes*. Hillsdale, NJ: Erlbaum, 1974.

Fry, W. F. The marital context of the anxiety syndrome, *Family Process*, 1962, *1*, 245–252.

Gallup, G. G. Self-recognition in primates. *American Psychologist*, 1977, *32*, 329–338.

Gergen, K. J. The social construction of self-knowledge. In T. Mischel (Ed.), *The self: Psychological and philosophical issues*. Oxford: Blackwell, 1977.

Guidano, V. F., & Liotti, G. *Cognitive processes and emotional disorders*. New York: Guilford Press, 1983.

Gur, R. C., & Sackeim, H. A. Self-deception: A concept in search of a phenomenon. *Journal of Personality and Social Psychology*, 1979, *37*, 147–169.

Hafner, J. R. The husbands of agoraphobic women: Assortative mating or pathogenic interaction? *British Journal of Psychiatry*, 1977, *130*, 233–239.

Hafner, J. R. Agoraphobic women married to abnormally jealous men. *British Journal of Medical Psychology*, 1979, *52*, 99–104.

Hamlyn, D. W. Self-knowledge. In T. Mischel (Ed.), *The self: Psychological and philosophical issues*. Oxford: Blackwell, 1977.

Haugeland, J. (Ed.), *Mind design*. Montgomery, VT: Bradford Books, 1981.

Hayek, F. A. *The sensory order*. Chicago, IL: University of Chicago Press, 1952.

Hayek, F. A. *New studies in philosophy, politics, economics, and the history of ideas*. Chicago, IL: University of Chicago Press, 1978.

Hayes, K. J., & Nissen, C. H. Higher mental functions in a home-raised chimpanzee. In A. M. Schrier & F. Stollnitz (Eds.), *Behavior of non-human primates* (Vol. 3). New York: Academic Press, 1971.

Hill, S. D., Bundy, R. A., Gallup, G. G., & McClure, M. K. Responsiveness of young nursery-reared chimpanzees to mirrors. *Proceedings of the Louisiana Academy of Science*, 1970, *33*, 77–82.

Jacob, F. Evolution and tinkering. *Science*, 1977, *196*, 1161–1166.

Katan, A. The role of displacement in agoraphobia. *International Journal of Psychoanalysis*, 1951, *32*, 41–50.

Kieras, D. Beyond pictures and words: Alternative information-processing models for imagery effects in verbal memory. *Psychological Bulletin*, 1978, *85*, 532–554.

Klein, D. F. The delineation of two drug-responsive anxiety syndromes. *Psychopharmacologia*, 1964, *5*, 397–402.

Kreitman, N. Mental disorders in married couples. *Journal of Mental Science*, 1962, *108*, 438–449.

Kreitman, N. The patient's spouse. *British Journal of Psychiatry*, 1964, *110*, 159–173.

Kuhn, T. S. *The structure of scientific revolutions.* Chicago, IL: University of Chicago Press, 1962.

Lakatos, I. Falsification and the methodology of scientific research programmes. In I. Lakatos & A. Musgrave (Eds.), *Criticism and the growth of knowledge.* Cambridge: Cambridge University Press, 1974.

Lamb, M. E. (Ed.). *The role of the father in child development.* New York: Wiley, 1976.

Leventhal, H. A perceptual-motor processing model of emotion. In P. Plines, K. R. Blankstein, & I. M. Spigel (Eds.), *Perception of emotion in self and others.* New York: Plenum Press, 1979.

Lewis, M., & Brooks-Gunn, J. *Social cognition and the acquisition of self.* New York: Plenum Press, 1979.

Lewis, M., & Lee-Painter, S. An international approach to the mother-infant dyad. In M. Lewis & L. Rosenblum (Eds.), *The effects of the infant on its caregivers.* New York: Wiley, 1974.

Linden, E. *Apes, men and language.* New York: Penguin, 1974.

Liotti, G., & Guidano, V. F. Behavioral analysis of marital interaction in agoraphobic male patients. *Behaviour Research and Therapy*, 1976, *14*, 161–162.

Liotti, G., & Reda, M. Some epistemological remarks on cognitive therapy, behavior therapy and psychoanalysis. *Cognitive Therapy and Research*, 1981, *5*, 231–236.

Lorenz, K. *Die Rückseite des spiegels.* Munich: Piper, 1973. *(Behind the mirror.* New York: Harcourt Brace Jovanovich, 1977.)

Luckman, T. Personal identity as an evolutionary and historical problem. In M. von Cranach, K. Foppa, W. Lepenies, & D. Ploog (Eds.), *Human ethology.* Cambridge: Cambridge University Press, 1979.

Lynn, D. B. *The father: His role in child development.* Monterey, CA: Brooks/Cole, 1974.

Mahoney, M. J. Psychotherapy and the structure of personal revolution. In M. J. Mahoney (Ed.), *Psychotherapy process.* New York: Plenum Press, 1980.

Mahoney, M. J. Psychotherapy and human change process. In *Psychotherapy research and behavior change.* Washington, D.C.: American Psychological Association, 1981.

Mahoney, M. J. Psychotherapy and human change processes. In J. H. Harvey & M. M. Parks (Eds.), *The Master Lecture Series: Psychotherapy Research and Behavior Change* (Vol. 1). Washington, D.C.: American Psychological Association, 1982.

Mahoney, M. J., & DeMonbreun, B. G. Psychology of the scientist: An analysis of problem-solving bias. *Cognitive Therapy and Research*, 1977, *1*, 229–238.

Marks, I. M. *Fears and phobias.* London: Academic Press, 1969.

Markus, H. Self-schemata and processing information about the self. *Journal of Personality and Social Psychology,* 1977, *35,* 63–78.

Mead, G. H. *Mind, self and society.* Chicago, IL: University of Chicago Press, 1934.

Meichenbaum, D. *Cognitive-behavior modification.* New York: Plenum Press, 1977.

Miller, G. A., Galanter, E., & Pribram, K. H. *Plans and structure of behavior.* New York: Holt, Rinehart & Winston, 1960.

Milton, F., & Hafner, J. R. The outcome of behavior therapy for agoraphobia in relation to martial adjustment. *Archives of General Psychiatry,* 1979, *36,* 807–811.

Mischel, W., Ebbesen, E. B., & Zeiss, A. M. Determinants of selective memory about the self. *Journal of Consulting and Clinical Psychology,* 1976, *44,* 92–103.

Montemayor, R., & Eisen, M. The development of self-conceptions from childhood to adolescence. *Developmental Psychology,* 1977, *13,* 314–319.

Newel, A., & Simon, H. A. *Human problem solving.* Englewood Cliffs, NJ: Prentice-Hall, 1972.

Nicolis, G., & Prigogine, I. *Self-organization in nonequilibrium system: From dissipative structures to order through fluctuations.* New York: Wiley, 1977.

Nisbett, R. E., & Wilson, T. D. Telling more than we can know: Verbal reports on mental processes. *Psychological Review,* 1977, *84,* 231–259.

Piaget, J. *L'epistemologie genetique.* Paris: Presses Universitaires de France, 1970.

Polyani, M. *The tacit dimension.* Garden City, NY: Doubleday, 1966.

Popper, K. R. *Objective knowledge: An evolutionary approach.* Oxford: Clarendon Press, 1972 (rev. ed., 1979.)

Popper, K. The rationality of scientific revolutions. In R. Harre (Ed.), *Problems of scientific revolutions.* Oxford: Clarendon Press, 1975.

Popper, K. R., & Eccles, J. C. *The self and its brain.* Berlin: Springer-Verlag International, 1977.

Pribram, K. H. *Languages of the brain.* Englewood Cliffs, NJ: Prentice-Hall, 1971.

Prigogine, I. Time, structure and fluctuations. *Science,* 1978, *201,* 777–785.

Pylyshyn, Z. What the mind's eye tells the mind's brain: A critique of mental imagery. *Psychological Bulletin,* 1973, *80,* 1–22.

Reber, A. A., & Lewis, S. Implicit learning: An analysis of the form and structure of a body of tacit knowledge. *Cognition,* 1977, *5,* 333–361.

Roberts, A. H. Housebound housewives: A follow-up study of a phobic-anxiety state. *British Journal of Psychiatry,* 1964, *110,* 191–197.

Rock, M. H., & Golberger, L. Relationship between agoraphobia and field dependence. *Journal of Nervous and Mental Disease,* 1978, *166,* 781–786.

Rogers, T. B., Kuiper, N. A., & Kirker, W. S. Self-reference and the encoding of personal information. *Journal of Personality and Social Psychology,* 1977, *35,* 677–688.

Rogers, T. B., Rogers, P. J., & Kuiper, N. A. Evidence for the self as a cognitive prototype: The "false alarm effect." *Personality and Social Psychology Bulletin,* 1979, *5,* 53–56.

Roth, M. The phobic-anxiety-depersonalization syndrome. *Proceedings of the Royal Society of Medicine,* 1959, *52,* 587–594.

Rutter, M. *Maternal deprivation reassessed.* Harmondsworth, England: Penguin Books, 1972.

Rutter, M. Maternal deprivation 1972–1978: New findings, new concepts, new approaches. *Annals Academy of Medicine,* 1979, *8,* 312–323.

Schaffer, H. R., & Emerson, P. E. The development of social attachments in infancy.

Monographs of the Society for Research in Child Development, 1964, *29* (Serial No. 94).

Shaw, R., & Bransford, J. D. (Eds.). *Perceiving, acting, and knowing: Toward an ecological psychology.* Hillsdale, NJ: Erlbaum, 1977.

Snaith, R. P. A clinical investigation of phobias. *British Journal of Psychiatry*, 1968, *114*, 673–697.

Sroufe, L. A. The coherence of individual development. *American Psychologist*, 1979, *34*, 834–841.

Sroufe, L. A., & Waters, E. Attachment as an organizational construct. *Child Development*, 1977, *48*, 1184–1199.

Swann, W. B., & Read, S. J. Self-verification processes: How we sustain our self-conceptions. *Journal of Experimental Social Psychology*, 1981, *17*, 351–372.

Tulving, E. Episodic and semantic memory. In E. Tulving & W. Donaldson (Eds.), *Organization of memory.* New York: Academic Press, 1972.

Turvey, M. T. Constructive theory, perceptual systems and tacit knowledge. In W. B. Weimer & D. S. Palermo (Eds.), *Cognition and the symbolic processes.* Hillsdale, NJ: Erlbaum, 1974.

von Senden, M. *Space and sight: The perception of space and shape in the congenitally blind before and after operation.* Glencoe, IL: Free Press, 1960.

Waddington, C. H. *The evolution of an evolutionist.* Edinburgh: Edinburgh University Press, 1975.

Wason, P. C. On the failure to eliminate hypotheses . . . A second look. In P. N. Johnson-Laird & P. C. Wason (Eds.), *Thinking: Readings in cognitive science.* Cambridge: Cambridge University Press, 1977.

Wason, P. C., & Johnson-Laird, P. N. *The psychology of reasoning.* Cambridge: Cambridge University Press, 1972.

Weimer, W. B. Psycholinguistics and Plato's paradoxes of the Meno. *American Psychologist*, 1973, *28*, 15–33.

Weimer, W. B. The psychology of inference and expectation: Some preliminary remarks. In G. Maxwell & R. M. Anderson (Eds.), *Induction, probability and confirmation*, Minnesota Studies in the Philosophy of Science, *VI*. Minneapolis, MN: University of Minnesota Press, 1975.

Weimer, W. B. A conceptual framework for cognitive psychology: Motor theories of the mind. In R. Shaw & J. D. Bransford (Eds.), *Perceiving, acting, and knowing: Toward an ecological psychology.* Hillsdale, NJ: Erlbaum, 1977.

Weimer, W. B. Hayek's approach to the problems of complex phenomena: An introduction to the theoretical psychology of the sensory order. In W. B. Weimer & D. S. Palermo (Eds.), *Cognition and the symbolic processes* (Vol. 2). Hillsdale, NJ: Erlbaum, 1981.

Weimer, W. B., & Palermo, D. S. (Eds.). *Cognition and the symbolic processes* (Vol. 1). Hillsdale, NJ: Erlbaum, 1974.

Weimer, W. B., & Palermo, D. S. (Eds.). *Cognition and the symbolic processes* (Vol. 2). Hillsdale, NJ: Erlbaum, 1981.

Weiss, E. *Agoraphobia in the light of ego psychology.* New York: Grune & Stratton, 1964.

Wolpe, J. *Theme and variations. A behavior therapy casebook.* New York: Pergamon Press, 1976.

Yarrow, L. J. Emotional development. *American Psychologist*, 1979, *34*, 951–957.

CHAPTER 5

Epistemological Therapy and Constructivism

LUIS JOYCE-MONIZ

THERAPIST: Here is your Pandora's box. Don't open it yet! Lean back until you feel really comfortable. Relax, take one or two deep breaths, and concentrate. When you open the box, I want you to concentrate on its interior space and examine the knowledge you have of your present difficulties. Try to understand which of your actions are in agreement with your thoughts and which actions contradict them. While maintaining this position and concentrating on the box's interior, I want you to examine the possibilities of solving the problem you told me about previously. This time, however, try to understand better the manner in which you analyze them. You may now open the box and begin.

CLIENT: Thank you, Doctor, but I would rather do this at home or on the beach and make use of my own epistemological inquiries.

It is clear that there is nothing fictitious about this type of dialogue. For a great number of us, clients and therapists alike, Pandora's box has made its way into clinical practice. It is a relatively good metaphor of epistemological inquiry and has nothing in common with the original box, which contained only human ills that flew forth when it was foolishly opened by Pandora. To save time and psychic energy, the therapist habitually analyzes the possibility of the client's agreeing to learn about the transformation of his cognitive processes

---

LUIS JOYCE-MONIZ • Faculty of Psychology, University of Lisbon, Rua Pinheiro Chagas 17, 1000 Lisbon, Portugal.

and considering the possibility of getting the therapist to understand the client's acquisition of knowledge.

The object of this chapter, however, is not to expound upon the rich metaphorical potential of the box itself but to examine something more significant contained within—the dialectic between the epistemology of the therapist and that of his client. The underlying concept behind Pandora's box is that, psychotherapy being a process of acquisition or modification of knowledge, its participants are active in epistemological confrontation even though they have no awareness of such knowledge and even less of the confrontation. One must not think, however, that Pandora's box lends itself to only one inflexible dialectic; on close examination one discovers that it can be opened in a variety of ways. In doing so, the participants discover that therapy is also a passageway from minor to major knowledge of self and the process can gradually cause a minor epistemological relationship to develop into a major one.

My experiences have been restricted essentially to those of epistemological therapy. Pandora has caused me to reflect on that which could prove to be a constructivist contribution to the epistemology of the client. On the other hand, as soon as I attempt to analyze the metaknowledge of the therapist, the lid slams shut.

THE EPISTEMOLOGY OF THERAPY AND THE THERAPY OF EPISTEMOLOGICAL ORIENTATION

The term *epistemology* became part of the philosophical lexicon in the middle of the nineteenth century, a few decades after the word *psychology* was granted the same privilege. Similarly, the epistemological question soon presented itself openly before the first *Areopagus* of psychotherapeutic controversies. It is popular to argue that psychotherapy inherited the epistemological inquiries of psychology and that psychology inherited those of philosophy. Such a progression could, however, be viewed in two ways. On one hand, the solution to the heuristic questions of therapy are to be found in philosophical contemplation and on the other hand, the great speculations of the *homo philosophicus* have their clarification in the reality of therapy. The truth of the matter is that philosophy of science, like its history, insists upon not wanting to repeat itself. Epistemological questions are born and formalized whenever a new scientific field comes into being and, above all, are reborn in each of the crisis periods through which that new field must inevitably pass (Kuhn,

1962). The classical problems concerning the possibility of knowledge which face the therapist (e.g., Pearls, Wolpe, Ellis) are different from the epistemological questions which their antecedents came across in psychology (Wertheimer, Hull, Adler), and, above all, in philosophy (Brentano, Spencer, Epictetus). Even Lacan's discourse on the duality of the subject and object may have little in common with the manner in which Freud presented the same issue in the psychoanalytical movement against mentalism. This epistemological affiliation becomes even more complicated if one wishes to take into consideration the empirical physicalism and associationism which had an influence on the advent of psychoanalysis.

The evolution of psychological therapies has confirmed this gradual differentiation. At each stage of the conceptual growth of a model, its advocates reconsider the possibility of developing new concepts and to determine under what conditions they might be established. Many times, however, the therapists conclude that their epistemological discussion is tedious and that a paradigmatic renovation would be excessively problematic. In effect, at the core of their reflections, the object to be transformed is inseparable from the subject capable of reflecting upon that transformation. Immersed in a dialectic pursuit which may or may not be beneficial to him, the therapist struggles for credibility in his practice with little regard for what his clients and colleagues might consider to be epistemologically "legal." The nature and independence of this epistemology generate various crises, however, which do not always contribute to the development of the therapeutic paradigm. For example, what are the consequences of the crisis of the practitioner who belongs to the behavioral tradition? It is difficult to give a direct answer to this question. But the interest which epistemological thought has generated among the therapists belonging to this tradition (e.g., Arnkoff, 1980; Liotti & Reda, 1981; Mahoney, 1974; Meichenbaum, 1977) indicates that they are most probably going through a healthy and productive crisis. And how could it be otherwise? The cognitivists feel the natural critical necessity to analyze the possibility of therapeutic knowledge by making use of the conceptual tools employed in this form of intervention. It is important to remember, however, that this question cannot be monopolized by cognitive therapies or even by those therapists who are especially given to theoretical speculation.

It is inevitable that every clinician, regardless of his creed or professed agnosticism, will commit himself to a distinct epistemological position. The clinician's definition of therapeutic knowledge influences his treatment strategies and these in turn contribute to the redefinition of that knowledge. Even if he is unaware of or does not concern himself with the epistemological fundamentals of his intervention, the fact that he thinks about gestalt formation processes, learning new reinforcement contingencies, dynamic restructuring, or operational regulation, indicates by implication that he poses the question of knowledge for himself and for his clients. In this way, the discrepancies so often spoken of between the scientific rationalization of the therapist and his clinical procedures do not necessarily lead to a lessening of his epistemological enthusiasm. On the other hand, the paradigmatic improvement, whatever it may be, never limits itself to the study of experimental or phenomenological modification of concepts or behavior but is deeply involved with the clinical process itself.

The process of the therapist's becoming epistemologically responsible suggests, therefore, an initial definition of the epistemology of psychotherapy which would become intertwined with the analysis of the cognitive acts which the therapist effects upon his client—the object of his action. In this case, the epistemological reflection would be limited to one of the interlocutors involved in the therapeutic relationship and would identify itself with the theoretical foundation of the intervention models. However, the golden rule of psychotherapy states that it is useless or at least insufficient to describe or unilaterally produce clinical results separate from the meaning they have acquired for the client. If it is the therapist who explains the client's knowledge to him, at least the model which is intended to represent that knowledge, then it seems to me that the client should be given an epistemic status so that he might be able to consider the value of the therapist's representation. The preceeding definition, therefore, can be enlarged to include an analysis of the client's cognitive acts which, in turn, would allow him to understand and remediate his difficulties. This analysis is equivalent to the metaknowledge of some of his psychological processes. In this chapter, thus, the term *knowledge of the client* is synonymous with his metacognitive capabilities. From this point of view, the goal of the epistemology of therapy is to solve the general problem of the relationship between the therapist's objective knowledge and the client's subjective knowledge.

A *theory of knowledge* for the therapist and a *philosophy of therapy* for the client have been meticulously developed in each therapeutic model in accord with its conceptual and methodological limits. The natural understanding of the therapeutic process granted to the client depends upon the formalization of the mechanisms by which that understanding is acquired, whether it refers to the transformation of libidinal energy, to the learning of reinforcement contingencies, to the substitution of irrational thoughts, or to the construction of adaptive structures. An intriguing question is raised by this subordination of the client's discourse to that of the therapist. How can one coordinate a positive learning process ("What should the client understand or learn?" "How should this knowledge be acquired?") with the epistemological evaluation of the clinical practice ("Under what conditions is there a scientific justification for the therapist's knowledge?" "What is the connection between the knowledge of the therapeutic process and the efficacy of the method employed?")?

The manner in which each therapeutic current seeks to respond to this problem is determined by the importance which it attributes to the epistemological status of the client, before, during, and after treatment. The *epistemological orientation* of a therapeutic strategy is thus connected to the processes utilized to develop this status. One strategy which is less committed to the preceeding leaves the causal and casuistic explanation of the constructs as well as the methods adopted to realize its goal entirely to the discretion of the clinician, thereby ignoring the role of the client's knowledge or filing it away under "incidents related to the clinical relationship" (e.g., treatment expectations, attitudinal characteristics, resistance or countercontrol of the client). In this context, the therapist relies on his knowledge in order to locate (topic activity) the client's knowledge of his own psychological processes, that is to say, to determine what the client can and should know about himself. A different strategy seeks, nevertheless, to facilitate the giving of information to the client—information not only about the therapist's activity and method but chiefly about the role of the client's cognitive processes (actual or to be developed) in the reformulation or expansion of that method. The objective of this strategy is to lead the client to a therapeutic epistemology of self. In this way, the client can locate the therapist's knowledge in relationship to the knowledge of his own psychological processes and the therapist can better contribute to the transformation of this metaknowledge.

Although incomplete, the conceptualization which follows attempts to demonstrate that the therapies of the behavioral and cognitive-behavioral tradition have progressed from one epistemological tendency to another and opened to a dialectic confrontation between the copartners in the clinical process. Other paradigmatic currents such as that of the dynamic or phenomenological persuasion were not considered because a true dialectic between the two types of knowledge is generally assumed not to exist; the client's epistemological status is unconditionally accepted or, inversely, it is entirely imposed by the clinician but without metacognitive references. But my principal motive lies in the fact that I include myself in the abovementioned tradition and am attempting to predict the direction it will take in the future.

CONJECTURES ON THE DIALECTIC BETWEEN THE TWO EPISTEMOLOGICAL DISCOURSES

If a therapy is never completely alien to the epistemology of the client, then a dialectic relationship between client and therapist always develops to one degree or another. This relationship, however, can be alien to a confrontation of metaknowledges. Be that as it may, the simple adherence of a client to treatment is a myth. From the behavioral and cognitive perspective, the therapist always wears the robes of the educator and reinforcer, even if the didactic procedure changes from the imposition of new neural connections among stimuli to the suggestion of alternative concepts, and even if the reinforcing function is able to occur over concrete actions, thought content, or metacognitive transformations. Independent of the method, the therapist *cognizes* the clinical process not only so that he might come to *recognize* himself epistemologically but also so that he might come to know or locate his client within these methodological and paradigmatic parameters. The topic activity is limited by the perspective the therapist holds on the two epistemic statuses, and when its time comes this will determine the type of information he is willing to provide. The explanation of the method and the role of the participants can vary from a description of the location and equipment used to the reading and discussion of a textbook on psychotherapy. In the majority of cases, the rationale is sufficiently complete. In a parallel fashion, the clinician gives further instructions, suggestions, and interpretations right in the consulting room, by telephone, or by means of recordings, during and after treatment. In spite of the fact that the clinical process has little to do with the quantity of interpretations (Sloane *et al.*, 1975), the feedback provided by the therapist can be reduced to a simple smile for his partner before he administers an emetic or before he wears himself out with the enumeration and explanation of his partner's irrational concepts. But by themselves these manifestations do not indicate where the epistemological discourse of the two should be placed. The integration of the preceeding into the clinical process is closely tied to the therapist's paradigmatic convictions which, within behavioral and cognitive currents, as one knows, are many.

It is possible to avoid an exhaustive analysis of dozens of procedures by considering only four major categories and by directing the reader who is eager for more references or details to the equally numerous reviews of literature in this field (e.g., Mahoney, 1974; Mahoney & Arnkoff, 1978).

1. *Direct and nonmediational conditioning:* The practitioner rejects the client's discourse either because he does not assign any procedural importance to it or because he considers it to be counterproductive. His ideas on the epistemic status of the client are simple: the acquisition, extinction, or maintenance of the target responses occur mechanically or automatically. Whether one attempts to modify inadequate behavior of the client by means of its antecedents or to control it through its consequences, it is useless to turn to the partner's knowledge, which indeed can have real inhibitory effects on therapy (Ekman, Krasner, & Ullmann, 1963). It is clear that in this context the clinician's beliefs are not threatened by the information eventually transmitted to the client. The therapist denies the client the right to a dialectic confrontation even if the therapist reveals the existence of a punishment or a reward, its intensity or duration, the detailed conditions of its application, or the alternative responses which allow one to avoid or engender stimulation.

2. *Indirect or mediational conditioning* (e.g., systematic desensitization, implosion, imagined covert sensitization, and participant modeling): The practitioner chooses not to change the discourse of the client. This is treated as simple feedback of the client concerning his answers (external or internal) which are necessary to the implementation of treatment or which confirm the discrimination, maintenance, and reproduction of the knowledge to which he was exposed. The epistemic status of the client continues to have a reduced function. While the therapist suggests real or fictitious, pleasant or unpleasant situations, the client has the opportunity to associate those images with his physical sensations or radically to cut off these visualizations. On the other hand, it does not seem to me that the overt or covert reproduction of the action of a model, even if it is a complex instrumental representation, presupposes an appreciable change in his metaknowledge.

3. *The development of coping skills* (e.g., self-monitoring, self-reward and self-punishment, self-instruction training, self-control variation of desensitization, stress inoculation): The practitioner analyzes

the knowledge that the interlocutor has of himself in his relationship to the world, teaching him new skills so that he may better adjust the world to his needs. The therapeutic dialectic is structured in such a way that it facilitates the client's confrontation not only with his social and physical surroundings, but with himself as well, which in turn leads to a change in the content of his metacognitions. In this context, he learns how to increase the knowledge that he possesses about himself through self-monitoring; to retain that knowledge, supporting or censuring his behavior; to use it rationally, relaxing or becoming active or even imagining himself in problem situations; to systematize it, giving himself instructions about what to do in various circumstances. The therapist is kept very busy organizing these threatening or painful encounters, giving illustrations of coping skills and devising a model with a new epistemic status in which the client can come to see himself.

4. *Metacognitive restructuring* (e.g., rational-emotional therapy, Beck's cognitive therapy, problem-solving therapies): The practitioner does not confine himself to pragmatic change in the client's knowledge but attempts to restructure it completely. The orientation given to this strategy is directed toward the dialectic exchange between the knowledge of both interlocutors. In effect, the therapist directly confronts the client's ideas, beliefs, rules, and norms and offers him a different philosophy. In addition, he arranges real or imaginary experiences for the client so that he may test concepts and strategies used to relate to the world and invent others. And he suggests crises so that the client may reexamine and transform his personal paradigm. The client's epistemic status is fully recognized and performs a crucial role in the clinical procedure. Through an open and diversified confrontation of knowledge, the two partners have the possibility of freeing themselves from the instrumental and conceptual obstacles which limit their individual growth and their relationship.

It remains to be seen how the client will react to these proposals of epistemological dialectics (or to their absence, as in the first example), prepared *a priori* by his educator and reinforcer. In effect, the client also cognizes the therapeutic process but only in order to recognize himself in it and solve his problem. His topic activity has a double function. On one hand, he indicates where the therapist's knowledge is to be located in relationship to other sources of knowledge such as previous therapeutic experiences, advice from friends, or the reading of books. On the other hand, he positions that knowledge according to the expectations of a new clinical experience and of the understanding which he has of his psychological processes. As I see it, the client's conception of the strategy depends upon the distinctions he makes among the therapist's knowledge, his own metaknowledge, and the overall epistemological scheme into which he places the treatment. There are at least three possibilities:

1. The client who is not able to make these distinctions places his expectations in the affective relationship which he establishes with his interlocutor. The therapeutic incidents which traditionally come under the headings of "nonspecific factors," "placebo influences," and "client variables" and which have produced a large body of literature (e.g., Frank, 1961; Garfield, 1978; Lazarus, 1961; Paul, 1966) allow one to understand this mythological perspective. Such a perspective states, for example, that a client, to a greater or lesser degree, is susceptible to the social influence, scientific status, and persuasive attitudes of his therapist; that he trusts the therapist's depth of experience and foresight; that he reacts to the therapist's warmth, genuine interest, and empathy (or coldness, disinterest, or antipathy); that he solicits an interpretation from the therapist concerning the subtle nature of his difficulties; and that he transfers his feelings and expectations to the therapist.

2. Similarly, the client is able to distinguish the explanation of the therapeutic paradigm from its actual utility without being able, nevertheless, clearly to place his knowledge in relationship to one or the other. His expectations are contractual in that he intends to define the therapist's functions and the concrete results of the process. However, he continues to be a relatively passive consumer. This pragmatic perspective is manifested, for example, in the expectation that his conception of treatment can be recognized in the rationale the therapist presents or in the actual process of change (Goldstein, 1962). Through an understanding of the instructions given to him and of the treatment progress, he is able to establish his responsibility within the therapeutic framework (Saltzman *et al.*, 1976). If his expectations are at variance with his initial experiences (Rickels & Anderson, 1967), or the promises made by the therapist are not kept (Storms & Nisbett, 1970), or if he becomes aware of the incorrect usage or of the uselessness of a strategy (Lazarus & Fay, 1982), the person involved considers the contract to be unfulfilled and the heuristic validity of the interlocutor's philosophy is of little importance to him.

3. Finally, the client is capable of differentiating among the three types of knowledge. For him therapy is no longer a process of intervention but one of dialectic collaboration. His expectations are concerned with determining the location and epistemological status of

the participants. As far as the therapist's knowledge is concerned, he can, for example, (a) refuse it either because he does not consider it to be important or because he believes that the therapist's "science" is counterproductive—most likely he will terminate treatment; (b) manipulate it because he transforms it into simple feedback in order to facilitate his use of his own knowledge—an attitude which leads to diversified resistance associated with the method and the paradigm whether implied or imposed; (c) accept it, supporting the therapist's "logic" and avoiding a confrontation of his knowledge with that of the interlocutor—the emergence of occasional resistance depends, however, upon the evaluation he makes of his capabilities in comparison with those of the therapist; (d) restructure it, because he believes that the transformation of his knowledge relies on that confrontation—the frequent, intense, and objective resistance expressed is, naturally, a part of the dialectic process.

The epistemological orientation of any therapeutic strategy is, it seems, closely linked to the confrontation between two types of knowledge. In practice, the client does not exclusively adhere to any of the positions delineated above. His overall attitude is determined by the balance he achieves among the three preceeding distinctions of knowledge. In this sense, the client is more eclectic (i.e., less dogmatic) than the therapist.

In my opinion, the evolution of cognitive-behavioral therapies corresponds to the passing from a dialectic relationship dominated by the therapist to an epistemological balance between the two participants. I feel, however, that it would be useful to examine some of the conceptual and methodological obstacles to this movement. Above all, I would like to address myself to three questions of a developmental nature which have important implications concerning the degree to which the two dialectic partners might be able to make use of this new freedom.

1. What are the limits which the client's metacognitive capacities impose on the implementation of clinical strategy?
2. What is the role given by the therapist to the client's cognitive structures in the process of epistemological restructuring?
3. How might the client and therapist participate in the construction of a dialectic relationship between their two types of knowledge?

It is evident that the complete answers to these questions are not to be found in Pandora's box. Nevertheless, an incursion into its interior invites further reflection.

CLIENTS' SOCIOCOGNITIVE CHARACTERISTICS AND THERAPEUTIC PROCEDURES

The advocates of the behavioral-cognitive therapeutic movement reject the thesis of the automatic nature of learning but, like the radical behaviorists, they seem to have as much confidence in the "almost limitless capacity for adaptive learning and for the learning of skills and dispositions" (Wolpe, 1980, p. 198). This faith in the inevitability of a type of learning which is democratically available to every person during any moment of his life has been the ruling dogma of a large sector of American psychology and is the principal reason for its resistance to the European psychogenetic views. Respect for tradition, however, does not adequately explain the fact that the cognitive therapists have not clearly denounced the standard classification of the client's intellectual potentialities and limitations along lines of the "placebo effects" or of the "test variables related to therapeutic outcomes" (Garfield, 1978). If the radical behaviorists place the role of the cognitive processes among the nonspecific factors of treatment (Wilson, 1980), could it be that the cognitive therapists do the same in relationship to the client's sociocognitive characteristics?

The conditions under which therapeutic learning occurs are, of course, connected with the relationship between a person's reasoning capabilities, the behavior and cognitions to be changed, and the clinical strategy utilized. It is true that in dynamic and personalist therapies the importance of a client's personality characteristics and traits is often exaggerated and the magnitude of treatment variables is ignored. On the contrary, the attempts to link a person's structural capacities to treatment modalities do not exist in strict behavioral therapies, in that their advocates believe in the determinism of specific contingencies of reinforcement. In principle, cognitive therapists oppose these two types of reductionism. In reality, with the exception of a few recommendations for adjusting the interventions to the cognitive capacities of the child (Kendall, 1977; Meichenbaum & Cameron, 1980), for all practical purposes, little or nothing has been accomplished, at least in developmental terms (Sollod & Wachtel, 1980).

All of this occurs as if the indisputable therapeutic successes already achieved in the CBTs (cognitive behavioral therapies) had caused the clinicians blindly to commit themselves to the principles of pragmatic rationalism: "If treatment is successful, it is because the clients are capable of responding to that which is taught to them! Everything depends on the way in which we proceed and not on the client's intelligence." In rational-emotive therapy (Ellis, 1962 and

1980), for example, there is absolute confidence in the rational capacities of any client to change his philosophy of life and replace his thoughts with others that are more suitable and rational. All that is necessary in order to realize the above is a good authoritarian therapist to push the client into this agreeable formalizing task. In a similar fashion, the practitioner who adheres to the cognitive therapy of Beck and his coworkers (1976, 1979) issues *a priori* a certificate of ability to the client so that he might examine his beliefs as hypotheses, differentiate distorted cognitions from adapted ones, and act accordingly. It would seem that with the aid of minor methodological adjustments the techniques of self-instruction (Meichenbaum, 1977) can be used with both children and adults. Whether they deal with techniques of self-control (Mahoney & Thoresen, 1974), with the self-control variation of desensitization (Goldfried, 1971), with systematic rational restructuring (Goldfried, Decenteo, & Weinberg, 1974), or· with assertive training (e.g., Gordon, 1970; Jakubowski & Lang, 1978), the procedures linked to the learning of coping skills also fail to include any reference whatsoever to the eventual structural limitations of their applicability. The situation is the same in an area as sensitive as that wherein the epistemological initiative is the client's, or in problem-solving therapies (D'Zurilla & Goldfried, 1971; Mahoney, 1974). Even the noteworthy developmental proposals for a better adjustment to intrapersonal relationships (Spivack, Platt, & Shure, 1976) do not make clear whether, within the context of each age period considered (early childhood, middle childhood, adolescence, adulthood), any individual has the ability to acquire the cognitive skills of the training needed to facilitate the solving of his relational problems.

One cannot refute the fact, however, that the different strategies of cognitive or rational restructuring, the acquisition of global skills, the resolution of complex problems, and the renovation of personal paradigms do involve sophisticated mental operations. The simultaneous examination of the different implications of a situation or of a concept, the formulation of hypotheses and inferences for solving a problem, the comparison of one's social and emotional perspective with that of someone else, the definition of norms and contemporary values and their replacement with values better suited to a confrontation with the environment—all are abilities which require formal thought. Nevertheless, various developmentalists (e.g., Kuhn, Langer, & Kohlberg, 1977; Lickona, 1976) have shown that only a very small percentage of adults succeed in attaining higher levels of abstract thought or sociomoral reasoning. Even adults included in this minority are not always able to function on a formally adequate level (Joyce-Moniz, 1978; Sollod & Wachtel, 1980).

Two studies done in Lisbon help to clarify the above subject (Joyce-Moniz, 1979a, 1980). In the first study, a group of soldiers with problems of self-esteem and self-assertion were counseled in self-monitoring and the elimination of depreciative and anxious thoughts and instructed in how to replace these thoughts with positive self-instruction. In the second, we used various "packets" of cognitive-behavioral techniques involving relaxation training, instruction in specific assertive skills, cognitive restructuring (modified RET), and a strategy for problem solving administered over a series of treatments to teachers of different grade levels. Each client's level of development of formal reasoning capacity was measured before and after these procedures with the aid of the operational tasks inspired by the work of Piaget, and each client's level of development of moral reasoning was measured by making use of dilemmatic situations of the Kohlbergian type. The results indicated that the clients who benefited most from the different strategies were those with higher levels of formal reasoning and postconventional moral reasoning. Apparently, these people's cognitive structuring capabilities significantly influenced the manner in which they monitored themselves and discussed and established strategies conducive to the modification of their attitudes and concepts. The therapist had proposed and the client disposed in accord with his logic abilities.

Mahoney (1980) is most likely correct when he argues that in CBTs rationality has been naively confused with sound reasoning (i.e., the therapist's good norms and values), instead of being considered a dialectic tool for maximizing the client's contact with reality. In effect, the acquisition of this type of rationality imposed by the practitioner has little to do with the developmental processes of human reasoning. A half-century of work in the area of psychogenetic constructivism (Piaget, Wallon, Bruner, Kohlberg, etc.) seems to illustrate that thought evolves by gradually opening itself up to a system of increasingly complex and integrated structures. When the process is not explicitly recognized by the therapist, it can be controlled or accelerated only with great difficulty.

In my opinion, a client's intellectual potential can no longer be viewed as a simple function of the clinical procedure by assigning it a secondary role or by trying to guarantee its acquisition beforehand by direct didactic means. Concretely, I think that the success of any cognitive therapy is to a great extent determined by the levels of sociocognitive reasoning to which the client has had the possibility to accede. These levels do not correspond to arbitrary slices taken from a continuum which would evolve through knowledge accumulation and even less to uniform stages composed of invariable age periods and fixed thought content. From the preceding perspective, the order of acquisition of those structures which make up the discontinuities is constant, but it is a nonchronological succession. The sequence is integrative, that is, the structures of a given level are incorporated into the structures of the following level and the logical operations of each structural group become progressively more complex. And lastly, a person does not always activate or make use of the same level of reasoning (and much less the highest level which he has attained). This apparent functional inconsistency will be examined later. Nevertheless, I would like to point out here that in an epistemological perspective of therapy, the clinician should seek to understand the manner in which the different levels coexist and are chosen.

By including the client's sociocognitive reasoning characteristics in the clinician's framework, one may perhaps facilitate the administration of cognitive procedures to an increasing number of children and adults who currently cannot benefit from these strategies. Otherwise, I fear that the majority of the CBTs will continue to submerge themselves in the sophistication of radical behaviorism, emerging only to treat very specific cases or, owing to its birth defect, to face problems of maintenance and generalization of results.

The preceding problem could rekindle the controversy over the relationship between competence and performance. I am reminded of the fact that the theorists of social learning (e.g., Bandura, 1977; Mischel & Mischel, 1976) have shown, for example, that their sociocognitive developmental pairs (e.g., Kohlberg, 1969; Selman, 1976) formalized different levels of personal competence within a general context but disregarded performance skills in specific situations. On the other hand, Kohlberg (1969) and Lickona (1976) among others have shown that they are less interested in the individual's convictions or specific experiences, which vary at the mercy of physical and cultural contingencies, than in his more general structures, which guide the way he organizes his thoughts about these beliefs and attitudes. This dilemma, however, has little to do with cognitive therapies. Obviously, a client's ability to reason is not the only determinant of the quality of his performance during treatment. But it does deserve to be raised to its proper place in relationship to other determinants of a personal nature, be they relational or cultural, owing to the mediational and structuring role attributed to the cognitive processes in controlling excessive emotion or in modifying inadequate performance. At the same time, as has already been mentioned, the client's competence of course determines his metacognitive skills—that is, his capacity to come to cognize and recognize himself through the clinical strategy.

The client's participation in the process of changing his epistemic status is, therefore, dependent upon his structures of reasoning. In principle, the person with advanced formal thought or with postconventional moral reasoning profits more easily from a dialectic confrontation with the therapist. Can it be that we are thus condemned to prefer and seek out educated clients who are intelligent and psychologically sophisticated (Garfield, 1978)? Or, in spite of everything (i.e., of the natural development of the client), can we overcome this difficulty through an energetic cognitive restructuring?

STRUCTURES AND COGNITIVE RESTRUCTURING

In the CBTs, restructuring and structures are constant topics of discussion, which is a new development within the behaviorist family. I have yet to understand if this is a semantic artifice or an operational reality. In effect, investigators such as Ellis (1962, 1980) and Goldfried (Goldfried et al., 1974) have made use of cognitive and rational restructuring procedures, but they make no references to structures. I presume we are dealing with more than a "restructuring without structures." On the other hand, other cognitive therapists speak of structures but it is difficult for me to perceive whether their reference and discussion contributes significantly to any cognitive restructuring process.

For example, for Meichenbaum and Butler (1980, p. 30), cognitive structures are "meaning systems or affective concerns that engender particular cognitive processes and overt behavior." Following Luria's developmental views (1961), Meichenbaum (1977) argues that discourse (self-verbalization) can modify and regulate the systems of meaning. Therefore, not only do cognitive structures identify themselves with affective mechanisms, but their acquisition is dependent upon speech functions as well. In the case of Beck, the concept of structure seems to be more diverse. On one hand, Beck and his collaborators (1979, p. 8) write:

> How a person appraises a situation is generally evident in his cognitions (thoughts and visual images). These cognitions constitute the person's "stream of consciousness" or phenomenal field, which reflects the person's

configuration of himself, his world, his past and future. Alterations in the
content of the person's underlying cognitive structures affect his or her
affective state and behavioral pattern.

In this case, the structures seem to correspond to more permanent
and deeper meanings than simple cognitions. On the other hand, they
argue that "relatively stable cognitive patterns form the basis for the
regularity of interpretation of a particular set of situations. The term
schema designates these stable cognitive patterns" (p. 12). These schemata or sets of structures seem to have here an organizing and regulating function. Beck, however, also assumes the existence of dere-
gularizing schemas: "In psychopathological states such as depression,
patients' conceptualizations of specific situations are distorted to fit
the prepotent dysfunctional schemas" (p. 13). In motor theory, Arnkoff (1980) makes an important distinction between surface structures, which correspond to observable behavior, and deep structures,
which determined the meaning of the surface structures and are virtually performed and formalized in abstract rules as an individual
map. Apparently, this is an even deeper structure.

From a constructivistic psychogenetic point of view, cognitive
structures are completely different constructs. In the first place, they
are clearly concerned with the forms of thought, not its content. This
distinction is of interest because cognitivist therapists, by manipulating irrational thoughts, self-instructions, imagined models, confrontation skills, or adaptive beliefs, have almost collectively precog-
nized the modification of specific cognitions as a *sine qua non* condition
for a rational performance in a general context. Although the objectives are different, this position differs little from that of radical behaviorism in that the control of specific external contingencies is
clearly parallel with the control of specific internal contingencies.
The determinism of the rules of the environment reigns in one case;
the rational determinism of the therapist governs in the other. This
preponderance of the specific is perhaps adequate when one intends
to change equally specific behavior. But it is even more difficult to
understand that the therapist can change the client's philosophy of
life, his system of values, and his regulative self-verbalization by
replacing the specific contents of thought.

In the second place, structures are not relatively permanent or
static totalities, but systems of transformations. These systems undergo
a change because they have a self-regulating function which brings
about certain states of balance between the cognitive capacities of
the person and the pressures of the environment, which are quali-
tatively different and pass through multiple disequilibriums and re-

structurings (Piaget, 1975). Although this slow and integrative process is characterized by abrupt leaps forward, digressions, and retrogressions, it makes it possible to explain, for example, how one progresses from sensory-motor levels to concrete ones and from these to formal levels in the process of understanding the physical world. Furthermore, it explains how preconventional levels of reasoning pass over to conventional ones and these to postconventional levels in the process of understanding sociomoral rules and norms (Kohlberg, 1969).

In my opinion, this structural perspective offers certain advantages. Most notably, it makes it possible to formulate a cognitive clinical practice in terms of sociocognitive development. Obviously, I am not advocating gearing the therapeutic strategy to the *tempo* of actual development, but rather the establishment of the objectives and limits of intervention in accord with the mechanisms of the developmental process. For example, in conjunction with an evaluation of a client's images, attributions, beliefs, expectations, and self-verbalizations, a meticulous appraisal of his sociocognitive development indicates what his structural and operative capacities are for moving toward the treatment objective, thus facilitating the selection and implementation of the cognitive strategy.

It is in this manner that the epistemological orientation of a therapy acquires its true value. Instead of the therapist's determining sophisticated therapeutic goals for the changing of one's philosophy of life or system of values, which sometimes are inaccessible to a client's comprehension, or determining what he should or should not believe in, the client has the opportunity to discover (or invent) his own concepts, beliefs, norms, and values in accord with his own sociocognitive structures. As mentioned before, the therapist cannot have the monopoly on reason and must acknowledge the difference between *believing* and *understanding*. Each level of logico-causal, social, moral, or other kind of reasoning involves different mental operations which in turn make possible certain judgments. The therapist who functions only on certain levels must give up the pretense of imposing such thought content on his clients, who frequently are operating on a different logical and phenomenological wavelength.

A correlative advantage of the preceding is related to the actual process of cognitive restructuring and it can be expressed in two forms:

By knowing the highest levels of reasoning which the client has reached, the therapist can help him to take proper advantage of his structural repertoire as it applies to different problematic contexts. As will be seen, this does not mean that the client should systematically make use of his most complex operative structures. An epistemological perspective of therapy is not synonymous with an abuse of formal rules. Nor is it, as Weimer writes (1980, p. 383), "tapping the abstract rules, which literally are the client's mind," which would involve a submission to a preformed logic. Rather, it is taking advantage of the best form of any operative structure which the person possesses. And it is only this person, by means of his metaknowledge, who is able rationally to administer his structural repertoire.

At the same time, the therapist, familiar with the sequences of development, implements his clinical strategy in such a way as to facilitate the client's passage to the highest levels of development. Previously, we thought that for this transition to take place it was necessary only to expose our clients to logico-causal, social, or moral patterns slightly superior to the highest level attained spontaneously (Joyce-Moniz, 1981a). Clinical practice caused us to realize that things are not quite so simple. In effect, this acceleration is subject in the same degree to laws of development, or rather, to the natural process of acquiring cognitive structures. Working on the premise that the preceding corresponds to transformational systems which possess the possibility of self-regulation, one understands that direct learning is unable by itself to activate this regulating mechanism. In the following paragraphs, I would like to propose other processes such as the epistemological confrontation within the therapeutic relationship as being much more conducive to the client's progression to the highest levels of reasoning.

From a constructivist-psychogenetic perspective, the restructuring process should lead the client to the transformation and autonomous control of his cognitions and not to the imposition of cognitive control as organized by the therapist. The latter, however, is condemned to have access only to the content of the client's thought. The therapist must question himself about the nature of the construction process if he is to predict which thoughts affect the generalization and transformation of a person's structural repertoire.

PSYCHOGENETIC CONSTRUCTIVISM AND THERAPY

The forms of constructivism are as numerous as the opinions on the way in which man purposely transforms reality. Some of the more conservative views assign a limited role to the constructive activity of the person:

> Social learning theory as proposed by Bandura (1977) is cognitive, constructivistic, and deterministic. . . . It is constructivistic in that previously

acquired cognitive rules are considered during responding in reciprocal conjunction with environmental sources of information. (Zimmerman, 1981, p. 41)

Other more radical views give rise to the enigma of a continuous and unlimited construction (Von Glasersfeld, 1981). Minimum or maximum constructivism has influenced the concepts of the cognitive-behavioral movement as much in its earliest beginnings, thanks to information processing (Mahoney, 1974), as in its most recent and audacious developments, of which the motor theory of the mind is an example (Arnkoff, 1980; Weimer, 1977). Nevertheless, the contribution of the constructivist ideal to therapy has been placed in doubt:

The cognitive notion of "construction" seemed to add very little to what clinicians already believed; it served more often as a rationalization than as a source of new insights. Moreover, it lends itself very readily to a kind of radical relativism, in which every perception and thought is as good as every other. If everyone's percepts are constructed, why are the therapist's constructions any more valid than the patient's? How can we distinguish sanity from insanity, truth from falsehood, or good from evil if all knowledge is of models in our heads rather than of the world itself? Of course no general theory can make such decisions for any particular case, but shouldn't there be some way to make them in principle? (Neisser, 1980, p. 365)

The same questions have been raised throughout this text. I feel that the client's constructions are more important than those of the therapist but that both work together toward the evolution of a therapeutic dialectic. A treatment which is oriented toward the development of the epistemic status of the client actually includes a double constructivism: the client generalizes or *constructs* the adaptive structures while participating in the construction of the confrontation between his metaknowledge and the therapist's knowledge. In principle, the dialectic within the clinical environment should take the form of guiding the dialectic between the individual and the actual environment. But what are the underlying mechanisms of this natural dialectic? The Piagetian conceptualizations of *decentration* and *compensation* can help one to understand this perspective.

The individual's gradual acquisition of self-knowledge, together with his knowledge of the physical and social world, is grounded in a structural differentiation. This differentiation is originally part of an egocentric point of view which is connected to obvious or readily perceived external features and to variable or incoherent personal or social attributes. If everything goes well, one arrives at a final distinction between the individual's point of view and that of someone else by means of subtle and anticipatory formal inferences about one's own feelings, norms, and attitudes and about those of other people. Piaget's work deals with the acquisition of structural mechanisms which come from this functional movement of decentration. But this acquisition is verifiable in the social world as well as the physico-causal world and includes the invariance of self-attributes (Joyce-Moniz, 1976, 1979b), feelings of empathy and altruism (Hoffman, 1976), social (Selman, 1976) and psychosexual (Kohlberg & Ullian, 1974) roles and attitudes, moral reasoning (Kohlberg, 1969), socio-political concepts (Connel, 1971), and so forth.

This opening up to the world of others is familiar to many therapeutic models. The client decenters when he tries to adopt the therapist's point of view (role reversal) or the perspective of an ideal model who is capable of effectively confronting perturbing situations (fixed-role therapy, Kelly, 1955, or exaggerated-role playing, Wolpe & Lazarus, 1966). Theoretically, the almost Brechtian distancing between the actor and the character represented facilitates the learning of a new role because the relationship is fictitious and can be changed at any point without any consequences. The process of decentration is also evident in the modern cognitivist therapeutic movement. The self-instruction training of Meichenbaum (1977), the covert modeling of Kazdin (1979), the cognitive modeling of Goldstein (1973), and even certain parameters of problem solving of D'Zurilla and Goldfried (1971) all have the client imagining or imitating the actions and the rationalizations of a model, which is, therefore, an attempt at the transformation of the person's initial viewpoint. Similarly, the rational-emotive therapy of Ellis (1962), the cognitive therapy of Beck (1976), and the systematic restructuring of Goldfried and his colleagues (1974) imply a similar movement in that the client is aided in identifying his inadequate, egocentric thoughts or helped not to consider himself as the center of the universe, and to replace these concepts with others that do not correspond to his logical, social, or moral points of view. Beck (1976, p. 244), for example, writes that "the technique of prying the patient loose from his pattern of regarding himself as the focal point of all events is called decentering."

It is obvious that psychogenetic constructivism assigns a different meaning to this process by placing it into an overall developmental framework. As a result, I shall emphasize those clinical procedures which can facilitate the increase or the control of decentration in different ways. In effect, many aggressive, depressive, obsessive, and compulsive reactions can be characterized by a marked lack of a decentering capacity, just as many phobic and hypomanic states, inadequate sexual behavior, and passive attitudes can be attributed to excessive decentration.

The reciprocal process of compensation requires a more detailed explanation.

The structures underlying an understanding of the contents of the physical world tend to be organized through discontinuities in equilibrium. This is what occurs with the so-called Piagetian stages. Nevertheless, the structures underlying an understanding of socio-affective content tend to be organized through changing discontinuities or discontinuities in incomplete equilibrium. That is to say, the characteristics of such sequences of development as self-attributes, social and psychosexual attitudes, and moral reasoning are not the same as those of the levels of development which correspond to the understanding of the physico-causal world. In this context, various investigators (e.g., Holstein, 1976), using Kohlbergian instruments and methods, have verified that half of a person's moral judgments are located in different levels of socio-moral reasoning and that a significant part of the individuals examined "inexplicably" skipped one or more levels of a sequence which was claimed to be invariable and integrative. In effect, a system of sociocognitive development produces, out of necessity, horizontal *décalages* between the structures underlying the various contents—that is to say, a person does not always demonstrate the same cognitive competence in every judgment rendered.

The fundamentals of Piagetian theory, especially as they pertain to the process of compensation (Piaget, 1975), allow one better to understand the nature of these displacements between levels of thought. During the preoperational period, the compensations are always approximate and characterized by incomplete regulations. For the child, it is a "hard" dialectic process. The child tries to compensate for the problems and disturbances imposed by the environment by directing his actions and concepts in the opposite direction (inversion) or by modifying his actions and concepts in order to accommodate the disturbing element (reciprocity). In both cases, there exists a final evaluation of the compensating attempt, which constitutes a beginning of metaknowledge. Later, the incomplete regulations are replaced by the operations which make up a prior correction of the problem, rather than compensating for it after the problem has occurred as in the previous period. This prior correction is therefore an anticipation which permits the system's complete equilibrium. In the second period, the precorrection is made directly over concrete objects, and in the third, it is realized in an abstract fashion which combines the compensations by means of inversion and reciprocity. Consequently, in this last period, the dialectic is internalized and the person succeeds in confronting not only the environment but himself as well.

The compensations encompassed by the integration process of socio-affective contents do not necessarily lead, therefore, to abstract operatory corrections and to dialectic equilibriums with disturbances which have been introduced from the exterior or interior. In these areas, and in comparison with the physico-causal world, the individual is less active or metaactive or has less possibility to manipulate and experiment autonomously those socioaffective situations. Many of the corrections made to compensate for emotional conflicts are realized from the exterior in the form of normative values; the person is subsequently incapable of freeing himself from that influence and as a result does not make appropriate use of his most adaptive structures. Moreover, ideas, beliefs, and principles of others are assimilated in an incoherent and unstable manner which has little in common with the causal regularity with which the physical phenomena always occur. Consequently, the compensating or the regulating activities can be insufficient to permit access to new levels of equilibrium once they arrange themselves in a probabilistic or nonessential fashion.

Usually, the client finds himself in diverse levels of reasoning in keeping with socioaffective contents for which he tries to compensate. For example, an obsessive-compulsive may respond by repeating an action, without any change whatsoever, only in those situations which involve an evaluation of his physical attributes; or a depressive may cease his activity, without any compensation, only in relationship to problems of a moral nature. These processes lie outside of consciousness but there are many compensations which can be a part of metaknowledge—especially when a person has the insight which comes from displacements. Many anxiety-ridden, unassertive, phobic (and so forth) individuals are surprised at times when they compare their "rationality" in certain situations with their "stupidity" (disturbance) in others. Insight arises because the compensating regulations are objectively successful in the first case but not in the second. This is the familiar consciousness of the phobic condition and, less frequently, of the obsessive and compulsive ones. I cannot stress strongly enough that these displacements between the various domains of structural competence do not in any way correspond to a system of set and unchanging skills. In the same problem context, an individual's compensating efforts may reach an equilibrium one day and may the next day lead to reactions of frustration, anxiety, avoidance, and aggressiveness. Therapists and educators alike are well acquainted with the alienating character of these regulating attempts. Obviously, this does not mean that the person has changed his structural repertoire. It indicates only that he has not made use of the appropriate operatory regulations or has done so only partially and that these regulations were unable to accommodate the disturbance.

If, from this perspective, symptoms, defense mechanisms, cognitive distortions, or inappropriate responses are equivalent to insufficient or inadequate compensations, then almost all therapeutic strategies strive to acquire *good* compensations which are able to bring about frequent self-regulation and dialectic equilibrium. Would that things were so simple. If they were, the integration of a therapeutic model into a developmental one would effortlessly lead to a translation of the former into the latter—and all would be solved. In reality, even within the context of the metacognitive strategies of the CBTs, it is very difficult to determine or speculate as to which suggested or imposed compensations may effectively contribute to the client's behavioral and epistemic autonomy. Nevertheless, this difficulty did not prevent us from attempting to systematize such compensations within the current constructivistic view. On the basis of an examination of work published in the last few years dealing with the various strategies of metacognitive restructuring (Joyce-Moniz, 1981b), it seemed to us that in making use of such methods as direct confrontation, self-instruction training, exposure to a model, and the like, the therapists involved attempted to have their clients internalize at least four types of compensation:

1. *Compensation through complete negation* corresponds to the old radical principle which holds that the best way to combat a disturbing thought or action is with an opposing thought or action. At the metacognitive level, such attempts at negation can correspond to beliefs ("When I feel pessimistic about the future, I try to fight that feeling by telling myself, for example, that it is useless and prejudicial to me") or to actions ("When I have difficulty in putting a plan into action, I do everything possible to realize that plan"). Extrapolating to the theory of Piaget (1975), this compensation through *inversion* is a form of regulation through negative feedback, which involves the direct annulment of the disturbance.

2. *Compensation through incomplete negation* corresponds to the traditional *sagesse* which holds that a good way to neutralize a disturbing thought or action is to establish a compromise based on gains and losses. Such compromise can strive for a balance between con-

cepts ("When I feel pessimistic, . . . I try to ward off this feeling by thinking of positive things that might happen to me") or between actions ("When I have difficulty in realizing a given option, I don't worry. I try to come up with a second option *as good* as the first"). At times, clients do not consider themselves competent enough to set up this balance compromise and settle for the solution of the lesser evil ("It is better to be pessimistic at first and then successful than the other way around" or "I try to effect a second option even though it is not as good as the first"). Again, with Piaget in mind, this compensation through *reciprocity* constitutes another form of regulation through negative feedback by means of a differentiation of the structural schema so it can accommodate the disturbance.

3. The compromise can also strive toward an *incomplete acceptance* of a disturbing thought or action. For example, the acceptance can work under the guise of a temporary postponement of confrontation ("I don't try to ward off my negative thoughts because I know that, whatever happens, positive things will happen to me in the future" or "I don't worry. I'll wait the time it takes to accomplish that which I had decided upon earlier"). In this case the regulation is the inverse of the reciprocal and the compensation can best be designated *correlative*.

4. The attempts to invalidate and compromise the disturbing thought or action can be obviated by a total acceptance, which is then assimilated into the existing conceptual framework through rationalization ("Negative ideas about the future or frustrations which naturally come with making plans are all part of a person's life. One must learn how to live with them"). This double negation is the equivalent of a nontransformation or compensation through *identity*. Nevertheless, these regulations through positive feedback are often replaced by *noncompensatory acceptance* because the people involved desist from confronting their thoughts ("If I feel pessimistic about the future, I won't try to fight it because I am unable to" or "I won't try to ward off negative thoughts because it doesn't do any good. Pessimism is part of me" or "When I run into difficulties in accomplishing the choice I have made, I give up because I'm not going to be able to overcome them"). If the metaknowledge is not sufficient to compensate for the disturbance, then the rationalization process can also be unsuccessful ("I try to analyze those factors which have made me a pessimist and which cause me to fail in the realization of my plan, but this doesn't make me feel better, nor does it help me find another solution").

The compensations through inversion (N), reciprocity (R), correlation (C) and identity (I) correspond to Klein's group and, according to Piaget and Inhelder (1968), are characteristic of formal thought in that they connect the two forms of reversibility, which during the previous period of concrete thought had been separated. The inversion was applied to the realm of classes (simple operations of inclusion, multiple classifications, etc.), and reciprocity to the realm of relations (operations of simple seriation, correspondence compositions, etc.). In the *INRC* group, the two reversibilities are connected by the correlative compensation which permits a return to the system's starting point. And, in a general way, the four transformations are associated commutatively. Piaget gives the example of a snail which crawls on a board in motion. If I is the movement of the snail to the right, R the movement of the board to the left, N the snail's movement to the left, and C the movement of the board to the right, then the transformations IR equal those of NC and the system is in equilibrium. Formal reasoning also presupposes the acquisition of another group of compensating regulations which allow the propositions to reflect back on themselves or upon an exhaustive *combinatory* of classifications and relations. As I have already pointed out, however, we must be careful when it comes to transposing the formalizations of the physical world to those of the socio-affective. In this process the coordination between different compensations never attains "equilibrium of the emotional states" or "stability between beliefs and values." In these domains, thought is truly idiosyncratic. But in so far as there should be only one logic underlying these various types of reasoning, it is only natural that the individual should strive for a certain coherency between the two worlds.

Responses to questionnaires on self-monitoring of confrontation strategies indicate that the people who respond best to logico-causal problems of the Piagetian approach (in principle, they attend to levels of full formal reasoning) are those who employ the largest variety of metacognitive compensating strategies and who use these strategies much more frequently than they do the noncompensating or partially compensatory strategies. This group is also characterized by a marked preference for the principle of compromise involving acceptance or negation through reciprocity. In this case, a form of clinical intervention could correspond to the identification, acquisition, and coordination of compensating regulations or confrontation strategies. This does not mean, of course, that these mechanisms are the only determinants of the development of the client's epistemic status. But, from our perspective, the dialectic confrontation between patient and therapist ought to facilitate the client's metacognitive confrontation with problem situations.

Although confrontation techniques have, of course, extensive traditions in gestalt, behavioral, cognitive, and family-system therapies, each has its own theoretical framework and methodology. In analogous terms, the strategies of compensatory confrontation can be seen as a metacognitive subclass of that which generically is referred to as coping skills.

CONFRONTATION STRATEGIES FOR NEGATIVE FEELINGS AND PROBLEMS IN DECISION MAKING

An epistemologically oriented therapy has, most likely, a larger incidence of correction of "pervasive disorders (e.g., generalized anxiety, chronic depression, existential dilemmas, negative self-concept, psychoses)" as Mahoney calls them (1980, p. 177), than of "specific adjustment problems (e.g., phobias)." Every human being, at one point or another in his life, faces these types of problematic situations or multiple disturbances. Preliminary results of a study using our clients allow us to describe constructivistically pervasive disturbances in the following manner:

A. Accentuated horizontal displacements among different levels of socio-cognitive reasoning (e.g., attributes of incoherence and dissociation; stereotyped concepts and existential dilemmas; inconsiderate attitudes or, on the contrary, excessive hesitation or lack of confidence prior to taking action).

B. Difficulties in decentration or in changing one's viewpoint (e.g., attributes of dependency or excessive responsibility; irrational thoughts or errors in implications, propositions, etc.; difficulties in imagining alternatives; unassertive or asocial behavior).

C. Prevalent utilization of noncompensating thoughts and actions on disturbances (e.g., attributes of insatisfaction, submission, passivity, etc., which lead to pervasive fear or anxiety; negative and depressive thoughts; problems of gaining or losing interest in people and things).

D. Weak coordination of attempts at regulation or of confrontation strategies (e.g., magico-phenomenological attributes which can cause more specific fears; obsessive or Manichean thoughts; lack of flexibility in making decisions; aggressive or compulsive behavior).

The above four characteristics are all involved in the formation of each of the problem situations enclosed within parentheses. These situations, however, were grouped according to the metacognitive dysfunction which they most closely resembled.

Our attention has been especially attracted to two types of disturbances because of the facility with which both lead to an avoidance of confrontation or to inadequate attempts at regulation: negative feelings and problems in decision making. The term *negative feelings* is a general one describing the negativism connected to emotions (to be sad, irritated), to expectations (to be pessimistic about one's health, the future), to attributes (to feel disillusioned, guilty). The phrase "problems in decision making" is an equally general term used to describe the difficulties connected with choosing an alternative, programming activities and making plans, and the like. The examples that follow were taken from our studies in order to illustrate the integration of confrontation strategies in the therapeutic process. This one is divided into four phases:

RATIONALE

As in other cognitivist approaches, our rationale provides an explanation for the interdependence among cognitions, affects, and behavior and for the role played by the former in correction and modification of the latter ones. The therapist strives to have his client gain confidence in his own ability to control and overcome his difficulties and emphasizes the importance which the identification of self-verbalizations and emotive reactions has in problem situations, the utility of elaborating alternatives and programming activities, and so forth. Nevertheless, in this beginning phase, a more epistemological perspective involves the development of expectations related to the regulating role of metaknowledge. In this manner, the person is informed that the awareness of his psychological processes can help him change a distressing, threatening, or indecisive sensation into a challenge to which he should respond. The openness to different points of view and the coordination of confrontation strategies are some of the components of this response. We have had occasion to confirm that an understanding of the role which metaknowledge plays in the treatment induces a majority of clients to lessen or eliminate any eventual anxiety or opposition to active participation in their treatment and, as a result, to increase their feeling of responsibility concerning the results obtained.

IDENTIFICATION OF DISTURBING ELEMENTS

These elements have their response in two themes already touched upon: negative feelings and areas of indecision. Self-evaluation instruments generally employed in CBTs, be they the regular recording of self-observations or the identification of negative thoughts, inadequate beliefs, or alternative actions in scales, integrate themselves perfectly into our orientation. In our work, some of the instruments developed by Beck (1976, 1979) have been used with satisfactory results, most notably a modified version of his Depression Inventory, the Daily Record of Dysfunctional Thoughts, which allows the client to record in three separate columns the situation which precedes or accompanies the disorder, the excessive emotion, and the disturbing thought, and the Mastery and Pleasure Monitoring, which aids the client in defining the activities in which he deems himself to be most skillful or from which he derives most satisfaction.

In addition, it is wise to conduct an assessment of the socio-cognitive reasoning levels the client attends to by presenting him with hypothetical problems. As has already been mentioned, the therapist can utilize abstract operatory exercises which include transformations of physical properties (combination or compensation of states, forces, and movements) as well as transformations of self-attributes (conservation and individualization of physical and psychological attributes) and of dilemmatic social and moral situations. The instruments at hand are still deficient but they do give the therapist some indications of the client's structural repertoire and the principal displacements among his most elaborated levels of reasoning.

In this phase, the therapist asks the client to decenter so that he may evaluate the frequency of his various negative feelings and difficulties in making decisions from a triple point of view: his, that of his family and friends, and, as long as this record is kept during the entire process, that of the therapist, beginning with the second or third session. This procedure has turned out to be an invaluable indicator of the client's opinion about the evolution of therapy and of his prospective agreement about the gravity of each specific disturbance with the therapist and with the social environment.

EVALUATION OF CONFRONTATION STRATEGIES

The various forms of acceptance or negation of negative feelings and of combining and evaluating of alternatives in the decision-making process are a few of the confrontation strategies which we have been studying. This evaluation can be realized in the same fashion as in the previous phase—that is to say, by using the self-monitoring instruments or by using questionnaires. For example, the Daily Record of Dysfunctional Thoughts can accommodate a fourth column in which a person learns to record strategies of confronting or avoiding negative feelings. Consider, for example, the observations made by two students taking an exam: In the second column subject *A* writes "impatience" and subject *B* "anxiety"; in the third column, *A* writes, "It's difficult. I'm not going to finish on time" and *B* writes, "It's extremely difficult. I'm not going to be able to begin." In the fourth column, *A* expresses an inversion or complete negation: "It's absurd to worry like this. It only makes me lose time" and *B*, a noncompensatory rationalization: "I am a nervous person and don't accomplish anything because I have too many expectations."

Among other procedures, to facilitate decision making we drew upon a scale of reasoning which covers various levels, from preoperatory (e.g., "When I have to make a decision, I follow my first impulse. There's nothing like spontaneity") to the formal combinatory ("When I have to make a choice, I imagine the greatest number of possible alternatives. After which, I study the advantages and disadvantages of each one and systematically compare it to the advantages and disadvantages of the others. It's a lot of work but it produces results").

The dialectic relationship between client and therapist is, however, the most effective means of helping the client become aware of his strategies of compensation or to think about the strategies of others. The client should have the feeling that the dialogue is free-flowing, but the therapist structures the conversation by making use of at least two procedures:

1. Confrontation of the client with real or hypothetical personal situations:

T: Why is it that you tell me you have such great difficulty in deciding what are you going to do with your professional life?

C: Because staying at the place where I work is no good. Leaving also may turn to be bad. Or worse. . . .

T: Are you quite sure that you only have these two choices?

C: I don't see any others. Either I leave or I stay.

T: Tell me something. What do you do when you want to go for a walk or take a trip?

C: Uh, I don't travel much. Never enough money.

T: But what if you had enough money to be able to travel at will?

C: I would talk with somebody who had already traveled a lot and then choose what I considered to be the most interesting trip on the basis of my conversation.

T: In other words, before you make a decision you would consider a variety of possibilities and choose the best only after you had considered the pros and cons of each one. (*C* agrees) Do you think you do the same thing when you consider future job possibilities?

C: I think I do sometimes but don't ask advice from anybody.

2. Confrontation with an epistemic model:

T: In our conversations, I will be telling you about other people with problems similar to yours who have been in our clinic. They tell themselves certain things in order to fight their negative thoughts. I'm not going to tell you if these expressions are good or not, or if they are effective or not. You must tell me what you think. For example: A little while ago you said you often feel sad without special reason. What do you do on such occasions?

C: Nothing. I'm unable to do anything. I'm almost always sad.

T: Another of our clients who is trying to fight sadness does so by telling herself that it doesn't do anybody any good to keep thinking about that.

C: I think that that attitude could be a healthy one but it doesn't work for me.

T: That means you have already tried it . . .

C: I don't believe so, but I know it won't work for me. I'm always depressed. That's the way I am.

T: Another client has already told me that nobody is like that. Everybody has moments when he is sad and others when he is cheerful.

C: That was true for me a long time ago. Now I'm always sad.

T: But you do remember the good things that happened to you in the past?

C: Yes.

T: And how do you feel when you remember those things?

C: Less sad.

T: Sometimes, then, you think you are unable to fight your sadness and other times you do the opposite by thinking of the good things that have already happened to you.

C: At times I think that things do change. And when that happens, probably I'm not so depressed.

If the client readily makes use of the same strategies of confrontation in various personal situations or rapidly adheres to the regulations of the models, then the therapist should adjust the dialogue to the levels of sociocognitive reasoning previously considered here. For example, the client considers the strategy employed effective because it satisfies the model's objectives point by point or because it satisfies his own objectives in a different context ("If it was successful with me in another situation, it's because it's a good thing which I also should have thought about already"). In this case, the therapist broadens the dialectic confrontation in order to test the client's power of resistance to an opposing argument and, in this way, of maintaining the previous strategy. This counterproof is made through the presentation of a model with a different perspective from that of the models which gave rise to adhesion, or through the presentation of a personal situation in which the client is accustomed to appraising himself from another point of view.

T: A while ago, we spoke about selecting a trip. But what do you do when you have to make an important sentimental decision?
C: Ah, it's my heart that makes the decision.
T: Does your heart also make the decision when it comes to your job?

On a more structured level, the client thinks that the strategy is correct because it is in compliance with the normative expectations that he has chosen concerning individual conduct or because he has aligned himself with the majority's behavior ("If these people are capable of knowing how things really work, I should adopt their ideas"). Confronted with this conventionalism, the therapist attempts to have the interlocutor think about his stereotypes, pointing out that it is normal for a person to change strategies, or he introduces a new model which underlines the necessity for these processes to become individualized.

T: I've already told you that I have a client who doesn't worry when he feels sad, because he knows that he will feel better when the sadness goes away. And you stated that you do the same thing. But I would like to call your attention to another client who believes that this attitude is worthless. What one must do is fight sadness in any way whatsoever. Which of these two clients do you think is correct and why?

COORDINATION AND IMPLEMENTATION OF CONFRONTATION STRATEGIES

This phase is that of metacognitive restructuring *per se*. As has already been mentioned, the therapist conducts the dialectic process so that the client is given the possibility to make adequate use of the previously identified compensatory strategies not only according to his different negative feelings and areas of indecision, but also to his structural repertoire. In effect, the acquired operatory structures determine the client's ability to accept, combine, or transform the mechanisms of compensation. The ongoing of process can occur in different ways, although once again by means of a confrontation with real or hypothetical situations or with models. Let us look at some:

a. In each problem situation, the person experiences the thoughts or the activities of confrontation identified in the previous phase. The overall objective is to help him think about the usefulness of replacing his noncompensatory strategies with the largest possible number of effective ones ("Now that you're already familiar with various ways of making a decision, you'll try to apply them, one by one, to your problem and see which ones help you most to put your choice into practice"). When it is impossible to confront directly a certain feeling during a session, the therapist should make use of other negative feelings that the interlocutor associates with the feeling in question ("You've mentioned that you're incapable of fighting against that feeling of dissatisfaction with everything you undertake because you also feel guilty. But we have already observed that people use a variety of thoughts to deal with the feeling of unfounded guilt. I'd like you to try them all").

b. The testing of strategies includes an investigation of their implications. For example, the client might consider that the same compensatory regulation gives different results in accord with the time or the situation to which it is applied, that two strategies used in succession turn out to be incompatible to one another, and so on. ("You told me that thinking about positive things works when you're distressed about the future, but has no effect when you feel disillusioned about your work. Let us see if we can't find another strategy which produces results in both instances"). Because contradiction itself is an incomplete compensation between acceptance and negation, the therapist checks to see if the client cannot make recursive compensations from other compensations by adopting strategies which are more and more open, flexible and generalizing, for example, combinations of different forms of compromise ("We've seen that when you're angry you tell yourself that it doesn't do any good to feel that way. Sometimes this works but at other times you feel even more angry. The same thing happens when you think about how you feel when you're calm. I'm sure that you'll successfully unite these two strategies so that you'll always get good results. Let us see how").

c. The coordination of strategies used at different moments or on different levels (for example, compensations of the combinatory type with those of the *INRC* type):

T: When a conflict with your family arises, you don't hesitate to follow what your instinct tells you in order to patch things up. Has this worked well?

C: It depends on the effort I make to realize that which I've decided at the moment. Sometimes I do everything I possibly can and at other times I give up because I know I'm not going to convince anybody.

T: I have a client who also does everything possible to put into practice that which she has decided to do. But instead of following her instinct, she imagines various ways of solving her conflict, examines each one very carefully, and then chooses the one that seems the best. Tell me if you think this procedure can be applied to your situation.

d. This phase also includes the implementation of strategies right in the real environment. The dialectic orientation should not be divorced from this process of transposition. An interesting way of prolonging the confrontation outside the consulting room is to systematize the utilization of a cognitive and behavioral *contract:* "Set up a contract with yourself in which you pledge to think in terms of strategy X when you feel pessimistic and if this doesn't work, think in terms of strategy Y" or "Set up a contract with the members of your family in order to put into practice the decision you all made together. If somebody doesn't respect that decision then make him pledge to employ strategy X. If the violation is but a minor one, then try to reach an understanding—strategy Y."

It has also been mentioned that although the therapist adapts the dialectic process to the person's structural repertoire, he seeks to facilitate the client's progression to more advanced levels of reasoning. After several unsuccessful attempts to attain this objective, we are trying out an adaptation of the devil's advocate technique (Goldfried & Davison, 1976). For example, at a certain level, the person is almost always unable to maintain his own perspective when he tries to put himself in someone else's place. The therapist, therefore, first requests the client to anticipate the compensatory strategies of the models already presented and then asks him to consider the points of view of these models favorably or negatively from his own point of view. On a more elaborated level, the client succeeds in seeing things from the perspective of one or two people, all the time maintaining his perspective with that of the others, but he has difficulty in taking the community's general viewpoint into consideration. In this case, after having anticipated the strategies people use the most, or the way they combine them, the client then examines this general perspective and argues in favor of it or against it, not only from his point of view but from that of each of the models presented.

FINAL COMMENTS

The suggestions or the considerations of the previous pages do not in any way pretend to exhaust the characterizations of the therapeutic change. Rather, they attempt only to delineate an approach to the process of natural transformation involved in sociocognitive development. Furthermore, the therapeutic strategy selected—that of confrontation—and the clinical examples presented—negative feelings and problems in decision making—permit only an incomplete response to the epistemological appeal made in the first part of this chapter.

As was suggested in the beginning, I think it is less important to invent new models than to rearrange already existing ones in such a way that they can be oriented epistemologically. A reader might remark that I have not done this and that I merely have cast more methodological novelties into Pandora's box. My purpose, however, is not to disclose a new and idyllic view of cognitive ability. In this regard, I am reminded of Manet's famous painting, *Le Déjeuner sur l'Herbe*. As all know, this painting caused a tremendous scandal when it was first displayed in the 1860s in Paris. Later, art historians realized that Manet had obviously based his work on an engraving of the judgment of Paris by Raimondi, who had taken the idea from his worthy master Raphael, who in turn had been inspired by a bas-relief of classical Rome. Over the centuries, a series of artists had made use of the same aesthetic lines, adapting the form to their personal style or to the taste of the period. Exactly the same thing happens with cognitive therapies. The same tricks of confrontation, reinforcement, modeling, self-instruction, or whatever are presented but enclosed within a wide variety of paradigmatic lines or Pandora boxes. Could this indicate that the underlying mechanisms involved in therapeutic change are always the same, that is, that we always paint the same picture but with different colors, light, and forms?

From my point of view, the answer to this question must be sought in the therapeutic frontier of the client's epistemology.

REFERENCES

Arnkoff, D. B. Psychotherapy from the perspective of cognitive theory. In M. J. Mahoney (Ed.), *Psychotherapy process*. New York: Plenum Press, 1980.

Bandura, A. *Social learning theory*. Englewood Cliffs, NJ: Prentice Hall, 1977.

Beck, A. T. *Cognitive therapy and the emotional disorders*. New York: International Universities Press, 1976.

Beck, A. T., Rush, A. J., Shaw, B. F., & Emery, G. *Cognitive therapy of depression.* New York: Wiley, 1979.

Connel, R. *The child's construction of politics.* Melbourne: University Press, 1971.

D'Zurilla, T. J., and Goldfried, M. R. Problem solving and behavior modification. *Journal of Abnormal Psychology,* 1971, *78,* 107–126.

Ekman, P., Krasner, L., & Ullmann, L. P. Interaction of set and awareness as determinants of response to verbal conditioning. *Journal of Abnormal and Social Psychology,* 1963, *66,* 387–389.

Ellis, A. *Reason and emotion in psychotherapy.* New York: Lyle Stuart, 1962.

Ellis, A. Rational-emotive therapy and cognitive-behavior therapy: Similarities and differences. *Cognitive Therapy and Research,* 1980, *4,* 325–340.

Frank, J. D. *Persuasion and healing.* Baltimore: John Hopkins University Press, 1961.

Garfield, S. L. Research on client variables in psychotherapy. In A. E. Bergin & S. L. Garfield (Eds.), *Handbook of psychotherapy and behavior change* (2nd ed.). New York: Wiley, 1978.

Goldfried, M. R. Systematic desensitization as training in self-control. *Journal of Consulting and Clinical Psychology,* 1971, *37,* 228–234.

Goldfried, M. R., & Davison, G. C. *Clinical behavior therapy.* New York: Holt, Rinehart & Winston, 1976.

Goldfried, M. R., Decenteo, E. T., & Weinberg, L. Systematic rational restructuring as a self-control technique. *Behavior Therapy,* 1974, *5,* 247–254.

Goldstein, A. P. *Therapist–patient expectancies in psychotherapy.* New York: Pergamon, 1962.

Goldstein, A. P. *Structured learning therapy: Toward a psychotherapy for the poor.* New York: Academic Press, 1973.

Gordon, T. *PET: Parent Effectiveness Training.* New York: Wyden, 1970.

Hoffman, M. L. Empathy, role-taking, guilt and development of altruistic motives. In T. Lickona (Ed.), *Moral development and behavior.* New York: Holt, Rinehart & Winston, 1976.

Holstein, C. B. Irreversible, stepwise sequence in the development of moral judgment: A longitudinal study of males and females. *Child Development,* 1976, *47,* 51–61.

Jakubowski, P., & Lange, A. J. *The assertive option: Your rights and responsibilities.* Champaign, IL: Research Press Company, 1978.

Joyce-Moniz, L. *Self-cognition: A cognitive-developmental approach to self-understanding.* Paper presented at the annual meeting of the American Educational Research Association, San Francisco, 1976.

Joyce-Moniz, L. Mécanismes de compensation et de rééquilibration dans le développement socio-affectif de l'enfant et de l'adulte. *Revue Suisse de Psychologie Pure et Appliquée,* 1978, *37,* 117–127.

Joyce-Moniz, L. *Développement socio-cognitif et auto-contrôle de la pensée.* Paper presented at the 9th European Congress of Behavioural Therapy, Paris, 1979. (a)

Joyce-Moniz, L. Perspectivas cognitivistas no desenvolvimento socio-afectivo do 'self'. In C. Jesuino, G. Pereira, & J. Moniz (Eds.), *Desenvolvimento psicológico da crianca* (Vol. *2,* 2 Tomo). Lisbon: Morais, 1979. (b)

Joyce-Moniz, L. *New decentering techniques in cognitive assertive training.* Paper presented at the Annual Conference of the British Association for Behavioural Therapy, Sheffield, 1980.

Joyce-Moniz, L. Perspectives constructivistes dans le mouvement thérapeutique cognitiviste. *Revue de Modification du Comportement,* 1981, *11,* 83–90. (a)

Joyce-Moniz, L. *From decentration to compensation: Toward a cognitive-constructivist therapy.* Paper presented at the First European Meeting on Cognitive-Behavioural Therapies, Lisbon: 1981. (b)

Kazdin, A. E. Imagery elaboration and self-efficacy in the covert modeling treatment of unassertive behavior. *Journal of Consulting and Clinical Psychology,* 1979, *47,* 725–733.

Kelly, G. A. *The psychology of personal constructs.* New York: Norton, 1955.

Kendall, P. C. On the efficacious use of verbal self-instructional procedures with children. *Cognitive Therapy and Research,* 1977, *1,* 331–341.

Kohlberg, L. Stage and sequence: The cognitive-developmental approach to socialization. In D. A. Goslin (Ed.), *Handbook of socialization theory and research.* Chicago: Rand McNally, 1969.

Kohlberg, L., & Ullian, D. Stages in the development of psychosexual concepts and attitudes. In R. Friedman, R. Richart, R. Wiele, & L. Stern (Eds.), *Sex differences in behavior.* New York: Wiley, 1974.

Kuhn, D., Langer, L., & Kohlberg, L. Attainment of formal operations. *Genetic Psychology Monographs,* 1977, *1,* 97–188.

Kuhn, T. S. *The structure of scientific revolutions.* Chicago: University of Chicago Press, 1962.

Lazarus, A. A. Group therapy of phobic disorders. *Journal of Abnormal and Social Psychology,* 1961, *63,* 504–512.

Lazarus, A. A., & Fay, A. Resistance or rationalization? A cognitive-behavioral perspective. In P. L. Wachtel (Ed.), *Resistance: Psychodynamic and behavioral approaches.* New York: Plenum Press, 1982.

Lickona, T. Critical issues in the study of moral development and behavior. In T. Lickona (Ed.), *Moral development and behavior.* New York: Holt, Rinehart & Winston, 1976.

Liotti, G., & Reda, M. Some epistemological remarks on behavior therapy, cognitive therapy and psychoanalysis. *Cognitive Therapy and Research,* 1981, *5,* 231–236.

Luria, A. *The role of speech in the regulation of normal and abnormal behavior.* New York: Liveright, 1961.

Mahoney, M. J. *Cognition and behavior modification.* Cambridge, MA: Ballinger, 1974.

Mahoney, M. J. Psychotherapy and the structure of personal revolutions. In M. J. Mahoney (Ed.), *Psychotherapy process.* New York: Plenum Press, 1980.

Mahoney, M. J., & Arnkoff, D. B. Cognitive and self-control therapies. In S. L. Garfield & A. E. Bergin (Eds.), *Handbook of psychotherapy and behavior change (2nd ed.). New York: Wiley, 1978.*

Mahoney, M. J., & Thoresen, C. E. (Eds.). *Self-control: Power to the person.* Monterey, CA: Brooks/Cole, 1974.

Meichenbaum, D. *Cognitive behavior modification: An integrative approach.* New York: Plenum Press, 1977.

Meichenbaum, D., & Butler, L. Egocentrism and evidence: Making Piaget kosher. In M. J. Mahoney (Ed.), *Psychotherapy process.* New York: Plenum Press, 1980.

Meichenbaum, D., & Cameron, R. Cognitive behavior modification: Current issues. In C. M. Frank & G. T. Wilson (Eds.), *Handbook of behavior therapy.* New York: Guilford, 1980.

Mischel, W., & Mischel, H. N. A cognitive social-learning approach to morality and self-regulation. In T. Lickona (Ed.), *Moral development and behavior.* New York: Holt, Rinehart & Winston, 1976.

Neisser, U. Three cognitive psychologies and their implications. In M. J. Mahoney (Ed.), *Psychotherapy process.* New York: Plenum Press, 1980.

Paul, G. L. *Effects of insight, desensitization, and attention placebo treatment of anxiety.* Stanford, CA: Stanford University Press, 1966.

Piaget, J. *L'équilibration des structures cognitives.* Paris: Presses Universitaires de France, 1975.

Piaget, J., & Inhelder, B. *La psychologie de l'enfant.* Paris: Presses Universitaires de France, 1968.

Rickels, K., & Anderson, F. L. Attrited and completed lower socioeconomic class clinic patients in psychiatric drug therapy. *Comprehensive Psychiatry,* 1967, *8,* 90–99.

Saltzman, C., Luetgert, M. J., Roth, C. H., Creaser, J., & Howard, L. Formation of a therapeutic relationship. *Journal of Consulting and Clinical Psychology,* 1976, *44,* 546–555.

Selman, R. L. Socio-cognitive understandings: A guide to educational and clinical practice. In T. Lickona (Ed.), *Moral development and behavior.* New York: Holt, Rinehart & Winston, 1976.

Sloane, R. B., Staples, F. R., Cristol, A. H., Yorkston, N. J., & Whipple, K. *Psychotherapy versus behavior therapy.* Cambridge, MA: Harvard University Press, 1975.

Sollod, R. N., & Wachtel, P. L. A structural and transactional approach to cognition in clinical problems. In M. J. Mahoney (Ed.), *Psychotherapy process.* New York: Plenum Press, 1980.

Spivack, G., Platt, J. J., & Shure, M. B. *The problem-solving approach to adjustment.* San Francisco: Jossey/Bass, 1976.

Storms, M. D., & Nisbett, R. E. Insomnia and attribution process. *Journal of Personality and Social Psychology,* 1970, *2,* 319–328.

Von Glasersfeld, E. The concepts of adaptation and viability in a radical constructivist theory of knowledge. In I. E. Sigel, D. M. Brodzinsky, & R. M. Golinkoff (Eds.), *New directions in piagetian theory and practice.* Hillsdale, NJ: Erlbaum, 1981.

Weimer, W. B. Science as a rhetorical transaction. *Philosophy and Rhetoric,* 1977, *10,* 1–29.

Weimer, W. B. Psychotherapy and philosophy of science: Examples of a two-way street in search of traffic. In M. J. Mahoney (Ed.), *Psychotherapy process.* New York: Plenum Press, 1980.

Wilson, G. T. Toward specifying the "nonspecific" factors in behavior therapy. In M. J. Mahoney (Ed.), *Psychotherapy process.* New York: Plenum Press, 1980.

Wolpe, J. Cognitive behavior and its roles in psychotherapy: An integrative account. In M. J. Mahoney (Ed.), *Psychotherapy process.* New York: Plenum Press, 1980.

Wolpe, J., & Lazarus, A. A. *Behavior therapy techniques: A guide to the treatment of neuroses.* London: Pergamon, 1966.

Zimmerman, B. J. Social learning theory and cognitive constructivism. In I. E. Sigel, D. M. Brodzinsky, & R. M. Golinkoff (Eds.), *New directions in Piagetian theory and practice.* Hillsdale, NJ: Erlbaum, 1981.

CHAPTER 6

The Role of Childhood Experience in Cognitive Disturbance

JOHN BOWLBY

The evidence that adverse experiences with parents during childhood play a large part in causing cognitive disturbance is now substantial. For example, at least some cases in which perceptions and attributions are distorted and some states of amnesia, both minor and major including cases of multiple personality, can be shown with considerable confidence to be the outcome of such experiences. Yet systematic research into these causal sequences is still scarce. Having myself recognized the importance of the area a little belatedly, all that I can do in this brief chapter is to open a door to a field calling urgently for a major research effort.

Before doing so, however, it is worth considering why the field has been so neglected.

Ever since 1897 when Freud changed his mind about the role of childhood seduction in the etiology of hysteria and decided, instead, that the alleged episodes were the fruits of fantasy, there has been reluctance to give weight to the real-life experiences of childhood. To do so has often been regarded as naive, or else as mere scapegoating of parents. Coupled with these prejudices has been the tendency of

This chapter is an expanded version of an article titled "On Knowing What You Are Not Supposed to Know and Feeling What You Are Not Supposed to Feel" which appeared in the *Canadian Journal of Psychiatry*, 1979, *24*, 403–408. Permission to reprint is gratefully acknowledged.

JOHN BOWLBY • Tavistock Institute, 120 Belsize Lane, London, NW 3, England.

those who have nonetheless looked for relevant real-life experiences to focus on such variables as bottle- versus breast-feeding or type of toilet training, which have subsequently been shown to be of negligible or at most marginal significance.

Added to that, moreover, is the undoubted difficulty of doing systematic research in the field. For example, those engaged in seeing only adult patients are usually ill-placed to investigate events alleged to have occurred many years earlier. Those whose childhoods have been spent amongst reasonably stable families and who, like all too many psychiatrists and psychotherapists, are ignorant of the recent family and child development literature, have no norms against which to match their patients' stories. Above all, clinicians are often faced with a blanket of silence, from patient and family alike, which neither training nor their experience has qualified them to penetrate. Little wonder, therefore, if the likelihood that many cases of psychiatric disorder, both mild and grave, having had their origins in adverse events of childhood have been discounted or else completely ignored—not only by general psychiatrists but by psychotherapists as well. Even the fact that some children are physically or sexually assaulted by their own parents, often repeatedly and over long periods, is missing from discussions of causal factors in psychiatry.

Today the scene is changing. First, knowledge of parent–child interactions in general, including a wide range of potentially pathogenic relationships and events, is increasing in both quality and quantity as systematic research is applied. Secondly, the psychological consequences for the children exposed to these relationships and events are becoming much better understood and documented. As a result, there are now many occasions when a clinician is on reasonably firm ground in drawing etiological conclusions. This is so especially when (a) his patient presents problems and symptoms which resemble the known consequences of certain types of experience and (b) when in the course of skilled history-taking, or perhaps much later during therapy, he is told of experiences of these same types. In reaching his conclusion, the reasoning a psychiatrist uses differs in no way from that of a physician who, having diagnosed a patient as suffering from mitral stenosis, proceeds unhesitatingly to attribute the condition to an attack of rheumatic fever suffered by the patient many years earlier.

When considering childhood antecedents of cognitive disorders, a good place to start is with amnesia.

In one of his classical papers on analytic technique, Freud (1914) made an important generalization, the truth of which probably every psychotherapist would endorse:

> Forgetting impressions, scenes or experiences nearly always reduces itself
> to shutting them off. When the patient talks about these "forgotten" things
> he seldom fails to add: "As a matter of fact, I've always known it; only
> I've never thought of it." (p. 148)

Such observations call for explanations of at least three kinds. First, are there special features that characterize the impressions, scenes, and experiences that tend to become shut off? Second, how do we best conceive of the processes by which memories become shut off and apparently forgotten? Third, what are the causal conditions, internal and external to the personality, that activate the shutting-off process?

The scenes and experiences that tend to become shut-off, though often continuing to be extremely influential in affecting thought, feeling, and behavior, fall into at least three distinct categories:

a. those that parents wish their children not to know about
b. those in which parents have treated children in ways the children find too unbearable to think about
c. those in which children have done, or perhaps thought, things about which they feel unbearably guilty or ashamed.

Since a great deal of attention has for long been given to the third category, here I discuss only the first two. We start with the first.

Children not infrequently observe scenes that parents would prefer they did not observe; they form impressions that parents would prefer they did not form; and they have experiences that parents would like to believe they have not had. Evidence shows that many of these children, aware of how their parents feel, proceed then to conform to their parents' wishes by excluding from further processing such information as they already have; and that, having done so, they cease consciously to be aware that they have ever observed such scenes, formed such impressions or had such experiences. Here, I believe, is a source of cognitive disturbance as common as it is neglected.

Yet, evidence that parents sometimes press their children to shut off from further, conscious, processing information the children already have about events that the parents wish they had never observed comes from several sources. Perhaps the most vivid concerns the efforts made by a surviving parent to obliterate his or her child's knowledge of the (other) parent's suicide.

Cain and Fast (1972) report findings from their study of a series of 45 children, aged between four and fourteen, all of whom had lost a parent by suicide and all of whom had become psychiatrically disturbed, many of them severely so. In reviewing their data, the authors were struck by the very large roles played in the children's symptomatology by their having been exposed to pathogenic situations of two types, namely situations in which intense guilt is likely to be engendered (not discussed here) and situations in which communications between parent and child are gravely distorted.

About one-quarter of the children studied had personally witnessed some aspect of the parent's death and had subsequently been subjected to pressure from the surviving parent to believe that they were mistaken in what they had seen or heard and that the death had not been due to suicide but to some illness or accident:

> A boy who watched his father kill himself with a shotgun ... was told later that night by his mother that his father had died of a heart attack; a girl who discovered her father's body hanging in a closet was told he had died in a car accident; and two brothers who had found their mother with her wrists slit were told she had drowned while swimming. (Cain & Fast, 1972, p. 102)

When a child described what he had seen, the surviving parent had sought to discredit it either by ridicule or by insisting that he was confused by what he had seen on television or by some bad dream he had had. Such confusion was sometimes compounded, moreover, by the child's hearing several different stories about the death from different people or even from his surviving parent.

Many of the children's psychological problems seemed directly traceable to their having been exposed to situations of these kinds. Their problems included chronic distrust of other people, inhibition of their curiosity, distrust of their own senses, and a tendency to find everything unreal.

Rosen (1955) describes an adult patient, a man of 27, who developed acute symptoms after his fiancée had jilted him because she had found him too moody and unpredictable. The patient began to feel that the world about him and also his own being were fragmenting and that everything was unreal. He became depressed and suicidal and experienced a variety of peculiar bodily sensations, which included a feeling that he was choking. His thoughts, he said, felt like cotton-wool. Some time during the second year of therapy, the analyst, struck by a series of associations the patient gave and bearing in mind the life history, ventured a reconstruction, namely that the patient's mother may have made a suicide attempt during the patient's childhood that he (the patient) had witnessed. No sooner had this suggestion been offered than the patient became racked with convulsive sobbing. The session proved a turning point. Subsequently, the patient described how it had seemed to him that, when the analyst made his suggestion, it was not so much that he was restoring a memory as giving him (the patient) permission to talk about something he had always in some way known about.

The authenticity of the memory was vouched for by the patient's father who admitted, when pressed, that the patient's mother had made several suicide attempts during the patient's childhood. The one the patient had witnessed occurred some time during his third year. His nurse had heard sounds in the bathroom and had arrived in time to prevent his mother from strangling herself. It was not clear just how much the little boy had seen. But whenever later he had mentioned the event both father and nurse had disconfirmed his memories by alleging that it was something he must have imagined or had simply been a bad dream. His father now claimed that he had felt it would have been harmful to his son to have remembered such an incident; but he also admitted that his attitude was dictated partly by his wish that the incident be kept secret from friends and neighbors. A year or so later the nurse had been discharged because the mother had found her presence too painful a reminder of the incident.

During one of the sessions before the vital reconstruction was offered, the patient had recalled the discharge of his beloved nurse as an event which he had always felt had been in some way his fault. Among many associations to it were recurrent references to his having been, as a child, witness to something that had changed his life, though he did not know what. He also had the notion that his nurse had been the one witness on his behalf. Thus, although the memory had been shut away from conscious processing, it continued to influence both what he thought and how he felt.

Elsewhere (Bowlby, 1973) I have drawn attention to the far from negligible incidence of suicidal attempts made by parents, and perhaps the even higher incidence of their threatening suicide, and have remarked how little attention has been given to either attempts or threats in the psychiatric and psychotherapeutic literature. Perhaps there are many more cases similar to Rosen's than has yet been realized.

Among the many other situations that parents may wish a child had not observed and that they may press him to suppose he never did are those concerning their sexual activities. An example of this was told me by a speech therapist who was trying to help an extremely disturbed little girl who hardly spoke at all. That she was well able to speak was, however, shown on certain dramatic occasions. She would sit a Teddy bear on a chair in a corner, then go over and, shaking her finger at him, would scold him in tones of extreme severity: "You're *naughty—naughty Teddy*—you *didn't* see that—you *didn't* see that, I tell you!" This she repeated again and again with increasing vehemence. What the scenes were that Teddy was being instructed he never saw was not difficult to guess: the little girl's mother was a teenage prostitute.

Clearly the purpose of these pressures by parents is to ensure that their children develop and maintain a wholly favorable picture of them. In the examples thus far given the form of pressure exerted is crude. More frequent perhaps and just as damaging are instances in which the pressures are more subtle.

During the past two decades renewed attention has been paid to incest, both to its unrecognized high incidence and to its pathogenic effects on children. Much the commonest forms are between father and daughter or stepfather and stepdaughter. Among the various problems and symptoms in the children and adolescents concerned that are believed to be due to these experiences, the commonest include withdrawal from all intimate relationships, sleep disturbances, and suicidal intentions (Adams-Tucker, 1982; Meiselman, 1978). An account of conditions likely to cause cognitive disturbance is given by MacCarthy (in preparation); he suspects disturbance to be especially likely when the children are prepubertal. In what follows I draw on his conclusions.

When a sexual liaison develops between a father and his adolescent daughter, MacCarthy reports, the liaison is usually acknowledged by the father during the course of daily life by such means as secret glances, secret touching and innuendoes. In the case of a younger child, however, a father is likely to make no such acknowledgments. Instead, he behaves during the day as though the nightly episodes never occurred, and this total failure to acknowledge them is commonly maintained even long after the daughter has reached adolescence.

MacCarthy describes the case of a married woman, Mrs. A., whom he treated for depression and reliance on tranquilizers and alcohol and who mentioned the ten years of sexual interference she had suffered from her adoptive father only after she had been in therapy for four months. It had begun when she was five or six, soon after her adoptive mother had died, and had continued until she was sixteen, when she had fled. Among her many problems were frigidity and finding intercourse disgusting, and a sense of inner blackness, of "a black stain." Her problems had become exacerbated when her own daughter was four years old. Whenever the daughter became affectionate to father and sat near him, Mrs. A. felt agitated, protective and jealous; on these occasions she could never leave them alone together. During therapy she was obsequious and terrified, and intensely vigilant of the analyst's every move.

In regard to the incestuous relationship, Mrs. A. described how her adoptive father would never at any time during the day allude to his nocturnal visits to her room, which had always remained darkened. On the contrary, he had lectured her incessantly on the dangers of allowing boys to go too far, and on the importance of chastity before marriage. When at the age of sixteen she had fled the home, he not only insisted she tell no one, but added sarcastically: "And if you do no one will believe you." This could well have been so since her adoptive father was a headmaster and the local mayor.

In commenting on this and similar cases, MacCarthy emphasizes the cognitive split between the respected and perhaps loved father of daytime and the very different father of the strange events of the night before. Warned on no account to breathe a word to anyone, including her mother, the child looks to her father for some confirmation of those events and is naturally bewildered when there is no response. Did it really happen or did I dream it? Have I two fathers? Small wonder if in later years all men are distrusted, and the professional stance of a male therapist is seen as a mere facade that hides a predatory intent. Small wonder also if the injunction on no account to tell anyone remains operative and if the expectation that in any case no one would believe you ensures silence. How often, we may wonder, do ill-informed therapists discourage a patient from telling the truth and, should she do so nonetheless, confirm her expectation that no one will believe her story?

In the examples so far described, the information a parent is pressing a child to shut away is information relating to events in the outside world. In other situations the information to be shut away relates to events in the child's private world of feeling. Nowhere does this occur more commonly than in situations of separation and loss.

When a parent dies, the surviving parent or other relative may not only provide the children with inadequate or misleading information but he or she may also indicate that it would not be appropriate for the child even to be distressed. This may be explicit: Miller (1979a) describes how, when a six-year-old's mother died, his aunt told him, "Don't cry; now go to your room and play nicely." At other times the indication is only implicit. Not infrequently widows or widowers, afraid to express their own distress, in effect encourage their children to shut away all the feeling they are having about their loss. Palgi (1973) describes how a small boy whose mother was chiding him for not shedding tears over his father's death retorted: "How can I cry when I have never seen your tears?"

There are in fact many situations in which a child is expressly told not to cry. For example, a child of five whose nanny is leaving is told not to cry because that would make it more difficult for nanny. A child whose parents leave him in hospital or a residential nursery insist he not cry, otherwise they will not visit him. A child whose parents are frequently away and who leave him with one of a succession of *au pair* girls is not encouraged to recognize how lonely, and perhaps angry, he feels at their constant absence. When parents separate it is often made plain to a child that he is not expected to miss the departing parent or to pine for the parent's return. Not only are sorrow and crying condemned as inappropriate in such situations, but older children and adults may jeer at a distressed child for being a crybaby. Is there any wonder that in such circumstances feeling should become shut away?

All these situations are plain enough but have, I believe, been seriously neglected as causes of information and feeling becoming excluded from consciousness. There are, however, other situations also, more subtle and hidden but no less common, that have the same effect. One such arises when a mother, who herself had a childhood deprived of love, seeks from her own child the love she has hitherto lacked. In doing this she is inverting the normal parent–child relationship—requiring the child to act as parent while she becomes the child. To someone unaware of what is going on it may appear that the child is being "overindulged," but a closer look shows that mother is placing a heavy burden on him. What is of special relevance here is that more often than not the child is expected to be grateful for such care as he receives and not to notice the demands being made upon him. One result of this is that, in conformity with his mother's wishes, he builds up a one-sided picture of her as wholly loving and generous, thereby shutting away from conscious processing much information also reaching him that she is often selfish, demanding, and ungrateful. Another result is that, also in conformity with his mother's wishes, he admits to consciousness only feelings of love and gratitude toward her and shuts away every feeling of anger he may have toward her for expecting him to care for her and for preventing him from making his own friends and living his own life.

A related situation is one in which a parent, having had a traumatic childhood, is apprehensive of being reminded of past miseries and so becoming depressed. As a result, her children are required always to appear happy and to avoid any expression of sorrow, loneliness, or anger. As one patient put it to me after a good deal of therapy: "I see now that I was terribly lonely as a child but I was never allowed to know it."

Most children are indulgent toward their parents, preferring to see them in a favorable light and eager to overlook many deficiencies. Yet, they do not willingly conform to seeing a parent only in the light the parent requires or to feeling toward him or her only in the way demanded. To ensure that, pressure must be exerted. Pressure can take different forms but all forms depend for their effectiveness on the child's insistent desire to be loved and protected. Miller (1979b), who has given these problems much attention, reports the words of an adult patient who was born the eldest child of an insecure professional woman:

> I was the jewel in my mother's crown. She often said: "Maja can be relied upon, she will cope." And I did cope. I brought up the smaller children for her so that she could get on with her professional career. She became more and more famous, but I never saw her happy. How often I longed for her in the evenings. The little ones cried and I comforted them but I myself never cried. Who would have wanted a crying child? I could only win my mother's love if I was competent, understanding and controlled; if I never questioned her actions nor showed her how much I missed her; that would have limited her freedom which she needed so much. That would have turned her against me.

In other families pressures are less subtle. One form, threatening to abandon a child as a means of controlling him, is an extremely powerful weapon, especially with a young child. Faced with such threats, how could a child do other than conform to his parents' wishes by excluding from further processing all that he knows they wish him to forget? Elsewhere I have given reasons for believing that threats of this sort are responsible for much acute and chronic anxiety (Bowlby, 1973) and also for a person responding to bereavement in later life with chronic depression in which the dominant belief is one of having been deliberately abandoned, as a punishment, by the dead person (Bowlby, 1980).

The hypothesis advanced, that various forms of cognitive disturbance seen in children and also in later life are to be traced to influences acting initially during the preadolescent years, is compatible with indications that during these years children's minds are especially sensitive to outside influence. Evidence of this, already emphasized, is the extent to which young children are vulnerable to threats by parents to reject or even abandon them. After a child has reached adolescence, clearly, his vulnerability to such threats diminishes.

The extent to which the minds of preadolescent children are prone to the influence of parents is well illustrated by an experiment of Gill (1970). The sample comprised 10-year-old children drawn from a London primary school and their parents. Of the 40 nonimmigrant families invited to participate, 25 agreed. Each family was visited in its own home and a series of ten pictures shown on a screen, each for two minutes.

Of the pictures used, five came from picture-book or film and the rest from thematic apperception tests. Some were emotionally benign; for example, a mother watching a small girl holding a baby. Some showed scenes of an aggressive and/or frightening sort. Three depicted a sexual theme: a woman obviously pregnant lying on a bed; a couple embracing on the grass; and a woman clutching the shoulders of a man who seems to be pulling away, with the picture of a seminude woman in the background.

The series of ten pictures was presented three times in succession. On the first showing, father, mother, and child were asked to write down, independently, what they saw happening in the picture. On the second, members of the family were asked to discuss each picture for the two minutes it was shown. During the third showing, each member was asked again to write down, independently, what they now saw happening.

When the children's responses to the three pictures depicting sexual themes were examined, it was found that whereas half the children (12) described the sexual themes in a fairly direct matter-of-fact way, the other half failed to do so. For example, to the picture of the obviously pregnant woman, one child's candid response ran: "She's having a rest. I can see that she's expecting a baby. She's asleep, I think." Descriptions of the same picture by other children omitted all reference to pregnancy: "Somebody is asleep in bed," and "There's a man on a bed. He is asleep."

A second step was to analyze how the parents discussed the picture in the child's presence during the second showing. This was done by a psychologist blind to the children's responses. Here again, it was evident that, whereas some parents were candid about the scene depicted, others made no reference to it and/or expressed disgust. For example, to the picture of the pregnant woman, the mother of one child remarked frankly and on three occasions that the woman was expecting a baby and was having an afternoon rest. By contrast, the parents of another child completed their two-minute discussion without any such reference. Instead, they concentrated on emotionally neutral details such as the woman's hairstyle, the material of her dressing gown, and the quality of the furniture. Not surprisingly, there was a high correlation between the way the children responded to the pictures and the way the parents had discussed them subsequently.

On the third showing, the descriptions given by all the children improved in accuracy, but those of the twelve who had responded candidly on the first showing improved more than did the descriptions given by the thirteen who had failed to report the pictures' content on the first occasion.

There could be little doubt that during their discussion of the pictures some of the parents were, consciously or unconsciously, avoiding reference to the content of the pictures. It was a reasonable inference also that their children's failure to describe the sexual themes on the first showing was in some way influenced by the "climate" they had experienced in their homes. What the experiment could not show, of course, was whether these children had truly failed to perceive the scene depicted or whether they had perceived it but had failed to report what they saw. Since preadolescent children tend to be slow and often uncertain in their perceptions, my guess would be that at least some of the children in the experiment had truly failed to register the nature of what was happening. Others may have known intuitively that the scene was one they were not supposed to know about and so avoided seeing it.

At first sight the notion that information of a certain meaning can be shut off, or selectively excluded from perception, appears paradoxical. How, it is asked, can a person selectively exclude from processing a particular stimulus unless he first perceives the stimulus which he wishes to exclude? This stumbling block disappears, however, once perception is conceived as a multistage process, as nowadays it is. Indeed, experimental work on human information processing undertaken during the past decade or so enables us to have a much better idea of the nature of the shutting-off processes we have been discussing than was possible when Freud and others in the psychodynamic tradition were first formulating the theories of defense that have been so very influential ever since. In what follows I give a brief sketch of this new approach.[1]

Studies of human perception (Erdelyi, 1974; Norman, 1976) have shown that before a person is aware of seeing something or hearing something the sensory inflow coming through his eyes or ears has already passed through many stages of selection, interpretation, and

---

[1] A fuller account is given in Bowlby, 1980.

appraisal, during the course of which a large proportion of the original inflow has been excluded. The reason for this extensive exclusion is that the channels responsible for the most advanced processing are of limited capacity and must therefore be protected from overload. To ensure that what is most relevant gets through and that only the less relevant is excluded, selection of inflow is under central or, we might say, ego control. Although this processing is done at extraordinary speeds and almost all of it outside awareness, much of the inflow has nonetheless been carried to a very advanced stage of processing before being excluded. The results of experiments on dichotic listening provide striking examples.

In this type of experiment, two different messages are transmitted simultaneously to a person, one message being transmitted to one ear and the other to the other ear. The person is then told to attend to one of these messages only, say the one being received by the right ear. To ensure that he gives it continuous attention, he is required to "shadow" that message by repeating it word for word as he is hearing it. Keeping the two messages distinct is found to be fairly easy, and at the end of the session the subject is usually totally unaware of the content of the unattended message. Yet there are significant exceptions. For example, should his own name or some other personally significant word occur in the unattended message, he may well notice and remember it. This shows that, even though consciously unattended, this message is being subjected to continuous and fairly advanced processing during which its meaning is being monitored and its content being appraised as more or less relevant, and all this without the person's being in any way aware of what is going on.

In the ordinary course of a person's life, the criteria applied to sensory inflow that determine what information is to be accepted and what is to be excluded are readily intelligible as reflecting what is at any one time in the person's best interests. Thus, when he is hungry, sensory inflow concerned with food is given priority while much else that might at other times be of interest to him is excluded. Yet, should danger threaten, priorities would quickly change so that inflow concerned with issues of danger and safety would take precedence and inflow concerned with food be temporarily excluded. This change in the criteria governing what inflow is to be accepted and what excluded is effected by evaluating systems central to the personality.

In thus summarizing the findings from a neighboring discipline, the main points I wish to emphasize are, first, that throughout a person's life he is engaged in excluding, or shutting out, a large proportion of all the information that is reaching him; second, that he does so only after its relevance to himself has been assessed; and third, that this process of selective exclusion is usually carried out without his being in any way aware of its happening.

Admittedly, so far most of these experiments have been concerned with the processing of current sensory inflow, namely, with perception, and not with the utilization of information already stored in memory, namely, with recall. Yet it seems likely that the same general principles apply. In each case, criteria are set by one or more central evaluating systems and it is these criteria that govern what information is passed through for further, and conscious, processing and what is excluded. Thus, thanks to the work of cognitive psychologists, there is no longer any difficulty in imagining and describing in operational terms a mental apparatus capable of shutting off information of certain specified types and of doing so without the person's being aware of what is happening.

Let us consider next the second category of scenes and experiences that tend to become shut off and forgotten while at the same time continuing to be more or less influential in affecting a person's thoughts, feelings, and behavior. These are the scenes and experiences in which parents have treated children in ways the children find too unbearable to think about or remember. Here again, not only is there amnesia, partial or complete, for the sequence of events, but also exclusion from consciousness of the thoughts, feelings, and impulses to action that are the natural responses to such events. This results in major disorders of personality which in their commoner and less severe forms tend to be diagnosed as cases of narcissism or false self and in their more severe forms may be labeled as a fugue, a psychosis, or a case of multiple personality. The experiences which give rise to such disorders have probably continued or been repeated over several years of childhood, perhaps starting during the first two or three but usually continuing during the fourth, fifth, sixth, and seventh years, and no doubt often for longer still. The experiences themselves include repeated rejection by parents combined with contempt for a child's desire for love, care, and comforting, and, especially in the more severe forms, physical violence (battering) repeated and sometimes systematic, and sexual exploitation by father or mother's boyfriend. Not infrequently, a child in this predicament is subjected to a combination of such experiences.

We start at the less severe end of what appears to be a spectrum of related syndromes.

An example of a patient labeled as "false self" which, on the basis of what the patient was able to recall during therapy can be attributed to repeated rejection by mother, is described by Lind (1973). The patient was a young graduate of 23 who, though severely depressed and planning suicide, maintained that his state of mind was less an illness than "a philosophy of life." He was the eldest of a large family; and by the time he was three, two siblings had already been born. His parents, he said, quarreled both frequently and violently. When the family was young, father had been working long hours away from home training for a profession. Mother was always unpredictable. Often she was so distraught by her quarreling children that she would lock herself in her room for days on end. Several times she had left home, taking the daughters with her but leaving the sons behind.

He had been told that he had been an unhappy baby, a poor feeder and sleeper, who had often been left alone to cry for long periods. His crying, it was said, had been just an attempt to gain control of his parents and to be spoiled. On one occasion he had had appendicitis and he remembered lying awake all night moaning, but his parents had done nothing and by next morning he was seriously ill. Later, during therapy, he recalled how disturbed he used to be at hearing his younger brothers and sisters being left to cry and how he hated his parents for it and felt like killing them.

He had always felt like a lost child and had been puzzled to understand why he had been rejected. His first day at school, he said, had been the worst in his life. It had seemed a final rejection by his mother; all day he had felt desperate and had never stopped crying. After that he had gradually come to hide all desires for love and support; he had refused ever to ask for help or to have anything done for him.

Now, during therapy, he was frightened he might break down and cry and want to be mothered. This would lead his therapist, he felt sure, to regard him as a nuisance and his behavior simply as attention-seeking; and, were he to say anything personal to her, he fully expected her to be offended and perhaps lock herself in her room.

Fortunately, he was in the hands of a therapist who understood his problem and gave full credence to the childhood experiences he described and sympathetic recognition to both his unrequited yearning for love and care and also the violent feelings toward his mother that her treatment of him had aroused and which initially were directed toward herself (the therapist). A patient with rather similar problems but whose experiences included also a period of 18 months in an impersonal institution, starting when she was four years old, is reported by Mintz (1976). Although both these patients made rewarding progress during treatment, both remained more sensitive than others to further misfortune.

A number of patients, both children and adults, whose disorders appear to have originated in similar though mainly worse experiences and to have resulted in personality splitting of an even greater degree have been described by therapists during the past decade. An example is Geraldine, aged 11, who had been found wandering in a dazed state and who had lost all memory both of her mother's terminal illness and of events of the three subsequent years. At the end of a long period of therapy, described in great detail by McCann (in Furman, 1974), Geraldine summed up the experiences which had preceded her amnesia:

> With Mama, I was scared to death to step out of line. I saw with my own eyes how she attacked, in words and actions, my Dad and sister and, after all, I was just a little kid, very powerless. How could I ever be mad at Mama—she was really the only security I had. . . . I blotted out all feelings—things happened that were more than I could endure—I had to keep going. If I had really let things hit me, I wouldn't be here. I'd be dead or in a mental hospital.[2]

The complex psychological state of Geraldine and also the childhood experiences held to have been responsible for it bear close resemblance to the states of patients suffering from multiple personality and to the childhood experiences held responsible for them.

In an article by Bliss (1980), based on clinical examinations and therapy carried out by means of hypnosis, a description is given of 14 patients, all female, diagnosed as suffering from multiple personality. The hypothesis Bliss advances is that the subordinate personalities that take possession of a patient from time to time are the cognitive creations of the principal personality when, as a child of between four and seven years, she was subjected for extended periods to intensely distressing events. According to Bliss, each such personality is created initially to serve a distinct purpose or role. To judge from the examples he gives, the roles are of three main kinds. The simplest and most benign is to act as a companion and protector when the creating personality is feeling lonely and isolated, as for example when parents are persistently hostile and/or absent and there is no one else to turn to. A second role is to be anesthetic to unbearably distressing events, as in the case of a child of four or five who shared a room with her mother who, dying of cancer, spent hours screaming in pain. The third role is more complex; namely, to shoulder the responsibility for thinking, feeling, and acting in ways that the patient cannot bear to accept as her own. Examples given by Bliss include feeling violent hatred of a mother who had attempted to kill the

---

[2]A long abstract of McCann's account is given in Bowlby, 1980, pp. 338–344.

patient when a child; a hatred amounting to an intent actually to murder her; feeling and acting sexually after having been raped as a child; and feeling frightened and tearful after crying had led to punishments and threats from parents.

Since findings derived from hypnotic procedures are controversial, it is important to note that a clinical research group at the University of California at Irvine, who use conventional procedures and who have studied a number of cases (see Reagor, in preparation), have reached conclusions very similar to those of Bliss. The therapeutic procedures proposed have much in common also and are, moreover, strongly in keeping with the concepts of therapy outlined briefly at the end of this contribution.

Lastly, a number of child psychiatrists and child psychotherapists (e.g., Bloch, 1978; Hopkins, 1984; Stroh, 1974; Rosenfeld, 1975) have described children whose thought and behavior make them appear either nearly or frankly psychotic, who show pronouncedly paranoid ideas, and whose condition, the evidence suggests, can be attributed to persistently abusive treatment by parents. Such children are often charming and endearing one moment and savagely hostile the next, the change occurring suddenly and for no apparent reason. Their greatest violence, moreover, is most likely to be directed against the very individual to whom they appear, indeed are, most closely attached. Not infrequently, these children are tormented by intense fear that some monster will attack them, and they spend their time trying to escape the expected attack. In at least some of these cases there is cogent evidence that what is feared is an attack by one or other parent but, that expectation being unbearably frightening, the expected attack is attributed to an imaginary monster.

As an example, let us consider the case of six-year-old Sylvia, reported by Hopkins (1984), one of whose principal symptoms was a terror that the chairs and other items of furniture, which she called Daleks, would fly across the room to strike her. "Her terror was intense and when she kept cowering and ducking as though about to receive a blow from a Dalek or some other monster, I thought she was hallucinating." From the first, Sylvia also expressed the fear that her therapist would hit her as her mother did. Not only did she constantly attack her therapist but she often threatened to kill her.

Sylvia's father had died in an automobile accident two years earlier. During many months of twice weekly interviews with a social worker, the mother was extremely guarded and told little of family relations. At length, however, after nearly two years the veil was lifted. She admitted her own massive rejection of Sylvia from the time of her birth, and the murderous feelings both she and father had had for her. Her treatment of Sylvia, she confessed, had been "utterly brutal." Father had had an extremely violent temper and in his not infrequent rages had broken the furniture and thrown it across the room. He had frequently beaten Sylvia and had even thrown her across the room.

Thus, the identity of the Daleks was not in doubt. Behind the "fantasy" of a Dalek attack lay the serious, reality-based expectation of an attack by father or mother. As Bloch (1978) has put it, a basic premise of the therapeutic approach that she and others like her advocate for these cases is that what is so facilely dubbed as fantasy be recognized as the reflection of a grim reality, and that an early therapeutic task is to identify the real-life experiences lying close behind the deceptive camouflage.

Not only are the childhood experiences of these near-psychotic children the same as those believed characteristic of adult patients with multiple personality, but the states of mind described by the respective therapists have features strikingly similar too. It seems highly likely, therefore, that the two conditions are closely related. It should be noted, furthermore, that these findings give support to the hypothesis advanced by Niederland (1959a, 1959b; discussed by Bowlby, 1973) that the paranoid delusions of Judge Schreber, on which Freud based his theory of paranoia, were distorted versions of the extraordinary pedagogic regime to which the patient's father had subjected him from the early months of life.

In this contribution, as in almost all my work, I have focused attention on psychopathology and some of the conditions that give rise to it. My reason for doing so is the belief that only with a better understanding of etiology and psychopathology will it be possible to develop therapeutic techniques and, more especially, preventive measures that will be at once effective and economical in skilled manpower.

My therapeutic approach is far from original. The basic hypothesis can be stated simply. So long as current modes of perceiving and construing situations, and the feelings and actions that ensue therefrom, are determined by emotionally significant events and experiences that have become shut away from further conscious processing, the personality will be prone to cognition, affect, and behavior maladapted to the current situation. When the yearning for love and care is shut away, it will continue to be inaccessible. When there is anger, it will continue to be directed at inappropriate targets. Similarly, anxiety will continue to be aroused by inappropriate situations and hostile behavior be expected from inappropriate sources. The therapeutic task is therefore to help the patient discover what these events and experiences may have been so that the thoughts, feelings, and behavior that the situations aroused and that continue to be so troublesome can be linked again to the situations that aroused them. Then the true targets of his yearning and anger and the true sources of his anxiety and fear will become plain. Not only will such discoveries show that his modes of cognition, feeling, and behavior are far more intelligible, given the circumstances in which they originated, than they had seemed before but, once the patient has grasped how and why he is responding as he is, he will be in a position to reappraise his responses and, should he wish, to undertake their radical restructuring. Since such reappraisal and restructuring can be achieved only by the patient himself, the emphasis in this formulation of the therapist's task is on helping the patient, first, discover *for himself* what the relevant scenes and experiences probably were and, second, spend time pondering on how they have continued to influence him. Only then will he be in a position to undertake the reorganization of his modes of construing the world, thinking about it, and acting in it which are called for.

The concepts of therapeutic process outlined here are similar to those described in much greater detail by others. Examples are recent publications by Peterfreund (1982) and by Guidano and Liotti (1983). Although the authors of these two books started their therapeutic work from radically different positions, namely traditional versions of psychoanalysis and of behavior therapy, respectively, the principles that now guide their work show a striking convergence. Similarly, current forms of bereavement therapy, which focus on distressing events in the comparatively recent past, are found to be based on the very same principles even when developed within equally different traditions (Melges & DeMaso, 1980; Raphael, 1977). However divergent tactics may still appear, strategic thinking is on a convergent course.

When applying these principles, the therapist has several roles to play, some of which I have sketched in a previous publication (Bowlby, 1977). Here I pick out two only. One is our role in sanctioning the patient to think thoughts that his parents have discouraged or forbidden him to think, to experience feelings his parents have discouraged or forbidden him to experience, and to consider actions his parents have discouraged or forbidden him to contemplate. In giving such sanction we have to be keenly aware that what we are doing is in flagrant opposition to what the patient's parents have constantly insisted on and that the patient may well regard our stance as, at best, misguided and morally mistaken and, at worst, as positively evil. A sensitive awareness of the patient's dilemma is therefore essential.

The second therapeutic role to which I draw attention here is that of providing a patient with a secure base from which he can explore.[3] For it is only when he can trust us sufficiently to respond to him and to what he has to say in a kindly and helpful way, instead of with the criticism and rejection that his earlier experiences have led him to expect, that he will be able to pluck up courage to undertake the explorations we are proposing, and which he quickly senses will be both frightening and painful.

There are, of course, still many disagreements about the most useful tactics for a therapist to adopt for different patients and different situations. Productive discussion of such disagreements turns, however, on prior agreement on what we are trying to do. It is to that issue that this contribution is addressed.

REFERENCES

Adams-Tucker, C. Proximate effects of sexual abuse in childhood: A report on 28 children. *American Journal of Psychiatry*, 1982, *139*, 1252–2356.

Bliss, E. L. Multiple personalities: A report of 14 cases with implications for schizophrenia and hysteria. *Archives of General Psychiatry*, 1980, *37*, 1388–1397.

Bloch, D. *So the witch won't eat me.* Boston: Houghton Mifflin, 1978.

Bowlby, J. *Attachment and loss* (Vol. 1). *Attachment* (2nd ed.). London: Hogarth Press, New York: Basic Books, 1982. (Also in Penguin edition, 1971)

Bowlby, J. *Attachment and loss* (Vol. 2). *Separation: Anxiety and anger.* London: Hogarth Press, New York: Basic Books, 1973. (Also in Penguin edition, 1975)

Bowlby, J. *Attachment and loss* (Vol. 3). *Loss: Sadness and depression.* London: Hogarth Press, New York: Basic Books, 1980. (Also in Penguin edition, 1981)

Bowlby, J. The making and breaking of affectional bonds. *British Journal of Psychiatry*, 1977, *130*, 201–210, 421–431. (Reprinted in Bowlby, *The making and breaking of affectional bonds.* New York: Methuen, 1979.)

Cain, A. C., & Fast, I. Children's disturbed reactions to parent suicide. In A. C. Cain (Ed.), *Survivors of suicide.* Springfield, IL: C. C Thomas, 1972.

Erdelyi, M. H. A new look at the New Look: Perceptual defense and vigilance. *Psychological Review*, 1974, *81*, 1–25.

Freud, S. Remembering, repeating and working through. *Standard Edition 12.* London: Hogarth Press, 1914, pp. 147–156.

Furman, E. *A child's parent dies: Studies in childhood bereavement.* New Haven and London: Yale University Press, 1974.

Gill, H. S. Parental influences in a child's capacity to perceive sexual themes. *Family*

---

[3]The concept of a secure base from which to explore is central to attachment theory (Bowlby, 1969, 1977).

Process, 1970, *9*, 41–50. (Reprinted in R. Gosling (Ed.), *Support, innovation and autonomy*. London: Tavistock Publications, 1973.)

Guidano, V. F., & Liotti, G. *Cognitive processes and emotional disorders*. New York: Guilford Press, 1983.

Hopkins, J. The probable role of trauma in a case of foot and shoe fetishism: Aspects of the psychotherapy of a six-year-old girl. *International Review of Psychoanalysis*, 1984, *11*, 79–91.

Lind, E. From false-self to true-self functioning: A case in brief psychotherapy. *British Journal of Medical Psychology*, 1973, *46*, 381–389.

MacCarthy, B. The psychoanalytic treatment of incest victims. In preparation.

Meiselman, K. C. *Incest—A psychological study of causes and effects with treatment recommendations*. San Francisco: Jossey-Bass, 1978.

Melges, F. T., & DeMaso, D. R. Grief resolution therapy: Reliving, revising and revisiting. *American Journal of Psychotherapy*, 1980, *34*, 51–61.

Miller, A. The drama of the gifted child and the psychoanalyst's narcissistic disturbance. *International Journal of Psychoanalysis*, 1979, *60*, 47–58. (a)

Miller, A. Depression and grandiosity as related forms of narcissistic disturbances. *International Review of Psychoanalysis*, 1979, *6*, 61–76. (b)

Mintz, T. Contribution to panel report on effects on adults of object loss in the first five years. Reported by M. Wolfenstein. *Journal of the American Psychoanalytic Association*, 1976, *24*, 662–665.

Niederland, W. G. The "miracled-up" world of Schreber's childhood. *Psychoanalytic Study of the Child*, 1959, *14*, 383–413. (a)

Niederland, W. G. Schreber: Father and son. *Psychoanalytic Quarterly*, 1959, *28*, 151–169. (b)

Norman, D. A. *Memory and attention: Introduction to human information processing* (2nd ed.). New York: Wiley, 1976.

Palgi, P. The socio-cultural expressions and implications of death, mourning and bereavement arising out of the war situation in Israel. *Israel Annals of Psychiatry*, 1973, *11*, 301–329.

Peterfreund, E. *The process of psychoanalytic therapy: Modes and strategies*. New York: The Analytic Press, 1982.

Raphael, B. Preventive intervention with the recently bereaved. *Archives of General Psychiatry*, 1977, *34*, 1450–1454.

Reagor, P. A. A reparenting model for management of therapeutic relationships with multiple personalities. In preparation.

Rosen, V. H. The reconstruction of a traumatic childhood event in a case of derealization. *Journal of the American Psychoanalytic Association*, 1955, *3*, 211–221. (Reprinted in A. C. Cain (Ed.), *Survivors of suicide*. Springfield, IL: C. C Thomas, 1972.)

Rosenfeld, S. Some reflections arising from the treatment of a traumatized child. In *Hampstead Clinic Studies in Child Psychoanalysis*. New Haven, CT: Yale University Press, 1975, pp. 47–64.

Stroh, G. Psychotic children. In P. Barker (Ed.), *The residential psychiatric treatment of children*. London: Crosby, 1974, pp. 175–190.

PART II

CHAPTER 7

Misconceptions and the Cognitive Therapies

VICTOR RAIMY

"Chaos prevails," declared Colby when prefacing his review of psychotherapy in the mid-1960s (Colby, 1964). By then, even many Freudians were questioning the effectiveness of psychoanalysis. And chaos still prevails, since by now the number of psychotherapies seems roughly to equal the number of its practitioners. For a cognitive therapist, however, the apparent chaos may simply mean that different techniques change the faulty cognitions that produce psychological disorders. This violates, of course, our expectation that there should be one best way to do anything—treat a medical disorder, learn how to read, or build a home. The single best solution stereotype is valid, if at all, only for limited and highly specified activities. Particularly in the psychological realm there are usually many different ways of solving problems. If psychotherapy is the modification or elimination of faulty conceptions, there is little reason for surprise that different treatment procedures produce similar results. There is even research support for the latter contention, as Smith and Glass (1977) have shown.

Such a proposition does not imply that anything one does is therapeutic. There must be limits, since persons with problems have retained them over long periods after having been "treated" informally by friends and relatives. Conversely, there is also a good likelihood that most psychological problems are solved spontaneously, without professional ministrations. This presents another challenge to theories of psychotherapy, since it makes highly improbable the necessity for formal techniques such as free association or systematic

VICTOR RAIMY • Clinical psychologist in private practice, 6770 Hawaii Kai Dr., Honolulu, Hawaii 96825.

desensitization. Formal techniques may be helpful but unnecessary. For if spontaneous recoveries occur, they must result from "experiments in nature," and nature though prodigal is unlikely to create formal techniques. Troubled people may, of course, think intensively about their problems, as in free association, or repeatedly picture themselves with feared objects, as in systematic desensitization, but these spontaneous mental activities are only prologues to techniques rather than techniques in themselves. Faced by spontaneous recovery plus the large number of apparently successful methods of treatment, whether we like it or not, therapists must live in a pluralistic universe of treatment methods and techniques. The same can be said for cognitive therapy. Wherever that appellation occurs in this article, it should be understood as a referent to the cognitive therapies.

The terminological waters have, however, been somewhat muddied. Beck (1976), for example, termed his approach Cognitive Therapy although it represents only one such approach. Others have also muddied the waters, particularly the cognitive behaviorists. Where that group is concerned, there seems to be a continuum from the behaviorists at one end who admit only a bit of cognition to their practice to the cognitivists at the other end who admit only a bit of the behavioral. The present paper is written from the cognitive end of the spectrum, but with due regard for a recent trend toward finding common factors in the various approaches to therapy. That trend is best exemplified by Goldfried's 1982 book on converging themes in psychotherapy. My book (Raimy, 1975) shows how many psychotherapists of different schools made major contributions to the cognitive therapies.

Cognitive therapists themselves have suggested many terms for the faulty beliefs or cognitions that constitute the core targets of a cognitive therapy. I tend to prefer *misconceptions* but feel equally at home with *irrational beliefs* or faulty *assumptions*, or even Janet's *fixed ideas*. Labeling is not, of course, a major issue. The cognitive therapies have much more basic questions, one of which is how misconceptions produce psychological problems, some as severe as the psychoneuroses.

MISCONCEPTIONS AS FAULTY GUIDES

Conceptions are the psychological tools we use to organize and deal with not only the world around us but also our thoughts and feelings. Faulty conceptions, however, are likely to defeat us in both the external and internal worlds because they are erroneous maps or guides. There is no need to show how faulty conceptions about the physical and biological worlds can lead to serious disruptions in our behavior, even to death. On the other hand, correct conceptions or adequate maps have produced awesome achievements such as the fifteenth-century voyages of discovery or the modern-day exploration of space in manned vehicles.

Misconceptions, however, may produce defeat and disruption in all realms, including our social lives. Mistaking the look-alike next door for one's wife can produce more or less disconcerting moments depending upon the circumstances. At a different level, misinterpreting an employer's veiled reproof as praise can eventuate in much misery and despair. Social maladjustment is often the result of the many stumbling blocks we encounter in trying to understand our significant persons who may be just as vague, inconsistent, unreliable, and ambivalent as we are.

Misconceptions about the self, however, are those most likely to produce defeat, disruption, maladjustment, and neurosis. These misconceptions become anchored in the self-concept, where as faulty guides to dealing with ourselves they often create havoc. Faulty beliefs about the self are particularly malignant because we always act upon them since they are the only guides we have to ourselves.

To illustrate, imagine someone who through life's vicissitudes develops a faulty belief about the self to the effect that, "No one could possibly like me if I reveal my true self." Such a person is likely to spend time endlessly avoiding others, avoiding spontaneous behavior, and eating his heart out in loneliness. Another set of circumstances may convince someone that continued "bad luck" means that whatever happens next is likely to be disastrous. Thereupon the individual becomes an impendiac, always fearful of the impending. Or after many frustrations and conflicts, the resulting anxiety convinces someone that a "nervous breakdown" is imminent. The person then tries to avoid all stress fearing that it will produce insanity, when the best cure would probably be subjection to normal stresses, as success in handling them would provide the only convincing evidence of mental well-being.

The doctrine that misconceptions are the villains mostly responsible for psychological problems is by no means a novelty. In the next section we shall look at a few of the major misconceptions proposed by mostly modern psychotherapists.

SOME COMMON MISCONCEPTIONS

Therapists often seem to fasten upon pet misconceptions as central to the problems of most of the people they treat. Freud, for example, fastened on his patients' unconscious misconceptions about sex and aggression, acquired in early childhood, as his primary therapeutic targets even though Freud did not write in cognitive terms. Adler (Ansbacher & Ansbacher, 1956) taught that the major error of neurotics was to believe mistakenly that personal superiority must be achieved without concern for others. Failure to contribute to the social interest was, for Adler, the result of pampering in childhood.

The list of major misconceptions proposed by various therapists can be expanded almost indefinitely. These, of course, constitute a major resource for the practitioner. Sullivan (Perry & Gawel, 1953) wrote of "parataxic distortions" which he thought were acquired in early childhood and which often persisted into adulthood side by side with more accurate conceptions learned at a later time.

Combs and Snygg (1959) describe the common retention of beliefs about the self that were appropriate in the past but are now inappropriate, such as the aging woman thinking of herself as still the young girl, or the troubled adolescent who still sees himelf as a young child. Ellis (1962) has proposed ten main irrational ideas he commonly finds in the people he treats. Among them are "I must be loved and approved of by everyone important to me" and "I am controlled by my history and my important past experiences." Rotter (1970) discusses "six generalized expectancies," each of which can be viewed as a misconception. The best known of the six is the belief that one's behavior is not under one's own control and that therefore one cannot control one's positive reinforcements.

I happen to be partial to three major misconceptions, or clusters of misconceptions, that will be discussed at greater length below. The three are phrenophobia, or the belief that one is verging on insanity; the Special Person misconception, or the notion that one is a superior person with special entitlements; and the incapability misconception, or the false belief that one lacks certain capabilities that most others possess.

Although faulty beliefs have played a prominent role in psychotherapy, they have been competing with the emotions for the role of principal villain of the psychological disorders.

EMOTION VERSUS COGNITION

The major bone of contention in the century-long struggle between emotion and cognition is the control of affect. For some years, research results have supported the contention that emotion depends upon the prior cognitive assessment of the situation. Arnold wrote in 1970, "There is hardly a rival in sight for cognitive theory in the field of emotion. . . . Today, most of the newer theories of feeling and emotion assume that [emotional] experiences depend upon the interpretation and evaluation of the situation" (p. 123). Acceptance of this conclusion today is, however, by no means universal. Two psychologists in particular, Tomkins (1981) and Zajonc (1980), have materialized as the archrivals Arnold failed to find in 1970. Even more recently, Lazarus (1982) has tried to rebut Zajonc's contentions that emotions can occur without perceptual and cognitive encoding and that emotion and cognition are controlled by different neural systems.

Zajonc's article provides an excellent critique of the cognitive viewpoint, but it seems to err much as do many clients when they infer or are told that therapy should consist of a discussion of their feelings. Everything is then prefaced with, "I feel. . . ." By such word magic they assume that they transform their thoughts, judgments, and conclusions, all good cognitive fare, into feelings. Although Zajonc denies that he does the same, a close analysis of his arguments makes it difficult to accept his conclusions. He assumes, for example, that preferences are content-free and are therefore affective experiences rather than cognitions. My problem is that ordinary preferences seem to me to be cognitions even though they have traditionally been regarded as affects. Preferences may have arisen from emotion-suffused situations and when ignored or violated may produce emotional responses, but simply because a statement is prefaced by "I prefer . . ." does not mean that arousal or emotion has occurred.

There is, nonetheless, little likelihood that theoretical, social, or experimental psychologists are about to resolve the century-old argument over the origins and control of affect; but at the moment cognitive appraisal, if only to a minimum degree, seems to be the leading contender for the control of affect. That at least is one currently acceptable answer to Bergin (Bergin & Strupp, 1972), who suggested that the central problem in psychotherapy is how to break the bonds between cognition and affect. If the cognition is changed, the affect alters.

Despite the differing positions on the relation of affect to cognition, there is, curiously enough, considerable agreement on a proposition first espoused by Leeper in 1970 when he wrote, "Emotions are perceptual processes. I mean this in the full sense of processes that have definite cognitive content" (p. 156). Leeper was joined by Zajonc, who wrote in his 1980 paper, "And perhaps all perceptions contain some affect" (p. 153). And in his 1982 article, Lazarus suggests that "cognition and emotion are usually fused in nature" (p. 1019).

In cognitive therapy, Leeper's statement that emotions have "definite cognitive content" has considerable practical application. Individuals, for example, frequently conclude that they must be "highly emotional as a person" after observing their emotional reactions based upon the "cognitive content" at the time of arousal. This aspect of their self-concept usually carries an implication, which is likely to be completely faulty, that they are unable to control their emotional reactions. This faulty conclusion has probably sanctioned as many sins as good intentions, perhaps more.

The failure to recognize that affect has cognitive content also leads to some curious consequences. In a 1980 critique of cognitive therapy, Mahoney, who labels himself a cognitive behavior modifier or cognitive therapist, discusses at some length the tendency of some cognitive therapists to neglect feelings. After some preliminary remarks indicating that he would probably accept Leeper's proposition, he comments, "A single traumatizing experience can sometimes override thousands of nontraumatic exposures" (p. 166). This illustration seems to join the issue. Does the single traumatic experience outweigh thousands of nontraumatic exposures only because of the added affect, or does the cognitive content of the trauma inform the individual that a hitherto harmless experience is potentially harmful? My conjecture is that people are likely to reject probabilities intellectually in ensuring their safety and welfare. This is often vividly brought to a therapist's attention when an attempt is made to convince a client that the chances are only one in ten that some untoward event will occur. The frequent and intelligent rebuttal is likely to be, "Yeah, and how do I know that I am not the *one* in ten?" a reply that fuses a cognitive base with some affect.

The general agreement on the fusion of cognition and affect may also account for my observation while reading verbatim accounts of therapy conducted by affect-oriented therapists that they are trying to bring about changes in beliefs although their efforts are ostensibly directed toward affect. Fritz Perls, whose emphasis upon increasing sensory awareness was implemented by having his patients act out their feelings, provided a good example of the affect-oriented virtuoso clinician trying to change misconceptions. Perls presents several verbatim treatment sessions with Liz (1969, pp. 82–89). In front of the group where he is treating Liz, Perls says that her problem is "I can only be important if I am perfect," an obviously faulty belief that was one of Perl's favorite targets. In the thirty-minute episode he was obviously trying to convince Liz that she should abandon the misconception. There is insufficient space here, but in my 1975 book (pp.

70–72) I have detailed the 26 sorties he made to change her belief by explanation, exhortation, derision, and even by enlisting group support.

This example is not an isolated one. In fact, as I read most verbatim accounts by therapists of all persuasions I am convinced over and over that much therapy consists of attempts, using a remarkable array of techniques, to root out or to change relevant misconceptions.

AFFECT PROVIDES CLUES TO MISCONCEPTIONS

Although we have argued that affect is controlled by cognitions, that does not mean that affect is unimportant in psychotherapy (see also Mahoney, 1980, pp. 164–167). Leeper's statement that "emotions are perceptual processes" supports the observation that reported or acted-out displays of feeling or emotion can be helpful in detecting misconceptions. Emotions tend to be associated with misconceptions because the latter are often challenged since they are misconceptions. The closer the belief to the core of the self-concept, the more affect is aroused. Not only do others challenge our faulty beliefs, but we do so ourselves, particularly when conflict occurs.

To illustrate, a 40-year-old client complained that he must have a "great well of meanness" because he was so upset by the lies and distortions from public characters during a recent election campaign. I was surprised that he would make such a self-reference, and also by his additional comment that he might be repeating a previous depressive episode "and this time I could lose my mind." I can see how people might kill during a campaign but hardly become severely depressed. The apparent irrationality of the two comments embedded in a strong emotional display alerted me to the possible presence of a significant misconception. It was quickly discovered. His anger and despair were actually displaced from a recent "first real argument with my new wife," for whom he felt great ambivalence. He had to displace his emotions because he was unaware of his ambivalence and could not, initially, express anger toward a wife whom he also loved and desired. Ambivalence is very difficult to deal with even for bright people who are not psychologically sophisticated.

In addition to providing clues to misconceptions, affect can also facilitate the bringing into focus of much cognitive content that might ordinarily go unremarked by the client. As a client becomes more emotional about an experience, redintegrative effects are likely to occur as more details are brought to mind. For example, a girl expressed great frustration and guilt because she could not bring herself to thank her mother for some recent gifts. When I asked her to describe the gift-giving scene, she became very emotional and raged, quite unlike herself, "She's always doing nice things for me. I feel like I'm nothing." When that elliptical outburst was examined, it appeared that she meant that she lost her integrity by accepting gifts from a mother for whom she had feelings of dislike. When I asked for still more details, she burst into tears and described the usual ambivalence. She then gained insight into the fact that she loved as well as hated her mother who, she claimed, made her develop many misconceptions about herself during adolescence. Thus an emotional display can be a good jumping-off point for detecting misconceptions, and the redintegrative effects can bring to the surface many of the hidden aspects of a cluster of misconceptions.

There are, of course, other ways to discover misconceptions in addition to the clues provided by emotion. Since the search for misconceptions usually occurs during treatment, their detection will be discussed in that general context.

COGNITIVE METHODS OF TREATMENT

There is little doubt that misconceptions can be changed in many different ways. Adherence to a cognitive approach does not, therefore, require the practice of any specific methods, although some cognitive therapists have marked preferences for certain techniques. Beck, Rush, Shaw, and Emery (1979) for example, have minutely detailed instructions for treating depression using Beck's form of cognitive therapy. Despite the detailed instructions, there is no reason to believe that those techniques are uniquely effective. Thus psychoanalysts with a cognitive orientation can continue to practice analytically if they are explicit in trying to change faulty cognitions. The same is true for therapists of other orientations. The only essential for cognitive therapy is the attempt to discover and change those misconceptions thought to be central to the client's problems.

This proposition that no specific techniques are required probably runs counter to the grain of most psychotherapists, for traditionally schools of therapy have prescribed certain methods of treatment thought to be uniquely effective. Such prescriptions now seem naive unless they are regarded simply as sometimes useful techniques that can be replaced by many other equally useful techniques. For example, I have counted at least ten different methods for bringing about fear or phobia reduction, all supported by studies cited in the research literature.

The cognitive therapist need not invent his own techniques for discovering relevant misconceptions. The psychotherapy literature contains a broad array of methods ranging from the straightforward interview to free association. Psychodiagnostic testing may be helpful, particularly those tests that elicit much content, such as the Thematic Apperception Test, the Minnesota Multiphasic Personality Inventory (if item answers are scrutinized), and various personality questionnaires. Sometimes such preliminary diagnostic procedures strike paydirt and permit work to begin immediately on the identified misconceptions. More often, however, finding the relevant misconceptions depends upon a more laborious search throughout the different phases of treatment. Attention to expressive behavior, such as displays of affect, is also useful.

In addition to using their preferred techniques for discovering misconceptions, cognitive therapists can also follow their own inclinations in selecting techniques for treatment. So many treatment techniques are described in the literature, it becomes necessary to lump them into broad categories for survey purposes. Each of the four categories selected for that purpose has its counterpart in educational methods. Education, as well as psychotherapy cognitively interpreted, is devoted to implanting, improving, correcting, or eliminating conceptions.

1. *Self-examination* in its purest form is practiced by hard-core client-centered therapists who are passionately devoted to a minimum of intervention and a maximum of nondirectiveness. In its purest form, the therapist tries only to facilitate the client's own search for, discovery of, and alteration of the relevant misconceptions. No interventions such as interpretations or confrontations are sanctioned. Less Spartan therapists may combine self-examination with other techniques, such as explanation. In so doing, periods of self-examination are followed by interpretations. Analysts and dynamic therapists often utilize such a combination. (In education, Socratic questioning is in many ways the counterpart of self-examination.)

2. *Explanation* is a far more active procedure in which the therapist tries to use whatever knowledge is at hand to convince the client that some of his beliefs are faulty. Explanation is not limited to formal explanations or mini-lectures. Interpretations and confrontations are also explanatory techniques. In its pure form explanation is likely to be quite directive, although it can usually be tempered by discussions

with the client. Explanation can also be combined with self-examination and is usually combined with self-demonstrations and modeling. (In education, lecturing is a clear example of explanation, while
the combined lecture-discussion method is the counterpart of combining self-examination with explanation.)

3. *Self-demonstration* consists of the therapist's arranging or proposing special situations either in real life or in approximations of
it, such as group therapy, where the client can observe himself in
action and discover, or perhaps change, his important misconceptions. (In education, any assigned activity, such as homework which
is more than just drill, can be considered the equivalent of self-
demonstration.)

4. *Modeling* as a therapeutic method was formally introduced by
Bandura (1969), although it was employed much earlier informally
by those therapists who were aware that their clients often identified
with them. In formal modeling, misconceptions are changed or eliminated by inducing the client to imitate a model either vicariously or
in reality. (When the teacher expects the class to imitate any kind of
demonstrated activity, the counterpart of modeling is being employed.)

All therapists can only try to modify beliefs, behavior, or affect.
Although the therapist proposes, the client always disposes. What
happens in the client?

THE PATIENT'S TASK—COGNITIVE REVIEW

Little is known of how the client disposes of the therapist's proposals. Most research and theory have been concerned with what the
therapist does and not with the client. Nonetheless, certain conjectures about the client's role in the change process can be ventured,
as belief modification is not confined to psychotherapy.

Since opinions, or beliefs, or conceptions are ordinarily formed
on the basis of evidence, adequate or inadequate, we can also assume
that beliefs are modified by evidence, adequate or inadequate. Thus
in successful modification of misconceptions clients must somehow
review their evidence in some fashion, be it slipshod or systematic.
The process, which is more often slipshod than systematic, we can
refer to as cognitive review. We can conjecture further that the reviews which occur must usually be repeated, often many times, as
one-trial learning is the exception.

An emphasis upon the review process as slipshod helps to avoid
the notion that cognitive review is a coldly mechanical process akin

to the systematic analyses performed by judges, scientists, and business experts. Their systematic analyses are the product of long-term training based upon concrete principles with appropriate criteria for judging the success of the analysis. Of perhaps greatest importance is the fact that they can be assured of external reviewers, whereas most of us conduct our review in secret. For most of us the rules of evidence are not even shattered; they never existed. Our wishes are taken as valid evidence. Leading questions are the rule for we are pleading before our own bars which are hopelessly prejudiced. We practice hearsay shamelessly. Affect is accepted as fact. An observer might wonder how anything ever gets done right.

What happens in typical cognitive reviews can be inferred to some extent by attending closely to what clients do in interviews. There is usually a hasty survey of what comes to mind, a tentative conclusion which is then tested against a tentative forecast of how a changed belief might affect the status quo, usually accompanied by interruptions to think about other pressing topics. Except when crises call for immediate decisions, there is always time to prevaricate, falsify the facts out of whimsy, fantasize impossible wish-fulfillments, and then to postpone some more. Cognitive review is rarely a formal kind of reckoning because people are rarely aware that they are weighing evidence against a possible faulty belief. They recognize only that they are dealing with a problem that requires some thought and that an immediate decision may entail some discomfort. Muddling through is not confined to governments.

Psychotherapy may, in fact, provide one of the few times when the individual is enticed or bullied into thinking somewhat systematically about some of his beliefs, particularly those about himself. Most clients under the scrutiny of the therapist try to behave like rational, responsible persons most of the time, since most therapists also expect clients to behave in that fashion most of the time. Therapists may protest that they accept the client totally, but carrying on a reasonable conversation at least some of the time requires constraints on both sides. What the therapist may not demand may be read into him by the client.

INSIGHT

The endpoint of the client's process of cognitive review, slipshod, helter-skelter, and biased as it may be, can be referred to as insight. Although insight has acquired a bad name in recent years, practitioners still work toward it. The reason for this seeming paradox is that insight probably does work, but perhaps not in the way specified by the analysts who laid so much store by it. Although there are many definitions of it, the most frequent refers to the discovering of developmental patterns that have produced current psychological difficulties. A more useful and more specific definition is needed to understand why many clients recover even when they still lack knowledge of the history of their disturbance.

From a cognitive standpoint, insight can be defined as *the recognition that one suffers from a specific misconception or a cluster of related misconceptions.* The client has insight if he says, "I display great compassion for others because I'm afraid of what people might say if I don't, not because I'm a great humanitarian." With such a definition of insight we need not get into the useless arguments over the necessary time frame for achieving insight. It can be achieved by dredging up and sorting out one's recollections, or it can occur following an examination of events in the psychological present. A longitudinal approach is no better or worse than a cross-sectional approach in therapy. Clients can escape into the present just as well as into the past. Intellectualizing can be practiced with either past or present material.

The definition of insight as recognition of a misconception also eliminates the need for concern over so-called "intellectual versus emotional insight." The latter somehow implies that emotion is welded onto understanding to promote conviction. From the present standpoint, however, either the individual who displays only intellectual insight is parroting words, or the insight is unrelated to the problem at hand, or the insight may be so partial and fragmented that it fails to explicate the relevant misconception. Passive acceptance of the doctrine of emotional versus intellectual insight deprives the therapist of the opportunity to stimulate the client to explore the misconception further. Freud referred to this as the need for working through. People respond with conviction when their problems have been worked through, but not necessarily when they emote.

The "aha!" experience is not necessarily characteristic of the insights achieved in therapy since such understanding ordinarily comes about slowly and hesitantly. Mahoney's "cognitive click" is much more descriptive of the usual insight, since it is simply a recognition that things have fallen into place. There are, of course, faulty insights, so that invalid clicking is certainly not unknown in this subjective game we call psychotherapy.

THE CLUSTERING OF MISCONCEPTIONS

The problems that bring people to therapy are usually so complex that the simple solutions have failed. The complexity may involve not only contradictory beliefs, such as ambivalence, but also a myriad of related events that have occurred over long periods of time. Because of this complexity, clustered misconceptions arranged in some loose hierarchy are usually found rather than isolated miconceptions.

For illustration, I have selected three clusters of misconceptions. Although by no means universal, each when present exercises a broad influence on its possessor and levies a considerable toll. The three are phrenophobia, the Special Person misconception, and the incapability misconception. The first two have been discussed at greater length in my 1975 book.

PHRENOPHOBIA

This belief that one is in danger of imminent mental collapse usually develops after inexplicable, recurring anxiety attacks. The accompanying fear of insanity probably sends a large proportion of clients into psychotherapy, but even more into physicians' offices in the hope of finding medical explanations. Thorne (1961) reported that 78% of the patients seen in his psychiatric practice had "fears of imminent mental breakdown." In several small studies with the help of graduate students we found that 75% of hospitalized mental patients had phrenophobia, and about 20% of college students reported having feared at one time that they might break down.

The disabling aspect of this cluster is largely due to the layman's fuzzy knowledge about "nervous breakdown" based largely on misconceptions. The layman usually thinks of psychotics as being homicidal, suicidal, sexually assaultive, and suffering from loss of identity. The consequences are seen as banishment to an asylum for life with permanent estrangement from family and friends. Those suffering from moderate to severe phrenophobia face enormous horrors. It is little wonder that denial of illness is as common in those with mental problems as in those with medical problems.

Treatment of this tenacious misconception is difficult. In direct treatment, which may be helpful to some, the therapist explains how constant apprehension, confusion, supposed loss of memory and concentration (the highly anxious concentrate on and remember their symptoms splendidly), and insomnia are products of anxiety usually resulting from severe stress. Direct reassurance can also be helpful, particularly during crises when fear is likely to become panic. Difficulties often arise in treatment because clients experience weird and subtle internal sensations from prolonged anxiety that are often impossible to describe to the therapist. Thus the client believes that the clinician's reassurance is based on partial evidence.

Indirect alleviation of phrenophobia occurs when the therapist consistently treats the client like a normal person. Those who live in fear of imminent breakdown become acutely sensitive to how others react to them. Thus when *the doctor* treats the phrenophobic as a normal individual, the fear of impending insanity tends to be dissipated and the phrenophobia relieved. Tranquilizers can also be helpful in reducing this concern, but a surprisingly large number of mental patients see medications as only temporary crutches. I usually castigate myself if I neglect to question clients about phrenophobia near the beginning of treatment. Direct treatment and reassurance act far more quickly than do the client's covert observations of the therapist's manner. When phrenophobia is reduced or eliminated, rational consideration of other misconceptions is possible.

THE SPECIAL PERSON MISCONCEPTION

One of the most puzzling aspects of neurotic behavior is the person's refusal to give in to or to compromise with reality. The neurotic who could solve many problems simply by accepting his place in line absolutely refuses to do so. This may represent a grandeur of temperament in the abstract but it hardly compensates for the misery endured in the concrete by the refusal to compromise.

This misconception is a conviction that one has special rights and should have special dispensations. Anderson (1981) writes of their belief in their "special entitlement." The Freudian narcissism, or enhancement of self-love, is a related phenomenon. Kohut (1971), building on the Freudian notion, has a related concept of the "grandiose self," which is "the grandiose and exhibitionistic structure which is the counterpart of the idealized parent imago" (p. 26). In all of these notions the core is an exaggerated belief in one's superiority or desirability.

There is no reason why the belief in one's superiority could not have several etiologies, among which I would emphasize the pampering of children or the direct indoctrination of specialness. Most mental health professionals, however, have been so indoctrinated with the Adlerian notion that a "superiority complex" is only a cover for an underlying "inferiority complex" that they reject out of hand any other etiology. Even Freud's narcissism is dependent upon the principle of compensation following rebuff, rejection, and pain from others.

Many Special Persons can be successful, at least for a time, in obtaining constant reaffirmation of their superiority, at least within their own reference group. As long as they succeed they are symptom-free. But when they fail to obtain such confirmation, the major handicaps of their misconception are borne in on them—devastated self-esteem and loss of specialness. The resulting depression and anxiety may become so severe that phrenophobia occurs, and the welter of symptoms obscures the underlying character disorder.

Often the Special Person finds different ways of maintaining the appearance of being special. Doing extensive homework before encounters with others is a favorite way of displaying intellectual superiortiy. Resorting to the hysteric's typical pattern of practicing constant and exaggerated charm is a less intellectual solution. Charm, real or fancied, brings its own reward in the attention it evokes from others, unless and until they sicken of the charm.

Treatment of this misconception is also difficult. The feeling of entitlement is so embedded that its possessor is ordinarily unable to perceive it even when it is salient to others. Direct confrontation is likely to be painful, for the Special Person sees this challenge as completely unfair and is then more likely to withdraw than to understand. I confront only when I have been able to collect a number of detailed incidents of rejection resulting from the client's inveterate practice of one-upmanship. With that ammunition I have at times been able at least to gain the client's attention. I usually also play it doubly safe by inserting at some point in the confrontation a brief description of the Special Person to which is appended, "Of course, you are not responsible for acquiring that misconception. . . . You did not pamper yourself, someone else pampered you." Some clients rapidly come to realize that they are pampered children grown up, but often their growth in this respect falters when giving up the satisfactions of the Special Person becomes intolerable.

THE INCAPABILITY MISCONCEPTION

The core of this misconception is an exaggerated belief in one's inabilities. The so-called inferiority complex is an extreme, generalized form of the incapability misconception. Although I have encountered few of the extreme forms, most clients I see have scattered patches of self-evaluated incapability that make it difficult for them to deal with problems. This misconception's development is nourished from two sources—real incapabilities and the confusion between inability and aversion, between "I cannot" and "I don't want to."

How much conscious deceit occurs in the incapability misconception is a vexing question. Keats took the skeptic's role when he suggested that "The fancy cannot cheat so well as she is famed to do." On the other hand, there must be many genuine beliefs about one's deficiencies that are factually incorrect. For example, there must be thousands, if not millions, of all ages who honestly believe they cannot learn mathematics, just as there are untold others who profess in all honesty their inability to perform painful or aggressive acts. The client, for example, who says, "I can't tell my mother that she is destroying my marriage," usually honestly believes it, even though he is confusing his aversion with his capability. Phobias represent a special and extreme form of this misconception.

Over the years I have become convinced that this belief is one of the most frequently encountered and troublesome of the common misconceptions. For some, it becomes a routine defense against any discomfort. There are standard phrasings such as, "I can't think about that because it's too painful," or "I can't learn how to do that, and my mother couldn't either." This misconception may protect one from much discomfort in the short run, but it tends to become an opiate used whenever discomfort intrudes. It is also intricately linked with the avoidance reaction, the tactic above all others that keeps the person from reassessing and confronting the reality underneath the faulty facade.

Treatment of the incapability misconception tends to be easier than that of phrenophobia, probably because concern about one's capabilities is unlikely to arouse intense fear except in special circumstances. Thus fewer avoidance reactions occur. It is also easier to deal with than the Special Person, since questioning incapabilities poses less threat to self-esteem than does questioning rights to special entitlement.

A SUMMING UP

The disadvantages encountered in employing a cognitive approach in psychotherapy are no different from those found with any other approach. Those unfamiliar with a cognitive approach may be dismayed by the prospect of trying to modify what they see as a dishearteningly large number of misconceptions. Fortunately, there is no need to treat all misconceptions since most are benign and have little influence on adjustment. Those held in common with one's reference group, for example, are probably benign, since they are accurate guides to the social milieu. The ones that create problems are primarily faulty beliefs about the self and the self in relation to others. As we have seen, offending misconceptions also tend to be clustered hierarchically, so that if one that subsumes many faulty beliefs is eliminated the whole structure collapses. Clients also tend to discuss symptoms and issues related to their important misconceptions, which helps not only in their discovery but also in narrowing down those in need of treatment.

Not only clients, however, suffer from misconceptions. Therapists may also hold faulty beliefs that may interfere with the course of treatment. The well-known countertransference is the therapist's misperception of the client, a counterpart of transference, or the client's misperception of the therapist. Another therapist misconception is the "teacher fallacy." Just as teachers are prone to assume that students must understand what has been carefully explained to them, therapists are likely to believe that their clients understand all that has been explained, interpreted, reflected, and posed in confrontation.

There appear to be few if any inherent disadvantges to a cognitive approach, but many advantages. One is that most therapists are familiar with a large number of misconceptions, even though they may not think of them as such. If a client says, "I'm sure no one could like me if he got to know me well," most therapists prick up their ears and begin to plan their strategy for changing this faulty belief. As a matter of fact, and for many reasons, nontherapists as well as therapists spend much of their lives listening for faulty beliefs, usually those of others.

Another advantage of the cognitive approach is that procedures for discovering relevant misconceptions have been proposed by many therapists of different persuasions, even though the proposals may not have emerged from a cognitive orientation. Misconceptions can be elicited by any method that encourages a client's verbal or expressive behavior, such as free association, nondirective interviewing, Gestalt therapy techniques for nonverbal behavior, dream interpretation, or straightforward history taking and questioning.

In cognitive therapy, identified misconceptions are usually phrased in the everyday language of the client so that the client's self-knowledge and language can be used imemdiately to discuss faulty beliefs.

No special language need be introduced, although occasionally technical terms, such as *ambivalence*, can be taught if they help to sharpen understandings and permit better communication.

Cognitive therapists also have a consistent orientation toward the tasks of therapy, as everything that happens there is grist for the cognitive mill. Initial unsatisfactory client attitudes toward therapy or the therapist are usually, but not always, the products of misconceptions, including those which create ambivalence. If history is taken, it may well provide clues to patterns or clusters of misconceptions from remote or recent times. Sudden changes in established patterns of normal behavior probably bear witness to the birth of important misconceptions following traumatic or other kinds of unusual life events.

Content-laden diagnostic tests, such as the TAT, the items of the MMPI, or personality questionnaires, can be scrutinized for relevant misconceptions.

The relationship between client and therapist provides rich opportunities for detecting misconceptions, particularly if the therapist is skilled at detecting transference reactions.

When clients put on an emotional display or report strong emotional reactions that occurred between sessions, they can usually be profitably examined for clues to important misconceptions. Problems may occur, however, as many clients are skilled ventriloquists who distort the therapist's perception of "where they are coming from." Ventriloquism is only one of many resistances. Resistance *per se* is based on misconceptions about the whole process of change. The defense mechanisms are also based on misconceptions, since they are devices for falsifying or avoiding one's true reactions.

Another advantage of the misconception approach is that changes in relevant misconceptions can often reorganize behavior rapidly and radically. Such changes are probably due to the elimination or modification of a misconception central to a cluster of faulty beliefs. The biblical story of Saul's transformation into Paul on the road to Damascus is a classic recognition of a radical transformation in personality brought about by insight.

Finally, there are three questions commonly asked about a cognitive approach that seem to represent genuine puzzlement. The most frequently asked implies that it is probably too "intellectual" for most clients. But this stems from a misunderstanding, for affect occurs as profusely or as sparsely as in any other approach, unless the therapist tries unwisely to dampen it. In view of their usefulness as clues to misconceptions, affective reactions play an important role in treatment. The second question asks whether cognitive therapy as I outline it is not just a matter of attitude, since its methods can be so varied. The third question, related to the second, is a query about cognitive therapy's being an eclectic approach, since so many methods can be used. Inasmuch as the last two relate to the wide array of methods they can be answered together. Cognitive therapy is not just a matter of attitude as the varied methods simply testify to the fact that there are many ways to change misconceptions. A cognitive approach can, therefore, be eclectic where methods or techniques are concerned, but its goal is certainly not eclectic. Finding and changing faulty beliefs that interfere with adjustment is a highly specific and concrete therapeutic activity, even though it may be accomplished in many different ways.

REFERENCES

Anderson, C. M. Self-image therapy. In R. J. Corsini (Ed.), *Handbook of innovative psychotherapies*. New York: Wiley, 1981.

Ansbacher, H. L., & Ansbacher, R. R. (Eds.). *The individual psychology of Alfred Adler*. New York: Harper & Row, 1956.

Arnold, M. (Ed.). *Feelings and emotions: The Loyola Symposium*. New York: Academic Press, 1970.

Bandura, A. *Principles of behavior modification*. New York: Holt, Rinehart & Winston, 1969.

Beck, A. T. *Cognitive therapy and the emotional disorders*. New York: International Universities Press, 1976.

Beck, A. T., Rush, A. J., Shaw, B. F., & Emery, G. *Cognitive therapy of depression*. New York: Guilford, 1979.

Bergin, A. E., & Strupp, H. H. *Changing frontiers in the science of psychotherapy*. Chicago: Aldine-Atherton, 1972.

Colby, K. M. Psychotherapeutic processes. In P. R. Farnsworth (Ed.), *Annual review of psychology*. Palo Alto: Annual Reviews, 1964.

Combs, A. W., & Snygg, D. *Individual behavior: A perceptual approach to behavior* (rev. ed.). New York: Harper, 1959.

Ellis, A. *Reason and emotion in psychotherapy*. New York: Lyle Stuart, 1962.

Goldfried, M. R. (Ed.). *Converging themes in psychotherapy: Trends in psychodynamic, humanistic, and behavioral practice*. New York: Springer, 1982.

Kohut, H. *The analysis of the self*. New York: International Universities Press, 1971.

Lazarus, R. S. Thoughts on the relation between emotion and cognition. *American Psychologist*, 1982, 37, 1019–1024.

Leeper, R. S. The motivational and perceptual properties of emotions as indicating their fundamental character and role. In M. Arnold (Ed.), *Feelings and emotions: The Loyola Symposium*. New York: Academic Press, 1970.

Mahoney, M. J. (Ed.). *Psychotherapy process: Current issues and future directions*. New York: Plenum Press, 1980.

Perry, H. S., & Gawel, M. L. (Eds.). *The interpersonal theory of psychiatry*. New York: Norton, 1953.

Perls, F. S. *Gestalt therapy verbatim.* Lafayette, CA: Real People Press, 1969.

Raimy, V. *Misunderstandings of the self: Cognitive psychotherapy and the misconception hypothesis.* San Francisco: Jossey-Bass, 1975.

Rotter, J. B. Some implications of social learning theory for the practice of psychotherapy. In D. J. Levis (Ed.), *Learning approaches to therapeutic behavior change.* Chicago: Aldine-Atherton, 1970.

Smith, M. L., & Glass, G. V. Meta-analysis of psychotherapy outcome studies. *American Psychologist,* 1977, *32,* 752–760.

Thorne, F. C. Personality: A clinical, eclectic viewpoint. *Journal of Clinical Psychology,* 1961, *18,* 172–176.

Tomkins, S. S. The quest for primary motives: Biography and autobiography of an idea. *Journal of Personality and Social Psychology,* 1981, *41,* 306–329.

Zajonc, R. B. Feeling and thinking: Preferences need no inferences. *American Psychologist,* 1980, *35,* 151–175.

CHAPTER 8

Cognition in Psychoanalysis

SILVANO ARIETI

In a paper published in 1965 in Volume 8 of *Science and Psychoanalysis*, edited by Masserman, I wrote:

> Cognition is or has been, up to now, the Cinderella of psychoanalysis and psychiatry. No other field of the psyche has been so consistently neglected by clinicians and theoreticians alike. Isolated studies and manifestations of interest have not so far developed into a definite trend. (Arieti, 1965)

Since then the attitude of the profession has changed but, until recent years, only to a modest degree. For a person like me, who wrote his first paper on cognition in the year 1949, these 32 years of waiting have been a taxing experience, but not a "waiting for Godot." Now cognition has become a growing stream of study and concern. And yet, if some colleagues who have been interested in this subject were to ask me to define cognition and then hear my answer, they would feel like Molière's famous character, M. Jourdain, who, when his teacher explained what prose was, said, "I spoke prose all my life without even knowing it." Similarly, even those of us psychoanalysts who have not been interested in cognition have done cognitive psychoanalysis every day, during every session, because cognition is the study of ideas and their precursors, that is, the study of the development, formation, content, interconnections, and dynamic effect of ideas. It is through ideas that we communicate with our patients; it is by hearing the content of their ideas that we get to know them and

"Cognition and Psychoanalysis" by S. Arieti originally appeared in the *Journal of the American Academy of Psychoanalysis*, 1980, *8*, 3–23. Copyright © 1980 by John Wiley & Sons, Inc. Reprinted with minor editorial ammendations by permission of John Wiley & Sons, Inc.

SILVANO ARIETI • Late of New York Medical College and William Alanson White Institute of Psychiatry, Psychoanalysis, and Psychology, New York, New York.

to know what ideas do to them. It is through ideas that we bring about improvement and cure. In the present paper, cognition will not be discussed as a medium by which we get to know and represent reality—this is the usual representation made by academic psychologists—but as a major component of our inner reality and as a dynamic force. Space limitations will compel me to make a cursory presentation and a selection of topics which may be arbitrary.

Under the influence of classic psychoanalysis, many psychoanalysts have stressed only the primitive—the bodily needs and instinctual or primitive behavior which can exist without a cognitive counterpart or with a very limited one. Simple levels of physiopsychological organization, such as states of hunger, thirst, fatigue, need for sleep and a certain degree of temperature, sexual urges, or relatively simple emotions, such as fear about one's physical survival, are undoubtedly powerful dynamic forces. They do not include, however, the motivational factors that are possible only at preconceptual levels of development.

Freud stressed how we tend to suppress and repress ideas which elicit anxiety. But we psychiatrists and psychoanalysts have suppressed or repressed the whole field of ideas, that is, cognition. We have repressed it apparently because it is anxiety provoking. As a matter of fact, as we shall see later, there would be very little anxiety in the human being without ideas or precursors of ideas. But psychoanalysts have for a long time preferred to think that cognition deals with those so-called conflict-free areas and therefore does not pertain to psychoanalysis. The contention of cognitive psychoanalysts is that very few conflicts, and only elementary ones, would exist in the human being if he were not able to think, to formulate ideas, old or new, to assimilate them, make them part of himself, face and compare them, distort them, attribute them to others, or finally, repress them.

When I stated that cognition has been neglected, some could have pointed out to me that this is not really so. At least three giants, Freud himself, Jean Piaget, and Hans Werner, have been very much interested in cognition. This is true, but let us see what kind of impact the contributions to cognition of these three giants have made on psychoanalysis.

One of Freud's great breakthroughs was his discovery of the primary process and the description of the primary and secondary processes. Freud, however, did not maintain a great interest in the primary process as a mode of cognition, but only as a carrier of unconscious motivation stemming from an instinctual source. Inasmuch as motivational theory in the Freudian system came to be interpreted in the function of the libido theory, the primary process came to be studied not in a framework of cognition, but in a framework of energetics. Primary and secondary processes came to be considered primarily not as two different ways of thinking, but as two different ways of dealing with cathexes. In the primary process the cathexis was described as free. In other words, cathectic quantities of energy are easily shifted from some objects to others. Inasmuch as this shifting may easily occur from realistic and appropriate objects to unrealistic and inappropriate ones, the primary process becomes an irrational mode of functioning.

These points of view leave many unexplored aspects, especially those which pertain more closely to cognition. Cognition is relegated to being a medium and is not considered as a source of conscious or unconscious motivation.

Piaget's contributions are very significant, especially in child psychology. But they have not made much impact on psychoanalytic therapy, mainly because they are difficult to integrate with a psychodynamic view of the human being. Piaget's works reveal very well the process of cognitive maturation and adaptation to environmental reality and disclose the various steps by which the child increases his understanding and mastery of the world. Although they are important, they do not represent intrapsychic life in its structural and psychodynamic aspects. They neglect affect as much as classic psychoanalytic studies neglect cognition and do not deal with motivation, unconscious processes, and conflicts of forces. The cognitive functions, as described by Piaget, seem really autonomous and conflict-free, as the ego psychologists have classified them. All attempts up to the present to absorb Piaget's contributions into the core of classic psychoanalysis—including the attempt made by Odier (1956)—have, in my opinion, not gone very far. The only contributions of Piaget that could be reconciled with classic psychoanalysis are those he made very early in his career when he was still under the influence of the psychoanalytic school (Piaget, 1919). For instance, his concept of the child's egocentrism is related to the psychoanalytic concept of the child's feeling of omnipotence.

The contributions of Hans Werner (1948) are perhaps more pertinent to psychiatric studies because, in following a comparative developmental approach, they take into consideration pathological conditions. However, like the works of Piaget, they do not make significant use of the concepts of the unconscious and unconscious motivation.

When my first writings on cognition appeared, from 1947 to 1955, such studies were looked at askance in America, whether they dealt with psychological structure or content (Arieti, 1947, 1948, 1953, 1955). And yet in France, Levy-Strauss (1951) was very well received for his structural approach, and in America, too, Chomsky (1957) introduced structuralism to linguistics. In the 1940s and in 1950s psychology, under the influence of behaviorism, was concerned mainly with overt behavior; classic psychoanalysis focused on energetics and instinctual precognitive life; and neo-Freudian, cultural psychoanalysis was concerned with the study of conflicts without considering their cognitive origin. In France in the meantime, Lacan (1966) started his cognitive studies of inner life and stressed the importance of the signifier in conscious and unconscious life. By *signifier* (in French, *signifiant*) he meant 'language' or the 'word', whatever gives a meaning to things. Unfortunately, his works are written in such a difficult style as to discourage many readers.

OTHERNESS AND INWARDNESS

Another reason that has induced many psychoanalysts to neglect cognition has been the assumption that a cognitive approach would neglect infancy and early childhood, a period of life during which there is little cognition and which in some respects can be called precognitive. It is a period during which sensations and elementary perceptions prevail. The child lives at what Piaget called a sensorimotor level, regulated mostly by the simple stimulus-response mechanism. In spite of this poverty of cognitive processes, many people rightly point out that at this level the baby and his mother are already capable of establishing a bond of love, with attachment, empathy, and mutal concern. Is not this bond of love, or the lack of it, or its vicissitudes, of fundamental importance for the subsequent life? A dialogue of love has already started in the first few hours of life. A large number of clues and signals are exchanged between the few-days-old baby and his mother. What is more meaningful than the eye-to-eye language, the body contact between mother and baby, contact established by sucking at the breast and by the embrace? What is more full of meaning than the reciprocal smile between the baby and his mother? The beauty of the embrace and the contact with the body of the mother cannot be spoiled even when we use our arid scientific language and call it an activation of sensorimotor systems in the infant (Harlow & Harlow, 1965). A cognitive approach does not deny the importance of this early stage of human life. However, the following considerations have to be made:

The dialogue of love between mother and baby is unequal. Even though the mother may not speak to the child, she touches him, feeds him, holds him, rocks him, smiles at him, sings to him, and she attributes an affective-cognitive meaning to these actions. For her, each gesture and action has a meaning. She does embrace her child with the warmth and love of her adulthood. When we see this beautiful scene, mother and baby together, and we call it a "dialogue" of love, we attribute to it our meanings, our words, and our word about words. Happy the baby who, in the smile on the face of his mother, intuitively perceives in a precognitive way a reflection of his own smile. But this precognitive intuition will not develop into a real and bilateral bond of love unless cognitive developments follow. This exchange between mother and child is a superb beginning; but no matter how superb and beautiful, in the human infant it will remain at a level not superior to that occurring in animal forms unless one of the two partners is a human adult, equipped with cognitive power, sowing cognitive seeds so that the primitive embrace does not remain primitive but becomes eventually an embrace capable of including other members of the family, the whole group of people with whom the child has significant contacts, and eventually, possibly, humankind. But how can the maternal embrace become a potentially worldwide embrace? By the gradual and subsequent acquisition of cognitive and symbolic forms. Language, concepts mediated through language, and emotions made possible by the acquisition of language will expand, deepen, transform the life of the child and give rise to a universe of ideas, mutual understandings, interpersonal ties, loves. The gradual independence from mother is accompanied by a gradual immersion in the big world. Thus whatever pain is involved in the gradual separation from mother is compensated for by the opening and joy of the world, which is gradually better understood and savored. But it must be a world from which mother is not absent. Mother is still there, symbol of the concrete precognitive attachment and as representative and intermediary of the world of incoming symbols. The openness to the big world has its earliest beginning when the child is approximately nine months old.

Mother becomes increasingly absent, but to the increasing absence of mother I shall return later. Now let us give another look at these early eight to nine months of life. In these early months, actually as soon as he is born, the baby is more or less receptive to some exchanges with the other. The other at first is only the mother, who becomes instantly the forerunner and representative of all future others: family members, people, mankind. So the first other is the person who is experienced the least as an other. Even those of us who do not believe the child considers himself part of mother do agree that the first Thou is the least other. It is through this relatedness to mother that the child starts to develop the I-Thou relation described by Martin Buber (1953). This relatedness is the prototype of subsequent meaningful interpersonal relations, leading to attachment, affection, friendship, intimacy, and love. Martin Buber also describes another encounter of the individual, the I-It, the encounter with the inanimate world, be it that of a simple object or a solar system. Buber rightly stresses the superiority of the I-Thou relation over the I-It.

Buber is the philosopher of what I call *otherness*, the relation with the other, which later was further explored by many authors, especially by George Herbert Mead and Harry Stack Sullivan. Buber's contribution is very important. Nevertheless, it has limitations. As a philosophical or psychological entity the human being cannot be defined exclusively in terms of the formulas I-Thou and I-It. Although Buber has made it clear that by reaching out to a fellow man a person reaches into himself, and that in reaching out to others one reaches oneself, this formulation is vague. The I, or self, needs a special consideration, a more profound treatment, which is not included in the concept of otherness. The I or self is a human being, too, but is not just an other. In reaching myself, I have an attitude different from the one I have in reaching others. The attitude toward oneself is based on introspection, or self-awareness, which other animal species have only to a rudimentary degree. It is only with the human being that this attitude or mental set expands to an enormous degree. Otherness requires openness to the world. Introspection and self-awareness require openness to oneself, that attitude or mental set that I call inwardness. Although in his otherness the human being is by far superior to, and extremely more complicated than, other animal species, in the beginning and first stages of otherness the human being is not completely dissimilar from other animals. Of course, he changes dramatically later when he is able to act, to embrace, to touch, to love, and to hate with words, too. Inwardness unfolds later and would not develop at all unless at least a rudimentary otherness already existed. Inwardness makes us reach for ourselves, inside, opens to us our inner life. I enter into a special dialogue with a special person, me, I face myself, speak to myself, and read myself. I am not an object to myself. I have a special encounter, I-I, and what I can discover can be unexpectedly new; a whole universe opens up to me, my own. But this inner universe consists of cognitive structures with cognitive content. If it were not for cognition, I could not have an inner life, or perhaps I could have only a very limited one. Moreover, if I want to discover my unconscious, I must do so in a cognitive way. For what I have repressed from consciousness is predominantly cognitive in nature; that is, I repress ideas, attitudes, mental dispositions, and in most cases the emotions derived from them. Many cognitive forms have a double entity; they consist of what seems to be a psychological bifurcation. One branch is interpersonal, reaching the other with a word, an idea, a complicated relation. The other branch is intrapsychic and makes it possible to retain such an idea, attitude, or disposition within oneself. When I acquire a new cognitive form, let us say a new word or a new concept, not only is it my otherness which expands but also my inwardness. I have a new way to reach not only others but also myself. The new word or concept, and the emotions which accompany it, will enrich my self as well and will become from now on part of my inner life.

IMAGERY

At this point I wish to give a bird's eye view of the development of cognition from babyhood to adulthood, as far as inner life is concerned. In the limited space at my disposal, I will be able to discuss the development of cognitive forms and their content only in a succinct way. I shall try to show how they are necessary for the origin of emotions and psychodynamic mechanisms. When we psychoanalysts interested in cognition stress the importance of ideas and systems of ideas, we do not minimize the importance of affective life, or of motivation, conscious or unconscious. On the contrary, we stress a fact which is very seldom acknowledged, namely, that at a human level most emotions would not exist without a cognitive substratum. The expansion of the neocortex and consequently of our cognitive functions has permitted an expansion of our affective life also. In a classic paper, published in 1937, Papez demonstrated that several parts of the rhinencephalon and archipallium are not usd for olfactory functions in the human being, but for the experience of emotion. In spite of the diminished importance of olfaction, these areas have expanded, not decreased, in man and have become associated with vast neocortical areas.

It is at approximately nine months of age that the "second birth" of the child occurs. This is when the child realizes that mother becomes more and more frequently absent. He gradually learns to understand language and to talk, but he acquires another faculty, which at first develops much more rapidly than language: imagery. The very first stage of internalization, that is, of inner life and inwardness, occurs through images. For the sake of simplification we shall consider only visual images. Brodmann's area 19 in the occipital lobes now becomes myelinized and capable of functioning. Visual sensations and perceptions which were mediated in areas 17 and 18 have left memory traces that assume the form of representation, that is, of images. The image is now an internal quasi-reproduction of a perception that does not require the corresponding external stimulus in order to be evoked. The image is indeed the earliest and one of the most important foundations of human symbolism. By *symbol* we mean something that stands for something else that is not present. Whereas previous forms of cognition and learning permitted an understanding based on the immediately given or experienced, from now on cognition will rely also on what is absent and inferred. Mother is now more and more frequently absent. But the child can endure her absence. Her image is with him; it stands for her. The image is based on the memory traces of previous perceptions of her. The mother acquires a psychic reality that is not tied to her physical presence.

Image formation is actually the basis for all the following higher mental processes. It enables the child not only to reevoke what is not present, but to retain an affective disposition for the absent object. For instance, the image of the mother may evoke the feelings that the child experiences toward her. If we adopt the terminology generally used in reference to computers, we can say that now the psyche or the brain is capable of analogic codification. The image thus becomes a substitute for the external object. It is actually an inner object, although it is not well organized. It is the most primitive of the inner objects if, because of their sensorimotor character, we exclude motor engrams from the category of inner objects. When the image's affective associations are pleasant, the evoking of the image reinforces the child's longing or appetite for the corresponding external object. The image thus has a motivational influence in leading the child to search out the actual object, which in its external reality is still more gratifying than the image. The opposite is true when the image's affective associations are unpleasant: the child is motivated not to exchange the unpleasant inner object for the corresponding external one, which is even more pleasant.

Imagery soon constitutes the foundation of inner psychic reality.

It helps the individual not only to understand the world better but also to create a surrogate for it. Moreover, whatever is known or experienced tends to become a part of the individual who knows and experiences. Thus, cognition can no longer be considered only a hierarchy of mechanisms but also must be seen as an enduring psychological content that retains the power to affect its possessor, now and in the future.

The child who has reached the level of imagery is now capable of experiencing not only such simple emotions as tension, fear, rage, and satisfaction, as he did in the first year of life, but also anxiety, anger, wish, perhaps in a rudimentary form even love and sadness, and, finally, security. Anxiety is the emotional reaction to the expectation of danger, which is mediated through cognitive media. The danger is not immediate, nor is it always well defined. Its expectation is not the result of a simple perception or signal. At subsequent ages, the danger is represented by complicated sets of cognitive constructs. At the age level that we are discussing now, it is sustained by images. It generally refers to a danger connected with the important people in the child's life, mother and father, who may punish or withdraw tenderness and affection. Anger, at this age, is also rage sustained by images. Wish is also an emotional disposition, which is evoked by the image of a pleasant object. The image motivates the individual to replace the image with the real object satisfaction. Sadness can be felt only at a rudimentary level at this stage, if by sadness we mean an experience similar to the one the sad or depressed adult undergoes. At this level, sadness is an unpleasant feeling evoked by the image of the loss of the wished object and by the experience of displeasure caused by the absence of the wished object. As I described in the mentioned paper, written in 1947, this is the stage when the child becomes capable of anticipating the future and is no longer capable only of expecting imminent events. This is also the stage when the baby becomes able to experience security, or the first forerunners of what will be security. As Sullivan (1953) was the first to point out, security is different from satisfaction. Satisfaction occurs when all the bodily needs, like food, sleep, rest, warmth, and contact with the body of mother, are satisfied. No cognition is necessary for the experience of satisfaction, but it is for the experience of security. Security does not consist only of removal of unpleasant emotions or removal of uncertainty, but also of pleasant anticipation, a feeling of well-being, a trust in people and things to come. Security is experienced by the year-old child not only by his contacts with his mother, but by the feeling that, if she is absent, she will return. The inner image of his mother, which he always carries inside himself, gives him this feeling of trust. Many other things could be said about images, imagery, and imagination. I shall limit myself to saying that imagery not only emerges as the first or most primitive process of reproducing, or substituting for, the real, but also is the first and most primitive process of creating the unreal. The French philosopher Gaston Bachelard has stressed this point repeatedly in his books (1960, 1971). It is true that the image does not reproduce reality faithfully; it emerges as an innovation, a state of becoming, a force of transcendence, and it is the beginning of human creativity (Arieti, 1976). Unfortunately, we cannot explore this subject but must pass on to the next stage of cognitive development, represented by the endocept or amorphous cognition.

THE ENDOCEPT

The endocept is a mental construct representative of a level intermediary between the image and the word. At this level, there is a primitive organization of memory traces, images, and motor engrams. This organization results in a construct that does not tend to reproduce reality, as it appears in perceptions or images: it remains nonrepresentational. The endocept, in a certain way, transcends the image, but inasmuch as it is not representational, it is not easily recognizable. On the other hand, it is not a motor engram that leads to prompt action. Nor can it be transformed into a verbal expression; it remains at a preverbal level. Although it has an emotional component, most of the time it does not expand into a clearly felt emotion.

The endocept is not, of course, a concept. It cannot be shared. We may consider it a disposition to feel, to act, to think that occurs after simpler mental activity has been inhibited. It is an interrelation of feelings and residues of former experiences which has not yet crystallized into a concept. The awareness of this construct is vague, uncertain, and partial. Relative to the image, the endocept involves considerable cognitive expansion; but this expansion occurs at the expense of the subjective awareness, which is decreased in intensity. The endocept is at times experienced as an "atmosphere," an intention, a holistic experience that cannot be divided into parts or words—something similar to what Freud called "oceanic feeling." At other times, there is no sharp demarcation between endoceptual, subliminal experiences and some vague primitive experiences. On still other occasions, strong but not verbalizable emotions accompany endocepts.

For the evidence of the existence of endocepts and for their importance in adult life, dreams, and creativity, the audience is referred elsewhere (Arieti, 1967, 1976). It is more likely that it is the right hemisphere that is mediating endoceptual activity.

MOVING TOWARD CONCEPTUAL THINKING

At this point I should open up the extensive area of cognition which includes the acquisition of language and the various stages of preconceptual thinking leading to the formulation of the mature concept. This is the stage in which, in addition to the analogic codification of imagery and the diffuse grouping of the endocept, the psyche or the brain becomes capable of digital codification, mediated chiefly by the left hemisphere. Entire libraries have been written on these subjects. From the acquisition of language (naming things) to a logical organization of concepts, various substages follow one another so rapidly and overlap in so many multiple ways that it is very difficult to retrace and individualize them. These intermediary stages are more pronounced and more easily recognizable in pathological conditions.

Some of them appear in the most fleeting way in ontogenesis (Arieti, 1967), and some of them reappear in schizophrenia (Arieti, 1974). In other writings (1967, 1970) I have described how the acquisition of language and concepts is necessary for the experience of high-level emotions like sadness, depression, hate, love, or joy.

In studying preconceptual stages of thinking, we view a vast cognitive realm which extends from the primitive cognition of the primary process to the elaborate one of the secondary process and Aristotelian logic. Unfortunately, I cannot deal here with this vast subject. I shall make only a few remarks. During these stages the child tends to explore more and more the external world, but also himself. The randomness of the cognitive experiences is more and more superseded by the gradual organization of inner constructs. These inner constructs at first consist of the forms we have already mentioned: images, endocepts, and preconceptual forms. Later they consist also of simple concepts and finally of complicated concepts with all their conscious and unconscious ramifications.

THE IMAGE OF MOTHER AND THE SELF-IMAGE

These constructs continuously exchange some of their components and increase in differentiation, rank, and order. A large number of them, however, retain the enduring mark of their individuality. Some of them have powerful effects and have an intense life of their own, even if at the stage of our knowledge we cannot give them an anatomic location or a neurophysiological interpretation. They may be considered the very inhabitants of inner reality. The two most important ones in the preschool age, and the only two to which I shall devote a few words, are the image of mother and the self-image. At this point the word *image* is used with a different meaning. It is no longer used exclusively to signify an attempted reproduction of a perception, but a complicated cluster of cognitive components. For instance, the image of the mother is a conglomeration of what the child feels and knows about her.

In normal circumstances the mother as an inner object will consist of a group of agreeable images: as the giver, the helper, the assuager of hunger, thirst, cold, loneliness, immobility, and any other discomfort. She becomes the prototype of the good inner object. At the same time she will become, as we have already mentioned, the representative of the Thou. Any other fellow human being, in his essential human qualities, will be modeled after her.

Much more difficult to study in early childhood is the self-image. At the precognitive sensorimotor level, the primoridal self probably consists of a bundle of relatively simple relations between feelings, kinesthetic sensations, perceptions, motor activity, and a partial integration of these elements. At the image level, the child who is raised in normal circumstances learns to experience himself not exclusively as a cluster of feelings and of self-initiated movements but also as a body-image and as an entity having many kinds of relations with other images, especially those of the parents. Inasmuch as the child cannot see his own face, his own visual image will be faceless—as, indeed, he will tend to see himself in dreams throughout his life. He wishes, however, to be in appearance, gestures, and actions like people toward whom he has a pleasant attitude or by whom he feels protected and gratified. The wish tends to be experienced as reality, and he believes that he is or is about to become like the others or as powerful as the others. As the child grows, his self-image will consist less and less of analogic images and preconceptual cognition, and more and more of concepts related to the self.

CONCEPTUAL LIFE

Struggling rapidly through preconceptual stages, the child finally reaches the conceptual level. As Vygotsky (1962) has illustrated, conceptual thinking starts early in life, but it is in adolescence that it acquires prominence.

Whereas psychiatrists and psychoanalysts study primitive and preconceptual types of thinking from the points of view of both form and content, they generally study concepts only in relation to their content. The study of conceptual forms remains almost exclusively an object of study for academic psychologists. I shall follow this tradition, and I shall discuss concepts only from the point of content.

In a large part of psychiatric, psychoanalytic, and psychological literature concepts are considered static, purely intellectual entities, separate from human emotions and unimportant in psychodynamic studies. I am among those who cannot adhere to this point of view. Concepts and organized clusters of concepts become depositories of emotions and also originators of new emotions. They have a great deal to do with the conflicts of man, his achievements and his frustrations, his states of happiness or despair, of anxiety or of security. They become the repositories of intangible feelings and values. Not only does every concept have an emotional counterpart, but concepts are necessary for high emotion. In the course of reaching adulthood, emotional and conceptual processes become more and more intimately interconnected. It is impossible to separate the two. They form a circular process. The emotional accompaniment of a cognitive process becomes the propelling drive not only toward action but also toward further cognitive processes. Only emotions can stimulate man to overcome the hardship of some cognitive processes and lead to complicated symbolic, interpersonal, and abstract processes. On the other hand, only cognitive processes can give origin to, and extend indefinitely, the realm of emotions (Arieti, 1967). Between known conceptual meanings there are gaps of potential meanings and consequently of potential emotions. Perhaps it is more accurate to say that clusters of meanings are islands in an uncharted ocean of potential meanings and emotions. Unstable clusters produce conflict-laden waves of anxiety, sorrow, and anger. A perennial effort is made to diminish the cognitive dissonance (Festinger, 1957) and to form new clusters which either do not make waves or repress the wave-making clusters. A perennial effort is made to diminish the contrast between the concepts which echo the objectivity of the universe and those which echo the inner subjectivity—the subjectivity which shifts between harmony and turmoil, craving and satisfaction.

From a psychiatric and psychoanalytic point of view, the greatest importance of concepts resides in the fact that to a large extent they come to constitute the self-image. When this development occurs, the previous self-images are not completely obliterated. They remain throughout the life of the individual in the forms of minor components of the adult self-image or as repressed or suppressed forms. In adolescence, however, concepts accrue to constitute the major part of the self-image. Such concepts as inner worth, personal significance, mental outlook, more mature evaluations of appraisals reflected from others, attitudes toward ideals, aspirations, capacity to receive and give acceptance, affection, and love are integral parts of the self and of the self-image, together with the emotions that accompany these concepts. Like other concepts, the concepts and emotions which constitute the self are generally not consistent with one another, in spite of a prolonged attempt made by the individual to organize them logically.

The motivation of the human being varies according to the various levels of development. When higher levels emerge, motivations originated at lower levels do not cease to exist. At a very elementary sensorimotor level, the motivation consists of obtaining immediate pleasure and avoidance of immediate displeasure by gratification of bodily needs. When imagery emerges, either phylogenetically or ontogenetically, the individual becomes capable of wishing something that is not present and is motivated toward the fulfillment of his wishes. Let us remember that no wish is possible without a cognitive component, perhaps one of the most primitive, the image. The child will continue to be wish-motivated as he moves on to more advanced stages of primary cognition, such as the prelogical stage. As I have already mentioned, although the motivation can always be understood as an attempt to retain pleasure and avoid unpleasure, gratification of the self or of the self-image becomes the main motivational factor at a conceptual level of development. Certainly, the individual is concerned with danger throughout his life: immediate danger, which elicits fear, and a more distant or symbolic danger, which elicits anxiety. However, whereas at earlier levels of development this danger is experienced as a threat to the physical self, at higher levels it is many times experienced as a threat to an acceptable image of the self. To reduce the emotional factors which accompany complicated cognitive processes to the status of cover-up of primitive instinctual drives is a reductionistic assessment of the human psyche; it is forcing a return to a presymbolic or prehuman level. Even feelings, sensations, bodily needs, which theoretically stand on their biological processes, become involved with systems of symbolism which give them special meaning and involve them in intricate networks of motivation. Let us take as an example the sexual need. It is obvious that sexual life cannot be considered only from a sensuous or instinctive point of view. Sexual gratification or deprivation become involved with such concepts as being accepted or rejected, desirable or undesirable, loved or unloved, lovable or unlovable, capable or incapable, potent or impotent, normal or abnormal. Thus sexual gratification and deprivation become phenomena that affect the whole self-image.

The self is a system of interrelated cognitive items and of the emotions to which they give origin. The value and identity of these items are defined not only by their history but by their place or distribution in the system. The historical identity, although extremely important, does not coincide with the present identity. The way I am today cannot toally be subsumed by my past. In other words, what counts is not only the sequence of historical events but their integration and cognitive transformation. Each of us to some extent is created by the acts of cognition which we initiate or at least in which we participate. We must study how each item is distributed and integrated with the others. Preexisting structures, or schemata, are brought to bear upon the present. Also schemata concerning the future are brought to bear upon the present, so that our present day may be brightened or darkened by the vision of tomorrow. Since the realm of cognitive symbolism is potentially infinite and consequently the distribution of these cognitive elements can vary in an infinite number of ways, complete or absolute knowledge of the psyche and sure predictability are impossible. What is possible, however, is presumable knowledge, and the assessment of probability.

In other writings I have shown the importance of cognitive life in schizophrenia. I have shown how the preschizophrenic, in a period of life which precedes the psychotic break, generally during adolescence or young adulthood, finds himself threatened on all sides, as if he were in a jungle (Arieti, 1974). It is not a jungle wherein ferocious animals are to be found, but a jungle of concepts that remain unconscious until shortly before the onset of the psychosis, or the phase that I have called the prepsychotic panic. The threat is again not to physical survival, but to the self-image. The dangers are concept-feelings, such as those of being unwanted, unloved, inadequate, unacceptable, totally dependent on others, inferior, awkward, clumsy, not belonging, peculiar, different, rejected, humiliated, guilty, unable to find one's own way among the different paths of life, disgraced, discriminated against, kept at a distance, suspected, and so forth. Some of these concepts were conscious even in earlier periods of life. What had remained unconscious was their full significance, their ramifications and connections, especially with similar concepts about the self, originated in early childhood. When these constellations of concepts are interconnected and become vividly conscious, they are experienced as unbearable and undergo drastic changes. At this point, the patient undergoes a conceptual transformation of cosmic magnitude. He either withdraws from the world or becomes possessed by a system of unusual beliefs which makes him see the world in a different way. In order to do so, he has to make a drastic shift: he must adopt a different type of cognition, the cognition of the primary process, of the dream. And then, no longer will he be besieged by the jungle of concepts which hurt his inner self, no longer will be consider himself inadequate, worthless, and deserving of contempt. The inner danger has now been transformed into a danger which comes from others. Inwardness is projected into otherness. I cannot possibly talk about schizophrenic cognition in the space at my disposal. But I shall mention only how the patient, at a certain period of his psychotic transformation, enters into the world of metaphor.

A patient thinks his wife is putting poison in his food. He really believes his wife is poisoning his life, but he cannot accept that belief. If she disturbs his life, he may have something to do with the marital difficulties. Another patient has an olfactory hallucination. He smells a bad odor that emanates from his body. We can be fairly sure that he attributes to his body what he thinks of himself. He has a rotten personality, one which stinks. It is easier for him to blame his body than his character. Another patient, while he was in a teenage camp, believed that at night people were going into his closet and drawers and putting female clothes in the place of his own. He was still concerned with his identity, especially gender and sex identity. Was he really a man? Another patient believes that a mysterious, unidentified person from another planet controls his thoughts. But this man is a symbol of the patient's father, toward whom he felt so emotionally distant, as if he were on another planet, and whom the patient experienced as wanting to control his ideas and the direction he wanted to give to his life. When another patient tells us that invisible rays pierce him and cause him harm, he refers to the hidden, or hard to detect, ways with which society has treated and harmed him.

The patient uses what is for us metaphorical language. From what he tells us, we can indeed learn some hidden truths, as we would learn from a poet. But is the patient a poet? He is not. The big discrepancy between him and the poet lies in the difference I described in the book *Creativity:* the magic synthesis between the cognition of the primary process of the schizophrenic and the cognition of the tertiary process of the creative person (Arieti, 1976). The patient is not at all aware of the metaphorical meaning of his delusions; he accepts them literally. The metaphors are for him metamorphoses. For him it is literally true that his wife poisons his food, that a bad odor emanates from his body, that a man controls his thoughts from a distant planet, that invisible rays go through his body. He is like a dreamer who, while he is dreaming, thinks the dream is true. The dream is true, of course, not just as an act of life, but also in its symbolic content. It is as true as the poetry which, in its metaphorical revelations, discloses to us ways and feelings deeper than those usually attached to a daily reality. It is one of our tasks to guide this pseudopoet, the patient, to return to the reality of the secondary process; but it must be a reality which is less anxiety provoking and, one hopes, not prosaic.

I regret that lack of space does not permit me to discuss further either schizophrenic cognition or creative cognition. I must also omit discussing the importance of cognition in depression, as Bemporad and I have illustrated (Arieti & Bemporad, 1978). I must overlook Barnett's studies on obsessive neurosis (Barnett, 1966, 1968, 1972), and I cannot even open the extremely important and vast topic of how culture provides the individual with innumerable basic concepts which lead to growth as well as to pathological conflicts. Before concluding, however, I want to refer again to an important issue to which I alluded in passing throughout my presentation: the relation between cognition and the unconscious. It is a basic tenet of the cognitive school of psychoanalysis that the unconscious and unconscious motivation include much more than infantile strivings. They include also a great deal of inner life, built in childhood, adolescence, and adulthood with cognitive forms.

Because of the enormous expansion of the neopallic areas, the human being is the first entity, at least in the history of our solar system, to be confronted with an infinite array of symbols and of emotions to which they give origin. We would not be able to bear this tremendous burden unless we had relief mechanisms. Other species have only the mechanism of nonattending or of reducing to tacit knowledge what they do not use at the moment. We, too, have the mechanism of nonattending. For instance, when I speak to you in English, I do not attend to my knowledge of Italian. As a matter of fact, I try not to let my Italian interfere with my English. But this is not equivalent to making conscious material unconscious, or transforming it into dynamically different forms. In other words, nonattending is not a mechanism of repression. But we do repress. As a relief mechanism, we do have the mechanism of repression, first described by Freud. Whatever disturbs one's cherished self-image tends to be modified, reevaluated, denied, or removed from consciousness. Whatever might make the individual appear to himself unworthy, guilty, inadequate, sadistic, vindictive, inconsistent with his ideas or ideals, escapist, or not living up to his ideals tends eventually to be repressed. Indeed, some of these evaluations of the self remain conscious; but even so, what is eliminated from consciousness is much more than the individual realizes. Psychoanalytic practice reveals how many of these cognitive constructs about oneself, and how many of their ramifications, are kept either in a state of unconsciousness or in dynamically acceptable or less unacceptable cognitive transformations.

Repression of the main motivation (protecting the self-image) is often achieved with the help of psychological mechanisms that detour consciousness toward other avenues of thought and behavior. Intricate cognitive configurations lead the patient to feelings, ideas, and strategic forms of behavior that make the self-image acceptable or at least less unacceptable. At times any form of self-criticism is repressed, and even benevolent criticism from others is restricted with awkward cognitive strategies.

We may thus conclude that we human beings are confronted not only by the infinite external cosmos but by the infinite cognition which reflects the cosmos, and the infinite cognition that we internalize, and the infinite cognition that we repress. The self remains a unity, a giant enriched and battered on all sides. We psychoanalysts must maintain a humble attitude, because no matter how much we explore and bring to consciousness, what we will clarify will be only a part of the psyche, the whole of which we shall never know. But we shall accept this limitation of our goals without a sense of defeat because cognition teaches us that the human being is *Homo symbolicus*, for which a small part becomes a symbol that stands for the whole. The proper symbol may be a little spark which sheds an intense light and guides us to a vast understanding and to the depths of our hearts.

REFERENCES

Arieti, S. The processes of expectation and anticipation. *Journal of Nervous and Mental Disease*, 1947, *106*, 471–481.

Arieti, S. Special logic of schizophrenic and other types of autistic thought. *Psychiatry*, 1948, *11*, 325–338. (Reprinted in Arieti, 1978, pp. 23–45.)

Arieti, S. *Some aspects of language in schizophrenia.* Paper presented at Clark University, November 25, 1953. Worcester, MA: Clark University Press, 1953.

Ariet;, S. *Interpretation of schizophrenia* (1st ed.). New York: Brunner, 1955.

Arieti, S. Contributions to cognition from psychoanalytic theory. In J. Masserman, Ed., *Science and Psychoanalysis* (Vol. 3). New York: Grune and Stratton, 1965.

Ariet;, S. *The intrapsychic self: Feeling, cognition and creativity in health and mental illness.* New York: Basic Books, 1967.

Arieti, S. The structural and psychodynamic role of cognition in the human psyche. In S. Arieti (ed.), The world bienniel of psychiatry and psychotherapy (Vol. 1). New York: Basic Books, 1970.

Arieti, S. *Interpretation of schizophrenia* (2nd ed., completely revised and expanded). New York: Basic Books, 1974.

Arieti, S. *Creativity: The magic synthesis.* New York: Basic Books, 1976.

Arieti, S. *On schizophrenia, phobias, depression, psychotherapy and the farther shores of psychiatry: Selected papers.* New York: Brunner/Mazel, 1978.

Arieti, S., & Bemporad, J. *Severe and mild depression: The psychotherapeutic approach.* New York: Basic Books, 1978.

Bachelard, G. *The poetics of reverie.* Boston: Beacon, 1960.

Bachelard, G. *On poetic imagination and reverie.* Indianapolis: Bobbs-Merrill, 1971.

Barnett, J. On cognitive disorders in the obsessional. *Contemporary Psychoanalysis,* 1966, *2,* 122–134.

Barnett, J. Cognition, thought and affect in the organization of experience. In J. Masserman (Ed.), *Science and psychoanalysis.* New York: Grune and Stratton, 1968.

Barnett, J. Therapeutic intervention in the dysfunctional thought processes of the obsessional, *American Journal of Psychotherapy,* 1972, *26,* 338–351.

Buber, M. *I and Thou.* Edinburgh: Clark, 1953.

Chomsky, N. *Syntax structures.* The Hague: Mouton, 1957.

Festinger, L. *A theory of cognitive dissonance.* Palo Alto, CA: Stanford University Press, 1957.

Harlow, H. F., & Harlow, M. K. The affective systems. In A. M. Schrier, H. F. Harlow, and X. X. Stollnitz (Eds.), *Behavior in nonhuman primates.* New York: Academic Press, 1965.

Lacan, J. *Ecrits,* Paris: Editions du Sevil, 1966.

Lévi-Strauss, J. Language and the analysis of social laws. *American Anthropologist,* 1951, 53, 155–163.

Odier, C. *Anxiety and magic thinking.* New York: International University Press, 1956.

Papez, J. W. A proposed mechanism of emotion. *Archives of Neurology and Psychiatry,* 1937, *38,* 725–743.

Piaget, J. La psychoanalyse dans ses rapports avec la psychologie de l'enfant. *Bulletin de la Société Alfred Binet de Paris,* 1919, *20.*

Sullivan, H. S. *Conceptions of modern psychiatry.* New York: Norton, 1953.

Vygotsky, L. S. *Thought and language.* Cambridge, MA: M.I.T. Press, 1962.

Werner, H. *Comparative psychology of mental development.* Chicago: Follet, 1948.

CHAPTER 9

Cognitive Therapy and the Individual Psychology of Alfred Adler

BERNARD H. SHULMAN

In our recent book, Forgus and I present Alfred Adler as a cognitive theorist with a constructionist viewpoint. Adler's theory

> emphasizes that the person is an active, creative agent in the construction of his own personality, not merely a passive reactor shaped by his environment. (Forgus & Shulman, 1979)

In its early stages, Adler's theoretical constructs were more motivational in nature than cognitive. He spoke, early on, about the striving for mastery, status, and significance in human beings and about the feelings of inferiority and its compensations. The origin of this striving was in the innate propensity of living organisms to expand, to develop, and to fulfill biological destiny. This striving, a continuously adaptive process, was also represented in Adler's concept of the Law of Compensation which said that it is the natural behavior of an organism to vary its behavior in such a way that it compensates for physical or psychic deficiences which impair its adaptive capacities.

These motivational constructs were not sufficient for a theory of human behavior, and Adler found a balancing set of propositions which allowed him to expand his set of hypotheses by introducing a

BERNARD H. SHULMAN • Stone Medical Center, 2800 North Sheridan Road, Chicago, Illinois 60657.

number of cognitive concepts. These eventually placed Adler securely among the cognitive personality theorists and cognitive therapists.

The key to casting the theory in cognitive terms came from the philosopher Hans Vaihinger's *Philosophy of "As If"* (1925). Vaihinger, a neo-Kantian, reasoned that each individual human being constructs for himself a set of guiding fictions which enable him to make sense of his world and which are derived from the person's own experiences in the world. Vaihinger used the word *fiction* not in the sense of 'falsehood' but in the sense of 'made' or 'manufactured'. A guiding fiction could be unrealistic or could be a reasonable approximation of reality. Vaihinger also proposed that these fictions could become more refined and eventually become dogma for the person who used them. In this way, convictions and beliefs could be formed.

Forgus and Shulman (1979) have schematized how such a process takes place. That the newborn human is soon capable of learning is obvious. The early learning comes from the responses the infant receives from its own built-in action programs and this information eventually leads to modification of these innate programs. Forgus and Shulman postulate the presence of the innate program for handling information—a perceptual program. New stimuli (external and internal) provide new information allowing the original innate program to become elaborated and modified in the service of the biological goal of adaptive striving.

This concept has a haunting similarity to Freud's concept of the ego splitting off from the id in order to cope with the demands of reality. The difference from Freud is the fact that Adler never saw the organism's attempt to cope with the real world as bringing one part of the mental life into conflict with another part. Instead, the modified perceptual program became the *plan* by which striving would take place, not a suppressor of organismic striving.

From this point, Adler developed the cognitive aspect of his theory, which we can now examine.

THE PRIMARY OF PERCEPTION IN ORGANIZING THE PURSUIT OF MOTIVES

"A person's behavior springs from his ideas," said Adler (1964, p. 19). As one construes the world, so does one act in it. One behaves as if one's self-constructed picture of the world is the true picture. These subjective beliefs guide the striving of the organism. They provide direction and goals for the striving. They constitute one's *definition of the situation*.

THE APPERCEPTIVE SCHEMA

Subjective beliefs have a relationship to each other. They form part of a schema for apprehending and coping with the demands of the real world. The schema is not limited to beliefs about the world but also includes beliefs about the self and the self–world interrelationship. Furthermore, it contains instructions for coping with the world, simple at first, then more complex. These instructions again grow out of early experiences.

Example of a simple instruction:

> If the stove is hot, don't touch it. It will hurt my hand if I touch it.

Example of a more complex instruction:

> If I tell mother something is wrong, she will ask me questions. If I don't tell her, she will leave me alone. When I want her to pay attention to me, I will tell her that something is wrong.

Both of these examples are apperceptive schemata. The schemata are used by the child in order to find its way in the world. As these schemata are used, they are continually refined to allow more accurate prediction of the outcome of events and hence of their meaning. Early learning consists of the construction of schemata and their meanings and values.

THE GUIDING IDEAL

Individual psychology holds that behavior is always a movement *toward* something; that behavioral movement always has a direction which is toward a goal. The goals are motivators; they act as a final cause for behavior; they are the end points of *intentions*. The goals themselves are often unconscious or at best dimly envisaged.

However, this is not only a motivational construct but also a cognitive one, since the goal which induces to action is perceived as a valuable object. The goal can become valuable because it gives pleasure or because it provides security or a feeling of superiority. Most important are those goals which the deepest convictions of the person say are crucial to his own worth—the striving for significance.

Thus, the organismic striving of the individual becomes embodied in a cognitive construct: an ideal. This guiding ideal, in turn, becomes a motive for directed movement. In its concrete forms, the ideal is found as an expression of the meaning assigned to life. Thus, one person's concrete form of the guiding ideal will be to have financial security, that of another to make a favorable impression on everyone, that of a third always to overcome challenges, that of a fourth always to avoid dangers, whereas that of a fifth may be a combination of two or more such concrete forms. The ideal shows the way in which the individual conceptualizes the meaning of life.

THE LIFE-STYLE

Apperceptive schemata grow in number and finally require integration into a master plan so that action in the world does not lose sight of the guiding idealized fiction. The overall direction of movement, no matter how many hesitations and detours occur, remains aimed at the guiding ideal. The master plan is actually a cognitive blueprint for striving in the world. This blueprint must contain certain elements: a set of constructs about the self, the world, and the relationship between the two; a construct about what the relationship should be; an image of ideal self; and a plan of action. All of these elements are attitudes, values, and meanings that the individual has conceived in the attempt to reduce life to manageable proportions.

PERCEPTUAL SELECTIVITY

The function of a blueprint is to provide direction for carrying out a task. The life-style gives direction for living life. The life-style begins as a rule of thumb for action in the world and becomes progressively refined. It contains what Kelly (1955) called "core constructs." It can be said to become the main modified perceptual program in the whole perceptual system in that it applies to a wider range of behavior than any other set of perceptions. Once it begins to operate, it leads to selective perceptual processing of all other incoming information. Since core constructs provide a basis for organizing the blueprint, these become the least modifiable part of the blueprint. The fictional ideal is shored up as the organism looks for information which confirms its rule of thumb, selectively perceiving information from events so that it proves to itself what it already suspects. Eventually, the rule of thumb takes on the character of the law for living which provides an assumed certainty about how to behave in life.

Early difficulties and insecurities (inferiority feelings) accentuate the tendency to give the rule of thumb a dogmatic character. When faced with a situation for which a plan of action is wanting or insufficient, the child tends to fall back on behavior which it already knows well (this is an individual psychologist's version of the psychoanalyst's concept of regression). At these times, the child holds on more tightly to its comforting "law of movement," which at least gives it a plan of action. One concrete form of such behavior is seen in the increased dogmatism and intolerance for ambiguity which are found in many people in times of insecurity.

COGNITIVE FUNCTIONS INFLUENCED BY PERCEPTUAL SELECTIVITY

Perhaps the great majority of cognitive functions are influenced by selective perception. *Memory* is a prime example of such a function. Subject to distortion in probably everyone, memory depends upon *attention, registration*, and *retrieval*, all of which operate selectively. What is watched for and what is later recalled will be influenced by the instructions in the master plan and subject to safeguarding tendencies which serve the master plan.

Learning, as such, is more attractive to the individual when it fits in with the person's own goals.

Expectancy is influenced by the person's constructs about himself in the world. *Fantasy* becomes a rehearsal, a preparation for what might happen. *Symbol creation* allows one to have a set of markers by which one can measure one's success or failure in reaching the goals. One patient recently told me, "I am thirty-five years old, I am unmarried, and I don't have job. That means I am a failure."

One result of the master plan is thus a private frame of reference by which the individual orients himself and arranges his coping strategies in the world-as-perceived.

CREATIVE SELF

The ability of the person to give meaning to life and to construct a master plan for coping with the world led Adler to conceive the theory of a *creative self*. By age three or four the child has formed a "prototypical life plan of action." The meanings contained in the prototypical plan are applied to subsequent experiences. In this way, the child creates its own law of movement which directs further psychic development. The person functions like an actor writing his own script and directing his own actions, forming his own personality through what Adler called *self-training*.

UNITY OF PERSONALITY

The basic dynamic force in Adler's theory is the striving for perfection or completion (Ansbacher, 1956). which in the social context of human life most often takes the form of striving for significance (*Geltungsstreben*) or superiority. Thought, affect, and cognition all work together in this striving. A motive (conscious or unconscious) evokes goal-directed behavior, which may be direct action response without emotional arousal, emotional arousal which catalyzes an action response, or a series of cognitions which can evoke an emotion and action together.

In humans, cognitive abilities are more fully developed than in any other animal; thought, therefore, can be expected to have correspondingly more influence on emotion and behavior in them.

SOCIAL INTEREST

The tendency of human beings to form attachments (social feelings) was considered by Adler to be a fact of life. The striving of the human is always in some way connected with human bonding. Social interest is the expression of this tendency in a way that promotes human welfare. Some aspects of social interest are innate as in the infant's tendency to bond to its mother. However, social interest is a potential that must be developed through training in cooperation with productive endeavor.

THE ROLE OF COGNITION IN PSYCHOPATHOLOGY

Psychopathology is characterized by heightened inferiority feelings, underdeveloped social interest, and an exaggerated uncooperative goal of personal superiority, which leads to striving in a self-centered way rather than in a cooperative and socially useful way. However, in its bare essence, psychopathology is the result of faulty training which leads to inappropriate fictions. Maladaptive behavior results from mistaken attitudes toward life. These mistaken attitudes have been described by Shulman (1973) as distorted perceptions about the self and life and distorted conclusions which result from these perceptions. A more extensive description of these attitudes as distorted cognitions has been provided by Ford and Urban (1964; see Table 1).

TABLE 1. Mistaken Attitudes as Distorted Cognitions[a]

Private perceptions	The use of private and idiosyncratic logic rather than common sense. Examples are seen most clearly in the psychotic patient. Sullivan's concept of prototaxic thinking will fit this category.
Perceptual sensitivity	An exaggerated tendency to make certain interpretations repeatedly from information that is more logically subject to different interpretation. Easily seen in the paranoid who uses almost any information as evidence to confirm his suspicion.
Antithetical mode of apperception	All black/all white thinking. The failure to appreciate shades of gray.
Analogical or "as if" thinking	Again seen most clearly in the psychotic. The psychotic depressive acts *as if* everything is hopeless because of some mistake he has made in the past.
Metaphorical thinking	An example would be conjuring up frightening images in order to feed and expand an anxious mood.
Rigidity of thought	The refusal to let facts interfere with one's previous assumptions.
Jumping to conclusions	Global/impulsive thinking.
Overdiscrimination	The opposite of global/impulsive thinking. One cannot see the forest for the trees.
Overambitious standards	Unrealistic aspirations for the self, unrealistic expectations from others.
Inappropriate self-image	A tendency to exaggerate inferiority or superiority feelings. The latter is seen in the narcissistic personality.
Pessimism	The tendency to focus on any information that confirms one's negative expectations.

[a]After Ford & Urban, 1964.

COGNITIVE MANEUVERS

The mistaken attitudes toward life invade the core constructs and are part of the personality style of the individual. In addition to these personality factors, psychopathological conditions display a wide use of cognitive maneuvers which help to sustain the pathology.

The life problem of the neurotic, according to Adler (1964), is not how to fit in with the demands of society but how to satisfy his own desires for superiority. The pathological symptoms are a creative arrangement designed to help the person achieve this goal. This arrangement partakes of a number of cognitive maneuvers, some of which are described below.

SAFEGUARDING AGAINST ANTICIPATED DIFFICULTIES

A simple example in such a maneuver is the technique of ignoring unwelcome information. Such selective perception is recognized in common speech when we say "Love is blind" to indicate that a person in love glosses over defects in the beloved. Another maneuver, often used for resisting therapeutic interpretations, is the *depreciation tendency*. In this maneuver, the person deflects threats to his own self-image by minimizing the threatening interpretation. A familiar example is Aesop's fox, who, after failing to reach the grapes, consoles himself that they were probably sour anyway.

The creation of obstacles is a maneuver which turns easy tasks into seemingly impossible ones so that one is excused from attempting them. This maneuver is not exclusively cognitive, since behavior such as procrastination can accomplish the same goal. A cognitive example is seen in the conjuring up of *disabling images*, which set obstacles in the way of the task. "How can I go to the party?" asks the socially insecure young man. "Everybody there will see that I am nervous and they will laugh at me." The image of others' knowing his inner thoughts is disturbing enough that he will not risk the experience.

A fourth example is the creation of a "resonance" between thought and an emotion by associating the two so that the occurrence of one brings on the other. Adler called this creation a *junktim* (an inappropriate) joining together of a thought and feeling for safeguarding purposes. The clearest example is in the phobic disorders, wherein a situation that does not frighten others is invested with such anxiety that the phobic person disables himself from functioning in the feared situation (Adler, 1968).

CARE AND FEEDING OF SYMPTOMS

This term coined by Mosak (1983) refers to the concept that symptoms will eventually tend to fade with time. Depressive reactions will eventually leave, anger will eventually subside, and anxiety will eventually diminish in the absence of new fearsome stimuli. Since the symptoms are an integral part of the creative arrangement, there must be some way of maintaining them so long as the original life problem exists. One such maneuver is arranging for experiences which will confirm the neurotic arrangement and exploiting them to justify one's behavior. Thus, the woman who believes that men will exploit her unconsciously invites her male friends to do so. We say of such a person that "he runs after his slap in the face."

OVERSENSITIVITY TO SMALL THINGS

The compulsive neurotic is disturbed if one small thing is out of place. The hypochondriac is alert to any body process he can notice and misinterprets normal physiological phenomena as symptoms of illness.

The *junktim* is also useful in maintaining symptoms. One patient suffering from frigidity did not reach orgasm during sexual contact with her husband. She reported a persistent connnection between loss of sexual arousal and a particular thought. She enjoyed the love-making every time and would always be aroused. In the middle of her enjoyment, she would think to herself, "I am sexually aroused. I wonder if I will be able to reach orgasm." This thought was immediately followed by the loss of the sexual arousal and disappointment.

Cognitive maneuvers are thus thoughts that are used in the immediate situation and have near-term effect. Beck's description (1976) of the thoughts of the depressive which evoke the depressed mood are excellent examples of such maneuvers.

O'Connell (1981) has described several cognitions that he calls "ego-constricting—that is, they lower self-esteen and lead to maladaptive behavior. He described "hidden demandments" by which a person abjures himself that he "must" or "must not" do, feel, or be something. In addition, he calls the tendency to place blame on the self or other "negative nonsense" which leads to no useful behavior, but instead to the "search for proof" which maintains the cycle of self-defeating cognitions. Continual practice, says O'Connell, leads to expertise in self-constriction. By means of unconscious invidious comparisons, self-esteem is lowered and cognitive "demandments" (similar to Ellis's irrational ideas and Horney's neurotic demands) follow. These demands on the self and life lead to feelings of defeat and discouragement. Then the blaming begins. Blaming, says O'Connell, serves no useful purpose except to provide one with adversaries. This is followed by the continuing search for proof, which, when found, leads to further lowering of the self-esteem and discouragement or to fictitious ways of proving one's superiority in the face of the feeling of defeat.

LIFE-STYLE (CORE) CONSTRUCTS IN VARIOUS PATHOLOGIC STATES

Adler described behavior in terms of movement—the action could be understood by understanding its goal and direction. However, throughout his writings on various pathological states, Adler described how the person perceived his situation in the world and the cognitive operations used. Thus, in discussing paranoia, Adler says:

> The patient blames others for lack of success in his exaggerated plans and his active striving for complete superiority results in an attitude of hostility to others. This expresses itself in ideas of reference and delusions. In these conditions, the patient sees himself as the center of the world. The ideas of the paranoiac are difficult to correct because he needs them in their very form to fortify his position. At the same time, they permit him to retain the fiction of his superiority without submitting them to the test. (1968, pp. 191–192)

In this example, we can see how Adler wove motivational and cognitive concepts together in accord with this theory that cognition always had motivational power and fit in with the dominant motives of the life-style. Another example can be seen in his description of euphoric mania as a state in which the patient decides, rather than to face the actual situation, to devalue reality and act as if he is already what he wants to be; and the schizophrenic as one who gives up hope of a successful life in the real world. (1929)

Forgus and Shulman (1979) have tried to convey the cognitive core of various psychopathological conditions by describing it in some of the personality disorders. The life-style constructs of the schizoid are described thus:

> I am a misfit. Life is a difficult place for me and human relationships are troublesome. Therefore, it is better for me to keep my distance and maintain a low profile. (1979, p. 332)

The compulsive personality has the following type of constructs:

> I am liable to be held responsible for whatever goes wrong. Life is unpredictable. Therefore, I have to be on guard against anything that might go wrong. (1979, p. 334)

Shulman (1968) has also described a paradigm of schizophrenia in which he infers a characteristic cognition that attends each phase. At the beginning, the schizophrenic is discouraged and feels unable to find significance in the real world. He gradually distorts and devalues common sense until after a period of agitated and confused thinking he loses his bearing. He then constructs his explanation for what has happened to him in such a way that he retains a fictitious feeling of worth even though surrounded by evidence that he is failing. He must then arrange distance between himself and consensual validation in order to protect his worth. Many of the symptoms of schizophrenia are attempts to keep distance and reify the private logic. In the development of schizophrenia, one could find the following cognitions: the belief that one is deficient as is, that one has to achieve some exalted position to feel secure in life, and the belief that the real world will not permit one's self to reach this exalted state.

COGNITIVE ASPECTS OF THERAPY

Since the theory pays so much attention to the cognitive aspects of personality, it is not surprising that psychotherapy has a strong cognitive cast. The Adlerian therapist does not think of his treatment as solely cognitive therapy because he sees cognition as part of the thinking-feeling-acting-organ language tetrad that constitutes behavior. However, in a psychotherapy which focuses on the patient's perceptions the amount of what can be called cognitive therapy is large indeed.

The main thrust of Adlerian therapy is to explain to the patient those subjective convictions that hamper his effective functioning in life and to encourage the patient to use his insights to meet the challenges of life with courage and cooperation. Clarification and explanation are used for the purpose of helping the patient to understand both that he *has* been mistaken and that he does not have to continue these mistakes. The therapist tries to build encouragement into this process by his manner of interpretation and clarification which is consistently ego-syntonic.

> A patient from a severely disturbed family had pulled himself out of the
> pathologic situation, attained an education and had become a respected
> university dean. He suffered from anxiety and feelings of inferiority about
> his acceptability to others. An ego-syntonic remark was very helpful to
> him. The therapist told him that, considering how he had started in life,
> he had overcome many more difficulties than most people had and had
> every right to be proud of himself.

This interpretation by the therapist is a deliberate attempt to
create in the patient's mind a different image of himself—to suggest
that the patient think about himself in a different way. The therapeutic intent is to correct the patient's mistaken apperception.

Some of the cognitive techniques used by Adlerians have been
described by Mosak (1979). One is instructing the patient to act "*as
if.*" When the patient complains, "If only I *could* . . .," the therapist
instructs him to act in a certain situation "as if" he *could* and observe
the results of the experience. *Creating images* is another technique.
Mosak reports the case of a patient who was afraid of being sexually
impotent. The therapist mused that he had never seen an impotent
dog. The patient concurred, saying, "Dogs just do it without worrying
about it." The therapist then suggested that the patient smile and
say "Bow-wow" before his next attempt. The patient returned the
next week to report that he had "bow-wowed" (Mosak, 1979, p. 72).

The push-button technique is another method. The patient is asked
to think of an unpleasant experience and to describe it. As expected,
this produces some unpleasant feelings in the patient. Next, the patient is asked to recall and describe a pleasant experience. Again, as
expected, this produces a more pleasant effect. This method is used
to teach that one can produce various affects within oneself by selecting various affect-laden topics to think about. The patient can
push the "happy button" or the "sad button" and it is his choice to
make.

PARADOXICAL RESPONSES

Mozdzierz, Macchittelli, and Lisiecki (1976) have discussed the
use of paradoxical techniques in Adlerian therapy. Paradox is used
to neutralize the patient's neurotic maneuvers by not responding to
them in the way the patient expects. Where the patient repeatedly
expresses a neurotic fear that he is going to die, for example, the
therapist says, "Well, if you are absolutely convinced of it, I guess
there's nothing I can do to change your mind." From the viewpoint
of the cognitive therapist, a paradoxical technique is intended to
create cognitive dissonance. The unexpected paradox intereferes with

the smooth flow of habitual cognitions and, one hopes, impels the patient to examine the implications of what he is saying.

Confrontation is an active therapeutic technique that is used to facilitate movement when the patient remains dead center or to bring movement up short where it is antitherapeutic. Confrontation asks the patient to consider what is going on *here* and *now* in the therapy situation. Shulman, (1971, 1972) has described a number of confrontations which utilized sudden questions. In confronting resistance, one may say:

"I notice you become defensive every time I wonder if you've made a mistake. Why is that?"

"You just changed the subject. Were we getting too close to something?"

Not only resistance, but other aspects of behavior can be noted:

"A look just passed over your face. What thought was on your mind?"

"Do you remember what I just said?"

"You just made a slip of the tongue. Did you catch it?"

Specific symptoms lends themselves to specific confrontations (always in a friendly tone of voice, of course):
(To the depressed patient):

"You are berating yourself again. Keep it up and you'll get yourself really depressed."

"I see you're telling yourself you're a failure again. Well, I guess you're trying to show me what high standards you have."

(To the anxious patient):

"You are very good at frightening yourself. You are truly creative. I am impressed at how you can create an atmosphere of fear. That you are so worried is really a tribute to your creativity."

COGNITIVE LEARNING IN FAMILY, GROUP THERAPY, AND CLASSROOM SITUATIONS

Influenced by Rudolf Dreikurs, Adlerians have done considerable work with family and school situations. The methods are described in Christensen and Schramski (1983), Dreikurs (1948, 1972), Dreikurs and Grey (1968), Dreikurs, Grunwald, and Pepper, (1971), and Dinkmeyer, Pew, and Dinkmeyer (1979). In addition to the usual Adlerian method of revealing goals and misconceptions, a number of specific cognitive behavioral techniques are used, of which two are listed below:

Changing one's own attitude. Dreikurs (1972) gives the example of an infant that cried excessively when put in the play pen. Dreikurs advised the mother that the infant was reacting to the mother's own insecurity in dealing with the infant and recommended that the mother be calm and realize that the crying would not harm the infant. In this example, the mother reported that as soon as she calmed her own behavior, the infant stopped crying when put into the play pen.

Keeping a list. On another occasion, Dreikurs, (personal observation by the author) noted a power contest between mother and child. The mother was constantly afraid the child would come to harm and kept telling him not to do things. The child was constantly doing whatever the mother told him not to. Dreikurs asked the mother, "How many times a day do you say 'don't' to the child?" The mother answered that she tried to stop the child about ten times a day. "I think it is more like five hundred," said Dreikurs. He then asked her to keep a list on the bulletin board in the kitchen. When the mother returned the next time, she reported that she had kept the list for only one day. She had reached fifty check marks and stopped, seeing that Dreikurs was right. She stopped the constant admonition and the child stopped the disobedience.

Changing the other's behavior by changing one's own first is a method applied to family, marital, group, and school situations by Adlerians working in these areas. The method includes (1) revealing the purpose of the behavior (as in the child's use of attention-getting mechanisms); (2) revealing the interaction by which one person provokes responses in others; (3) prescribing a change in attitude and behavior that will not reinforce the objectional behavior, and (4) prescribing new behavior that will reinforce cooperative responses from others.

Group-learning formats are extensively used by Adlerian counselors working with families, school teachers, and personnel situations. The group members study a book and discuss it intensively under the guidance of a trained group leader. At first glance, such a method may seem far from traditional psychotherapy, but it contains important identical ingredients; an atmosphere of openness and self-disclosure, discovery of the meaning of behavior in self and others, information about alternative attitudes and methods of behavior, and encouragement to change.

SUMMARY

Murray and Jacobson (1978), discussing early cognitive theorists, state:

> The most notable of these early congnitivists was Alfred Adler. Adler believed that the neurotic person had unrealistic and often anti-social goals, such as wanting to be superior to all others or to dominate others. In his therapy, Adler would attempt to change the patient's belief that he or she had to attain such goals, and he would try to encourage more socially productive ideas. In fact, Adler may be viewed as the forerunner of many modern cognitive therapists such as Albert Ellis, Julian Rotter, George Kelly, Eric Berne and Aaron Beck. (p. 66)

Since the Adlerian theory assigns to perception the task of giving meaning to the world and to cognition the power to program movement and evoke emotions, the Adlerian therapist seeks to understand in each patient the basic cognitive map of the world and the instructions for coping with it—what the Adlerian calls "the life-style." In addition, the maintenance of any systematic behavior that flies in the face of common sense requires a set of supporting cognitions. It is these faulty plans and supporting cognitions that the therapist seeks to ferret out and display to the patient.

REFERENCES

Adler, A. *Social interest: A challenge to mankind*, New York: Putnam, 1964.

Adler, A. *The practice and theory of Individual Psychology*. Totowa, NJ: Littlefield Adams, 1968.

Adler, A. *Problems of neurosis*. London: Kegan Paul, 1919.

Ansbacher, H. L., & Ansbacher, R. R., *The Individual Psychology of Alfred Adler*. New York: Basic Books, 1956.

Beck, A. T. *Cognitive therapy and the emotional disorders*. New York: International Universities Press, 1976.

Christensen, O. C., & Schramski, T. C., *Adlerian family counseling*. Minneapolis: Educational Media Corporation, 1983.

Dinkmeyer, D. C., Pew, W. L., & Dinkmeyer, D. C., Jr. *Adlerian counseling and psychotherapy*. Belmont, CA: Wadsworth, 1979.

Dreikurs, R. *The challenge of parenthood*. New York: Duell, Sloan, and Pearce, 1948.

Dreikurs, R. & Grey, L., *Logical consequences*. New York: Meredith, 1968.

Dreikurs, R., Grunwald, B., & Pepper, F. C., *Maintaining sanity in the classroom*. New York: Harper & Row, 1971.

Dreikurs, R. *Coping with children's misbehavior.* New York: Hawthorn, 1972.

Ford, D. H., & Urban, H. B., *Systems of psychotherapy: A comparative study.* New York: Wiley, 1964.

Forgus, R., & Shulman, B. H. *Personality: A cognitive view.* Englewood Cliffs, NJ: Prentice-Hall, 1979.

Kelly, G. A. *The psychology of personal constructs.* (Vol. 1), New York: Norton, 1955.

Mosak, H. H. *Personal communication,* 1983.

Mosak, H. H. Adlerian psychotherapy. In *Current psychotherapies,* R. J. Corsini (Ed.). Itasca, IL: F. E. Peacock, 1979, pp. 44–94.

Mozdzierz, G. J., Macchittelli, F. J., & Lisiecki, J., The paradox in psychotherapy: An Adlerian perspective. *Journal of Individual Psychology, 1976, 32,* 169–184.

Murray, E. J., & Jacobson, L. T., Cognition and learning in traditional and behavioral therapy. In *Handbook of psychotherapy and behavior change.* S. L. Garfield & A. E. Bergin (Eds.). New York: Wiley, 1978, pp. 661–687.

O'Connell, W. E. Natural high therapy. In *Handbook of innovative psychotherapies,* R. J. Corsini (Ed.). New York: Wiley, 1981, pp. 554–568.

Shulman, B. H. *Essays in schizophrenia.* Baltimore: Williams & Wilkins, 1968.

Shulman, B. H. Confrontation techniques in Adlerian psychotherapy. *Journal of Individual Psychology,* 1971, *27,* 167–175.

Shulman, B. H. Confrontation techniques. *Journal of Individual Psychology,* 1972, *28,* 177–183.

Shulman, B. H. *Contributions to Individual Psychology.* Chicago: Alfred Adler Institute, 1973.

Vaihinger, H. *The Philosophy of "As If."* New York: Harcourt, Brace, 1925.

CHAPTER 10

Logos, Paradox, and the Search for Meaning

VIKTOR E. FRANKL

In a paper presented to the Second World Congress of Logotherapy, Alfried A. Laengle came up with the contention that "by its main term and program, logotherapy is the first cognitive psychotherapy." In fact, when logotherapy was launched in the late 1920s, the idea behind it was to overcome so-called psychologism, which represents one among the various outgrowths of reductionism, namely, the tendency to interpret a psychological phenomenon by "reducing" it, that is, tracing it back to its alleged emotional origin, thereby totally neglecting the question of its rational validity. As early as in 1925, I cautioned against this one-sided approach by pointing out (Frankl, 1925) that renouncing *a priori* any dispute of the patient's *Weltanschauung* on rational grounds results in giving away one of the most powerful weapons within our therapeutic armamentarium. Anyway, the very name coined to denote the new approach, namely, logotherapy, was intended to signify the shifting emphasis from the affective to the cognitive aspects of human behavior.

In the paper mentioned above, however, Laengle went on also to state that "the idea of logos is only partly outlined by the classical cognitive terms of cognition," indicating that during the development of logotherapy (better to say, of the logo-theory underlying it) logos included the cognition, or perception, of meaning. This ingredient of logotherapy is that which accounts for its appeal in an age such as ours, when a feeling of meaninglessness is so pervasive and predominant.

VIKTOR E. FRANKL • University of Vienna Medical School, 1 Mariannengasse, Vienna 1090, Austria.

Let me clarify from the start that meaning, as well as its perception, as seen from the logotherapeutic perspective, is something completely down to earth rather than anything floating in the air or residing in an ivory tower. Sweepingly, I would locate the cognition of meaning (that is, the personal meaning of a concrete situation) midway between an "Aha" experience along the lines of Karl Buhler's concept and a *Gestalt* perception. The *Gestalt* implies the sudden awareness of a "figure" on a "ground," whereas, as I see it, the perception of meaning boils down to becoming aware of a possibility against the background of reality, or, more simply, becoming aware of what can be done about a given situation.

In addition to the paper I had published in 1925 in the journal edited by Alfred Adler, another paper of mine (Frankl, 1924) was published, upon the initiative of Sigmund Freud, in the *International Journal of Psychoanalysis* (1924). But why this historical digression? The Freudian and the Adlerian views on psychotherapy were diametrically opposed to one another. But this is not unusual, for wherever you open the book of the history of psychotherapy you are confronted with two pages, a left page and a right page, and both pages show pictures—pictures of man, that is—that not only differ from one another but even contradict one another. Let us symbolize such mutual contradictions by a square on one page and a circle on the facing page (Figure 1). And now remember what you know from mathematics, namely, the fact that the age-old problem of squaring the circle has been proven to be unsolvable. But if I may come up with a suggestion—what about turning the left page into a perpendicular position (Figure 2)? All of a sudden you can imagine that the square and the circle are but the (two-dimensional) projections of a (three-dimensional) cylinder inasmuch as they represent its profile view and its ground-plan, respectively (Figure 3). And then we notice that the

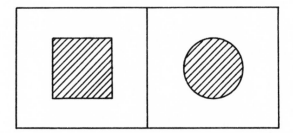

FIGURE 1

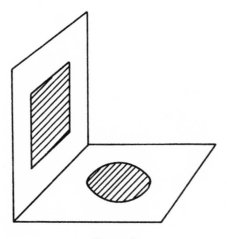

FIGURE 2

contradictions between the pictures need no longer contradict the oneness of what they depict.

Incidentally, there is another contradiction that disappears as soon as we conceive the pictures as mere projections. If we assume that the cylinder is not a solid but rather an open vessel—say, an empty cup—this openness, too, disappears in the lower dimensions;

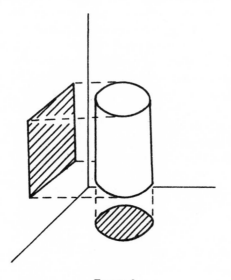

FIGURE 3

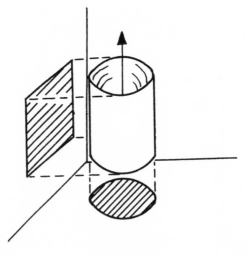

FIGURE 4

both, the square and the circle, are closed figures (Figure 4). But once we view them as mere projections, their closedness no longer contradicts the openness of the cylinder.

But how shall we now apply all this to our concept, our theory, of man, to our anthropological theory as it—explicitly or implicitly— underlies our psychotherapeutic practice? Well, similarly, the contradictions between the disparate pictures of man as they are propounded by the different psychotherapeutic schools cannot be overcome and surpassed unless we proceed into the next higher dimension; that is to say, as long as we remain in those lower dimensions into which we have projected man in the first place, there is no hope for a unified concept. Only if we open up the next higher dimension, which is the human dimension, the dimension of the specifically human phenomena—only if we follow man into this dimension is it possible to catch the oneness as well as the humanness of man. Further, entering the human dimension becomes mandatory if we are to tap and muster those resources which are available solely in the human dimension in order to incorporate them in our therapeutic armamentarium.

Among these resources, there are two which are most relevant for psychotherapy: man's capacity for self-detachment and his capacity for self-transcendence. As to the first, it could be defined as the capacity to detach oneself from outward situations, to take a stand toward them; but man is capable of detaching himself not only from the world but also from himself. And it is this very capacity which is mobilized in the logotherapeutic technique of *paradoxical intention* (Frankl, 1939, 1947).

From what I wrote in 1947 I would like to quote the following passage in order to show on what theoretical grounds the practice of paradoxical intention had been based. (In addition, the quotation may build a bridge of mutual understanding between logotherapists and behavior therapists.)

> All psychoanalytically oriented psychotherapies are mainly concerned with uncovering the primary conditions of the "conditioned reflex" as which neurosis may well be understood, namely, the situation—outer or inner—in which a given neurotic symptom emerged the first time. It is this author's contention, however, that the full-fledged neurosis is caused not only by the primary conditions but also by secondary conditioning. This reinforcement, in turn, is caused by the feedback mechanism called anticipatory anxiety. Therefore, if we wish to recondition a conditioned reflex, we must unhinge the vicious cycle formed by anticipatory anxiety, and this is the very job done by our paradoxical intention technique.

This technique lends itself to the treatment of phobic and obsessive-compulsive conditions. I am used to explaining its therapeutic effectiveness to my students by starting with the mechanism called anticipatory anxiety. A given symptom evokes on the part of the patient a phobia in the form of the fearful expectation of its recurrence; this phobia provokes the symptom actually to recur; and the recurrence of the symptom reinforces the phobia (Figure 5).

There are cases in which the object of the "fearful expectation" is—fear itself. Our patients spontaneously speak of a "fear of fear." Upon closer interrogation it turns out that they are afraid of the consequences of their fear: fainting, coronaries, or strokes. But as I pointed out in 1953 (Frankl, 1953) they react to their fear of fear by

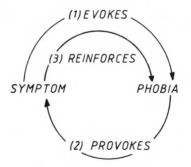

FIGURE 5. The first circle formation: phobias.

a "flight from fear"—what you would call an avoidance pattern of behavior. By 1960 I had arrived at the conviction that "phobias are partially due to the endeavour to avoid the situation in which anxiety arises." Since that time, this contention has been confirmed by behavior therapists on many occasions.

Along with the phobic pattern which we may circumscribe as a flight from fear, there is another pattern, the obsessive-compulsive one which is characterized by what one may call a "fight against obsessions and compulsions." The respective patients are afraid that they might commit suicide or homicide or that the strange ideas haunting them might be the precursors, if not already the symptoms, of a psychosis. In other words, they are not afraid of fear itself but rather afraid of themselves.

Again, a circle formation is established. The more the patient fights his obsessions and compulsions, the stronger they become. Pressure induces counterpressure, and counterpressure in turn increases pressure (Figure 6).

In order to unhinge all the vicious circles discussed, the first thing to do is to take the wind out of the anticipatory anxieties underlying them, and this is precisely the business to be carried out by paradoxical intention. It may be defined as a procedure in whose framework the patients are encouraged to do, or wish to happen, the very things they fear—albeit with tongue in cheek. In fact, "an integral element in paradoxical intention is the deliberate evocation of humor," as Lazarus (1971) justifiably points out. After all, the sense of humor is one of the various aspects of the specfically human capacity of self-detachment. No other animal is capable of laughing.

In paradoxical intention, the pathogenic fear is replaced by a paradoxical wish. The vicious circle of anticipatory anxiety is un-

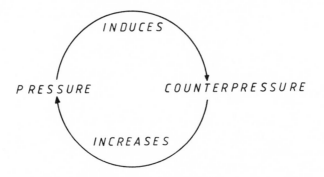

FIGURE 6. The second circle formation: obsessions and compulsions.

hinged. For illustrative case material, the reader is referred to the pertinent literature. As an example, take the following letter I once received from a reader (Frankl, 1978):

> Two days after reading *Man's Search for Meaning*, a situation arose which offered the opportunity to put logotherapy to the test. During the first meeting of a seminar class on Martin Buber, I spoke up saying I felt diametrically opposed to the views so far expressed. While expressing my views I began to perspire heavily. When I became aware of my excessive sweating I felt even more anxiety about the others seeing me perspire, and this caused me to sweat even more. Almost instantly I recalled a case study of a physician who consulted you, Dr. Frankl, because of his fear of perspiring, and I thought, "Here I am in a similar situation." Being ever skeptical of methods, and specifically of logotherapy, in this instance I determined the situation was ideal for a trial and put logotherapy to the test. I remembered your advice to the physician and resolved to deliberately show those people how much I could sweat, chanting in my thoughts as I continued to express my feelings on the subject: "More! More! More! Show these people how much you can sweat, really show them!" Within two or three seconds after applying paradoxical intention I laughed inwardly and could feel the sweat beginning to dry on my skin. I was amazed and surprised at the result, for I did not believe logotherapy would work. It did, and so quickly! Again, inwardly, I said to myself, "Damn, that Dr. Frankl really has something here! Regardless of my skeptical feelings, logotherapy actually worked in my case. (p. 131)

Hand, Lamontagne, and Marks (1974), who had treated chronic agoraphobia patients in groups, observed that they spontaneously used humor as an impressive coping device—"When the whole group was frightened, somebody would break the ice with a joke, which would be greeted with the laughter of relief." They reinvented paradoxical intention, one may say.

Paradoxical intention may be effective even in severe cases. Lamontagne (1978) for one instance, cured a case of incapacitating erythrophobia that had been present for 12 years, within four sessions. Niebauer (Kocourek, Niebauer, & Polak, 1959) successfully treated a 65-year-old woman who had suffered from a hand-washing compulsion for 60 years. And Jacobs (1972) cites the case of Mrs. K. who for 15 years had suffered from severe claustrophobia and was cured by him within a week. His treatment was a combination of paradoxical intention, relaxation, and desensitization, a fact that should demonstrate that paradoxical intention, or for that matter logotherapy, does in no way invalidate any other, or previous, psychotherapies but rather presents a means to maximize their effectiveness. In the same vein, Ascher (1980) points out that "most therapeutic approaches have specific techniques" and "these techniques are not especially useful for, nor relevant to, alternative therapeutic systems." But there is "one notable exception in this observation," namely, paradoxical intention. Which "is an exception because many professionals representing a wide variety of disparate approaches to psychotherapy have incorporated this intervention into their systems both practically and theoretically." In fact, "in the past two decades, paradoxical intention has become popular with a variety of therapists" who had been "impressed by the effectiveness of the technique." Even more important, "behavioral techniques have been developed which appear to be translations of paradoxical intention into learning terms."

Yalom (1980), too, holds that paradoxical intention is an "effective" technique which "anticipated the similar technique of symptom prescription and paradox employed by the schools of Milton Erickson, Jay Haley, Don Jackson, and Paul Watzlawick.

I would recommend to take heed not to confound "the similar technique of symptom prescription" with paradoxical intention. They are two different things. When I apply symptom prescription, I want the patient to increase, say, anxiety. When I use paradoxical intention, however, I want the patient to do, or wish to happen, *that of which* he is afraid. In other words, not fear itself but rather its *object* is dealt with. Let me invoke a case published by the logotherapist Byung-Hak Ko (1981), a professor at the National University of Korea. The patient had been suffering from fear of death. Treating him by paradoxical intention, the psychiatrist did in no way recommend for him to increase the thanatophobia but, to quote from the paper, the respective instructions read: "Try to be more dizzy, have faster palpitations, and choke more. Try to *die* in front of the people." And the next time, in fact, the patient entered the psychiatrist's "office cheerfully and reported success."

Compare this type of intervention with what I would call symptom description although it was intended by a professor at the University of Nebraska to serve as an illustration of paradoxical intention: "For example, a person who had an obsession to wash his hands ten times a day will be invited to do so thirty times a day." Of course, this is symptom prescription rather than paradoxical intention.

How much the treatment would have been different if paradoxical intention had been enacted should be illustrated by a case of washing compulsion that I myself published in German (Frankl, 1947). The patient felt compelled to wash her hands several hundred times a day. Thereupon a doctor on my hospital department suggested that, "for a change," the patient, instead of being afraid of bacteria should wish to contract an infection. "I can't get enough bacteria," she was advised to tell herself, "I want to become as dirty as possible. There is nothing nicer than bacteria." And the patient really followed the advice. She asked the other patients at the hospital department to let her borrow from them as many bacteria as possible and came up with the resolution no longer to wash "the poor creatures" away but, instead, to keep them alive. But certainly no one on my staff would have dreamt of recommending that the patient no longer wash her hands several *hundred* times a day, but, along the lines of symptom prescription, that she do so several *thousand* times a day.

Ascher and Turner (1979) were the first to come up with a "controlled experimental validation of the clinical effectiveness" of paradoxical intention in comparison with other behavioral strategies. But Solyom *et al.* (1972) also proved experimentally that paradoxical intention works.

Inasmuch as the two human capacities, self-detachment and self-transcendence, equally derive from logotherapy's concept of man, both, paradoxical intention and the business of finding meaning in life, belong to one another. It is true that paradoxical intention is not "specifically related to life meaning" (Yalom, 1980). Yet I cannot subscribe to the statement made by Weisskopf-Joelson (1978) to the effect that "paradoxical intention is not closely related to the logotherapeutic position in ways other than owing its origin to Frankl." I rather think that the effectiveness of the technique, in the final analysis, is due to some basic trust in *Dasein*, ultimately, to some sort of faith which is reinstalled and reinstated by the technique. As far, however, as fear is concerned, faith proves to be the very antagonist. In fact, there is an old saying that reads: "Fear knocked at the door. Faith answered, and no one was there."

Nor can Yalom (1980) persuade himself "that paradoxical intention is specifically related to life meaning." Yet to the extent that it "allows one to assume responsiblity for one's symptoms, it may be considered within the domain of existential therapy." Regarding logotherapy, however, Lukas (1932) makes the following statement:

> In my twelve years of practicing logotherapy I have never doubted that paradoxical intention is a true child of logotherapy, even though it is frequently adopted, under various names, by other schools of psychotherapy. Its logotherapeutic origin, however, can easily be identified. The concept of self-distancing legitimizes paradoxical intention as a true child of logotherapy because this method constitutes ninety percent of a ther-

apeutic dialogue with the self. This legitimacy is not invalidated by the
many "illegitimate children"—practices used by other schools which do
not admit the paternity for methods strikingly similar to paradoxical
intention.

But let us turn to the second human capacity, that of self-transcendence. It denotes the fact that being human always points, and
is directed, to something other than oneself, namely, to meanings to
fulfill, or to other human beings lovingly to encounter. And only to
the extent to which a human being lives out this, his self-transcendence, is he really becoming human and actualizing his self. This always reminds me of the ironic fact that the capacity of the eye visually
to perceive the surrounding world is contingent on its incapacity to
perceive itself, to see anything of itself. Whenever the eye sees anything of itself, its function is impaired. When does the eye see anything
of itself? If I am affected by a cataract, I see something like a cloud—
then my eye sees its own cataract. Or if I am affected by glaucoma,
I see rainbow halos around the lights—then my eye perceives, as it
were, the heightened tension that causes the glaucoma. The normally
functioning eye does not see itself but rather is overlooking itself, and
similarly man is human to the extent to which he overlooks and
forgets himself by giving himself to a cause to serve or another person
to love. By being immersed in work or in love, we are transcending
ourselves and thereby actualizing ourselves.

Why has the self-transcendent quality of the human reality been
so completely ignored and neglected by psychology? As I see it, this
has something to do with the Heisenberg law—provided that I am
allowed to restate it, a bit freely, as follows: The observation of a
process unavoidably and automatically influences the process. Something similar holds for the strictly scientifically (rather than phenom-
enologically) oriented observation of human behavior in that it cannot escape making a subject into an object. But, alas, it is the inalienable
property of a subject, I would say, that it has objects of its own.
(According to the phenomenological terminology [Brentano, Husserl,
and Scheler], they are called intentional objects or intentional referents.)[1] Understandably, at the moment the subject is made into an
object, its own objects disappear. And inasmuch as the intentional
referents form *the world in* which a human being *is* as a "being-in-
the-world," to use Heidegger's more often than not misused phrase,
the world is shut out as soon as man is seen no longer as a being, so
to speak, acting into the world but rather as a being reacting to stimuli

---

[1]Intentionality may be viewed as the cognitive aspect of self-transcendence.

(the behavioristic model) or abreacting drives and instincts (the psychodynamic model). In either way, the human being is dealt with as a worldless monad or a closed system, and now we remember what was said at the outset, namely, that the openness of a vessel projected into lower dimensions disappears.

To repeat, human behavior is really human to the extent to which it means acting into the world. This in turn implies being motivated by the world. In fact, the world toward which a human being transcends itself is a world replete with meanings that constitute the reasons to act and full as well of other human beings to love. As soon as we project human beings into the dimension of a psychology conceived in strictly scientific terms, we cut them off from the world of potential reasons. Instead of reasons there are only causes. The difference? Reasons motivate me to act in the way I choose. Causes determine my behavior unwillingly and unwittingly, whether I know it or not. When I cut onions I weep. My tears have a cause. But I have no reason to weep. When a loved one dies I have a reason to weep.

And what are the causes that are left to the psychologist with a blind spot for self-transcendence and consequently for meanings and for reasons? If he is a psychoanalyst, he will substitute for motives drives and instincts as that which causes human behavior. If he is a behaviorist, he will see in human behavior the mere effect of conditioning and learning processes. If there are no meanings, no reasons, no choices, determinants must be hypothesized, one way or another, to replace them. To be sure, the humanness of human behavior is done away with, in the circumstances. And if psychology, or for that matter psychotherapy, is to be rehumanized it must remain cognizant of self-transcendence rather than blotting it out.

One of the aspects of self-transcendence is what is called in logotherapy the will to meaning. If man can find and fulfill a meaning in his life he becomes happy but also capable of coping with suffering. If he can see a meaning he is even prepared to give his life. On the other hand, if he cannot see a meaning he is equally inclined to take his life even in the midst, and in spite of, all the welfare and affluence surrounding him. Just consider the escalating suicide figures in welfare states such as Sweden and Austria. Deliberately to quote a behaviorist, namely, L. Bachelis (1976), director of the Behavioral Therapy Center in New York, "many undergoing therapy at the Center tell [him] they have a good job, they're successful but they want to kill themselves, because they find life meaningless." I do not intend to say that most suicides are undertaken out of a feeling of meaninglessness, but I am convinced that people would have overcome the impulse to kill themselves if they had seen meaning in their lives. Meanwhile, people have the means to live but no meaning to live for. As you see, logotherapy squarely faces the situation confronting us "in a post-petroleum society" and even "has special relevance during this critical transition," to quote Wirth (1980).

Happiness is not only the result of fulfilling a meaning but also more generally the unintended side effect of self-transcendence. It therefore cannot be *pursued* but rather must ensue. The more one aims at it the more one misses aim. This is most conspicuous with sexual pleasure and it is the characteristic of the third pattern to be discussed, the sexually neurotic, that people strive directly for sexual performance or experience, male patients trying to demonstrate their potency and female patients their capacity of orgasm. In logotherapy, we are used to speaking of *hyperintention* in this context. Since hyperintention is often accompanied by what we call in logotherapy *hyperreflection*, that is, too much self-observation, both, hyperintention and hyperreflection join to form another, the third, *circle formation* (Figure 7). In order to break it up, centrifugal forces must be brought into play. Hyperreflection can be counteracted by the logotherapeutic technique called *de-reflection*, that is to say, the patients, instead of watching themselves, should forget themselves. But they cannot forget themselves unless they give themselves.

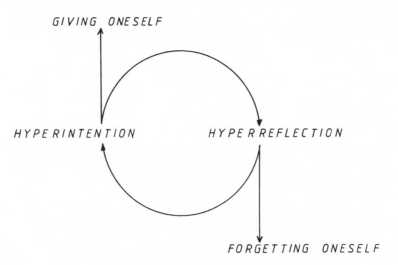

FIGURE 7. The third circle formation: sexual dysfunctions.

Again and again, it turns out that the hyperintention of sexual performance and experience is due to the patient's sexual achievement orientation and tendency to attach to sexual intercourse a "demand quality." To eliminate the tendency is the very purpose of a logotherapeutic strategy that, along with the dereflection technique, I described in English for the first time in 1952 (Frankl, 1952) and more elaborately in *The Unheard Cry for Meaning* (1978). Sahakian and Sahakian (1972) were the first to point out what later on was confirmed by Ascher (1980) and finally by Bulka (1979) who sees in dereflection "a clear anticipation of the approach of Masters and Johnson."

The feeling of meaninglessness not only underlies the mass neurotic triad of today, that is, depression–addiction–aggression, but may also eventuate in what we logotherapists call a "noogenic neurosis." Thus far, ten researchers have estimated independently of each other, that about 20 percent of neuroses are noogenic (c.f. Klinger, 1977). In such cases, logotherapy comes in as a specific procedure devised to assist the patient in finding meaning. As such, logotherapy is based on a logotheory and the logotheory in turn is empirically based. The logotherapist never prescribes meaning but he may well describe how the process of meaning perception is enacted by the man or woman in the street, more specifically, by virtue of their "prereflective ontological self-understanding," as I am used to calling it. In other words, logotherapists neither preach meaning nor teach it but learn it from people who for themselves have discovered and fulfilled it.[2] And a phenomenological analysis reveals that there are three main avenues on which one arrives at meaning in love. The first is finding it by creating a work or by doing a deed.

However, in addition to the meaning potential inherent and dormant in creating and doing, a second avenue to meaning in life is available in experiencing something or encountering someone; in other words, meaning can be found not only in work but also in life. Weisskopf-Joelson (1980) observes in this context that the logotherapeutic "notion that experiencing can be as valuable as achieving is therapeutic because it compensates for our one-sided emphasis on the external world of achievement at the expense of the internal world of experience."

Most important, however, is a third avenue to meaning in life: It finally turns out the even the helpless victim of a hopeless situation,

---

[2]To quote C. Buhler (1971), "All we can do is study the lives of people who seem to have found their answers to the questions of what ultimately a life was about."

facing a fate he cannot change, may rise above himself, may grow beyond himself, and by so doing change himself. He may turn a personal tragedy into a triumph. To quote a pertinent example from the Texarkana Gazette of April 15, 1980:

> Jerry Long has been paralyzed from his neck down since a driving accident which rendered him a quadruplegic three years ago. He was 17 when the accident occurred. Today Long can use his mouth stick to type. He "attends" two courses at Texarkana Community College via a special telephone. The intercom allows Long to both hear and participate in class discussions. He also occupies his time by reading, watching television and writing.

In a letter I received from him he writes:

> I view my life as being abundant with meaning and purpose. The attitude that I adopted on that fateful day has become my personal credo for life: I broke my neck, it didn't break me. I am currently enrolled in my first psychology course in college. I believe that my handicap will only enhance my ability to help others. I know that without the suffering, the growth that I have achieved would have been impossible.

For a quarter of a century I was running the neurological department of a general hospital, and I bear witness to my patients' capacity to turn their predicament into a human achievement. Who tells the story of the young men who yesterday were skiing in the Austrian Alps or riding a Yamaha and today are paralyzed from the neck down? Or of the girls who yesterday were dancing in a disco and today are confronted with the diagnosis of a brain tumor?

Weisskopf-Joelson (1958) once expressed the hope that logotherapy "may help counteract certain unhealthy trends in the present-day culture of the United States, where the incurable sufferer is given very little opportunity to be proud of his suffering and to consider it ennobling rather than degrading so that he is not only unhappy, but also ashamed of being unhappy."

But also empirical evidence is available regarding the possibility of finding meaning even in suffering. Researchers at the Yale University School of Medicine (Sledge, Boydstun, & Rabe, 1980)

> have been impressed with the number (61%) of POWs of the Vietnam war who explicitly claimed that although their captivity was extraordinarily stressful—filled with torture, disease, malnutrition, and solitary confinement—they nevertheless benefited from the captivity experience seeing it as a growth experience. They believed they are wiser than before their captivity, stronger, and more mature. (p. 731)

By virtue of the fact that meaning may be squeezed out even from suffering, life proves to be potentially meaningful literally up to its last moment, up to one's last breath. Even death may be turned into something potentially meaningful. Again, empirical evidence is available. Thomas and Weiner (1974) reported that patients who were critically ill had higher Purpose in Life Test (PIL) scores than had patients with a minor ailment or nonpatients. Thus, not only life itself is potentially meaningful but also "the end of life is always a time of unparalleled potential for personal and interpersonal growth," as the surgeon Balfour Mount of McGill University once said, adding the words "for the patient and his family." How true. Let me cite an example: An elderly general practitioner consulted me because of his severe depression. He could not overcome the loss of his wife who had died two years before and whom he had loved above all else. I confronted him with the question, "What would have happened, Doctor, if you had died first, and your wife would have had to survive you?" "Oh," he said, "for her this would have been terrible; how she would have suffered!" Whereupon I replied, "You see, Doctor, such a suffering has been spared her, and it is you who have spared her this suffering; but now you have to pay for it by surviving and mourning her."

Of course, this was no therapy in the proper sense since his despair was no disease. But in that moment I did succeed in changing his attitude toward his unalterable fate inasmuch as from that time on he could at least see a meaning in his suffering. In fact, despair could be defined as suffering without meaning. And that is why in the courses that I give to my medical students, I write on the blackboard the equation:

$$D(espair) = S(uffering) - M(eaning)$$

But let me make it perfectly clear that in no way is suffering *necessary* to find meaning. I only insist that meaning is possible even in the presence of suffering. Provided, to be sure, that we have to deal with unavoidable suffering—if it were avoidable, the meaningful thing to do would be to remove its cause, bet it psychological, biological, or political. To suffer unnecessarily is certainly masochism rather than heroism. But if you really cannot change a situation that causes your suffering, what you still can choose is your attitude. And I will not forget an interview I once heard on Austria's television given by a Polish cardiologist who during World War II had organized the Warsaw ghetto upheaval. "What a heroic deed," exclaimed the reporter. "Listen," calmly replied the doctor, "to take a gun and shoot is no great thing; but if the SS leads you to a gas chamber or to a mass grave to execute you on the spot, and you can't do anything about it—except for keeping head high and going your way with dignity, you see, this is what I would call heroism." He should know.[3]

So life is potentially meaningful under any conditions, be they pleasurable or miserable, and precisely this cornerstone of logotherapeutic teaching (which had been based solely on the intuitions of a teenager named Viktor E. Frankl) has lately been corroborated on strictly empirical grounds, through tests and statistics applied to tens of thousands of subjects. The overall result (of research conducted by Brown, Casciani, Crumbaugh, Dansart, Durlak, Kratochvil, Lukas, Lunceford, Mason, Meier, Murphy, Planova, Popielski, Richmond, Roberts, Ruch, Sallee, Smith, Yarnell, and Young) was that meaning is in principle available to each and every person irrespective of sex, age, IQ, educational background, character structure and environment and, last but not least, irrespective of whether one' is religious or not, and, if religious, irrespective of the denomination to which one belongs.

Those suffering from obsessive-compulsive and phobic conditions to be aided by paradoxical intention are but a minority. As to the majority, however, it is not a silent one. To those who know to listen, it is rather a crying majority—crying for meaning! For too long a time the cry has remained unheard. Psychotherapy must give a hearing to the unheard cry for meaning.

REFERENCES

Ascher, L. M. Paradoxical intention viewed by a behavior therapist. *International Forum for Logotherapy*, 1980, *1*(3), 13–16.

Ascher, L. M. Paradoxical intention. In A. Goldstein & E. B. Foa (eds.), *Handbook of behavioral interventions*. New York: Wiley, 1980.

Ascher, L. M. and R. M. Turner. Controlled comparison of progressive relaxation, stimulus control, and paradoxical intention therapies for insomnia. *Journal of Consulting and Clinical Psychology*, 1979, *47*(3), 500–508.

Bachelis, L. Depression and disillusionment. *APA Monitor*, May 1976.

Buhler, C. Basic theoretical concepts of humanistic psychology. *American Psychologist*, 1971, *26*, 378.

Bulka, R. P. *The quest for ultimate meaning: Principles and applications of logotherapy*. New York: Philosophical Library, 1979.

Frankl, V. E. Zur mimischen Bejahung und Verneinung, *Internationale Zeitschrift für Psychoanalyse*, 1924, *10*, 437–438.

---

[3]An empirical study recently conducted by Austrian public opinion pollsters evidenced that those who are held in highest esteem by most of the people interviewed were neither the great artists nor the great scientists, neither the great statesmen nor the great sports figures, but those who master a hard lot with dignity.

Frankl, V. E. Psychotherapie and Weltanschauung, *Internationale Zeitschrift Für Individualpsychologie*, 1925, *3*, 250–252.

Frankl, V. E. Zur medikamentosen Unterstutzung der Psychotherapie bei Neurosen, *Schweizer Archiv für Neurologie und Psychiatrie*, 1939, *43*, 26–31.

Frankl, V. E. *Die Psychotherapie in der Praxis*. Vienna: Deuticke, 1947.

Frankl, V. E. The pleasure principle and sexual neurosis. *International Journal of Sexology*, 1952, *5*, 128–130.

Frankl, V. E. Angst und Zwang. *Acta Psychotherapeutica*, 1953, *43*, 26–31.

Frankl, V. E. Paradoxical intention: A logotherapeutic technique. *American Journal of Psychotherapy*, 1960, *14*, 520–535.

Frankl, V. E. *The unheard cry for meaning*. New York: Simon and Schuster, 1978.

Hand, I., Lamontagne, Y., & Marks, I. M. Group exposure (flooding) in vivo for agoraphobics. *British Journal of Psychiatry*, 1974, *14*, 588–602.

Jacobs, M. An holistic approach to behavior therapy. In A. A. Lazarus (ed.), *Clinical behavior therapy*. New York: Brunner/Mazel, 1972.

Klinger, E. *Meaning and void*. Minneapolis: University of Minnesota Press, 1977.

Ko, Byung-Hak. Applications in Korea. *International Forum for Logotherapy*, 1981, *4*(2), 89–93.

Kocourek, K., Niebauer, E., & Polak, P., Ergebnisse der klinischen Anwendung der Logotherapie. In V. E. Frankl, V. E. von Gebsattel, & J. H. Schultz (eds.), *Handbuch der Neurosenlehre und Psychotherapie*. Munich: Urban & Schwarzenberg, 1959.

Lamontagne, Y. Treatment of erythrophobia by paradoxical intention. *Journal of Nervous and Mental Disease*, 1978, *166*(4), 304–406.

Lazarus, A. A. *Behavior therapy and beyond*. New York: McGraw-Hill, 1971.

Lukas, E. The "birthmarks" of paradoxical intention. *International Forum for Logotherapy*, 1982, *5*(1), 20–24

Sahakian, W. S. & Sahakian, B. J. Logotherapy as a personality theory. *Israel Annals of Psychiatry*, 1972, *10*, 230–244.

Sledge, W. H., Boydstun, J. A., & Rabe, A. J., Self-concept changes related to war captivity. *Archives of General Psychiatry*, 1980, *37*, 430–443.

Solyom, L., Garza-Perex, J., Ledwidge, B. L., & Solyom, C. Paradoxical intention in the treatment of obsessive thoughts: A pilot study. *Comprehensive Psychiatry*, 1972, *13*(3), 291–297.

Thomas, J., & Weiner, E. Psychological differences among groups of critically ill hospitalized patients, noncritically ill hospitalized patients and well controls. *Journal of Consulting and Clinical Psychology*, 1974, *42*(2), 274–279.

Weisskopf-Joelson, E. Logotherapy and existential analysis. *Acta Psychotherapeutica*, 1958, *6*, 193–204.

Weisskopf-Joelson, E. Six representative approaches to existential therapy: A. Viktor E. Frankl. In R. S. Valle & M. King (eds.), *Existential-phenomenological alternatives for psychology*. New York: Oxford University Press, 1978.

Weisskopf-Joelson, E. The place of logotherapy in the world today. *International Forum for Logotherapy*, 1980, *1*(3) 3–7.

Wirth, A. G. Logotherapy and education in a post-petroleum society. *International Forum for Logotherapy*, 1980, *2*(3), 29–32.

Yalom, I. D. *Existential psychotherapy*. New York: Basic Books, 1980.

CHAPTER 11

Cognition and Psychoanalysis
A Horneyan Perspective

MARIO RENDON

> Adam knew Eve, his wife, and she conceived.
> —Genesis 4:1

Cognition concerns how humans reflect the real world in which they live. It is a complex issue because humans can transcend simple perception and can therefore evoke a nonpresent situation or even create a new one. Most often the concern of the psychoanalyst is how humans distort their world because of past experiences. Reality has been penetrated and known by humans through ever-advancing technology, the ultimate aim of which is perfecting the perception and the knowledge of the world. The reality external to the individual is called *objective*, and that reality mapped on the basis of the individual's experience is called *subjective*. Subjective cognition comprises the knowledge not only of external reality, but also of the part of reality which we call *internal* and which constitutes the individual himself. The word *cognition* has a scientific connotation as opposed to terms such as *consciousness*, *spirit* or *soul*; it derives from the Latin prefix *co* which means 'together, with,' and *gnoscere*: 'to come to know'. Implicit in the word *cognition* is the fact that knowledge is always a relationship. Dialectically, modern science has emphasized relationships as opposed to the old focus on isolated things or parts. Epistemology is the theory of the nature and grounds of knowledge and paradigms are the patterns followed by it.

The growing extent of cognition is facilitated by a dialectical interaction between technological advance and neocortical growth. It has been pointed out by Piaget, for example, that the Greek phi-

MARIO RENDON • Montefiore Hospital and Medical Center, 3412 Bainbridge Avenue, Bronx, New York 10467.

losophers, for the first time in history, reached the state of formal operational thinking (Inhelder & Piaget, 1958), which allowed them to deal with concepts such as nonbeing. Today, children in certain privileged environments reach that state at about the age of eleven.

Philosophers such as Plato and Aristotle were concerned with knowledge as being the making of the *thinking* identical with the *thought*. Those philosophers, however, saw passion as opposed to reason, and Plato gave the ego a function of mediating between those (see, for example, the metaphor of the charioteer in the *Phaedrus*) in a manner which seems strikingly reminiscent of Freud. Although philosophy remained concerned with issues of cognition, emotion, volition, and so forth, these were considered to be discrete and isolated entities, in the abstract and often without a dialectical interaction. The fact that humans are characterized not only by sensory but also by rational cognition was explained, as in Descartes and Kant, by an obscure spiritual principle.

The advent of psychology did not change this outlook significantly. For example Wundt, the most important psychologist of the nineteenth century, although scientifically studying the elementary clinical processes of sensation, feeling, perception, attention, and memory, also ultimately resorted to ineffable higher spiritual phenomena beyond the reach of science in his attempts to explain rational cognition. Wundt, however, with his theory of apperception, paved the way for further epistemological advance. Others who had already contributed in this respect were the Hegelian philosophers—particularly Hegel himself, with his theory of history, process, and totality; Marx, with his theory of consciousness as determined by historical socioeconomic formations; Feuerbach, with his understanding of theology as anthropology and his concept of God as a projection of man; and Kierkegaard, with his delicate insight into subjective experience and morality. Darwin contributed evolutionary theory and challenged creationism, while, finally, nineteenth-century European physics and physiology set out to combat the spiritual principle, the soul, or any similar construct not susceptible of measurement. Freud's teacher Bruckner, belonged to the last movement.

Let me emphasize the fact that Sigmund Freud revolutionized epistemology to an extent that will continue to affect us for a long time to come. Psychology and psychiatry have been clearly and substantially modified since Freud and this is generally accepted; what is less well known—at least by us psychoanalysts—is the Freudian influence in the fields of epistemology and logic. From the point of view of cognition, Freud gave shape to a concept which had occupied philosophers (e.g., Leibnitz) for quite some time already, and for which the time was ripe: the concept of unconscious mentation. In dealing with such a difficult concept, Freud was most daring and innovative in his early writings. He postulated, as we well know, a locus or topography which lent itself to spatial representation or mapping and which was, in all probability, more important in psychic determinism than the sphere of consciouness. In opposition to the later structural concepts, the early concept of unconscious was a noun rather than an adjective since it referred to an entity and not merely to a quality.

The unconscious as initially postulated by Freud was a conceptual construct which broke off from the classic principles of formal logic. According to the laws governing the unconscious, something could, for example, contradicting the law of identity, simultaneously be itself and something else or, overruling the law of noncontradiction, be and not be at the same time. The Freudian unconscious was timeless—thus overriding linear causality. It was nonverbal, wish-ridden, infantile, closely connected to instinctual life, and inaccesible to consciousness. Yet it was not alogical or lawless since it was governed by such important laws as condensation and displacement, which Lacan (1971) has noted are isomorphic with the universal language polarities of metonymy and metaphor. This led Lacan to state that the unconscious is structured like a language.

Reality and certainty, concepts so sacred to formal logic, were also radically shaken. The bulk of our psychological life, cognition included, was deemed to be determined by a subordination to pleasure–unpleasure forces which supposedly aimed only at the restitution, by the shortest available route, of *perceptual identity*. In other words, an experience of satisfaction of a need would connect the idea of a special object to a satisfying discharge, which would, in turn, seek repetition and go to the extent of usurping reality by means of hallucinatory wish-fulfillment (Freud, 1900).[1]

The concept of perceptual identity and thought identity are cen-

---

[1]Piaget has a similar concept which runs approximately as follows: Every new stimulus creates a schematic disequilibrium between assimilation and accommodation. Such a state of disequilibrium creates a certain hunger for repetition of such a stimulus until equilibrium is reached again. Then the hunger for the repetition stops. For Freud, however, if the stimulus had a certain intensity (i.e., was traumatic), equilibrium (i.e., lack of symptomatic pressure) occurred only by the appropriate release—consciously—of both the memory or idea and the affect. We see clearly that what is missing in Piaget's conceptualization is the quantitative, affective component, and the idea of dynamic repression. Otherwise the concepts are very similar. Piaget also discovered alternate logical systems according to which children operate. See for example, J. Piaget and B. Inhelder *The Psychology of the Child*. New York: Basic Books, 1969.

tral to Freud's epistemology. Higher in heirarchy than the former, thought identity concerns itself with connecting paths between ideas without regard for their intensity. Thought identity leads, through a roundabout path, to deferred wish-fulfillment. This path is created by individual experience, and particularly by the acquisition of language.

Philosophers before Freud had of course introduced such a scale of cognitive complexity going from sensation to perception to thought. Hegel's phenomenology (1966) is a synthesis of such efforts;[2] Freud integrated such seemingly abstract concepts into the concrete clinical approach and also, and perhaps more important, into the dramatics of everyday life. Freud's monumental discoveries were, however, hampered by his inability completely to overcome his Cartesian paradigm, one of the main characteristics of which was the individual nature of the mind. I qualify my statement with the word "completely," because in most other ways Freud did in fact move on to the nineteenth-century Hegelian paradigm. Witness to this are his conceptualization of the mind as dynamic and an attempt to conceptualize knowledge as a returning circle.[3]

Freud's later structural theory, as well as the theories of the post-Freudians who concentrated on ego psychology, turned again to issues of conscious cognition, normality, intelligence, and so on. Most of what had been *the* unconscious was allocated to the id but cognition became by and large an autonomous function within the sphere of the ego. A new concept, the self, reminiscent of Hegel's processes of self-consciousness and self-realization, did emerge with Horney. Eminently cognitive, the theory of self shifted the focus toward the degree of congruity between the individual's reality and the distortion of such reality in the individual's mapping of it, leading to the individ-

---

[2]Many efforts have been made, largely by European scholars, to correlate Freud and Hegel. An interesting example of such attempt is given by Clark Butler, who correlated Freudian periods (i.e., oral-anal-phallic-oedipal-latency-adolescence-adulthood) to Hegelian stages of consciousness in the phenomenology, (i.e., desire–life and death struggle–lordship and bondage–stoicism–sketpticism–self-realization). As we can see, while Freud related those developmental periods to the body, Hegel clearly dealt with them from an intersubjective vantage point. This is an area which needs further integration. See C. Butler, "Hegel and Freud: a comparison." *Philosophy and Phenomenological Research*, 1976, *36*, 506–522.

[3]See I. Markova *Paradigms, thought and language*. New York: Wiley, 1982, for an in depth study of the Cartesian and Hegelian paradigms in psychology. Unfortunately, the author left out all psychoanalytic references from her otherwise erudite and comprehensive book.

ual's alienation from his real self. The lack of self-congruity led to distortion in the perception of reality at large.

When we talk about cognition we are talking really about re-cognition, or the matching of reality and our representation of it whether it is at the basic animal level of sensation or at the more developed human levels, where rational thought, self-consciousness, and fantasy are present. It is surprising that Freud, so much inspired by Darwin and his evolutionary theory, did not put more emphasis on the concept of the fight-or-flight reaction and survival of the fittest in his theory of perceptual identity (issues that Hegel had already stressed regarding the self in his life–death struggle concept). In this respect Karen Horney, with her concept of basic anxiety, is closer to both Darwin and Hegel. Here her difference with Freud stems from a fundamental philosophical premise regarding the *primum movens* of psychological life. As we know, Horney was critical of what she saw as Freud's excessively biological orientation and substituted a predominantly sociological one. That animals have to rely on accurate perception of reality for purposes of their survival nobody would argue; how animals arrive at the capacity to discriminate between enemy and prey is far from clear however, although it is difficult to imagine that they do so on only an instinctual basis. Modern ethology has shown us that the social life of animals and their systems of communication are far more advanced that was thought during Freud's lifetime. Although biology provides the scope of capacity for animal development, learning processes in interaction with the environment produce more or less optimal behavior.[4]

Human development is unique, as pointed out repeatedly, in part because of the immaturity of the infant at birth and its dire dependency on a caretaker. Were such dependency not highly complex and psychologically complementary, we would call it parasitism but, appropriately instead, we call it symbiosis. The uniqueness of this human bond between caretaker and child wherein dependency is so paramount may have been one of the reasons why Freud started from

[4]Attachment theorists such as Bowlby and Ainsworth postulate a genetic component to the attachment bond which may serve the purpose of protection–security for the newborn as well as securing early exploratory behavior. This is, however, quite different from Freud's instinctual constructs, placing emphasis on the social rather than the biological. Thus the face and the sound of the mother's voice are stressed, rather than the breast or feeding, for example. For an excellent review of attachment research and its particular relevance to Horney's theory see the recent article by Candice Feiring, "Behavioral Styles in Infancy and Adulthood: The Work of Karen Horney and Attachment Theorists Collaterally Considered" *Journal of the American Academy of Child Psychiatry* 1983, *22*, pp 1–7.

love and libido—unfortunately translated as 'instinct' rather than as 'need'—and not from fight-or-flight survival issues as could have been the case for, let us say, pure animal psychology. The bonus of inferiority at birth is human history, which contains the recording of millennia of generational experience and civilization, which is global concretization of such experiences necessary for the continuation of a superb but brittle machine: the human being.

As an aside, let me point out why the concept of culture (so dear to Horney) is better fitted to psychoanalytic thinking than those of civilization or socioeconomic formation. The latter notion is closer to the fields of ideology and politics or political economy and refers to macroscopic or molar historical formations. Civilization is the total process of historical advance, including all socioeconomic formations, and involves a global and unitary concept of process. Culture, on the other hand, refers to the unique characteristics, personality, so to say, of either molecular or microscopic social formations or groups.

We know that cultures value certain behaviors, mores, conventions, and the like while discouraging others. Whether it is love and sharing, or war, competitiveness, and aggression, or else asceticism or retirement or whatever, those values are enforced through socialization in the family and ultimately become individual cognitive and affective structures that help maintain the particular society's homeostasis. In like manner, families, as small cultures, deviate from the social norm within certain range and develop systems of value which make them differ among themselves. Furthermore, individuals in families develop differing value orientations leading to a variety of characterological types. Some of these observations, made by anthrophologists and sociologists contemporary to Horney, were among other factors at the basis of her divergence from Freudian theory.

The caretaker–infant bond thus already brings into the picture an adult with a certain psychological structure in the context of a certain cultural background. In other words, the caretaker has a personality which is value-laden and belongs to a culture which has certain value biases. Through a complex and dynamic process which involves the caretaker's personality and defenses as well as the child's temperament, the child emerges in a gradual fashion as a psychological being with a unique personality, developed largely from the interaction with the surrounding adults. In this process, the child has learned certain values which are crucial for survival in a human world. Those values are eminently relative to the cultures and personalities involved.

The concept of value was not developed by Freud, even though he was the first to point out that values were often determined by unconscious defenses such as sublimation, reaction formation, and denial. It was not until Karen Horney's writings that this thorny issue was extensively tackled in psychonanalytic psychology.

After 15 years of struggling with Freudian metapsychology, Horney started to write about the influence of culture in neurotic development. Through a series of publications (Horney, 1937, 1939, 1942, 1945) she arrived at her latter theroetical formulation which postulates the creation of an unconscious "idealized self image" in the neurotic, the obverse of which is an unconscious "despised self image" (1950). Horney was thus clearly concerned with re-presentation and re-cognition of the self, leading either to self-realization or to self-alienation.

Although Horney gave credit to Adler for first addressing the issue of the self, she in fact pioneered the development of a self-psychology. Also, opposite to Freud, Horney by and large sidestepped psychiatric nosology and became instead interested in an exclusive psychoanalytic personology. From a cognitive viewpoint what was crucial for Freud was whether or not certain mental elements, such as wishes for pleasurable gratification or libidinal discharge, were accessible to consciousness. If dynamically repressed, rather than just forgotten, and if powerful enough—in economic terms— such drive elements will create neuroses manifested by compromise formations such as symptoms. The latter would produce neuroses styled by the particular set of defenses used and the points of fixation–regression in the libidinal development.

For Horney, in contrast, neurosis is determined within a certain "morality of evolution." According to the degree of "basic anxiety"— the experience of feeling oneself helpless and isolated in a world perceived as potentially hostile— repression of certain parts of the self occur, as well as overvaluation and expansion of certain other parts. What parts are repressed and which ones are overvalued is determined by strategic needs, namely, by what significant others value. The matter is far from simple, however, since what others value has to do with their distortions of reality, including *their* externalizations and *their* effect on the child-to-be-perceived. In other words, the child tries to make a collusion with the caretaker in order to assume the role assigned him or her through the latter's externalizations, with the purpose of gaining approval—however paradoxical such approval may be at times—and of feeling secure and belonging.

The values in question—whether love or mastery or freedom—

were initially conceptualized by Horney in an interpersonal frame-work as moving toward, moving against, and moving away from others; later on those values were translated intrapsychically as the "self-effacing solution," the "expansive solution (narcissistic, perfec-tionistic, arrogant-vindictive)," and the "resigned solution." Those values are neurotic in character because they are indiscriminate, rigid, and compulsive, supressing their opposites, and making no allowance for a flexible repertiore of behaviors; in other words, they leave no room for spontaneity. Pushed by those neurotic values, the self splits itself into idealized and despised images which are distorted cognitive and affective mappings of the self, constituting what Horney called "actual self." The purpose of the therapeutic process is to restore true freedom and spontaneity by introducing congruity or identity be-tween the self and its image, leading to a certain utopia called "real self." I say utopia not pejoratively, but to connote the fact that the therapeutic process works in an asymptotic fashion.

The life course of all humans is composed of experiences which are more or less pleasurable, more or less traumatic. Based on this, the personality of the child develops around two poles: the positive one leads to feeling secure, happy, and part of a "we," which ulti-mately constitutes the source of what Horney calls "constructive forces" which lead to the realization of the self. The negative pole stems from experiences wherein the child may feel threatened, insecure, and alone. This negative nucleus gives origin to neurotic trends or destructive forces which obstruct the growth of the self and produce basic anxiety and neurosis. The relative equilibrium between these forces then de-termines in what direction developmental processes are to occur and how the person's energies are going to be spent, whether predomi-nantly defensively or creatively, and to what extent either way. The strategic compulsive moves toward closeness, away from others, or against others have the purpose of reducing anxiety. When fully in-ternalized in the form of the idealized image, the individual spends his energies in the "search for glory" which is the attempt at ac-tualizing the work of fiction or imagination constructed in the indi-vidual's mind about his self. The individual lives *as if*, compelled by "the tyranny of the should," a set of rigid mandates geared to accom-plishing idealization. The "shoulds" are imperatives aimed at per-fecting the idealized image. The individual value of such image is reflected in "neurotic pride." This pride needs constant reinforcement from outside and is highly vulnerable, leading, when hurt, to intense self-hate and identification with the despised self. The "pride system" includes the above-mentioned shoulds and also the neurotic "claims" which are wishful distortions of external reality or a version of externalized shoulds.

Thus, the individual becomes fragmented and alienated from himself, shifting in his neurotic values and identifications and trying to achieve a neurotic equilibrium through pursuing the phantom of his idealized image. The general measures employed to relieve tension are externalization, compartmentalization, or psychic fragmentation, automatic self-control to keep up the distorted self-image, and supremacy of the mind, which is the ultimate cognitive maneuver whereby the self detaches into the position of a sadistic observer of itself.

The expansive solution leads the person to identification with his or her pride and aims at mastery. It may be subclassified into narcissistic, perfectionistic, or arrogant-vindictive types according to the predominant value orientation. The self-effacing solution prides itself on love and submission, surrender and compliance. Here the value is placed on a subdued self. The third major solution, resignation, places premiums on detachment, noninvolvement, and freedom. It is a sort of further retreat from conflict already created by the first two solutions and it may be persistent and/or rebellious, sometimes leading to shallow living.

Horney did not elaborate on the stages of the formation of the self; she described adult processes, and the basic assumption in her theory was that the culture and the family provided the aliment for growth of the self, including the interpersonal strategies leading to neurotic or more or less normal adaptive outcomes. She did postulate that certain personality structures in the caregiver would produce certain neurotic patterns in the child, but at the same time allowed for the child's own temperamental contributions to the personality outcome.

There are three ways of representing reality. One is through action, which ontogenetically is the first and is called *enactive representation*. With the development of intelligence a second form is developed called *iconic representation* which uses images; the third way is *symbolic representation*, which uses thought and language, mostly mediated through the latter (Bruner, 1964). I pointed out how Freud was concerned with iconic representation as being the main mode of the unconscious. Horney, with her concept of idealized and despised images, remains in that tradition, although she never explicitly elaborates her thoughts along those lines; her choice of the word *image* however, refers to the mode of mentation which is predominantly iconic. Had Horney been concerned only with the issue of conscious value, she could have used terms such as *self-esteem* or *self-assessment*.

It is noteworthy that the conceptualization of the idealized image by Horney is referred to as a solution, a comprehensive one, to neurotic conflict. As a solution, the idealized image involves the concepts of equilibrium or homeostasis, remaining eminently dynamic, and skirting the type of reification involved in the concept of *imago* which had been used by other analysts in the Freudian tradition after its introduction by Jung. The concept of idealized image does not simply refer to something like a picture or even a statue of the self. It is rather an imaginary set which distorts the perception of the self, of others, and of reality at large.

Approaching the issues of cognition, we are concerned with their psychoanalytic meanings. Cognition is a loose and comprehensive concept which involves, among other things, perception, imagery, conceptual thinking, language, memory, recognition, evaluation, symbolism, semiotics, and behavior. Psychologists have experimentally dealt with many of these component parts in the laboratory, and some of those areas such as linguistics have taken on a definite scientific body of their own. As psychoanalysts, we are concerned with the part of cognition which refers to the self and which becomes misrecognition. The self is a core psychoanalytic concept which assumes a system of structures in the psychological order which color human experiences according to its form and which determine individual personality. It can only be partially conscious. We can discover self-misrecognition or alienation because part of the meaning involved in our communication with patients is couched in common semiotic systems such as language and folklore. This cultural aspect is a counterpoint to purely individual idiosyncratic or autistic symbolism arising from subjective experience. Since we have had cultural experiences similar to those of our patients, we have known or lived either personally or vicariously much of the patient's drama and thus we can understand it. We also have several channels of communication open to us from our patient and we receive the orchestration of messages as either euphonic (congruous) or cacophonic (incongruous). We have been trained to put aside convention in communication, that is, the complementary or reciprocal response to the manifest level, in order to put into practice our unique operational tool: interpretation.

Thus the object of our scientific endeavors is man, an object that we share with other sciences, and our point of departure is the unconscious, or that part of the self which remains alien to the subject and which, however, can be heard and discovered through our specific procedures, and which can then be reintegrated by the subject through our main instrument—interpretation, the scientific study of which, hermeneutics, is in our domain. It is true that our young psychoanalytic science remains preparadigmatic (Kuhn, 1970) as shown by the fact that interpretations vary according to the schools. The advance of psychoanalytic investigation and the mutual communication of results, along with changing scientific paradigms, will necessarily lead to a unitary psychoanalytic theory in the hopefully not too distant future.

Let me for the sake of illustration propose the hypothesis that with the refreshing advent of systems and structuralist theories, which have paralleled the rise of computers and cybernetics, we might take a fresh look at psychoanalytic theory, keeping in mind the contributions of those new fields and their methodologies. Essentially the focus in these new methodologies is the relationship between parts, and their possible translocations, reversibilities, permutations, and so on. Piaget has illustrated much of this in his discussion of intelligence, particularly regarding formal operational thinking and the group of four operations.

In a fascinating article, mathematician Michael Barbut (1966) has shown how structuralist thinking has been applied not only in mathematics and linguistics, but also in anthropology (Lévi-Strauss), psychology (Piaget), logic, and geometry. He uses as an illustration the so-called group of four (which is somewhat different from Piaget's and in mathematics has also been called the group of Klein) which is represented in Figure 1.

If we take *Value* ($+$ = idealized, $-$ = despised) and *Self* (x) and *Other* $\left(\dfrac{1}{x}\right)$ as opposites, we could use such a logical construct to illus-

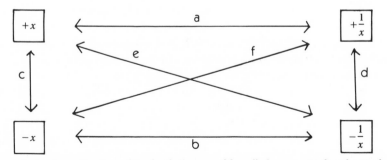

FIGURE 1. A schematization of Barbut's "group of four:" where $+x$ is the Identical, $-x$ the Opposite, $+\dfrac{1}{x}$ the Inverse, and $-\dfrac{1}{x}$ the Inverse of the Opposite, the horizontal arrows represent opposition, the vertical inversion and the oblique opposition of the inverse or vice versa. For a syntax of such group I refer the reader to Barbut (1966).

trate the representation of self and other *vis à vis* value systems. Let us assume that $+x$ means idealized $(+)$ self (x) and $-x$ despised self; $+\dfrac{1}{x}$ would be idealized other and $-\dfrac{1}{x}$ despised other. Where the person is located in this system may determine the clinical psychoanalytic picture being dealt with at the time. The upper horizontal arrow (a) would indicate that both self and other are idealized, as may occur in purely manic states; whereas if the self is predominantly idealized at the expense of the other then narcissistic states may develop. Where the other is idealized and the self devalued, states of religious ecstasy or merger with another may prevail as seen, for example, in borderline or narcissistic positive transference situations. The opposite is true for horizontal arrow (b) where both self and other are endowed with negative value, and disdain prevails, with impoverishment of both internal and external worlds. This is seen in extreme depressive states, with hopelessness and helplessness predominating. But it may be that self-hate outweighs devaluation of the other, leading to self-destructive and self-punishing behavior, which constitutes moving against the self. It may be, contrariwise, that devaluation of the other predominates and paranoid behavior would ensue, as can be seen in negative transferential reactions or paranoid pictures (moving against the other). Let us now take vertical dynamic (c) which would represent excessive detachment from others and self-imbeddedness. The most extreme form in this realm would be autistic states, but less severe forms of detachment are more frequent in psychoanalytic practice; these are the so-called resigned states, in Horney's terms. The other extreme, arrow (d), would represent in its extreme form symbiotic states, but more frequently morbid dependency an self-effacing states, where externalization is predominant. The oblique arrows would thus represent combinations of narcissistic to paranoid states (e), and states of overvaluation of others, and self-hate (f).

In summary, then, we have two axes, one of which refers to value and which could help explain those clinical pictures in which affect predominates (depression, dysthymia, hypomania, mania), and the other of which is eminently cognitive, a continuum from symbiosis (through phobia, obsessive-compulsive states, etc.) to autistic states. *Affect* and *Boundaries* would be the genetic precursors of *Value* and *Self*. In other words, primitive states of euphoria–dysphoria would be genetically related to the experience of self as valued or devalued, and primitive mechanisms of externalization–internalization would predate what is experienced as self and what as alien. I have elaborated some of these points in a previous paper (Rendon, 1981).

In terms of the genesis of the self, there is no doubt that it orig-inates in the other through a process of internalization best described by Lacan in his Mirror Stage postulate. We develop a schema of what we are like by apprehending the gestalt of the other. Marx, a Hegelian thinker, had already envisioned such development while developing the theory of value in commodities:

> In a sort of way, it is with man as with commodities. Since he comes into the world neither with a looking glass in his hand, nor as a Fichtian philosopher, to whom "I am I" is sufficient, man first sees and recognizes himself in other men. Peter only establishes his own identity as a man by first comparing himself with Paul as being of like kind. And thereby Paul, just as he stands in his Pauline personality, becomes to Peter the type of genus homo.[14]

Although Freud had the merit of discovering the unconscious and inaugurating a new era in the study of man, he was caught within the limitation of his paradigm and his ideology. A dialectician at times, Freud had to struggle with limitations imposed by his frame of reference as well as by the peak of individualism in the history of civilization. Freud has the merit of stressing the fact that our material basis of existence is our body and that in that body our history is written. What Freud did not stress enough was the fact that our higher cortical functions are developed eminently in a social culture (in the widest sense of the word, as in connotations of husbandry or milieu for growth (Luria, 1982), and that our self, as opposed to the body ego, originates in the other, with all the ambiguity of the last term which, as Lacan has pointed out (1978) may mean interlocutor, generic man, virtual image, or alienated self.

Along with other so-called culturalists or neo-Freudians, Horney created a new substantial way of psychoanalytic discourse which emphasized human relationships and self-relationships, culture, growth, and self-realization. Since such concepts already had their roots in previous philosophical thinking, a return to such areas as philosophy, and particularly dialectical logic, epistemology, axiology, and hermeneutics, would seem most appropriate for psychoanalysis in this age of creationism and genetic engineering. Along with careful scrutiny of new paradigms, this course may assure the continued advance of psychoanalysis as a unitary and unique science.

REFERENCES

Barbut M. Le sens du mot structure en mathematiques. *Les Temps Modernes*, 1966, *246*, 791–814.

Bruner, J. The course of cognitive growth. *American Psychologist*, 1964, *19*, 1–15.

Freud, S. The interpretation of dreams. In *The standard edition of the complete psychological works of Sigmund Freud* (Vols. 4–5). London: Hogarth Press, 1900.

Hegel, G. W. *Fenomenologia del espiritu*. Mexico: Fondo de Cultura Economica, 1966.

Horney, K. *The neurotic personality of our times*. New York: Norton, 1937.

Horney, K. *New ways in psychoanalysis*. New York: Norton, 1939.

Horney, K. *Self analysis*. New York: Norton, 1942.

Horney, K. *Our inner conflicts*. New York: Norton, 1945.

Horney, K. *Neurosis and human growth*. New York: Norton, 1950.

Inhelder, B., & Piaget, J. *The growth of logical thinking from childhood to adolescence*. New York: Basic Books, 1958.

Kuhn, T. S. *The structure of scientific revolutions*. (2nd ed.) Chicago: University of Chicago Press, 1970.

Lacan, J. La Instancia de la letra en el inconsciente, o la razon desde Freud, en *Escritos 1*. Mexico City: Siglo Vientiuno Editores, 1971.

Lacan, J. *Escritos II*. (3rd ed.) Mexico City: Siglo Veintiuno Editores, 1978.

Luria, A. *Language and cognition* New York: Wiley, 1982.

Marx, K. *Capital*. New York: International Publishers, 1967.

Rendon, M. *The structures of character*. Unpublished manuscript.

CHAPTER 12

Cognition in Interpersonal Theory and Practice

RALPH M. CROWLEY

Interpersonal psychiatry was Harry Stack Sullivan's term for his theory of interpersonal relations from which his practice directly flowed (1953). Sullivan was described by Michels variously as "that most creative of American born psychoanalysts" (1981) and as "America's most important and unique contributor to psychiatry" (1976). It is proper, therefore, to begin discussing the role of cognition in interpersonal psychiatry with Sullivan.

Before discussing the role of cognition, I will define what cognition is and what it meant to Sullivan. Dictionaries give meanings to cognition of perceiving, recognizing, noticing, sensing, being aware, and knowing. These terms give scant recognition to the complexity of processes involved in so-called knowing. Arieti (1965, 1967a, 1972), an avowed interpersonalist, recognized as did Sullivan before him, that cognitive processes can be both conscious and out of awareness, or unformulated. Arieti, however, tends to restrict cognition and cognitive domains to ideas and beliefs, which in turn give rise to emotions and feelings. He discusses cognition as separable from affect and conation, that is, the striving, wishing, desiring, willing, and impulsive aspect of the self. Perhaps this is only an artifact arising from Arieti's didactic approach in his writings, as he does profess a holistic view of human functioning.

Sullivan, on the other hand, was explicit in his view that affect

RALPH M. CROWLEY • Late of William Alanson White Institute of Psychiatry, Psychoanalysis, and Psychology, New York, New York.

(feelings and emotions), cognition, and conation were inseparable. In one of his earliest papers, written in 1925, he wrote (1962, p. 28 note):

> Cognitive elements must be dealt with before the conative and affective aspects of mental situations can be elucidated. At the same time it is unduly easy to lose appreciation of the artificial abstraction by which we come to speak of cognition as if it were in itself some independent faculty of mind.

With this caveat, he continued:

> One cannot but appreciate that it is by cognitive characters that we achieve intelligibility in thought and in conversation; so by attention to the cognitive aspect of mental activity in schizophrenia, one may perhaps learn to talk with the victims. (1962, p. 28)

In this paper, "Peculiarity of Thought in Schizophrenia," Sullivan demonstrated that schizophrenic thought was not archaic, nor even autistic, but had meaning derived by its clear connections with experience in the various developmental eras through which the person had passed. True, the meaning was disguised by the peculiarity of the thinking. Along with Adolf Meyer, he believed that problems in psychopathology are problems of symbol functioning. He quoted Meyer to the effect that symbols appeared "in the form of gestures, emotional display and language, and in their silent forms," that is, thought. He defined thought (1962, p. 83) as "activity by the implicit functioning of symbols, themselves abstracts ... from events."

Several writers (Chrzanowski, 1973, p. 137; Lincourt & Olczak, 1979, p. 10, Rappoport, 1972) regard Sullivan as emphasizing emotional over cognitive aspects of human functioning. Even Sullivan himself writes (1962, pp. 96–97), "the writer is inclined to believe that conative factors will prove fundamental in explaining schizophrenia." In his latest formulations of interpersonal theory (1948, 1949, 1953), one finds little or no mention of affect, cognition, or conation as such. He clearly believes, however, that experience is filtered through cognitive processes, verbal and nonverbal, witting and unwitting, primitive or logical. The result is a compound of affective, conative, and cognitive elements not readily separable. Cognition, for Sullivan, was not only a symbolic process, but an organizing principle. No idea occurs without some feeling behind it, and any feeling always has some idea at the basis of it.

To continue with Sullivan's views of thinking, he wrote (1962, p. 92), "Schizophrenic thinking shows in its symbols and processes nothing exterior to the gamut of ordinary thinking, including therein that of revery and dreams." Further on, he writes (1962, p. 113):

> The schizophrenic's cognitive operations deal with perceptions of reality, personal and impersonal. All these—like the figures in the dream—are distorted into use for representing the personal situation and for efforts at solving it.

He was indebted to Kempf for a similar approach. Kempf wrote (1921), "There is no such thing as an undetermined, absurd or non-sense expression in a psychosis."

In a lucidly written article on the language of schizophrenia, Sullivan stated (1944) that the schizophrenic, having lost all hope of satisfaction in the world of people, used language altogether for purposes of interpersonal security. He perceived schizophrenic language only as a further refinement on language used among intimates, with all its mutually understood undercurrents. This spoken and often nonverbal language deviates in the direction of the personal language of the child's sign language and magic.

After studying obsessive-compulsive personalities and neurotics, Sullivan came to much the same conclusion about their use of language as a means not of communication but of attaining interpersonal security with the therapist and many others (1956, p. 239, p. 250).

Spiegel (1964) points out that this view of schizophrenic thought is opposed to that of Arieti, who insists on its phylogenetic, paleologic, and archaic nature. Although Sullivan agrees that primitive forms of thought exist which are not in a consensually validatable syntaxic mode of experience (such as "archaic preconcepts" or prototaxis modes of experience), he strongly disagrees with applying phyletic theory to schizophrenic thinking (Spiegel, 1964).

In this same discussion of a paper by Arieti on cognitive theory, Spiegel says of Sullivan:

> In his very first paper, "The Oral Complex," presented in 1924 when he was thirty-one, Sullivan states with the force of a postulate that mind as an attribute of the living organism is not limited to the forms of awareness of adult human experience, and, particularly for the human being, that *psychologic experience precedes birth*. Preconcept . . . connotes experience structure which is formed prior to birth . . ., complex . . . identi-structures which are acquired during the life of the individual as such (Spiegel, 1964).

---

[1]Although this paper was not published until 1925, it was the first paper to be presented before a professional psychiatric audience, namely the May 1924 meeting of the American Psychiatric Association. H. S. Perry writes that it was written at the same time as "Schizophrenia: Its Conservative and Malignant Features," read before the June 1924 meeting of the American Psychopathological Association. The two papers constituted a unit in Sullivan's thinking (Perry, 1962, p. 3).

Spiegel further points out:

> Sullivan later gave up terminology which might suggest a topologic view
> of the psyche, as 'structure' does. 'Preconcept,' the term he had coined,
> was fused later in its meaning with and gave way to 'prototaxic', part of
> his enterprise of setting up a consistent and individual terminology for a
> hierarchy of modes of experience. (Spiegel, 1964, p. 4)

In speaking of Sullivan's lasting interest in symbolization, she writes:

> Here he also elaborates on his theory that the first symbol in human
> experience is that of the nipple, a symbol formed out of visual, kinesthetic
> and tactile experience, and is the nearest approach of the subjective in-
> dividual to the emancipation represented in the preconcept cosmos.

Sullivan related the basic most primitive experience to the formation of symbol cadres, and he stated that "we can see in the ontogenesis of personality, cadres of these symbols. The fundamental differentia among them reside in the order of abstraction from the experiential basis." In connection with discussing "paleomentality," Sullivan wrote of the language of the 18-month-old child:

> It is ... much more related to the magic sense of power which occurs not
> only in these days of childhood ... but in the religious beliefs of diverse
> peoples (e.g., the Yogi of 'om') and in the behavior of schizophrenia in
> which case also some primordial awe has been attached. (1925, p. 36)

Interpersonal theory has been interpreted, fallaciously, as omit- ting the intraphyschic. For Sullivan, however, the *mind*, the intra- psychic, had its basis in experience, in its past history (Sullivan, 1962, p. 8). So *interpersonal* for him subsumes the intrapsychic. In a footnote (1962, p. 10, note) he states:

> Experience is used here in the sense of the ultimate psychical "unit." It
> is purely subjective in fact, regardless of its known or unknown objective
> relation. "Thought," "percept," sensation," "image," or what not, all are
> terms of particular experience.

His early papers are usually neglected for his later writing be- cause many of them are available only in periodicals or in unpub- lished form.[2] In connection with the "cognitive *aspect* of mental ac- tivity in schizophrenia" quoted above, Sullivan (1962, p. 28) is dealing with the "primitive-archaic" character of thought. Although he was

[2]Unpublished papers of Sullivan's and his complete bibliography are obtainable on request from the William Alanson White Psychiatric Foundation, 1610 New Hamp- shire Avenue, N.W., Washington, D.C. 20009. There is a charge for xeroxing and the bibliography costs $3.00.

aware of the phylogenetic approach as later amplified by Arieti, he regarded it as unsubstantiated and offered as an alternative that the facts could possibly be explained on the basis of regression to an earlier mode in the person's experience.

Sullivan's explicit concern with cognitive processes manifests itself when he writes:

> The student of cognitive processes . . . could show us by what processes our notions of particular "external reality" grew from elementary sentience to its terminus in more or less marvellous information.

He is discussing the importance of symbols in psychiatry, and comments further, "One cannot but realize that the symbol activities of which the tree was the root are not only strikingly private to the individual, but in fact pertain enormously more to the individual than to the tree" (Sullivan, 1926, pp. 87–88). Sullivan is emphasizing here a person's private symbolic activity, an intrapsychic element in the psyche.

To describe thought processes and symbols subsumed in elementary sentience, Sullivan invented such terms as *prehension* (1938, p. 124n; 1947, p. 39; 1953, pp. 76–77; 1972, pp. 10, 118) and *preconcepts* (1962, pp. 9–10; 1972, p. 39n). Spiegel (1962) shows how in the later Sullivan these cognitive concepts are fused in their meaning with the prototaxic mode of experience, corresponding, according to Lincourt and Olczak (1974, 1979), to C. V. Peirce's firstness and Lincourt's monadic situation, and more roughly to Freud's primary process, at least in terms of the phenomenology with which these terms deal. For fuller discussion of Sullivan's prototaxic, parataxic, and syntaxic modes of experience, consult Sullivan (1947, pp. 45, 45n, 101, 116, 117), Mullahy (1947, pp. 125–27, 134, 136–39), Spiegel (1964) and Green (1961, pp. 733–35; 1962, pp. 7–8).

Sullivan dealt explicitly with cognition in his earlier papers and later implicitly in his discussions of modes of experience. As Spiegel (1964, p. 14) writes:

> Sullivan had respect for secondary process and almost an anxiety about the patient and his psychiatrist being submerged in primary process. Sullivan was keenly aware of and concerned with cognitive process, be it in the schizophrenic disorder, anxiety, or in the development of the person.

In his practice, Sullivan clearly operated in the cognitive sphere. Emotional and conative dispositions are dealt with through the medium of the patients' cognitive and therefore, integrative interpretations of their experience. Sullivan stated explicitly in 1947 (pp.

46–49) the conscious, cognitive preconceptions with which he operated. In summary, they are:

1. The patient is a stranger and is to be treated as a stranger.
2. The interrogation proceeds insofar as possible from a given point in a direction easy for the patient to follow.
3. Little can be learned as to "what manner of man is this" by direct questioning. By this he meant that the significant aspects of personality were not elicited by direct questioning along lines which the patient could not follow. Needless to say, he believed much useful information could be obtained by directly questioning a patient.
4. Nothing is static, everything changes—in velocity or in organization, in the general dynamic view of interpersonal relations.
5. One assumes that everyone is much more human than different or unique, and that no matter what ails a patient, be he happy and successful, contented and detached, miserable and mentally disordered, he is mostly a person like the psychiatrist, much more simply human than otherwise. This is an elaboration of what many thinkers have said in other ways before and after Sullivan, for example, Terence as quoted by Cicero: *"Homo sum; humani nihil a me alienum puto."*[3]
6. In an indefinite field, where we do not know much, one accommodates as simply as possible to the apparent prevailing tendencies. If a patient has to fight, one accommodates oneself to his having to fight. If a patient needs to disassociate or deny, one accommodates to this tendency, at least for the present moment.
7. In general, one cannot accomplish good by increasing a patient's anxiety.
8. Personality tends toward mental health or interpersonal adjustive success, handicaps by way of acculturation notwithstanding, that is, in spite of the person's false pride or sense of uniqueness.

Sullivan's instructions to patients (1947, p. 99), that is what the psychiatrist can reasonably expect a patient to do, typify his cognitive approach to his practice, by which I mean becoming aware or sensing:

- First: Note changes in one's body, by which he meant increase or decrease in tension, changes in one's gross movements, and in one's voice.

[3]Translated: "I am a man; I think therefore nothing human is alien to me."

- Second: Note marginal thoughts, those that are usually unspoken in telling a story.
- Third: State promptly that which comes to mind. In other words, trust the situation to the extent of expressing the thoughts provoked by and in the therapeutic situation.

He repeatedly expressed his opinion (1947, pp. 4, 91) that one has information about one's experience, one's state of being, only to the extent that one has tended to communicate it to another, or has thought about it in the manner of communicative speech. He also claimed (1947, p. 91), "Much of that which is ordinarily said to be *repressed* is merely unformulated." He also believed that much that was dynamic could be completely dissociated, that is, unconscious.

Therapy, Sullivan taught (1949), must always effect changes in the person and his situation. The dichotomy of the personal situation and the personality is a figment of logical thinking. Let us note, in summary again, what Sullivan thought therapy consists in doing (1949, pp. 4–6).

1. Provides information
2. Corrects misinformation
3. Functions in rectifying impractical evaluational systems
4. Acts in reducing or augmenting personal distance
5. Corrects the parataxic or transference phenomena, the nucleus of psychoanalytic technique
6. Functions in reintegrating dissociated and suppressed experience systems, by releasing personal awareness from inhibitions
7. Acts not to restrict communication to logical thoughts and furthers communication in terms of implicit activity of patients
8. Acts to further forward movement toward an expansion of satisfactions and to limit the reliance on needs for security

From the above summaries relating to Sullivan's theory of therapy and technique, it is obvious that secondary process or cognition in the syntaxic mode was significantly important to him. Does Sullivan practice what he preaches? Let me portray him in action.

The first patient (1954, pp. 24–25) is a college boy, schizophrenic, whose parents are pleased that he is so much better, although all that has happened is that he has found someone who is enquiring. Sullivan then applies pressure to learn the young man's responses to his mother. These turn out to be quite hostile ones, in spite of the patient's view that he has great love for his mother. Under this pressure, the patient becomes insecure and says, "There are times I really hate her," which realization shatters the patient still more. At this point, Sullivan says,

"How could it be otherwise when your mother is the person who has always prevented your spending time in the evening away from home among people of your own age, from whom you could have learned to act like a person of your own age?" In saying this, he shows the patient, who had become quite anxious on realizing how much he hated his mother at times, that this feeling was quite natural and inevitable and would have been experienced by anyone in his situation.

Being able in this way to allay a patient's anxiety is what Sullivan meant when he advised that a therapist should not increase insecurity deliberately, unless the therapist has an answer that will obviate destructive self-recrimination which would only augment insecurity and anxiety.

Sullivan reports (1953, pp. 338–39) a dream of a schizoid, obsessional patient who had a vaguely annoying, depressing mother. He dreamed of a Dutch windmill, a very beautiful scene, with a carefully cared-for lawn on which the windmill revolved. Suddenly he was within the windmill. There everything was wrack and ruin, with rust inches deep; it was obvious that the windmill had not moved in years. Sullivan said, "That is, beautiful, active on the outside—utterly dead and decayed within. Does it provoke anything?" The patient said, "My god! my mother." Sullivan added, "We made fairly rapid progress in getting some lucidity about the mother. . . . You will note that I have not discussed latent content . . . but in psychiatry one is occupied chiefly in benefiting the patient."

Sullivan was explicit as to the usefulness of the concept of "the unconscious as representing gaps in consciousness" (1964, p. 204). The story of the man who dreamed of the Dutch windmill illustrates Sullivan's experience that the unconscious is often that which has never been formulated here, for instance, the reality of his mother; it also reminds us of Sullivan's view that unverifiable speculation as to latent content, that is, as to the furniture of the unconscious, is more satisfying to the analyst's needs than it is helpful to the patient.

Another example (Chatelaine, 1981)[4]: Sullivan tells a schizophrenic patient in response to his obsession about salvation:

SULLIVAN: Worry is a way of standing still in front of a problem.
PATIENT: Worry causes pretty serious mental sickness, doesn't it?
SULLIVAN: On the contrary. It is a perfect way of standing still. All that happens is that one gets older.

[4]This and the subsequent example are quoted with specific permission by Chatelaine (1981) and by Schulz (1978) and are not to be republished without permission by them.

Then Sullivan explains to him in response to questions as to what he can do about his worrying:

SULLIVAN: Take stock of the actual situation before you and you will probably find something really distressing that would be harder to deal with than worrying.

PATIENT: But you would certainly save my life if you would give me one method of trying to cut out this worrying.

SULLIVAN: I have already given it to you.

PATIENT: That is to just stop.

SULLIVAN: Nothing of the kind. What do you suppose I have been talking to you for—to be misquoted that way. I mean just what I said. That everyone worries is a way of standing still rather than meeting the thing that is in front of him or seems to be in front of him. That whenever you get around to it, figure out what is ahead of you, what you are afraid to meet and when you get busy on that, your worry, of course, will disappear and I hope you will do well. But while you may kid yourself by stewing about all this sort of thing, so far as I am concerned, it is merely your way of standing still.

PATIENT: Immediately when I stop worrying I can sleep.

SULLIVAN: Anybody can sleep when he hasn't anything more interesting to do.

Another example of Sullivan's cognitive methodology (Chatelaine, 1981; Schulz, 1978), that of perceiving or paying attention to what one fears in a worrisome situation, is that of his interview with a hospitalized 23-year-old schizophrenic who, in his fifth hospital day, was not talking. Finally, in response to Sullivan's observation that he was acting odd, the patient said,

"I know who you are all right." After some conversation, Sullivan remarks:
"I don't think you have the faintest idea who I am."

PATIENT: I know you are a policeman all right. And he grins. Sullivan then asks him why, and he says something about everybody trying to get him into prison and Sullivan asks him why he thinks this, and he responds:

"Just because I said it, that's all."

SULLIVAN: Do you believe everything you say? Do you never make
    any mistakes in what you say? . . . Are you always right?

Patient shakes his head no. Sullivan then pursues persistently why
this man thinks Sullivan is a policeman and receives seemingly irrelevant responses.

SULLIVAN: Why should you connect me with the police? I should love
    to know. Isn't that a bit cuckoo?

Patient grins faintly and Sullivan continues:
    Isn't it a little bit weird to connect me with the police? Doesn't
    that require considerable imagination on your part? Or maybe
    you have seen the blue cross on my car. Is that it?
PATIENT: I know your car—sure.
SULLIVAN: You know those blue crosses are physicians' permits from
    the police. All the doctors who want them can get blue crosses
    from the police in Baltimore. The same as ambulances. Did you
    know that or didn't you? They are known as right-of-way signs.
    I put mine on the tail end because I want the right-of-way over
    speed cops. But the fact that I have a blue cross doesn't make
    me a policeman.[5] Mr. Clark [a fictitious name], do you feel every-
    one is against you—that you have no friends—that everybody
    has it in for you—is that the notion?

Patient shakes his head no. And they go on from here about the patient's suspicions of the man who is taking the notes on the interview.[6]
    So much for examples of Sullivan's cognitive approach, the use
of thinking and perception in therapy.
    Before we continue with post-Sullivan interpersonally oriented
contributors, Andras Angyal (1941) merits consideration. Like Sullivan, he attempted to outline a basis for a science of human behavior.
He agreed with Sullivan's view that personality disorders are disturbances in interpersonal relations (p. 331). He laid the foundations
for a holistic theory of personality, in which separation of individual
and environment was rejected. In believing in the "universally symbolic nature of all conscious phenomena" he was at one with Sullivan
and at odds with psychoanalysis. His is essentially a cognitively ori-

[5]The blue crosses, I am informed by Leon Salzman, M.D., had inscribed on them
    "Baltimore Police Department" or something like.
[6]Much of the foregoing material from Sullivan is taken from a previous article by
    Crowley (1980, pp. 119–123).

ented approach, although, like Sullivan's, not one that separates cognition, affect, and conation except for didactic purposes.

I turn now to some of those writers who, having studied Sullivan and adhered to his interpersonal orientation, have emphasized and/or amplified various aspects.[7] Some have applied the orientation to realms that Sullivan did not.

Arieti, an interpersonal theorist, stresses cognition in psychoanalytic theory much more explicitly than did Sullivan. As early as 1947, he wrote on the processes of expectation and anticipation in psychopathology. Later on (1948, 1955, 1963, 1967a, b) he continued to stress the role of cognition in schizophrenia, psychoanalysis, and psychiatry. In schizophrenics he noted (1948, 1955, 1974) their use of predicates rather than subjects as the basis of identity (Von Domarus principle as contrasted with Aristotelian logic). However he attributed the logic of schizophrenics to a regression to an inherited, paleologic form of thinking, as has been mentioned. This is antithetical to Sullivan's view of such peculiarities of thought as regression to an earlier mode of thinking in the person's experience (Spiegel, 1964). In 1965, Arieti wrote, "Cognition is or has been, up to now, the Cinderella of psychoanalysis and psychiatry." He focuses (1968), like Beck (1976) after him, on a person's conscious thoughts, wishes, ideals, and conceptual constructs such as self-image, self-esteem, self-identity, and projection of the self into the future. These, according to Beck and Arieti, engender the important emotional factors which disturb human beings (Arieti, 1965, p. 34). Beck stresses cognition as a therapeutic tool; Arieti develops it also in terms of psychoanalytic theory. In addition to primary and secondary process, Arieti has introduced a third cognitive process, the tertiary process, to account for creative thinking (Arieti, 1967a, b).

In summarizing his view of cognitive processes, Arieti writes (1965, p. 34):

> The most important emotional factors, which motivate and disturb men, are those which are sustained or actually engendered by complicated cognitive symbolic processes. To think that these cognitive processes are only displacements, detours or rationalizations which cover more primitive instinctual drives, is a reductionist point of view.

Frieda Fromm-Reichmann became a close associate of Sullivan's on emigrating to the United States in 1935. In her book, *Principles of*

Intensive Psychotherapy, (1950) she followed him closely in adopting the term *intensive psychotherapy* instead of psychoanalysis. Not only was she expert at following a psychotic's verbal communications, but she worked intensively with his nonverbal ones. In her advice on interpretation and its application, she was ever alert to the differences between what the psychiatrist might intend to mean and what the patient heard. She taught the best ways of communicating to a patient, so that the therapist would not feel put down or otherwise misunderstood (1950, Chapter 8).

Stanton and Schwartz (1954) studied the effects of differences among staff members of a private psychiatric hospital, especially between the therapeutic and administrative psychiatrists, on disturbances in patients' behavior. They found that when these cognitive differences were resolved by adequate communication the patient's behavior returned to a more usual and productive level.

The interest in countertransference as an interpersonal phenomenon, although not one of Sullivan's, became one of certain of his followers. Cohen (1952), Tauber (1954), Searles (1955, 1979), and Weigert (1958) are illustrations of investigators who used interpersonal theory in this way.

Tauber (1954) pioneered in calling attention to countertransference–transference issues in the supervisor–supervisee relationship, making explicit what was implicit in Sullivan's formulations.

Searles (1955) elaborated on the same theme in terms of the informational value of the supervisor's emotional experiences. He stressed, like Tauber before him, how the supervisor's private subjective fantasy experiences and his personal feelings in respect to the supervisee could accurately reflect what was going on between the supervisee and patient. It could provide clarification for the supervisee of the treatment situation existing at the time with him and his patient. Searles has also written and spoken extensively on how the therapists' own personal feelings may illuminate what the patient is more or less unwittingly feeling and communicating to the therapist (Searles, 1979). He has also extended the interpersonal point of view to patients' nonhuman environment, which becomes personalized, and a defense against personal involvements (Searles, 1960).

Another emphasis emerging from the interpersonal framework is that of family therapy and dynamics as exemplified by Wynne and his colleagues (1958) and Lidz (1973), which, as Schulz (1978) has pointed out, is broader than Sullivan's stress on parental influences, resulting in patients' feelings of guilt and low self-esteem.

Schulz (1978, p. 127) has cited the concept of a need–fear dilemma (Burnham, Gladstone, & Gibson, 1969) as illustrated in the Sullivan interviews but not formulated by Sullivan. Schulz himself is interested in integrating this dilemma with aspects of self-object differentiation.

Hill, a colleague of Sullivan's, elaborated his own interpersonal approach in his contribution *Psychotherapeutic Intervention in Schizophrenia* (1955). His appreciation of the role of cognition is shown in his statement, "It may well be that the urge to help is not so productive as is the willingness to be of use to the patient" (p. 4). He goes on, not only to the historical derivation of the word *cure*, as meaning care of souls, that is, persons (p. 12), but also to various meanings of *treat* as in treatment, especially the concept of "an artist who works with a living medium toward creative ends" (pp. 12–14). When a schizophrenic patient in a therapeutic session regarded herself as hallucinating because she felt her father in the room, Hill was sensitive enough to enquire further, with the result that it was the hair tonic from Hill's recent visit to a barber shop that was the reality basis for her feeling of her father in the room (p. 160). However interpersonal Hill was in treating patients, he at times wrote in terms of classical psychoanalysis. When he wrote about therapy and the therapist's contribution, it was in terms of two people, participant observation or, in short, communication (p. 192).

Weinstein and Kahn, (1955) study the cognitive processes manifested by brain-injured people in an interpersonal context. Weinstein (1962), in a psychiatric study of communications of Caribbean patients in psychotic states, establishes their symbolic meaning in terms of the culture. Thus, he carries out Sullivan's operational approach and also his view of the importance of symbolism in the behavior of human beings. In regard to the latter, he concludes: "The content of such delusions is not determined primarily by universal biological forces, but is selected in accordance with the preferred channels of relatedness in a culture" (p. 204).

Although cognition is not mentioned in the index of Tauber and Green's book *Prelogical Experience* (1959), they deal with cognitive experience, not in the sense of discursive language, but in terms of what Sullivan has called marginal thoughts and the parataxic mode of experience, as distinguished from parataxic distortion. Langer (1942) referred to the same material as presentational or nonverbal symbolism. Tauber and Green urge psychoanalysts to exploit the subthreshold communication, represented by dreams and poetic and artistic expression of all kinds, altered states of consciousness, memory lapses, confabulations, and reduplication in brain-injured persons

(Weinstein & Kahn, 1955), hallucinations, extrasensory perceptions, use of the analysts' own emotional reactions to patients (counter-transference), analysts' dreams of patients, and their intuitions and hunches. They find that Sullivan overemphasizes communication in the syntaxic or logical discursive mode and limits use of dreams in therapy to what might be formulated in a consensually valid state-ment, despite his contradictory opinion that one cannot expect to convert dreams into such statements (Sullivan, 1953, p. 343, Tauber & Green, 1959, pp. 77–78).

Artiss upholds an interpersonal tradition that symptoms of schizophrenics have communicative meaning. He and several coau-thors demonstrated this from their army patients (Artiss, 1959). From later research at Chestnut Lodge, Artiss concludes that *"the schizo-phrenic's quandary results from a relative deficit in the connotative as-pect of language"* (Artiss, 1966, p. 46). He is referring to inability to deal with metaphors. He comments:

> what a shaking thought that our children might someday come to know what we today call schizophrenia as something like "the behavior syn-drome resulting from words wrongly combined and misconstrued" Is it possible that . . . by classifying delusions and hallucinations . . . as symp-toms, we have been required to postulate a disease entity, by the language logic itself rather than by the phenomenology? (pp. 53–54)

He is referring, of course, to the label *schizophrenia*.

Barnett (1966), an interpersonalist, called attention to cognitive disorders in the obsessional as "central to the obsessional way of living" and as "appearing to be core phenomena" (p. 122). He quotes Fenichel, Hartman, Sullivan, Rado, Fromm-Reichmann, and Spiegel as commenting on thought disturbances in the obsessional (pp. 123–25) and states, "The primary defect in the life of the obsessional is not in the sphere of affect but in the area of inference making" (p. 129). In order to avoid inference making, obsessionals utilize a mechanism, *affective implosion*, "by which affect is forced inward on the psycho-logical processes and disorganizes those processes" (p. 130). He de-velops therapeutic implications of his theory in terms of opposition to getting the patient to express feelings and in favor of a direct approach and analysis of the cognitive and inferential gaps and dis-tortions in this thinking. In a later paper, Barnett (1980) writes not only of "cognitive repair" in the obsessional but also in treatment of neruosis in general. Although Horney (1950) and Fromm (1941) omit discussion of cognition as such, Barnett (1980, p. 41) points out that they, having abandoned the libido theory, have shifted meaning to experience and language, as did Sullivan. Barnett sees all neuroses as related to issues of character formation and regards all psychoanlaysis as analysis of character traits and needs. He differs with those who regard character analysis as a prelude to "real" analysis. Self is a cognitive experience which is patterned by one's character structure, which in turn is involved in issues of knowing and meaning, subject to cognitive repair in the process of psychoanalytic therapy (p. 49). He applies this theory to the treatment of both the explosive disorders, in which affect is exploded outward, and to the implosive disorders, in which affect is forced inward, as discussed above (1980, pp. 49–51).

Green (1961) has expanded on Sullivan's advice to attend to marginal thoughts in conscious mental life in order to investigate prelogical cognitive processes. He writes, "Logical structure does not characterize consciousness any more than . . . magical structure or superstitious structure" and that logical processes can occur without consciousness (p. 727). He stresses the importance of play in human life, noting that it never occurs in response to external compulsion but only to a spontaneous, self-initiated stimulus. He follows Dewey in maintaining that emotion, thinking, remembering, and imagination, as well as perception, are all modes of consciousness; thus he avoids a dichotomous position in regard to affect and cognition.

In another paper (1970), he traces human cognitive and perceptual development in children's dreams. He concludes (p. 81), "However, it may not be the drives and unconscious conflicts with the pleasure principle that are the issue, but the normative developmental sequences of various levels of cognition." Interesting too in connection with Artiss's views of schizophrenic thinking is Green's reference to Miller and Jesperson, linguistically oriented, who demonstrate that metaphor is the most vital principle of language and perhaps of all symbolism (p. 68).

In a paper on children's dreams, Green writes (1971a, p. 80), "All feelings aroused by an event are cognitive because they express an emotional or felt appraisal either of the degree of fulfillment or of the threat offered to both short- and long-term values in living." He notes that "feelings by definition are conscious, but their reference implications and sources may not be."

Green is especially known for his application of the interpersonal approach to child therapy, which he describes in an encyclopedic article (1971b). Sullivan (1953) described six ways in which learning takes place, and these Green develops in their application to children (p. 519, 520).

Colm (1966), who also worked with children, bases her theoretical and technical approach on Sullivan.

Searles has developed interpersonal therapy particularly in the sphere of transference–countertransference feelings in working with schizophrenics and others. He discusses (1970) the meanings of things to very ill patients and how and when to communicate with the patient in terms of those meanings. He expatiates on the analysts' feeling experiences in terms of their informationally empathic value (1955, 1976). Like Fromm-Reichmann (1950) before him, he emphasizes the strengths and power of the seemingly helpless ill, especially in their ability to thwart the analyst's efforts and to make him feel useless and helpless (1966). And more than anyone else he has stressed the role of the nonhuman environment in transference reactions (1960).

Will, a student of Sullivan's, also carries on the tradition of Sullivan and Fromm-Reichmann in working with psychotics. He elaborates (1961) on the years of work it takes to get a paranoid patient to distinguish between himself and others, between himself and the analyst (p. 85). He also demonstrates the need of the psychotic patient for a dependable but reactive human presence in order to begin getting well. As he puts it, "The comforting, protective presence of another person is of vital importance in restoring equilibrium to the personality" (1972, p. 35).

Cognition is an abstract concept used in developing theory of the workings of the human mind and technical procedures based on a theory of the role cognition occupies. As Witenberg, Reich, and Mazer, interpersonalist theorists, assert (1959, p. 1418), Sullivan "is more concerned with developing formulations which will facilitate his purpose—the development of an effective therapy—than with theoretical 'systems' of a high order of abstraction." This is why Sullivan fails to satisfy those who wish he were more explicit on the role of cognition. It also explains his selective inattention to theoretical difficulties in abandoning the unique individual self to a delusion, except for "the real unique individuality of each psychobiological organism" (Sullivan, 1964, p. 16). Since he attributes real unique individuality to the *psycho*biological organism, he contradicts himself in saying that the unique individual self is a delusion, or illusion (Sullivan, 1964, pp. 198–226).

Chrzanowski (1973) cites as "one more limitation . . . in Sullivan's psychiatric ecology . . . the relative neglect of cognitive processes" and asks for a more detailed account of the 'proto- , para- , and syntaxic modes of experience" in which the "pathological thought processes" would be correlated "to personal experiences and their genetic origin." In his 1977 work he makes no mention of this criticism, nor does he respond to his own request for a detailed account of the origin of the modes of experience. He does give a more detailed account of cognition in interpersonal theory and how it contrasts with Freudian and ego psychology. He also expands on interpersonal theory in developing his concept of a total self, which he terms the "interpersonal self," a broader concept than Sullivan's dynamism of the "self-system." However, this concept includes "self-system" as well as Sullivan's concepts of cognitive modes of experience and the cognitive patterns of good-me, bad-me, not-me. He regards Sullivan's emphasis on the self-system as reductionistic and energetic in a way different from that in Freudian theory. Chrzanowski hypothecates an interpersonal self "as transcending energetic principles" and being more of a transactional concept. He criticizes Sullivan's concept of participant observation as being too mechanistic, energetic, and overinstrumental. He prefers a more transactional concept of direct emotional interchange, communicative observation, so to speak, a person-to-person relationship rather than interpersonal or between-person relationship. For him, Sullivan's stress on the illusion of personal individuality confuses individuality with "real self," that is, an immutable self which has nothing to do with other persons. Chrzanowski's interpersonal self includes individuality but avoids the implications of being some essence above and beyond influence and change. Chrzanowski notes that "cognition and anxiety assume a complementary role in interpersonal theory" (1977, p. 45). He rejects a rigid division of personality theory into intrapsychic, interpersonal, and transactional, opting instead for use of all three vantage points. Sullivan's interpersonal theory alone is not sufficiently transactional, in that it does not pay "adequate attention to the highly individualized personal coding of experience" (p. 153).

Lincourt and Olczak (1974, 1979), a philosopher, cites Chrzanowski's criticism of Sullivan for neglecting cognitive processes and referes to C. V. Peirce, one of Sullivan's intellectual antecedents, as having supplied a basis for remedying the defect in his concepts of firstness, secondness, and thirdness, also discussed by Green (1961, 1962). Lincourt suggests the terms *monadic, dyadic,* and *triadic situations* and expands on them as a means of preserving the self-correcting character of interpersonal psychiatry.

Wolstein (1981a, b), like Chrzanowski and others, emphasizes the inadequacy of Sullivan's concepts of the self, opting for "a psychology of the self in terms of first-personal psychic activity" (p. 133). In no way does Wolstein abandon an interpersonal or transactional view of the self, but he redefines psychoanalysis, not in terms of either its biological or socio-anthropological borders, but in terms of the "first-personal psychic activity of the uniquely individual self" (pp. 140, 601), thereby differing in his cognitive emphasis.

Attempting also to formulate the self in terms of an integrating,

organizing principle, rather than to delineate another part of the self,
Pearce and Newton (1963), in their exposition of interpersonal theory,
write of an "integral self."

Although Leston Havens never knew Sullivan personally, he has
carefully studied him. As a result, he has re-presented him to us in
some of his own words, thus explaining, interpreting, systematizing
and amplifying his work at the same time (Havens, 1973). In a following contribution, he expands Sullivan's therapeutic methods into
a technique from which the book, *Participant Observation*, is named
(1976). He describes a rational and coherent technique in cognitive
terms. He contrasts the method with psychoanalysis, in that paranoid
delusions are regarded as "disguised reproductions of actual events"
(p. 103), much as Niederland (1960) does in discussing the Shreber
case. Havens describes Sullivan's interventions as counterprojective,
that is, counter to the maximal fantasy and transference development
which is typical of classical psychoanalysis in its emphasis on the
production of a transference neurosis. "The appeal is to experience,
not to the content of spontaneous thought, as in analysis," writes
Havens (p. 103). He has expanded even further his systematic studies
of ways to say things to patients in his papers on "Explorations in
the Uses of Language in Psychotherapy" (1978, 1979, 1980). He acknowledges that Beck's cognitive therapy has counterprojection in
common with Sullivan and other interpersonalists (1980, p. 56). His
contributions help enormously to make psychotherapy teachable, as
does also Bruch (1974).

Bruch (1969, 1980) develops interpersonal theory in regard to
eating disorders, such as bulimia and anorexia nervosa. She stresses
listening to patients, in contrast to interpretation of their feelings and
the meaning of their communications (Bruch, 1961; Bruch & Palombo, 1961). Giving insight, she thinks, "reinforces basic deficiencies
in their personality structure." She recognizes that interpretation of
content is "less important than reconstruction of the developmental
interactional patterns and correction of childhood misconceptions"
(p. 1538).

Sullivan's interpersonal theory was open-ended and expressed in
terms lending itself to outside verification, in contrast to enclosed
and only internally verifiable theories. Therefore the many contributors to interpersonal theory and its cognitive aspects discussed in
this chapter vary considerably in their interests and in the particular
elements in Sullivan's works they choose to explore further. Many
interpersonalists, such as Will and Searles, have been interested mainly
in what is most therapeutically effective, as was Sullivan. Their writ-

ings lend themselves only with difficulty to discussion of their theoretical position, as the role of cognition requires (Cameron, 1938; Crowley, 1975; Fromm, 1951; Schactel, 1959).

REFERENCES

Angyal, A. *Foundations for a science of personality.* New York: Viking Press, 1941.

Arieti, S. Special logic of schizophrenia and other types of autistic thought. *Psychiatry,* 1948, *4,* 325–338.

Arieti, S. *The interpretation of schizophrenia.* New York: Brunner, 1955.

Arieti, S. *The psychotherapy of schizophrenia in theory and practice* (Psychiatric Research Report 17, pp. 13–29). American Psychiatric Association, 1963.

Arieti, S. Contributions to cognition from psychoanalytic theory. In *Science and psychoanalysis* (Vol. 8), J. Masserman (Ed.). New York: Grune Stratton, pp. 16–37, 1965.

Arieti, S. Some elements of cognitive psychiatry. *Amrican Journal of Psychotherapy,* 1967, *21,* 723. (a)

Arieti, S. *The intrapsychic self: Feeling, cognition and creativity in health and in mental illness.* New York: Basic Books, 1967. (b)

Arieti, S. The present status of psychiatric therapy. *American Journal of Psychiatry,* 1968, *124,* 52–61. Reprinted in Arieti (1978).

Arieti, S. *The will to be human.* New York: Quadrangle Books, *The New York Times,* 1972.

Arieti, S. An overview of schizophrenia from a predominantly psychological approach. *American Journal of Psychiatry,* 1974, *131,* 241–249.

Artiss, K. The symptom as a communicative device (pp. 9–39) and The symptom during therapy (pp. 172–178). In K. Artiss (Ed.), *The symptom as communication in schizophrenia.* New York: Grune Stratton, 1959.

Artiss, K. Language and the schizophrenic quandary. *Contemporary Psychoanalysis,* 1966, *3,* 39–54.

Barnett, J. On cognitive disorders in the obsessional. *Contemporary Psychoanalysis,* 1966, *2,* 122–134.

Barnett, J. Cognitive repair in the treatment of neurosis. *Journal of the American Academy of Psychoanalysis,* 1980, *8,* 39–56.

Beck, A. *Cognitive therapy and the emotional disorders.* New York: International Universities Press, 1976.

Bruch, H. Some comments on talking and listening in psychotherapy. *Psychiatry,* 1961, *24,* 269–272.

Bruch, H. *Learning psychotherapy.* Cambridge: Harvard University Press, 1974.

Bruch, H. Hunger and instinct. *Journal of Nervous and Mental Disease.* 1969, *149,* 91–114.

Bruch, H. Anorexia nervosa: Therapy and theory. *American Journal of Psychiatry,* 1980, *139,* 1531–1538.

Bruch, H., Palombo, S. Conceptual problems in schizophrenia. *Journal of Nervous and Mental Disease,* 1961, *132,* 114–117.

Burnham, D., Gladstone, A., Gibson, R. *Schizophrenia and the need–fear dilemma.* New York: International Universities Press, 1969.

Cameron, N. *Reasoning, regression, and communication in schizophrenics.* Psychological Monographs, 1938, No. 221.

Chatelaine, K. *Harry Stack Sullivan—The formative years (1892–1930). Washington, D.C.: University Press of America, 1981.*

Chrzanowski,G. Implications of interpersonal theory. In E. Witenberg (Ed.), *Interpersonal explorations in psychoanalysis*. New York: Basic Books, 1973.

Chrzanowski, G. *Interpersonal approach to psychoanalysis*. New York: Gardner Press, 1977.

Cohen, M. Countertransference and anxiety. *Psychiatry*, 1952, *15*, 231–243.

Colm, H. *The existential approach to psychotherapy with adults and children*. New York: Grune and Stratton, 1966.

Crowley, R. Harry Stack Sullivan: the complete bibliography. *Contemporary Psychoanalysis*, 1975, *11*, 83–99. Reprinted in Chrzanowski (1977).

Crowley, R. Cognitive elements in Sullivan's theory and practice. *Journal of American Academy of Psychoanalysis*, 1980, *8*, 115–126.

Fromm, E. *Escape from freedom*. New York: Rinehart, 1941.

Fromme, E. *The forgotten language*. New York: Rinehart, 1951.

Fromm-Reichmann, F. *Principles of intensive psychotherapy*. Chicago: University of Chicago Press, 1950.

Green, M. Prelogical processes and participant communication. *Psychiatric Quarterly*, 1961, *35*, 726–74.

Green, M. The roots of Sullivan's concept of self. *Psychiatric Quarterly*, 1962, *36*, 271–282.

Green, M. Maturational features in children's dreams. In E. Witenberg (Ed.), *Interpersonal explorations in psychoanalysis*. New York: Basic Books, 1970.

Green, M. Clinical significance of children's dreams. In J. Masserman (Ed.), *Science anpsychoanalysis* (Vol. 19). New York: Grune and Stratton, 1971. (a)

Green, M. The interpersonal approach to child therapy. In B. Wolman (Ed.), *Handbook of child psychoanalysis*. New York: Van Nostrand Reinhold, 1971. (b)

Havens, L. *Approaches to the mind*. New York: Little, Brown, 1973.

Havens, L. *Participant observation*. New York: Aronson, 1976.

Havens, L. Explorations in the uses of language in psychotherapy: Simple empathic statements. *Psychiatry*, 1978, *41*, 336–345.

Havens, L. Explorations in the uses of language in psychotherapy: Complex empathic statements. *Psychiatry*, 1979, *42*, 40–48.

Havens, L. Explorations in the uses of language in psychotherapy: Counterprojective statements. *Contemporary Psychoanalysis*, 1980, *16*, 53–66.

Hill, L. *Psychotherapeutic intervention in schizophrenia*. Chicago: University of Chicago Press, 1955.

Horney, K. *Neurosis and human growth*. New York: Norton, 1950.

Kempf, E. *Psychopathology*. St. Louis: Mosby, 1921, p. 390 (as quoted by H. S. Perry in Sullivan, 1972, p. xvii).

Langer, S. *Philosophy in a new key*, Cambridge: Harvard University Press, 1942.

Lincourt, J., Olczak, P. C. S. Peirce and H. S. Sullivan on the human self. *Psychiatry*, 1974, *37*, 78–87.

Lincourt, J., & Olczak, P. H. S. Sullivan and the phenomenology of human cognition. *International Journal of Psychiatry*, 1979, *25*, 10–16.

Lidz, R. *The origin and treatment of schizophrenic disorders*. New York: Basic Books, 1973.

Michels, R. Comment on flyleaf of Havens (1976).

Michels, R. Psychoanalysis and psychiatry—the end of the affair. *The Academy Forum*, 1981, *25*, 6–10.

Mullahy, P. A theory of interpersonal relations and the evolution of personality. In

Conceptions of modern psychiatry, H. S. Sullivan, Washington, D.C.: William Alanson White Psychiatric Foundation, 1947.

Neiderland, W. Schreber's father. *Journal of the American Psychoanalytic Association*, 1960, *8*, 492–499.

Pearce, J., Newton, S. *The conditions of human growth*, New York: Citadel Press, 1963.

Perry, H. Commentary in Sullivan (1962, p. 3).

Rappaport, L. *Personality development: the chronology of experience*. Glenview, IL: Scott, Forsman, 1972.

Schachtel, E. *Metamorphosis*. New York: Basic Books, 1959.

Schulz, C. Sullivan's clinical contributions during the Sheppard–Pratt era—1923–1930. *Psychiatry*, 1978, *41*, 117–128.

Searles, H. The informational value of the supervisor's emotional experiences. *Psychiatry*, 1955, *18*, 135–146.

Searles, H. *The Non-human environment in normal development and in schizophrenia*. New York: International Universities Press, 1960.

Searles, H. Feelings of guilt in the psychoanalyst. *Psychiatry*, 1966, *29*, 319–323.

Searles, H. Autism and the phase of transition to therapeutic symbiosis. *Contemporary Psychoanalysis*, 1970, 7, 1–20.

Searles, H. Psychoanalytic therapy with schizophrenic patients in a private–practice context. *Contemporary Psychoanalysis*, 1976, *12* 387–406.

Searles, H. *Countertransference and related subjects*: Selected papers, New York: International University Press, 1979.

Spiegel, R. Sullivan's contributions to a theory of cognitive processes. Unpublished discussion of Arieti (1965) presented at a meeting of the American Academy of Psychoanalysis, December 1964.

Stanton, A. & Schwartz, M. *The mental hospital*. New York: Basic Books, 1954.

Sullivan, H. S. The oral complex. *Psychoanalytic Review*, 1925, *12*, 30–38.

Sullivan, H. S. The importance of a study of symbols in psychiatry. *Psyche* (London), 1926, *8*(1), 8193.

Sullivan, H. S. Psychiatry: Introduction to the study of interpersonal relations. *Psychiatry*, 1938, *1*, 121–134.

Sullivan, H. S. The language of schizophrenia. In J. Kasanin (Ed.), *Language and thought in schizophrenia: Collected papers*. New York: Norton, 1944.

Sullivan, H. S. *Conceptions of modern psychiatry*. New York: Norton, 1947 (reprinted, 1953).

Sullivan, H. S. The meaning of anxiety in psychiatry and in life. *Psychiatry*, 1948, *11*, 1–13. (Reprinted in Sullivan, 1964).

Sullivan, H. S., The theory of anxiety and nature of psychotherapy. *Psychiatry*, 1949, *12*, 3–12.

Sullivan, H. S. *The interpersonal theory of psychiatry*, New York: Norton, 1953.

Sullivan, H. S. *The psychiatric interview*. New York: Norton, 1954.

Sullivan, H. S. *Clinical studies in psychiatry*. New York: Norton, 1956.

Sullivan, H. S. *Schizophrenia as human process*. Introduction and Commentaries by Helen Swick Perry. New York: Norton, 1962.

Sullivan, H. S., *The Fusion of psychiatry and social science*. Introduction and commentaries by Helen Swick Perry. New York: Norton, 1964.

Sullivan, H. S. *Personal psychopathology*. Introduction by Helen Swick Perry. New York: Norton, 1972.

Tauber, E. Exploring the therapeutic use of countertransference data. *Psychiatry*, 1954, *17*, 331–336.

Tauber, E. & Green, M. *Prelogical experience*. New York: Basic Books, 1959.

Weigert, E. Problems of communication between doctor and patient in psychotherapy. *Psychiatry*, 1958, *21*, 241–248.

Weigert, E. *The courage to love*, New Haven: Yale, 1970.

Weinstein, E. A. & Kahn, R. L. *Denial of illness: Symbolic and neurophysiologic aspects*. Springfield, IL: Thomas, 1955.

Weinstein, E. A. *Cultural aspects of delusions*. New York: Free Press of Glencoe, a division of Crowell Colier, 1962.

Will, O. Jr. Paranoid development and the concept of self: Psychotherapeutic intervention. *Psychiatry*, 1961, *24* 74–88.

Will, O. Jr. Catatonic behavior in schizophrenia. *Contemporary Psychoanalysis*, 1972, *9*, 29–58.

Witenberg, E., Rioch, J., & Mazer, M. The interpersonal and cultural approaches. In S. Arieti (Ed.), *American Handbook of Psychiatry*, (Vol. II) New York: Basic Books, 1959.

Wolstein, B. Psychology of the self and immediate experience. *Contemporary Psychoanalysis*, 1981, *17*: 136–143. (a)

Wolstein, B. Psychic realism and psychoanalytic inquiry. *Contemporary Psychoanalysis*, 1981, *17*: 545–606. (b)

Wynne, L., Ryckogg, I., Day, J., & Hirsch S. Pseudo-mutuality in the family relations of schizophrenics. *Psychiatry* 1958, *21*, 205–220.

CHAPTER 13

Expanding the *ABC*s of Rational-Emotive Therapy

ALBERT ELLIS

The *ABC*s of rational-emotive therapy (RET) go back to its very beginnings in 1955, and I continually used them with my early rational-emotive therapy clients (Ellis, 1962). When the Institute for Rational-Emotive Therapy in New York founded its psychological clinical in 1968, cognitive homework forms were printed for its clients, and they added *D* and *E* to the original *ABC*s (Ellis, 1968). As explained in Chapter 3 of *Humanistic Psychotherapy: The Rational-Emotive Approach* (Ellis, 1973). *A* stands for Activating events, Activating experiences, Activities or Agents that people disturb themselves about. *B* stands for rational Beliefs or realistic Beliefs about the Activating events that tend to lead to a *C*, appropriate Consequences. *IB* stands for irrational Beliefs about the Activating events and tends to lead to *iC*, inappropriate Consequences (especially, emotional disturbances and dysfunctional behaviors). *D* stands for Disputing irrational Beliefs—Detecting them, Discriminating them from rational Beliefs, and Debating them (Phadke, 1982). *E* stands for Effective rational Beliefs to replace people's irrational Beliefs and also for Effective appropriate emotions and Effective functional behaviors to replace their disturbed emotions and dysfunctional behaviors.

The *ABC*s and the *DE*s have served RET very well over the last three decades and have been copied in hundreds of books and articles and used with many thousands of clients. In their original form, however, they are oversimplified and omit salient information about human disturbance and its treatment. Several RET writers have tried

ALBERT ELLIS • Institute for Rational-Emotive Therapy, 45 East 65th Street, New York, New York 10021.

to expand them, with some degree of success (Dryden, 1984; Wessler & Wessler, 1980). In this chapter I shall try to give my own version of how I think they can be usefully expanded.

DEFINITIONS OF THE *ABC*s OF RET

Let me start with some definitions involved in the RET outlook on human personality and behavior and particularly in its view of emotional disturbance. RET holds that humans are purposeful, or goal-seeking creatures (Adler, 1927, 1929; Ellis, 1973) and that they bring to *A* (Activating events or Activating experiences) general and specific goals. (*G*). Almost always, their basic Goals are (1) to stay alive and (2) to be reasonably happy and free from pain while alive. Their main subgoals as they strive for happiness include: to be happy (a) when alone, by themselves, (b) when associating with other people, (c) when engaging in intimate relationships with others, (d) when earning a living, and (e) when engaging in recreational activities (e.g., sports, study, art, music, drama).

Rational Beliefs (*rB*s) in RET mean those cognitions, ideas, and philosophies that aid and abet people's fulfilling their basic or most important Goals.

Irrational Beliefs (*iB*s) are those cognitions, ideas, and philosophies that sabotage and block people's fulfilling their basic or most important Goals.

Nonevaluative observations, descriptions, and cold cognitions are people's observations of what is going on (*WIGO*) in the world and in their own thoughts, feelings, and actions.

Evaluative assessments, inferences, expectations, and conclusions are people's evaluations of what is going on (*WIGO*) in the world. These may be either:

1. Warm evaluations—involved with people's desires, wishes, and preferences.
2. Hot evaluations—involved with people's absolutistic demands, commands, musts, and necessities.

ACTIVATING EVENTS OR ACTIVATORS (*A*) OF COGNITIVE, EMOTIONAL AND BEHAVIORAL CONSEQUENCES (*C*)

The RET theory of personality and of personality disturbances begins with people's trying to fulfill their Goals (*G*s) in some kind of environment and encountering a set of Activating events or Activators (*A*s) that tend to help them achieve or block these Goals. The *A*s they encounter are normally present or current events or their own thoughts, feelings, or behaviors; but they may be imbedded in (conscious or unconscious) memories or thoughts about past experiences. People are prone to seek out and respond to these *A*s because of (a) their biological or genetic predispositions (b) their constitutional history, (c) their prior interpersonal and social learning, and (d) their innately predisposed and acquired habit patterns (Ellis, 1976, 1979).

*A*s (Activating events) virtually never exist in a pure or monolithic state but almost always interact with and partly include *B*s and *C*s. People bring *themselves* (their goals, thoughts, desires, and physiological propensities) *to A*s. To some degree, therefore, they *are* these Activating events and the *A*s (their environments) *are* them. They can only think, emote, and behave in a material milieu—as Heidegger (1962) notes, only have their being-in-the-world; and they almost always exist in and relate to a *social* context—live with and relate to other humans. They are never, therefore, pure individuals, but are *world-centered* and *social* creatures.

BELIEFS (*B*s) ABOUT ACTIVATING EVENTS (*A*s)

According to RET theory, people have almost innumerable Beliefs (*B*s)—or cognitions, thoughts, or ideas—about their Activating events (*A*s); and these *B*s importantly and directly tend to exert strong influences on their cognitive, emotional, and behavioral consequences (*C*s). Although *A*s often *seem* directly to "cause" or contribute to *C*s, this is rarely true, because *B*s normally serve as important mediators between *A*s and *C*s and therefore more directly cause or create *C*s (Bard, 1980; Beck, 1976; Ellis, 1957, 1962, 1968; Goldfried & Davison, 1976; Griegor & Boyd, 1980; Grieger & Grieger, 1982; Guidano & Liotti, 1983; Mahoney, 1974; Raimy, 1975; Walen, DiGuiseppe, & Wessler, 1980; Wessler & Wessler, 1980). People largely *bring* their Beliefs to *A*; and they prejudicially view or experience *A*s in the light of these biased Beliefs (expectations, evaluations) and also in the light of their emotional Consequences (*C*s) (desire, preferences, wishes, motivations, tastes, disturbances). Therefore, humans virtually never experience *A* without *B* and *C*, but they also rarely experience *B* and *C* without *A*.

People's *B*s take many different forms because they have many kinds of cognitions. In RET, however, we are mainly interested in their rational Beliefs (*rB*s), which we hypothesize lead to their self-helping behaviors, and in their irrational Beliefs (*iB*s), which we theorize lead to their self-defeating (and society-defeating) behaviors. We can list some of their main (but not only) kinds of *B*s as follows:

1. Non-evaluative observations, descriptions, and perceptions (cold cognitions). *Examples*:
    a. "I see people are laughing."
2. Positive preferential evaluations, inferences, and attributions (warm cognitions). *Examples*: Because I prefer people to like me and they are laughing—
    a. "I see they are laughing with me."
    b. "I see they think I am funny."
    c. "I see that they like me."
    d. "I like their laughing with me."
    e. "Their liking me has real advantages, which I love."
3. Negative preferential evaluations, inferences, and attributions (warm cognitions). *Examples*: Because I prefer people not to dislike me and they are laughing—
    a. "I see they are laughing at me."
    b. "I see they think I am stupid."
    c. "I see that they don't like me."
    d. "I dislike their laughing at me."
    e. "Their disliking me has real disadvantages, which I abhor."
4. Positive absolutistic evaluations, inferences, and attributions (hot cognitions; irrational Beliefs). *Examples*: "Because people are laughing with me and presumably like me and I must act competently and must win their approval—
    a. "I am a great, noble person!" (*overgeneralization*)
    b. "My life will be completely wonderful!" (*overgeneralization*)
    c. "The world is a totally marvelous place!" (*overgeneralization*)
    d. "I am certain that they will always laugh with me and that I will therefore always be a great person!" (*certainty*)
    e. "I deserve to have only fine and wonderful things happen to me!" (*deservingness and deification*)
    f. "I deserve to go to heaven and be beautified forever!" (*deservingness and extreme deification*)
5. Negative absolutistic evaluation, inferences, and attributions (hot cognitions; irrational Beliefs). *Examples*: "Because people

are laughing at me and presumably dislike me and because I must act competently and must win their approval—

   a. "I am an incompetent, rotten person!" (*overgeneralization*

   b. "My life will be completely miserable!" (*overgeneralization*)

   c. "The world is a totally crummy place!" (*overgeneralization*)

   d. "I am certain that they will always laugh at me and that I will therefore always be a rotten person!" (*certainty*)

   e. "I deserve to have only bad and grim things happen to me!" (*deservingness and damnation*)

   f. *"I deserve to roast in hell for eternity!" (deservingness and extreme damnation*)

6. Common cognitive derivatives of negative absolutistic evaluations (additional hot cognitions and irrational Beliefs). *Disturbed ideas*: "Because I must act competently and must win people's approval, and because their laughing at me shows that I have acted incompetently and/or have lost their approval—

   a. "This is *awful, horrible,* and *terrible!*" (*awfulizing, catastrophizing*)

   b. *"I can't bear it, can't stand it!"*, (*I-can't-stand-it-itis, discomfort anxiety, low frustration tolerance*)

   c. "I am a thoroughly incompetent, inferior, and worthless person!" (*self-downing, feelings of inadequacy*)

   d. "I can't change and become competent and lovable!" (*hopelessness*)

   e. "I deserve misery and punishment and will continue to bring it on myself!" (*damnation*)

7. Other common cognitive derivatives of negative absolutistic evaluations (additional irrational Beliefs). *Logical errors and unrealistic inferences*: "Because I must act competently and must win people's approval, and because their laughing at me shows that I have acted incompetently and/or have lost their approval—

   a. "I will always act incompetently and have significant people disapprove of me." (*overgeneralization*)

   b. "I'm a total failure and completely unlovable." (*overgeneralization; all-or-none thinking*)

   c. "They know that I am no good and will always be incompetent. (*non sequitur; jumping to conclusions; mind reading*).

    d. "They will keep laughing at me and will always despise me." (*non sequitur; jumping to conclusions; fortune telling*)

    e. "They only despise me and see nothing good in me." (*focusing on the negative; overgeneralization*)

    f. When they laugh with me and see me favorably that is because they are in a good mood and do not see that I am fooling them" (*disqualifying the positive; non sequitur*)

    g. "Their laughing at me and disliking me will make me lose my job and lose all my friends." (*catastrophizing; magnification*)

    h. "When I act well and get them to laugh with me that only shows that I can occasionally be wrong; but that is unimportant compared to my great faults and stupidities" (*minimization; focusing on the negative*)

    i. "I strongly feel that I am despicable and unlovable; and because my feeling is so strong and consistent, this proves that I really am despicable and unlovable." (*emotional reasoning; circular reasoning, non sequitur*)

    j. "I am a loser and a failure." (*labeling; overgeneralization*)

    k. "They could only be laughing because of some foolish thing I have done and could not possibly be laughing for any other reason." (*personalizing; non sequitur; overgeneralization*)

    l. "When I somehow get them to stop laughing at me or to laugh with me and like me, I am really a phony who is acting better than I am and who will soon fall on my face and show them what a despicable phony I am." (*phonyism; all-or-nothing thinking; overgeneralization*)

People can learn absolutistic evaluations, inferences, and conclusions (hot cognitions and irrational Beliefs) from their parents, teachers, and others—for example, "I must have good luck, but now that I have broken this mirror fate will bring me bad luck and that will be terrible!" But they probably learn these irrational Beliefs *easily* and *rigidly* retain them because they are born with a strong tendency to think irrationally. More important, people often learn family and cultural rational standards—for example, "It is *preferable* for me to treat others considerately"—and then overgeneralize, exaggerate, and turn these into irrational Beliefs—for example, "Because it is *preferable* for me to treat others considerately I *have* to do so at all times, else I am a *totally unlovable, worthless person!*" Even if all humans were reared utterly rationally, RET hypothesizes that virtually all of them would often take their learned standards and their rational preferences and irrationally escalate them into absolutistic demands on themselves, on others, and on the universe in which they live (Ellis, 1958, 1962, 1971, 1973, 1976, 1984; Ellis & Grieger, 1977; Ellis & Whiteley, 1979).

CONSEQUENCES (*C*s) OF ACTIVATING EVENTS (*A*s) AND BELIEFS (*B*s) ABOUT *A*s

*C*s (cognitive, effective, and behavioral Consequences) follow from the interaction of *A*s and *B*s. We can say, mathematically, that A × B = C; but this formula may actually be too simple and we may require a more complex one adequately to express the relationship. *C* is almost always significantly affected or influenced but not exactly caused by *A*—because humans naturally to some degree react to stimuli in their environments. Moreover, when *A* is powerful (e.g., a set of starvation conditions or an earthquake) it tends profoundly to affect *C*.

When *C* consists of emotional disturbance (e.g., severe feelings of anxiety, depression, hostility, self-deprecation, and self-pity), *B* usually (not always) *mainly* or *more* directly creates or causes *A*. Even emotional disturbance, however, may at times stem from powerful *A*s—for example, from environmental disasters such as floods or wars. And they may follow from factors in the organism—hormonal or disease factors, for instance—that are somewhat independent of or may actually cause Beliefs (*B*s).

When strong or unusual *A*s significantly contribute to or cause *C*s or when physiological factors create *C*s, they are usually accompanied by contributory *B*s as well. Thus, if people are caught in an earthquake or if they experience powerful hormonal changes and they therefore become depressed, their *A*s and their physiological processes probably are strongly influencing them to create irrational Beliefs (*iB*s), such as "This earthquake *shouldn't* have occurred! Isn't it *awful*! I can't stand it." These *iB*s, in turn, add to or help create their feelings of depression at *C*.

*C*s (thoughts, feelings, and behavioral Consequences) that result from *A*s and *B*s are virtually never pure or monolithic but also partially *include* and inevitably *interact with A* and *B*. Thus, if *A* is an obnoxious event (e.g., a job refusal) and *B* is first, a rational Belief (e.g., "I hope I don't get rejected for this job") and second an irrational Belief (e.g., "I must have this job! I'm no good if I don't get it"), *C* tends to be, first, a healthy feeling of frustration and disappointment and, second, unhealthy feelings of severe anxiety, inadequacy, and depression.

So $A \times B = C$ But people also *bring* feelings (as well as hopes, goals, and purposes) to A. They would not *apply* for a job unless they *desired* or *favorably evaluated* it. Their A therefore, partially includes their C. The two, from the beginning, are related rather than completely disparate.

At the same time, people's Beliefs (Bs) also partly or intrinsically relate to and include their As and their Cs. Thus, if they tell themselves at B, "I want to get a good job," they partly created the Activating event at A (going for a job interview) and they partly create their emotional and behavioral Consequence at C (feeling disappointed or depressed when they encounter a job rejection). Without their *evaluating* a job as good they would not try for it nor have any particular feeling about being rejected.

A, B, and C, then, are all closely related and none of them tends to exist without the other two. Another way of stating this is to say—as some psychologists have recently clearly stated—that environments only exist for humans (who are quite different from certain other animals); and humans only exist in certain kinds of environments (e.g., where temperatures are not too hot or too cold) and are *part* of their environment. Similarly, individuals usually exist in a society (rarely as hermits) and societies are only composed of humans (and are quite different when composed, say, of ants or birds). As the systems theory devotees point out, individual family members exist in a family system and change as this system changes. But RET also points out that the family system is composed of individuals and may considerably change as one or more of the individual family members change. In all these instances *interaction* is a key, probably an essential, concept for understanding and effectively helping people to change.

Similarly with cognition, emotion, and behavior thinking as I pointed out in 1956 (Ellis, 1958, 1962) importantly includes feeling and behaving. We largely think because we desire (a feeling) to survive (a behavior) and to be happy (a feeling). Emoting significantly *includes* thinking and behaving. We desire because we *evaluate* something as good or beneficial and, as we desire it, we move toward rather than away from it (act on it). Behaving to some degree usually *involves* thinking and emoting. We perform an act because we think it is advisable for us to do it and because we concomitantly feel like doing it. Occasionally, as certain mystical-minded people claim, there may be 100% *pure* thoughts, emotions, or behaviors which have no admixture of the other two processes. If so, they seem to be exceptionally rare. Even when they occasionally appear to occur—as when a person is tapped below the knee and gives a knee jerk response without any apparent concomitant thought or feeling—the original response (the knee jerk) seems to be immediately followed by a thought ("Look at that! my knee jerked!") and a feeling ("Isn't that nice that my nerves function well!"). So pure cognitions, emotions, and behaviors may exist, but rarely during normal waking (or conscious) states; and even when they do they are quickly followed by related cognitive-affective-behavioral states (Schwartz, 1982).

Humans uniquely are involved in cognitive processes and these often instigate, change, and combine their emotive and behavioral reactions. When they feel and behave, they almost always have some thoughts *about* their feelings and actions; and these thoughts lead them to have other feelings and behaviors. Thus, when they feel sad about, say, the loss of a loved one, they usually *see* or *observe* that they are sad, evaluate this feeling in some way (e.g., "Isn't it good that I am sad—this proves how much I really loved this person" or "Isn't it bad that I am sad—this shows that I am letting myself be too deeply affected").

When people feel emotionally disturbed at *C*—that is, seriously anxious, depressed, self-downing, or hostile—they quite frequently view their symptoms absolutistically and awfulizingly and irrationally conclude, "I should not, must not be depressed. It's awful to feel this way! I can't stand it. What a fool I am for giving in to this feeling!" They then develop a secondary symptom—depression about their depression or anxiety about their anxiety—that may be more severe and more incapacitating than their primary symptom and that may actually prevent them from understanding and working against their primary disturbance. RET assumes, on theoretical grounds, that they often use their cognitive processes in this self-defeating manner— because this is the way they *naturally, easily* tend to think—and it routinely looks for secondary symptoms and treats them prior to or along with dealing with clients' primary symptoms. The observable fact that people tend to spy on themselves and condemn themselves when they have primary symptoms, and thereby frequently develop crippling secondary symptoms, tends to support the RET hypothesis that cognition is enormously important in the development of neurotic feelings and behavior and that efficient psychotherapy had better usually include considerable rational-emotive methodology.

When people develop secondary symptoms—for example, feel very anxious about their anxiety, as agoraphobics tend to do—their secondary feelings strongly influence their cognitions and their behaviors. Thus, they feel so strongly that they tend to conclude, "It really *is* awful that I am panicked about open spaces!" and they tend to behave more self-defeatingly than ever (e.g., they withdraw all the more from open spaces). This again tends to demonstrate that *A* (Activating events), *B* (Beliefs), and *C* cognitive, emotive, and behavioral consequences) are interactive—that thoughts significantly affect feelings and behaviors, that emotions significantly affect thoughts and feelings, and that behaviors significantly affect thoughts and feelings.

In RET, we are mainly concerned with people's emotional disturbances—both their primary and secondary disturbances. But the *ABC* theory also is a personality theory that shows how people largely create their own normal or healthy (positive and negative) feelings and how they can change them if they wish to and work at doing so. I hope that the formulations in this paper will add to the *ABC* theory and make it more complex and more useful.

REFERENCES

Adler, A. *Understanding human nature*. New York: Greenberg, 1927.

Adler, A. *The science of living*. New York: Greenberg, 1929.

Bard, J. A. *Rational-emotive therapy in practice*. Champaign, IL: Research Press, 1980.

Beck, A. T. *Cognitive therapy and the emotional disorders*. New York: International Universities Press, 1976.

Dryden, W. *Rational-emotive therapy: Fundamentals and innovations*. London: Croom Heim, 1984.

Ellis, A. *How to live with a "neurotic."* New York: Crown, 1957. Rev. ed.: North Hollywood, CA: Wilshire, 1975.

Ellis, A. Rational psychotherapy. *Journal of General Psychology*, 1958, *59*, 35–39.

Ellis, A. *Reason and emotion in psychotherapy*. Secaucus, NJ: Lyle Stuart and Citadel Press, 1962.

Ellis, A. *Rational self help form*. New York: Institute for Rational-Emotive Therapy, 1968.

Ellis, A.*Growth through reason*. North Hollywood, CA: Wilshire, 1971.

Ellis, A. *Humanistic psychotherapy: The rational-emotive approach*. New York: Crown and McGraw-Hill Paperbacks, 1973.

Ellis, A. The biological basis of human irrationality. *Journal of Individual Psychology*, 1976, *32*, 145–168.

Ellis, A. The theory of rational-emotive therapy. In A. Ellis & J. Whiteley (Eds.), *Theoretical and empirical foundations of rational-emotive therapy*. Monterey, CA: Brooks/Cole, 1979.

Ellis, A. *Rational-emotive therapy and cognitive behavior therapy*. New York: Springer, 1984.

Ellis, A., & Grieger, R. (Eds.). *Handbook of rational-emotive therapy*. New York: Springer, 1977.

Ellis, A., & Whiteley, J. M. (Eds.) *Theoretical and empirical foundations of rational-emotive therapy*. Monterey, CA: Brooks/Cole, 1979.

Goldfried, M., & Davison, G. *Clinical behavior therapy*. New York: Holt, Rinehart & Winston, 1976.

Grieger, R. & Boyd, J. *Rational-emotive therapy: A skills-based approach*. New York: Van Nostrand Reinhold, 1980.

Grieger, R., & Greiger, I. *Cognition and emotional disorders*. New York: Human Sciences Press, 1982.

Guidano, V. F., & Liotti, G. *Cognitive processes and emotional disorders*. New York: Guilford, 1983.

Heidegger, M. *Being and time*. New York: Harper & Row, 1962.

Mahoney, M. *Cognition and behavior modification*. Cambridge, MA: Ballinger, 1974.

Phadke, K. M. Some innovations in RET theory and practice. *Rational Living*, 1982, *17*(2), 25–30.

Raimy, V. *Misunderstandings of the self*, San Francisco: Jossey-Bass, 1975.

Schwartz, R. M. Cognitive-behavior modification: A conceptual review. *Clinical Psychology Review*, 1982, *2*, 267–293.

Walen, S. R., DiGiuseppe, R., & Wessler, R. L. *A practitioner's guide to rational-emotive therapy*. New York: Oxford, 1980.

Wessler, R., & Wessler, R. L. *The principles and practice of rational-emotive therapy*. San Francisco: Jossey-Bass, 1980.

CHAPTER 14

Cognitive Therapy, Behavior Therapy, Psychoanalysis, and Pharmacotherapy

A Cognitive Continuum

AARON T. BECK

PHILOSOPHICAL SYSTEMS AND PSYCHOPATHOLOGY

To a large degree our scientific interpretations are based on a particular, often tacit, philosophical system. The philosophical system that we use as investigators may differ widely from that we use as clinicians. Thus, the laboratory investigator who studies depression may work within the trappings of a materialistic (or monistic) model while he is in the laboratory. When he takes off his lab coat and replaces it with his sports jacket as he prepares to treat a patient in psychodynamic therapy, he switches to a new philosophical system— either dualism or mentalism.

Moreover, the philosophy that guides our scientific or clinical endeavors may be completely different from that which shapes the view of the practical realities of everyday life. Thus, when our investigator arrives home to confront a troubled wife, he may advise her to stop worrying or she will get an ulcer (interactionist system). In

This chapter is an extended version of the Paul Hoch Award Address, American Psychopathological Association, March 3, 1983.

AARON T. BECK • Department of Psychiatry, University of Pennsylvania, 133 South 36th Street, Room 602, Philadelphia, Pennsylvania 19104.

sum, we may jump from materialism in the laboratory, mentalism in psychotherapy, and interactionism outside our professional activities.

In order to find the common ground among the psychotherapies and pharmacotherapy we need to have some understanding of the philosophical background that shapes the quite diverse approaches to an individual case.

Psychopharmacology has drawn on a materialistic (or monistic) system; behavior therapy, also, predominantly utilizes a materialistic system; psychoanalysis depends primarily on a mentalist system; cognitive therapy has been primarily interactionist.

Despite the obvious philosophical, theoretical, and technical differences among cognitive therapy, psychoanalysis, behavior therapy, and pharmacotherapy, there are enough subtle but important similarities to justify attempts to construct a maximodel to encompass those systems of therapy.

As a springboard for clarifying these similarities, let us take a typical case of a patient who showed a marked change during and after a particular intervention in cognitive therapy.

I will condense the description of the patient and interview to a few salient points in order to save space.

The patient was a 40-year-old married attorney who had been depressed for at least six months. He finally sought psychiatric evaluation after continuous prodding by his wife. Among the most salient features were insomnia, loss of gratification from any of the kinds of experiences that had brought gratification in the past (anhedonia), loss of appetite, loss of weight, early morning awakening, loss of libido, general slowing down, and difficulties in concentration. He was highly self-critical and pessimistic and did not think that any kind of psychiatric treatment would be helpful because his depression was "realistic"—that is, was derived from his basic inadequacy and ineffectiveness on the job, his failure in all spheres of his life.

On interview, the patient appeared to be very depressed and slowed down in all of his observable behaviors. He scored near the top on the Depression Inventory (50). The patient's pervasive view of himself was that he was totally inadequate and incapable of dealing with even minimal demands or expectations. He believed firmly that he was incapable of performing any of his work at the office, that this would always be the case, and if indeed he did attempt to do something he would be incapable of completing it or of doing an adequate job. His sense of hopelessness, inadequacy, and self-criticism also spread to his role as a husband and parent (he had two teenage sons).

Because of his sense of inadequacy and failure, he had been spending progressively less time at the office and had accumulated a pile of work that he had not attended to. He expected that he would be fired by the senior partners at any time and thus he and his family would be destitute. He saw suicide as a way of relieving his family of the emotional burden (he believed) he had imposed on them and also as a way to provide them with some financial support from his life insurance policy.

The only indication of precipitating factors had been the death of a senior partner of the firm a few months prior to the onset of the depression. The patient had been very attached to, and probably dependent on, him and "took his death very hard."

The patient was so suicidal that it was obvious that a quick intervention was indicated. This consisted essentially of starting cognitive-behavioral procedures immediately in the first interview. I discovered that the patient's belief that he would be fired in a day or two had a realistic basis. He was unprepared to try a case coming up for trial the next day and he had felt incapable of doing the necessary paperwork to request a continuation (that is, postponement) of the trial. He had tried many times to draft a letter or to make the appropriate phone call to the clerk of the court but felt incapable of mobilizing the degree of concentration for either action. He also had evaded telling his senior partners of the problem because of his sense of shame.

The therapeutic approach consists essentially of modified graded task assignments (Beck, Rush, Shaw, & Emery, 1979). Since he felt incapable of writing the letter, I asked him to give me some idea what he would say in the letter. As he "warmed up" to the project, he became unusually fluent and in a few minutes was able to produce orally an appropriate request. I took notes during this period of time and then handed him the written letter. He was surprised at this "success" and then we went on to dictate several other more complicated letters that he had been unable to attend to previously. After leaving the office he felt considerably better, more "alive" and more energetic. He started to walk through the campus and noted a number of buildings that had been erected since he graduated from the University of Pennsylvania. On an impulse he decided to go to the student cafeteria to see what the students were up to. As he went through the cafeteria line, he began to feel hungry and he had his first complete meal in several months. He later reported that he had enjoyed the meal and also enjoyed seeing various old familiar sights on the campus. These were the first experiences of pleasure that he recalled having had since his depression started.

APPLICATION OF PHILOSOPHICAL SYSTEMS

How can we understand this particular case?

From the standpoint of the materialistic system (centralist type), we could say that the patient had some kind of biochemical disturbance that was responsible for his symptoms. The basic problem, according to current theories, might be variously ascribed to a disturbance in functioning, a decreased sensitivity of specific receptors, a deficiency in steroid metabolism, some imbalance in the regulation of growth or thyrotropic hormones—or any combination of these or some other endocrine or normal neurochemical disturbance. According to the materialistic system, the treatment would consist of an administration of a drug to correct the deficiency or imbalance.

The psychodynamic approach would work within a mentalistic system and assume that the symptoms evolved from certain unconscious forces such as "loss of a love object" or retroflected hostility. Behavior therapy would use a materialistic model (peripluralist type) and look for a deficit in reinforcements of positive behaviors. By environmental modification, the individual would be given positive reinforcements, particularly in constructive behaviors, and nonreinforcements for self-defeating behaviors.

The usual cognitive model is interactionist (Mahoney, 1982), although I personally favor the model I shall present in this chapter. Thus, the cognitivist assumes that the individual's primary problem has to do with his construction of reality. The remedy lies in modifying the cognitive set. This psychological modification then produces biochemical changes which in turn can influence cognitions further.

There are a number of reasons why none of the aforementioned philosophical systems can totally "explain" a phenomenon such as depression. For instance, the philosophical system dictates what type of instruments one uses for making observations, what kinds of observations are actually made, and how these observations are interpreted. If the investigator is interested in the phenomenon as a psychological entity, then all of the data and conceptualizations would be shaped to conform to the psychological mold. If he perceives of it as a biochemical entity, then the observations and inferences will deal with tangibles (neurons, synapses, neurotransmitters, etc.). This philosophical position may be illustrated by aligning the cognitive approach to the preceding case with the neurochemical.

The philosophical system that I endorse rests on the following postulates:

1. Nonmaterial, nonspatial phenomena or processes are just as *real* as material, spatial phenomena. *Nonspatial* means that the particular process cannot be located in space. *Nonmaterial* means that the phenomena or process does not consist of stuff that we can touch, see, or taste. Further, these phenomena are private and dependent on the introspective report of the individual who is experiencing the phenomena and thus cannot be directly validated by another individual.

2. A phenomenon such as depression may be viewed alternately from either a biochemical perspective, a psychological perspective, a behavioral perspective, or other perspectives. The biochemical and behavioral perspectives are similar insofar as they deal with public, spatial stimuli. The cognitive and psychoanalytic perspectives deal primarily with private, nonmaterial, nonspatial data. Neither perspective is more correct or more real than the other perspectives.

3. The various perspectives have varying degress of explanatory power. By relating them to each other, we can attempt to construct an integrated model that will have greater explanatory power than the individual perspectives.

It is important to recognize that the thoughts and beliefs of the patient do not constitute the cognitive process any more than do the neurochemical changes that are taking place simultaneously. Thoughts do not cause the neurochemical changes and the neurochemical changes do not cause the thoughts. Neurochemical changes and cognitions are the same process examined from different perspectives. However, correspondences between one perspective and the other tend to validate the formulations of each perspective and provide a more complete explanation of the phenomenon.

We can now apply this unitary system to understanding how the cognitive-behavioral intervention improved the patient's anhedonia, sadness, and loss of appetite. We can conceptualize this as follows: The psychological intervention by the therapist was processed by the patient's information-processing apparatus. This processing involved changes in the brain, reflected in a biochemical modification and simultaneously modification in the cognitive set. If we took a "psychological biopsy" after the cognitive-neurochemical modification, we would obtain cognitions such as "He really believes he can help me," and "I didn't believe I could write this letter—but I did." If we took a neurochemical biopsy at that point in time, we would find an intricate pattern of neurons firing and chemical changes at the synapses.

If we conceptualize depression as an abnormal or dysfunctional phenomenon, the cognitive processes *and* neurochemical processes are abnormal. This abnormality may be corrected in a variety of ways.

The cognitive approach, expressed in terms of the verbal and non-verbal behavior of the therapist, produces cognitive-neurochemical changes. Similarly, the pharmacological approach, specifically the administration of an antidepressant drug, leads to cognitive-neuro-chemical changes.

As we will see later, biochemical interventions have the same type of cognitive impact as does cognitive therapy. How do we explain the biological changes in this case after a psychological intervention? We can take anhedonia as an example. The lawyer patient had a rigid idea: "Nothing matters. . . . Life has gone stale. . . . How can I enjoy anything when I'm a failure?" The cognitive-behavioral intervention reversed the cognitive set to "I can experience pleasure" and the patient did experience pleasure. A successful pharmacological inter-vention would produce the same cognitive changes (Simons, 1982). Couched in biological terms, the improvement in cognitive processing is expressed in a reversal of a biochemical chain reaction, leading further to a reversal of those biochemical processes involved in the experience of dysphoria.

THE UNIVERSAL DEFICIT

We can approach this case from the vantage point of the treat-ments listed in the title of this chapter. Each of these systems qualifies as a system of therapy, by which we mean a coherent theoretical framework, a body of clincial data to support it, and a therapeutic approach intrinsically related to the theory. As we shall see, each theory revolves around the concept of loss and deficit and each ap-proach includes a replacement therapy to fill in the gaps.

The psychoanalytic formulation of the case would rest largely on the loss of the "loved object" (death of the partner) and a consequent negative affect. This negative affect, presumably anger, is not overtly expressed but is turned against the self and is transformed into de-pressive affect. Similarly, behavior therapy would postulate that the-loss of reinforcements from his senior partner and other members of the firm led to a reduction in the spontaneous behaviors (Lewinsohn, 1975); Rehm's self-control model (1977) would indicate that the pa-tient's termination of self-reinforcement for achievement led to neg-ative affect. Seligman's learned helplessness model (1975) would ex-plain the patient's depressive behavior as the basis of loss of control over reinforcement (the partner) and attribution of responsibility to himself. According to these models, the positive reinforcement of constructive behavior by the therapist increased the patient's positive behavior (Lewinsohn) and the self-reinforcement (Rehm) and concept of control over reinforcement (Seligman).

The cognitive model postulates a similar deficit in this patient. As a by-product of the serious loss, the individual begins to overinterpret his experiences as losses; the usual positive constructions of reality have been deleted and, thus, negative constructions become dominant. Since the negative constructions are presumably tied to negative affect, not only does the individual make negative appraisals of himself and his present, past, and future experiences, but he also experiences unpleasant affect and loss of constructive motivation and suicidal impulses. According to the cognitive model, the positive deficits were counteracted by providing for more positive constructions of experience.

The psychopharmacological approach would also rest on an analogous hypothesized deficit. It would propose, for example, that the patient suffered from some disturbance in the availability or utilization of certain chemical transmitters at synaptic junctions in the brain. The derived remedy (not employed in this case) would be the administration of a monoamine oxidase inhibitor or tricyclic compound to counteract this defect. Other hypothesized deficiencies might involve defects in regulation of the entire neuroendocrine system or insufficient output of brain cells bearing noradrenergic receptors to meet increased demands resulting from stress (Stone, 1983).

THE KEYS TO THE BLACK BOX

As was indicated above, clinicians of the major schools of thought have focused on the concept of loss or deficit in depression. In general, an external loss is postulated (loss of reinforcements or of control over them or loss of loved object). If the loss leads to depression, there are certain processes that need to be stipulated to bridge the gap between the external deprivation and the depressive behaviors. Each of the theories either directly describes or alludes to some type of structure that mediates between the external situation (loss) and the ultimate depressive reaction. This intervening structure has been described in elaborate detail (psychoanalysis), in simplified terms (cognitive model), or simply alluded to as the "black box" (behavioral model).

The concept of the black box was applied originally to the unspecified "location" in the conditioning model in which stimuli connect up with the conditioned response. According to behavioral theories, it is here that the positive inputs (reinforcements) make their connections and produce the positive outputs (constructive behaviors). If the positive inputs (reinforcements) are inadequate for a sufficient period of time, then the outputs (behaviors) become extinguished and, according to the theory, the individual shows the typical slowing down of depression. The treatment prescribed by Lewinsohn attempts to increase the number of reinforcements through exposing the patient to potentially pleasant activities and thus increasing the positive outputs. In the case described above, the patient's constructive activities were positively reinforced by the therapist and this led to more activity. Rehm's approach is to activate the patient to engage in activities for which he will reinforce himself, and this will tend to increase positive behavior.

The psychoanalytic and cognitive models presuppose several levels of organization, the lowest of which corresponds to the black box. Thus, the psychoanalytic version of the black box is represented by the complex formulation of the Unconscious, as the repository of the Id, or as the site of Primary Process thinking. Through the process of interpretation, the patient is able to lift the lid off the box and use his mature Ego to counteract these disruptive forces. The attempt is to "make the unconscious conscious" or to fulfill the dictum "where the Id was, there the Ego shall be." From a different standpoint, the Primary Process thinking (lower level) is subjected to contact with reality in the form of the Secondary Process (higher level) and is brought into a more logical and less disruptive framework. One psychoanalytic explanation of the lawyer's rapid symptomatic response is that he found a long lost father figure in the therapist, with whom he could identify. Another interpretation is that the therapist's nurturance neutralized the patient's overwhelming sense of emptiness and satisfied his dependence and/or needs.

The theoretical framework of cognitive therapy is somewhat similar to that of psychoanalysis (Beck et al., 1979). The constructs of "mature thinking" (higher level) and "immature or primitive thinking" (lower level) correspond to Secondary Process and Primary Process. The mechanism of successful treatment may or may not involve introspection. The thrust in this case was (a) to negate the hopelessness through behavioral experiments and thus undermine the negative bias, (b) to promote, through the doctor–patient relationship and the assignment of success and pleasure experiences, a build-up of positive behavioral and affective experiences. According to the underlying rationale, as the patient's negative constructions diminish, the negative feelings diminish; as the positive constructions increase, the positive feelings increase.

In summary, in addition to having a common thematic content relevant to depression, the three systems of psychotherapy have a similar structural basis. The black box of the behavioral model corresponds to the Primary Process of psychoanalysis and the primitive thinking of the cognitive model. The neurochemical correlates of this construct constitute an area for future research.

THE COMMON PATHWAY: COGNITIVE PROCESSING

Another commonality among the systems of psychotherapy is the mechanism by which the specific therapy produces therapeutic results. There is considerable evidence accumulating that each of the effective therapies has an impact on cognitive processes. When measures of these cognitive processes show a shift from negative to positive, they are accompanied by a general improvement in depression and anxiety. Since only a few studies have been reported to date, I will have to cite disparate reports to illustrate my point.

Psychoanalytic therapy has not been studied to an extent using the kinds of measures that have been applied in other studies. However, a study by Carrington (1979) which used insight therapy based on psychodynamic principles, demonstrated that the depressed patients who improved on insight therapy showed changes in the cognitive items on the Depression Inventory.

A study by Hammen, Jacobs, Mayol, and Cochran (1981) using social skills training for the treatment of socially anxious individuals showed significant positive changes on the Dysfunctional Attitude Scale, an instrument developed by Weissman and Beck (1978) to define the dysfunctional attitudes in depression.

If you randomly select two groups of depressed patients and one receives cognitive therapy and the other receives antidepressant medication, what changes take place? Cognitive therapy presumably affects cognition; antidepressant medication allegedly affects physiological processes. Is there a common denominator?

The most appropriate study to illustrate the cognitive impact of successful treatment was Simons' analysis (1982) of an outcome study conducted by Murphy and his associates at Washington University. She analyzed the data on the depressed outpatients who received cognitive therapy alone and those who received antidepressant medication alone. In looking at the change scores in the instruments specifically designed to measure, respectively, automatic thoughts, dysfunctional attitudes, and negative expectancies, she found that the clinically improved patients showed a corresponding improvement in these measures of cognitive phenomena. More significantly, perhaps, the patients who did not improve did not show a change on the cognitive measures. What is most salient for our present discussion is that pharmacotherapy had essentially the same impact on the cognitive content as did cognitive therapy.

These findings are in line with those reported by Eaves and Rush (1982) in a study of depressed outpatients and inpatients. It should also be noted that Eaves and Rush found the endogenous depressions showed as much cognitive distortion as did nonendogenous depressions, a result supporting the thesis that cognitive processes are an intrinsic component of depressions, even those assumed by some writers to be biological in origin.

ANHEDONIA: FUSION OF THE PERSPECTIVES

A promising area for examining the overlap of the systems of psychotherapy with psychopharmacology is anhedonia, specifically as related to depression. Investigators have linked the presence of high concentrations of norepinephrine and dopamine to hypothetical pleasure centers in the brain. More recently, evidence that stimulation of specific brain areas containing high concentrations of the endorphins acts as a powerful positive reinforcer of behavior has suggested the importance of these substances as mediators of pleasure. By inference it could be hypothesized that depletion of the catecholamines or endorphins could lead to anhedonia. In fact, drugs designed to counteract the reduced availability or utilization of catecholamines in depression have been shown to be effective in this disorder.

In view of the progress in expanding the biochemical perspective, it would seem valuable to broaden the *psychological perspective*. Moreover, comparison of these perspectives can serve as a guide to further research. Ultimately, the fusion of the perspectives on anhedonia should provide a more comprehensive model than is currently available.

A good deal of publicity lately has been attached to the biochemistry of anhedonia (Belson, 1983). Some writers appear to regard this condition as a primary biological phenomenon presumably due to some aberration of neuroendocrine. The reductionist models of this disorder seem to rest on the assumption that biochemical processes of the brain proceed in splendid oblivion of environmental demands. It is more in keeping with contemporary concepts to analyze the phenomenon in terms of its functions and its relationships to normal processes. Furthermore, it would seem that anhedonia may well have— or has had—evolutionary value in order to have survived a multitude of selective pressures. Thus, a broad view of anhedonia should include not only concepts regarding internal regulatory mechanisms but also notions regarding adaptation to changing environmental stressors.

It should be noted that the reductionist explanation may also dictate notions regarding the appropriate therapy for this condition. Thus, part of the skepticism about the impact of cognitive therapy on primary affective disorders has been based on the notion that these are biochemical in origin. However, it has been found that even the endogenous depressives, characterized largely by loss of responsiveness to pleasurable stimuli, respond well to this type of psychological intervention (Rush, Beck, Kovacs, & Hollon, 1977). Further, the item on the Beck Depression Inventory relevant to anhedonia shows an early responsiveness to cognitive therapy.

Anhedonia may be analyzed in terms of an elevation of the threshold for positive experience. This relative imperviousness accounts, in part, for the selective focus on the negative. This type of response may be precipitated by an absolute subtraction from the domain (for example, being abandoned by a loved one) or by a hypothetical, relative loss (specifically, a disappointment, such as not performing as well as expected or not getting as much affection or approval as expected). Following a significant meaningful loss, the depression-prone individual is likely to make an overgeneralized *absolute* judgement (for example, "I can never get what I want") even though the loss is only partial or relative, representing the discrepancy between anticipated gain and actual gain.

Such a conceptualization indicates the formation of a negative congitive set, sometimes a prelude to depression. Positive experiences are blacked out, interpreted negatively, forgotten, or devalued on recall. Negative experiences are selectively abstracted or exaggerated. If the cognitive blockade becomes fixed, it sets in motion a sequence of other cognitive, motivational, and affective symptoms of depression.

It should be noted that in many situations we function with bias toward the positive: We tend to be optimistic and have a somewhat elevated hedonic tone ("the illusory glow"). The dominance of positive processing appears to be a function, in part, of the reduction in negative processing. As the positive apparatus becomes less active (shows increased thresholds), the negative organization becomes relatively more prominent.

THE COGNITIVE BLOCKADE

Let us analyze the psychological mechanisms by which anhedonia and dysphoria may be produced in depression. Anhedonia, which is present in 92% of cases of severe depression, may be described along a dimension ranging from "I feel bored most of the time" to "I am dissatisfied with everything" (Beck, 1967), and dysphoria, present in 88% of cases of severe depression, from "I feel sad" to "I am so sad I can't stand it" (Beck, 1967).

The experimental and clinical studies cited below have suggested that there is a *cognitive blockade* that interferes with the reception and/or integration of positive data in depression. The term *cognitive* is used because the interference may occur at various points along the cognitive continuum: perception, recognition, interpretation, integration, learning, immediate recall, long-term memory. This refractoriness to the integration of positive aspects of experience increases with the severity of depression. The blockade against utilization of positive experiences may account for the loss of pleasure response associated with depression. If the positive experiences do not "get through," are diverted from active storage, or are minimized on recall, they are prevented from having any impact on the hedonic system. Sadness is a consequence of the relative predominance of negativity as a result of the blockage of the positive inputs. Thus, the elimination of positive factors from the conception of past, present, and future leaves the patient with an exclusively negative view, which leads to sadness.

The evidence suggesting a cognitive blockade in depression may be pieced together for a variety of experimental paradigms. Alloy and Abramson (1979) have reported that normal subjects have an "illusion of control" in contrast to realistic self-appraisals by nonclinical depressives. If generalized to normal experiences, their experiments suggest that we are generally inclined to be optimistic and thus maintain a somewhat pleasurable hedonic tone. If our bias toward the positive (e.g., the illusion of control) is negated, however, our hedonic tone is likely to drop to or below the baseline, as in the case of Alloy and Abramson's depressives. Thus, in the mildly depressed state we have dropped our positive illusions and process negative information as readily as positive. Further, increasing depression is associated with increased refractoriness to positive inputs and a relative negative bias.

Analogue studies using induced mood procedures to produce sadness or "minidepressions" indicate that normals or "elated" subjects have a positive bias that is eliminated in the sad subjects (Bower,

1981; Clark & Teasdale, 1982; Goodwin & Williams, 1982; Rholes, Riskind, & Lane, 1982).

Stiles (1978) reported that depressed subjects recall experiences less positively with the passage of time. Although initial appraisals of enjoyment, performance and success following an experience task were realistic, these assessments declined at subsequent testing up to two weeks following the task.

A different type of experiment (by Muller, 1982) supports the notion that normals have a positive bias that is vitiated in depressives. Using tachistoscopically presented scenes, he found that normals had a greater sensitivity to positive than to negative words. This positive bias (or, more precisely, antinegative bias) was eliminated in the depressed student volunteers who showed the same latency for positive exposures as for negative exposures.

An interesting study by Gilson (1983) presented evidence suggestive of the cognitive blockade. Using a binocularscope, he showed unpleasant and neutral or pleasant slides to "depressed" students and normals. The depressed subjects showed a significant main effect for the depressive slides (i.e., the "perception" of only depressed slides and "nonperception" of positive or neutral slides when presented simultaneously). The normals, in contrast, showed a main effect for the slides with the positive or neutral scenes. A subsequent unpublished study by Gilson showed the same results with hospitalized depressed patients.

A variety of state-dependent studies indicate that *clinically* depressed patients have impaired recall of favorable feedback (e.g., DeMonbreun & Craighead, 1977), of pleasant events (Lloyd and Lishman, 1975; Clark & Teasdale, 1982), self-referent positive adjectives (Bradley & Mathews, 1983), or of pleasant schemes in stories (Breslow, Kocsis, & Belkin, 1981).

Further support for the notion that depressives selectively block out positive aspects of experiences is found in a study by Butler and Mathews, 1983). They reported that depressive and anxious patients attached much higher probabilities to mishaps occurring to them than did normals. Of interest to the present review, they found a trend for depressives to attach lower probabilities for positive events than did either anxious patients or normals. This finding is in line with Giles and Shaw's report (1982) that depressives underestimate probabilities of success on an experimental task.

The tendency of normals to block out negative self-references and of depressives to block out positive self-references is born out in tests of social desirability response style. The normals tend to eschew items reflecting unfavorably on them, whereas depressives generally will not endorse favorable items. This tendency of depressives to give a fairly accurate statement of socially undesirable characteristics, such as symptoms, accounts for the validity of certain types of self-report instruments, such as the Depression Inventory.

Some of the aforementioned studies are reminiscent of an earlier trend in psychology subsumed under the rubric, the "New Look in Perception." The newer concepts of raising and lowering thresholds for recognition are suggestive of earlier notions of "perceptual defense" and "perceptual vigilance." More recently, Erdelyi (1974) has reformulated these two phenomena as a special instance of selectivity in cognitive processing. His concepts are close to those presented here. Selectivity consists of multiple processes operating through varied mechanisms brought into play at multiple loci of the information-processing sequence. Anticipating the studies reported here, he states (p. 1): "Thus, selectivity is pervasive throughout the cognitive continuum, from input to output, and no single site is likely to provide exhaustive explanations of any substantial selective phenomenon." Thus, the slide studies cited above fit into the notion that a complex of sites and functions is involved in the selectivity observed in the cognitive processing of favorable and unfavorable information by the depressed individual. The influence of the negative cognitive set may be detected at multiple points along the pathway from perception to long-term memory. Thus, the depressives show a bias against positive at the level of recognition (Muller, 1982; Gilson, 1983), recent memory (Clark & Teasdale, 1982; DeMonbreun & Craighead, 1977), more remote memory (Lloyd & Lishman, 1975; Stiles, 1978), and expectancies (Butler & Mathews, 1983; Giles & Shaw, 1982).

MECHANISMS OF COGNITIVE BLOCKADE IN ANHEDONIA

The addition of a positive factor to the personal domain represents a gain and ordinarily produces gladness; the subtraction of a positive (e.g., the departure of a valued person or the nonfulfillment of a positive expectancy) leads to sadness. If the subtraction is significant, the individual adjusts to the loss by reducing his expectations of pleasure or gain. Consequently, his overall goal-oriented striving, which is derived from his expectations, is reduced. Another adjustment also occurs. The threshold for subjective satisfaction is raised ("loss of reinforcer effectiveness"—Costello, 1972). The previously cited experimental evidence suggests that this hedonic adjustment is drived from an increased threshold for the integration of positive inputs. In addition, there seems to be relative loss of the ability to assign positive *meaning* to events ordinarily regarded as positive. These cognitive changes may be regarded as expressions of the change from a positive to a negative cognitive set.

A serious question raised by this formulation is: Why does a loss lead to an *increased* threshold for positives? The increased threshold may, conceivably, be understood as a response to hemeostatic or cybernetic regulation. The organism is "wired" to achieve a balance between action and passivity. The function of activity is related to goals relevant to long-term survival and reproduction. If the organism was not deterred by disappointment, it might continue in unending attempts to gain satisfaction and thus would be eventually exhausted (as in manic states).

The shift to negative expectations and the raising of minimal level of satisfaction following disappointment damp down spontaneous motivations and activity and thus serve as a check against the runaway quest for gratification. The individual experiences dysphoria not only following a deprivation but also in anticipation of a future deprivation. The individual consequently anticipates further dysphoria if he attempts to undertake a project and thus retreats further into an anhedonic passivity.

In a broader sense, we may view the intricate process of increasing and decreasing thresholds for positive experiences as playing a role in overall adaptation (and reproduction). The system of "rewards" regulated by enhanced sensitivity to positive stimuli enhances behavior directed toward these goals. The reduction of rewards reduces such behavior. Thus, in depression the increased thresholds for perceiving satisfying activities plus the negative expectancies lead to reduction in appetite for activities relevant to long-term survival (eating) and reproduction (sex).

In cognitive therapy of depression we attempt to exceed the thresholds along the cognitive continuum by providing a series of selected positive experiences ("the mastery and pleasure principle"). In "running the cognitive blockade," we seek to increase positive expectancies, which in turn increase motivation, leading to more success experiences and consequent positive feedback. By swamping the thresholds with a series of immediate, concrete, unmistakable success experiences, we "force" the threshold and inject a positive view of the immediate and near future. We also instruct the patient to write down experiences relevant to pleasure and mastery and to repeat them during the therapy sessions. These successful experiences stimulate increased positive expectancies and the threshold for perceiving positives consequently drops; the writing down and forced recall increases the integration of positive experiences; and the patient experiences a gradual return of gratification.

Anhedonia is an interesting phenomenon to discuss from the perspectives of the various psychotherapies and psychopharmacology. The psychoanalytic perspective would focus on the antitheses between the pleasure principle and the reality principle. It could be suggested, for instance, that as a result of a series of disconfirmations of expectations, the pleasure principle is suspended temporarily: In order to bring cognitive processes more in line with the reality, the expectations are switched to a more realistic but negatively tinged "data-processing apparatus."

In essence, excesses resulting from regulation by the pleasure principle are counteracted by the imposition of the reality principle which directs attention to scarcity rather than abundance, to failure and deprivation rather than success and fulfillment. The displacement of the pleasure principle by the reality principle inactivates the pleasure response mechanism. The adjustment to reality, however, may overshoot the mark and lead to a negative cognitive set.

The cognitive model, as indicated above, spells out the consequences of the switch from positive to negative cognitive set. The behavioral model can account for anhedonia in terms of the removal of external reinforcements (Lewinsohn, 1975). As the self-reinforcing has become switched off, the individual no longer receives satisfaction for activities that were previously reinforcing.

It is of interest that the sequence of positive cognitive set→realistic set→ negative set may culminate in depression. The road back to normal functioning appears to be based on a reversal of this sequence. Thus, cognitive therapy and psychoanalysis use techniques calculated to inject a more realistic perspective into the patient's thinking. It is of interest that the realistic perspective which is a link in the chain leading to depression is a crucial link in the chain back to normality.

The overlapping psychological theories of anhedonia may point the way for further brain research. It may be possible through some of the recent advanced techniques to pinpoint particular areas in the brain or neurochemical systems involved with the experience of pleasure. It would be interesting to demonstrate what effects manipulating the cognitive set would have on the activity of such systems.

COGNITIVE COMPONENTS OF SPECIFIC TREATMENTS

BEHAVIOR THERAPY

We are now ready to analyze the various therapies within the framework of the model I have just presented.

The traditional formulation of behavior therapy bypasses the role of cognitive processes in the therapeutic process. More recent writings by Wolpe (1982) suggest that in some cases of phobia, specifically those in which the patient has been exposed to erroneous information about the phobic situation, cognitive restructuring is valuable. However, Wolpe tends to equate cognitive with "conscious" ideas. The more comprehensive view presented in this paper treats the cognitive organization as composed of several levels. Only the higher levels (mature level) are characterized by free decision-making, objectivity, rationality, and the like.

According to the scheme I have presented (Beck *et al.*, 1979) the lower levels of cognitive organization (primitive level) are characterized by features attributed to *conditioned emotional responses*— the cognitive reaction occurs as if by reflex, is automatic and maladaptive, and occurs despite the patient's considering it irrational and consciously opposing it. Hence, Wolpe's initial notion regarding cognitive processes is correct as far as it goes, in that *the higher-level* cognition is bypassed in the reflex arc, but he overlooks the concept of low-level cognition, a significant component of the conditioned emotional response (Beck, 1976). The agoraphobic demonstrates graphically how a patient can recognize at the higher "rational" cognitive level that a situation is safe but the lower primitive level generates a sequence of automatic thoughts relevant to losing control or dying. The patient's experience and interpretation of physiological feedback such as rapid heartbeat or faintness further reinforce the primitive cognitive content such as fear of dying, losing control, and being abandoned, and swamps attempts at the mature level to view the situation realistically.

The therapeutic mechanism of behavior therapy may be readily analyzed within a cognitive framework. Let us turn to the treatment of the agoraphobic. Exposure therapy—*in vivo* flooding, for example—switches on the primitive level: The individual experiences a sense of danger and intensification of symptoms of anxiety. The symptoms themselves trigger further cognitions about danger (Last & Blanchard, 1982). At that point the individual believes with close to 75–100% certainty that he is having or is about to have a heart attack, stroke, loss of control, loss of sanity, or whatever.

Within a therapeutic structure, that is, with a therapist present, he is enabled to assimilate the experience. Given a sufficient period of time during the exposure therapy, he receives cumulative feedback that indicates that he is *not* dying, losing control, having a heart attack, or going crazy and that the fear of disaster is unwarranted.

Even without coaching, he can recognize increasingly that his fright is a false alarm. Incidentally, it is crucial that the patient experience anxiety in order to ensure that the primitive cognitive levels have been activated (since these levels are directly connected to the affects).

The repeated, direct, immediate recognition that the danger signals do not lead to catastrophe eventually provides sufficient disconfirming evidence to enable the patient to switch off the alarm reaction. Subsequent practice sessions further reinforce the new learning experience. They enhance the responsivity of the primitive level to more realistic inputs from "above" (that is, from the mature cognitive level) which then turn off the alarm reaction. In the course of time, the agoraphobic is able to switch off the alarm reaction at an early stage because he has learned that the physiological reactions are not signs of danger and that he can ignore his fearful cognitions. There is obviously much more to the cognitive component of behavior therapy than the foregoing, but this brief analysis demonstrates how its action can be brought within a cognitive framework.

Behavior therapy has shown that it is possible to "cure" a neurosis without the person's having insight into the origin of the disorder. Although behavior therapy explicitly shortcuts the high-level cognition insofar as it focuses exclusively on direct exposure to threatening situations, it actually provides the patient with a powerful framework to correct—cognitively—his unrealistic fears. The patients are aware of the unreasonableness of the primitive belief system as indicated by statements such as "I know that nothing will happen to me (in the crowded store), but I am still afraid of suffocating," and thus exposure therapy is able to produce cognitive restructuring.

It is important to emphasize the overlap between cognitive therapy and behavior therapy despite differences in terminology. The concept of primitive level (in the cognitive model) has much in common with the notion of conditioned reflex. The conditioning model postulates that the inappropriate response is due to the previous pairing of an innocuous stimulus with a realistically dangerous one. The cognitive model posits that the innocuous stimulus is construed as dangerous because of an idiosyncratic (low-level) cognitive set. Both the conditioning and cognitive models require low-level cognitive mediation because of the rapid stereotyped, inappropriate response.

In both models, the response to the innocuous stimulus involves immediate motivational and affective components. In the cognitive model the automatic cognitive structuring determines the affect (anxiety) and the behavioral response (avoidance). In behavior therapy the affect (anxiety) and behavioral response (avoidance) are chained to the specific stimulus situation.

PSYCHOANALYSIS

The theory of cognitive therapy differs from psychoanalysis in several ways but shares many similar concepts. Psychoanalysis postulates that the content of the unconscious is diametrically opposite to that of the content of consciousness—in fact, that a variety of defenses such as reaction formation, displacement, rationalization, and sublimation are used to disguise any unconscious material that might leak through the wall of repression.

In cognitive therapy, in contrast, the distorted content is exposed (for example, by eliciting automatic thoughts) and the bulk of the work from there on is spent on fortifying this reality testing through behavioral experiments, checking observations, looking for evidence and so forth. Thus, the dominant emphasis is on the technical procedures sometimes referred to in the psychoanalytic literature as "ego support" or "ego analysis."

In sum, psychoanalysis attempts to expose the unconscious processes (primary process) and assumes that the ego, relieved of the burden of trying to seal off the taboo material, will then spontaneously provide realistic corrections. Cognitive therapy explicitly attempts to induce the patient to draw continually on his rationality (logic, empiricism, etc.) to correct the irrationality.

PSYCHOPHARMACOLOGY

The system of psychopharmacology has been primarily empirically derived and is not theoretical in any systematic sense. Many of the somatic treatments such as insulin coma therapy and electroconvulsive therapy were discovered serendipitously. When a drug was found to work, it was then refined to be more effective, with fewer side effects, and an attempt was made to map out mechanisms of actions. Some of the current neurochemical theories of depression have been based in part on the known neurochemical effects of antidepressant drugs.

There has been a concerted attempt to apply findings regarding the nervous system as a basis for developing new and effective drugs. Progress has been limited by several factors: (a) the integrated knowledge of the central nervous system (CNS) is still limited although rapidly growing, (b) a broad schema which emphasizes a systems approach to CNS function is lacking and (c) there has been little attempt to utilize psychological findings or schemas as a guide for searching for or integrating biochemical findings. As a result of the tendency toward reductionist thinking prevalent in much scientific work, neurochemical abnormalities have often been labeled as *the* cause or *the* explanation for depression. An example of an attempt to link psychological and pharmacological data has been the development of the Dexamethasone Suppression Test and attempts to correlate neuroendocrine deviations with specific subtypes of depression.

Thus far, neuropsychopharmacotherapy has adopted a deficiency model for understanding depression. Certain deficiencies have been found (for example, in pre- or post-synaptic neurotransmitter function) or in neuroendocrine response (as in the Dexamethasone Suppression Test). As the abnormal findings have not been woven into an adequate explanatory model, a comprehensive psychobiological model would integrate the psychological and neurochemical perspectives. It would enable the researcher to look at the psychological levels and correlate them with neurochemical findings and drug actions on the basis of these levels. It would also correlate neurochemical findings with the major spheres: cognitive, affective, motivational and behavioral.

This maximodel might, for example, prompt the investigator looking for the equivalent of an ego deficit to search for an abnormality in the neocortex. Or he might consider a dysfunction of the paleocortex contributing to the cognitive distortions. We found that the initial change with drug therapy was in cognitions, not the affect of depression (Rush, Beck, Kovacs, Weissenburger, & Hollon, 1982). What are the cognitions being affected by drugs? Are they low level (primary process) or high level (secondary process) or both? A better model for understanding psychopharmacology may be found.

There is increasing evidence of a rapprochement between biological and psychological approaches. The theme of the 1983 meeting of the Society of Biological Psychiatry was the biology of information processing. Gevins (1983) proposed a new model of neurocognitive functioning.

A promising line of research attempting to bridge the gap between psychosocial and psychopharmacological approaches has been the work by Kraemer and McKinney (1979), who found that the combination of a psychosocial stressor (maternal deprivation) and a drug (AMPT) that depletes brain catecholamines had a synergistic effect in producing depression in monkeys. This is an example of how loss or deprivation at an abstract symbolic level may be brought into apposition with loss or deficiency at the concrete biochemical level. Studies such as this by investigators well versed in the psychological perspectives as well as the biochemical perspectives may advance the day when the understanding and treatment of the psychiatric disorders can be encompassed within a sophisticated comprehensive model.

SUMMARY

Psychological observations are just as real as biological observations. The biological and psychological systems are different perspectives of the same phenomonen and use, respectively, a public, spatial, concrete focus and a private, nonspatial, nonmaterial focus. Despite differences in the level of abstraction, there should be correspondences between the two, and a unified theory should provide clues as to where to look for these correspondences.

Commonalities across the systems of psychotherapy and pharmacotherapy and their underlying theories may be delineated. When we examine specific disorders such as depression, we find that each theory focuses on a relative deficit of the positive components of experience. This common concept is represented by terms such as loss of reinforcement (behavior therapy), loss of object (psychoanalysis), deprivation or defeat (cognitive therapy). It is speculated that the concept of psychological deficit may have some relationship to deficits in neuroendocrine function.

Although different terms are used, there are other similarities in theory and therapy. Structurally, the locus of the problem in a disorder such as depression can be ascribed to the primary process or unconscious; to the "black box" of behaviorism, or to the primitive cognitive organization. The key to therapy consists of correcting the negative balance through insight, through reestablishing positive reinforcements, through changing the negative cognitive set, or through increasing the availability of catecholamines and/or serotonin.

A common denominator of the various systems is the ascription of cognitive mechanisms to the process of therapeutic change. Research has indicated that improvement in the clinical condition is associated with changes in cognitive structuring of experience irrespective of the type of therapy. It is suggested that changes in the cognitive processes play an essential therapeutic role with each type of treatment.

REFERENCES

Alloy, L. B., & Abramson, L. Y. Judgment of contingency in depressed and nondepressed students. *Journal of Experimental Psychology: General*, 1979, *108*, 441–445.

Beck, A. T. *Depression: Clinical, experimental and theoretical aspects.* New York: Hoeber, 1967. (Republished as *Depression: Causes and treatment.* Philadelphia: University of Pennsylvania Press, 1972.)

Beck, A. T. *Cognitive therapy and the emotional disorders.* New York: International Universities Press, 1976.

Beck, A. T., Rush, A. J., Shaw, B. F., & Emery, G. *Cognitive therapy of depression.* New York: Guilford, 1979.

Belson, A. A. New focus on chemistry of joylessness. *The New York Times*, March 15, 1983, Science Times section, p. 1

Bower, G. H. Mood and memory. *American Psychologist*, 1981, *36*, 129–148.

Bradley, B. & Mathews, A. Negative self-schemata in clinical depression. *British Journal of Clinical Psychology*, 1983, *22*, 173–181.

Breslow, R., Kocsis, J., & Belkin, B. Memory deficits in depression: Evidence utilizing the Wechsler Memory Scale. *Perceptual and Motor Skills*, 1980, *51*, 541–542.

Butler, G., & Mathews, A. Cognitive processes in anxiety. *Advances in Behavior Research and Therapy*, 1983, *5*, 51–62.

Carrington, C. *A comparison of cognitive and analytically oriented brief treatment approaches to depression in black women.* Dissertation, University of Maryland, 1979.

Clark, D. M. & Teasdale, J. D. Diurnal variation in clinical depression and accessibility of memories of positive and negative experience. *Journal of Abnormal Psychology*, 1982, *91*, 87–95.

Costello, C. G. Depression: Loss of reinforcers or loss of reinforcer effectiveness? *Behavior Therapy*, 1972, *3*, 240–247.

DeMonbreun, B. G., & Craighead, W. E. Distortion of perception and recall of positive and neutral feedback in depression. *Cognitive Therapy and Research*, 1977, *1*, 311–329.

Eaves, G., & Rush, A. J. Cognitive patterns in symptomatic and remitted unipolar major depression. *Journal of Abnormal Psychology*, 1984, *93*, 31–40.

Erdelyi, M. H. A new look at the new look: Perceptual defense and vigilance. *Psychological Review*, 1974, *81*, 1–25.

Gevins, A. *Shadows of thoughts: Towards a dynamic network model of neurocognitive functioning.* Paper presented at the meeting of the Society of Biological Psychiatry, New York, April 1983.

Giles, D. E. & Shaw, B. F. *A test of the cognitive triad in Beck's cognitive theory of depression.* Unpublished manuscript.

Gilson, M. *Depression as measured by perceptual dominance in binocular rivalry.* Manuscript submitted for publication, 1983.

Goodwin, A. M. & Williams, J. M. G. Mood-induction research—Its implications for clinical depression. *Behavior Research and Therapy*, 1982, *20*, 373–382.

Hammen, C. L., Jacobs, M., Mayol, A., & Cochran, S. D. Dysfunctional cognitions and the effectiveness of skills and cognitive-behavioral assertion training. *Journal of Consulting and Clinical Psychology*, 1981, *48*, 685–695.

Kraemer, G. W. & McKinney, W. T. Interactions of pharmacological agents which alter biogenic amine metabolism and depression. *Journal of Affective Disorders*, 1979, *1*, 33–54.

Last, C. G. & Blanchard, E. B. Classification of phobics versus fearful nonphobics: Procedural and theoretical issues. *Behavioral Assessment*, 1982, *4*, 195–210.

Lewinsohn, P. M. The behavioral study and treatment of depression. In M. Hersen, R. M. Eisler & P. M. Miller, (Eds.), *Progress in behavior modification*, Vol. 1 New York: Academic Press, 1975.

Lloyd, G. G. & Lishman, W. A. Effect of depression on the speed of recall of pleasant and unpleasant experiences. *Psychological Medicine*, 1975, *5*, 173–180.

Mahoney, M. Personal communication, 1982.

Muller, R. L. *The recognition times to depressive and neutral stimuli by the depressed and non-depressed*. Unpublished master's thesis, Farleigh Dickinson University, 1982.

Rehm, L. P. A self-control model of depression. *Behavior Therapy*, 1977, *8*, 787–804.

Rholes, W. S., Riskind, J. H., & Lane, J. W. Emotional states and memory biases: The effects of cognitive priming on mood. *Journal of Personality and Social Psychology*, in press.

Rush, A. J., Beck, A. T., Kovacs M., & Hollon, S. D. Comparative efficacy of cognitive therapy and pharmacotherapy in the treatment of depressed outpatients. *Cognitive Therapy and Research*, 1977, *1*, 17–37.

Rush, A. J., Beck, A. T., Kovacs, M., Weissenburger, J., & Hollon, S. D. Differential effects of cognitive therapy and pharmacotherapy on hopelessness and self-concept. *American Journal of Psychiatry*, 1982, *139*, 862–866.

Seligman, M. E. P. *Helplessness*. San Francisco: W. H. Freeman, 1975.

Simons, A. *The process of change during the course of congitive therapy or pharmacotherapy of depression: Changes in mood and cognitions*. Dissertation, Washington University, 1982.

Stiles, J. C. *Cognitive devaluation of past experiences in depression*. Dissertation, University of Texas, 1978.

Stone, E. A. Problems with current catecholamine hypotheses of antidepressant agents: *Behavioral and Brain Sciences*, 1983, *6*(4), 535–577.

Weissman, A. & Beck, A. T. *Development and validation of the Dysfunctional Attitude Scale*. Paper presented at the meeting of the Association for Advancement of Behavior Therapy, Chicago, 1978.

Wolpe, J. *The practice of behavior therapy* (3rd Ed.) New York: Pergamon Press, 1982.

Index

Transcendance, 28
Transference, 306
Transformational processes, 29
Transmutation, 29–30
Triadic reciprocality, 83–84

Unconscious
  change process and, 21–25
  epistemology and, 279
  motor theories of mind and, 104

Values
  Horney, 283–285
  learning and, 65–66
  structuralism and, 287–288
  See also Culture
Vicarious capability, 88–92
Vitalism, 37–39

Youth
  self-knowledge and, 113
  See also Adolescence; Children;
    Infancy